THREE CRITICS OF THE ENLIGHTENMENT

Vico, Hamann, Herder

ISAIAH BERLIN

Edited by Henry Hardy

incorporating
Vico and Herder
and
The Magus of the North

PIMLICO

Published by Pimlico 2000

2 4 6 8 10 9 7 5 3 1

Vico and Herder © Isaiah Berlin 1960, 1965, 1976
The Magus of the North © Isaiah Berlin and Henry Hardy 1993
Editorial matter © Henry Hardy 1997, 2000

First published by
Pimlico in 2000

Pimlico
Random House, 20 Vauxhall Bridge Road,
London SW1V 2SA

Random House Australia (Pty) Limited
20 Alfred Street, Milsons Point, Sydney,
New South Wales 2061, Australia

Random House New Zealand Limited
18 Poland Road, Glenfield,
Auckland 10, New Zealand

Random House South Africa (Pty) Limited
Endulini, 5A Jubilee Road, Parktown 2193, South Africa

The Random House Group Limited Reg. No. 954009
www.randomhouse.co.uk

A CIP catalogue record for this book
is available from the British Library

ISBN 0 7126 6492 0

Papers used by Random House are natural,
recyclable products made from wood grown in sustainable forests;
the manufacturing processes conform to the environmental
regulations of the country of origin

Typeset by Deltatype Ltd, Birkenhead, Merseyside
Printed and bound in Great Britain by
Mackays of Chatham PLC

CONTENTS

EDITOR'S PREFACE

Next year we are publishing a book by Sir Isaiah Berlin called *Three Critics of the Enlightenment*.

Elizabeth Jennings of the Hogarth Press to
the Italian Institute, London, 31 May 1960

BETWEEN 1960 and 1971 a somewhat disorienting series of announcements in the seasonal lists of the Hogarth Press increasingly tantalised the many readers who looked forward to any new publication by Isaiah Berlin. The first in the series appeared in the catalogue for autumn 1960: headed *Three Critics of the Enlightenment*, it promulgated a book comprising studies of Giambattista Vico, Johann Gottfried Herder and Joseph de Maistre.[1]

Not only did this book not materialise in this form or according to the projected time-scale, but its contents underwent a sequence of transformations that amounted almost to a case of Chinese whispers – almost, because just one element in the original conception, namely the study of Vico, did continuously survive all the changes, and duly appeared, rejoined by the essay on Herder, in the volume finally published sixteen years later as *Vico and Herder: Two Studies in the History of Ideas*.

The intervening stages may be briefly summarised. In autumn 1965 Herder was replaced by Johann Georg Hamann. In spring 1967 *Three Critics* was supplanted by two other proposed books, *Three Studies in the Philosophy of History* (essays on Vico and Herder, together with 'The Concept of Scientific History')[2] and *Two Enemies of the Enlightenment* (Hamann and Maistre). In autumn 1968 *Three Studies* became simply *Studies*, with the addition of a fourth essay, on Montesquieu.[3] In autumn 1971, *Studies* was cut back to two essays, becoming – and remaining until publication in 1976 – *Vico and Herder*. *Two Enemies* did not

---

[1] The contract, dated 31 December 1959, specifies only essays on Vico and Maistre.

[2] The latter study was eventually included in *Against the Current: Essays in the History of Ideas* (London, 1979; New York, 1980).

[3] Also later included in *Against the Current*.

reappear, though I was able to publish its intended contents as 'Joseph de Maistre and the Origins of Fascism' (in *The Crooked Timber of Humanity*) and *The Magus of the North* (Hamann) in the 1990s.[1]

This compressed account of some of the vicissitudes that have attended the publication of Isaiah Berlin's work[2] provides a basis for explaining the genesis of the present volume, which rescues his original title and the intention that underlay it (though not quite his original contents) forty years on. As will be seen, each of the three studies collected here was at one stage or another due to form part of a volume under the present title, devoted to key figures of the Counter-Enlightenment. The views held by the Enlightenment's opponents were a lifetime's preoccupation of Berlin's, and their examination produced some of his best and most characteristic work. For this reason, as well as because he had for so many years hoped to publish a book that would bring a number of his essays in this field together, it is fitting that his long-deferred project should be realised at last.

The opportunity to do this has arisen because in their original published incarnations the three studies included here are either out of print or soon to become so. Had one been starting from scratch, one might have devised a larger selection of studies by Berlin devoted to anti-Enlightenment thinkers, and such a volume might have signalled more obviously the centrality of this theme in his intellectual agenda. But the other possible candidates, including the three other essays mentioned in the Hogarth announcements, are all readily available in collections that are still in print, and likely to remain so for some time to come. It seemed best, then, to reissue the less available material, without duplicating essays from other volumes. (Besides, the titles of those other volumes – *Against the Current* and *The Crooked Timber of Humanity* – themselves

---

[1] *The Crooked Timber of Humanity: Chapters in the History of Ideas* (London, 1990; New York, 1991) and *The Magus of the North: J. G. Hamann and the Origins of Modern Irrationalism* (London, 1993; New York, 1994).

[2] Berlin was himself only too aware of the extent to which he tested the endurance of his publishers by the long delays, the unrealistic predictions and the changes of plan that characterised his experience of authorship: as he wrote to Hugo Brunner at the Hogarth Press on 24 July 1975, 'anyone dealing with me must be armed with considerable reserves of patience'. That was no exaggeration, but the eventual outcome always more than compensated for the preceding frustrations.

reflect, if less perspicuously, the anti-Enlightenment tendency of some of the thinkers examined in their pages.)

Had one been starting from scratch with these particular studies, one would have printed them in the chronological order of their subjects' lives, as indicated in the book's subtitle. But since Vico and Herder were already linked by the introduction specially written by Berlin for *Vico and Herder* – and reproduced here – it seemed inappropriate to disturb their adjacency.

In a letter to Elizabeth Jennings dated 8 March 1960, written in response to her request for a description of *Three Critics* to appear in the Hogarth Press catalogue, Berlin expresses the book's linking theme in a way that fits this descendant volume equally well:

> My thesis is that what unites these three writers is their antipathy to the fundamental ideas of the French Enlightenment, and the depth and permanent force of their critical reflections on them ... The issue between the advocates of the Enlightenment and these critics is today at least as crucial as it was in its beginnings, and the fashion in which the rival theses were stated in their original form is clearer, simpler and bolder than at any subsequent time.

For this new volume I have taken the opportunity to make a number of editorial revisions in the section on Vico, and in particular to check and amend quotations and references, adding or amplifying the latter where appropriate. Translations have also been scrutinised, and sometimes added where this seemed helpful. The essay on Herder had already received similar treatment for its appearance in *The Proper Study of Mankind*,[1] and it is the version from that volume, *mutatis mutandis*, that appears here. The study of Hamann is reproduced in essentially the same form that it took when first published, with the addition of the foreword specially written by the author in 1994 for the German edition.[2]

Very few of my editorial changes affect the substance of what Berlin wrote, but perhaps I may be permitted to advise any readers who wish to follow up the references in the footnotes that it will be worth their while to consult the revised versions of the essays on Vico and Herder rather than, or at least alongside, the previous versions; by this means they will save themselves a number of

---

[1] *The Proper Study of Mankind: An Anthology of Essays* (London, 1997; New York, 1998).

[2] *Der Magus in Norden* (Berlin, 1995).

problematic, sometimes fruitless, attempts to track down quotations or other sourced remarks.

Leon Pompa has helped me prodigiously with Vico, and my debt to him is especially great. I am also most grateful to Andrew Fairbairn, Roger Hausheer (who has in addition kindly read the proofs), Michael Inwood, Raymond Klibansky, T. J. Reed and Donald Phillip Verene for help with various recalcitrant problems.

Wolfson College, Oxford   HENRY HARDY
July 1999

NOTE ON REFERENCES

VICO

References for quotations from Vico cite the relevant page (or, in the case of the *New Science*, paragraph) from the relevant volume of the Scrittori d'Italia edition of Vico's works:

G. B. Vico, *Opere*, ed. Benedetto Croce, Giovanni Gentile and Fausto Nicolini, 8 vols in 11 (Bari, 1911–41: Laterza)

This edition is referred to hereafter as *Opere*. Page references to vol. 5, which contains Vico's autobiography, are to the second edition of that volume (1929), which was reset throughout, so that its pagination differs unsystematically from that of the first edition (1911).[1] References for quotations from Vico's main works do not mention *Opere* by name, but use the following abbreviations:

A   Autobiography (in *Opere*, vol. 5)
DA   *De antiquissima italorum sapientia ex linguae latinae originibus eruenda* (in *Opere*, vol. 1)
DN   *De nostri temporis studiorum ratione* (in *Opere*, vol. 1)
DU   *De universi iuris uno principio et fine uno* (in *Opere*, vol. 2, part 1)
IO   Inaugural Orations (in *Opere*, vol. 1)
NS   *Scienza nuova*, 1744 edition (*Opere*, vol. 4, in two parts)
NS1   The first (1725) edition of the *Scienza nuova* (in *Opere*, vol. 3)

[1] For completeness I should perhaps mention that a revised edition of vol. 4 (1928), the *Scienza nuova* of 1744, appeared in 1942 – rather misleadingly called a third edition, because the 1928 edition was itself a revision of an earlier edition by Nicolini. But this does not affect the citation system explained here, since this work is referred to by paragraph, and the paragraph numbering was not altered.

Wherever possible (except in the case of NS and NS1, where the paragraph numbers in the Italian edition are also used in the English translations), the page reference to the Italian edition is followed, after an oblique stroke, by a page reference to the relevant English translation from the following list (though the actual translations used by the author, except in the case of A and NS, are of varying origin, and sometimes his own):

A   *The Autobiography of Giambattista Vico*, trans. Max Harold Fisch and Thomas Goddard Bergin (Ithaca, New York, 1944: Cornell University Press; reprinted with corrections 1944 [*sic*]; reissued in 1963 [Great Seal Books, with further corrections] and 1975); the pagination is not affected by the corrections

DA   Giambattista Vico, *On the Most Ancient Wisdom of the Italians Unearthed from the Origins of the Latin Language*, trans. L. M. Palmer (Ithaca and London, 1988: Cornell University Press)

DN   Giambattista Vico, *On the Study Methods of Our Time*, trans. Elio Gianturco (Indianapolis etc., 1965: Bobbs-Merrill; reissued with additional material, Ithaca and London, 1990: Cornell University Press); the pagination of the translation is not affected by the additions, but Gianturco's introduction has been repaginated, and references are to the 1990 edition (subtract xii for a reference to the 1965 edition)

IO   Giambattista Vico, *On Humanistic Education (Six Inaugural Orations, 1699–1707)*, trans. Giorgio A. Pinton and Arthur W. Shippee (Ithaca and London, 1993: Cornell University Press)

NS   *The New Science of Giambattista Vico*, trans. Thomas Goddard Bergin and Max Harold Fisch (Ithaca, New York, 1968: Cornell University Press); this is a revised edition of a translation of Vico's third edition (1744) first published in 1948, and uses Nicolini's paragraph numbers; there is also a 1984 reissue, adding 'Practic of the New Science'. Berlin tended to use the 1948 edition: where relevant his quotations have been brought into line with the 1968 edition.

NS1 *Vico: Selected Writings*, ed. and trans. Leon Pompa
(Cambridge, 1982: Cambridge University Press), which
contains translations of large extracts from NS1, as well
as alternative translations of parts of DA, DN and NS

Thus 'DA 145/60' indicates that the passage in question is from *De
antiquissima*, and is to be found on p. 145 of the first volume of
Opere, while a translation appears on p. 60 of Palmer's volume.
References to translators' introductions and notes cite only one
page-number, e.g. 'A 40', 'DN xliii'; in the case of NS, 'p.' is added
to make clear that the reference is not, on such an occasion, to a
paragraph, e.g. 'NS p. xxxix'.

HERDER

References for quotations from Herder are to *Herder's sämmtliche
Werke*, ed. Bernhard Suphan (Berlin, 1877–1913: Weidmann), by
volume and page, thus: viii 252.

HAMANN

References to Hamann's writings, and to letters written to
Hamann, are to the following editions:

WORKS: Johann Georg Hamann, *Sämtliche Werke*, ed. Joseph
Nadler (Vienna, 1949–57: Herder), 6 vols. The last volume is
an invaluable analytical index.

LETTERS: Johann Georg Hamann, *Briefwechsel*, ed. Walther
Ziesemer and Arthur Henkel (Wiesbaden and Frankfurt,
1955–79: Insel), 7 vols. Unfortunately there is as yet no
subject index to these volumes, and no consolidated name
index.

These editions are referred to as W and B respectively, and passages
are cited by volume, page and first line, thus: W iii 145.13.

VICO AND HERDER

To the memory of
Leonard Woolf

AUTHOR'S PREFACE

THE ESSAYS in this book originate in lectures delivered respectively to the Italian Institute in London in 1957–8 and to Johns Hopkins University in 1964. The original version of the essay on Vico[1] was published in *Art and Ideas in Eighteenth-Century Italy* (Rome, 1960: Edizioni di Storia e Letteratura); that on Herder appeared in Earl R. Wasserman (ed.), *Aspects of the Eighteenth Century* (Baltimore, 1965: Johns Hopkins Press), and was later reprinted with minor modifications in *Encounter*, July and August 1965. Both essays have since been revised, and the first has been considerably expanded. I should like to take this opportunity of thanking Dr Leon Pompa for discussing with me his views of Vico, particularly Vico's conception of science and knowledge, and Professor Roy Pascal for an illuminating letter about Herder – from both of these I have greatly profited. Dr Pompa's book on Vico[2] unfortunately appeared only after my book was already in proof, too late to enable me to make use of it here.

As will be plain from the references in the text, I have relied on the admirable translation of Vico's *Scienza nuova* by Professors T. G. Bergin and M. H. Fisch for the quotations from, and references to, it in this book. My thanks are also due to Professors B. Feldman and R. D. Richardson, Roy Pascal, and F. M. Barnard for the use of their renderings of texts by Herder quoted in this work. My debt to Professor Barnard's excellent anthology, *Herder on Social and Political Culture*,[3] is particularly great: some of his renderings are reproduced verbatim, others in a form somewhat altered by me. I also wish to thank Mr Francis Graham-Harrison

---

[1] [Treated in this edition as two separate essays rather than as a single essay in two parts.]

[2] Leon Pompa, *Vico: A Study of the 'New Science'* (Cambridge, 1975: Cambridge University Press).

[3] (Cambridge, 1969: Cambridge University Press).

for his valuable help in reading the proofs of this book, Mr Hugo Brunner of the Hogarth Press for the care, courtesy and above all infinite patience displayed by him in his dealings with me, and finally Mrs Patricia Utechin, my secretary, for generous and unflagging help when it was most needed.

July 1975   I.B.

INTRODUCTION

HISTORIANS ARE concerned with the discovery, description and explanation of the social aspects and consequences of what men have done and suffered. But the lines between description, explanation and analysis, selection and interpretation of facts or events or their characteristics, are not clear, and cannot be made so without doing violence to the language and concepts that we normally use. Goethe remarked long ago that no statement of fact is free from theory; and even though some conceptions of what shall count as fact are less theory-laden than others, yet there is no complete consensus on this. Criteria of what constitutes a fact differ between fields of knowledge and between those who engage in them. Even within one field, history for instance, there are obvious differences in this regard between Christian and pagan historians, or post-Renaissance historians of different outlooks; what was incontrovertible evidence for Bossuet was not so for Gibbon, what constitutes a historical fact is not identical for Ranke, Michelet, Macaulay, Guizot, Dilthey. It is not the same past upon which nationalists and Marxists, clericals and liberals, appear to be gazing: the differences are even wider when it comes to selection and interpretation. This is equally true of the methods of those who rely principally upon quantitative and statistical methods as opposed to those who engage in imaginative reconstruction; of writers guided, not always consciously, by the maxims of this or that school of social psychology, or sociology, or philosophy of culture, or those who find illumination in the doctrines of functional anthropology or psychoanalysis or structuralist theories of language or imaginative literature.

This book examines the work of two thinkers whose ideas played a major part in transforming the canons of selection and interpretation of historical facts, and thereby affected the view of the facts themselves. Both wrote in the eighteenth century, but their doctrines did not achieve their full effect until the nineteenth, in both cases mainly through the labours of their disciples. These studies are not intended as an examination of the entire *oeuvre* of either Vico or Herder: only of those among their theses which seemed to me the most arresting, important and suggestive. For this reason I have made no attempt to submit the more technical philosophical ideas of either thinker to critical examination, even though some among them raise issues of considerable importance. So – to take but three examples – Vico's notion of *scienza*, which involves the conception of explanation *per caussas*, seems to embody a view of causality which differs from those of Descartes or Hume or Kant or modern positivists, and leads him to a doctrine of motives and causes *par excellence* which is highly relevant to problems that are in hot dispute today. So, too, is the distinction he draws between *scienza* and *coscienza*, *verum* and *certum*, which, in its turn, is highly relevant to much Hegelian and post-Hegelian – materialist, Marxist, Freudian – discussion and controversy about historical and sociological methods. Again, Herder's conceptions of teleological or cultural explanation made, or at least widened, conceptual and psychological paths not open to tough-minded and consistent materialists, positivists and mechanists – and this, too, leads to the widely varying positions of, among others, thinkers influenced by Marxism, by the doctrines of Wittgenstein, by writers on the sociology of knowledge or phenomenology. But a discussion of these philosophical developments, like that of anticipations of modern linguistic structuralism in Vico's *New Science*, although both interesting and seminal, would take one too far from Vico's and Herder's own discussions of issues on which they propounded their most original and influential theses – the nature and growth of human studies in general, and the nature of history and culture in particular. I have not attempted to trace the origins of these ideas, save in somewhat tentative fashion, nor to give an account of the historical or social circumstances in which they were conceived, nor their precise role in the *Weltanschauung* of the age, or even that of the thinkers themselves.

No one stressed the importance of comprehensive historical treatment more boldly or vehemently than Vico; no one argued more eloquently or convincingly than Herder that ideas and outlooks could be understood adequately only in genetic and historical terms, as expressions of the particular stage in the continuing development of the society in which they originated. A good deal of light has been shed on the intellectual and ideological sources of these ideas by scholars far more erudite than I can ever hope to be: Benedetto Croce, Antonio Corsano, Max H. Fisch, Nicola Badaloni, Paolo Rossi, A. Gerbi and, above all, Fausto Nicolini have done much of this for Vico; Rudolf Haym and, more recently, H. B. Nisbet, G. A. Wells, Max Rouché, V. M. Zhirmunsky and Robert Clark (to choose the most important) have provided an indispensable framework for Herder's teaching. I have profited greatly by their labours even where I disagreed with some of their assessments of the ideas themselves. Ideas are not born in a vacuum, nor by a process of parthenogenesis: knowledge of social history, of the interplay and impact of social forces at work in particular times and places, and of the problems which these generate is needed for assessing the full significance and purpose of all but the strictly technical disciplines and, some now tell us, even for the correct interpretation of the concepts of the exact sciences. Nor do I wish to deny the importance of considering why it is in the Kingdom of the Two Sicilies, and still more in East Prussia, usually described as cultural backwaters in an age of intense intellectual and scientific activity, that original ideas of major importance were generated. This is a historical problem for the solution of which knowledge of social, ideological and intellectual conditions is clearly indispensable, and which, so far as I know, has not been adequately examined. But it is not directly relevant to the purpose of these essays. But even though such historical treatment is required for full understanding, it cannot be a necessary condition for grasping the central core of every historically influential doctrine or concept. The Neoplatonists in the later Roman Empire or during the Renaissance may not have interpreted Plato's doctrines as faithfully as more erudite and scrupulous commentators of a later period, who paid due attention to the relevant social and historical context of his thought, but if Plato's main doctrines had not transcended their own time and place, they would scarcely have had expended on them – or, indeed, deserved – the labours of gifted scholars and interpreters; nor would the imagination of distant posterity – of Plotinus or Pico della Mirandola or Marsilio Ficino or Michelangelo or Shaftesbury – have been set on fire by them; nor would they have had enough life in them to provoke major controversies in our own time. Accurate knowledge of the social, political and economic situation in England in the second half of the seventeenth century is certainly required for a full understanding of a particular passage in Locke's *Second Treatise* or of a letter to Stillingfleet. Yet what Voltaire (who did not go into such details), or the Founding Fathers of the American Republic, supposed him to mean nevertheless derives from his writings, and not solely, or even mainly, from their own minds or problems. The importance of accurate historical knowledge to the understanding of the meaning, force and influence of ideas may be far greater than many unhistorical thinkers, particularly in English-speaking lands, have recognised, but it is not everything. If the ideas and the basic terminology of Aristotle or the Stoics or Pascal or Newton or Hume or Kant did not possess a capacity for independent life, for surviving translation, and, indeed, transplantation, not without, at times, some change of meaning, into the language of very disparate cultures, long after their own worlds had passed away, they would by now, at best, have found an honourable resting-place beside the writings of the Aristotelians of Padua or Christian Wolff, major influences in their day, in some museum of historical antiquities. The importance of historical hermeneutics has been greatly underestimated by historically insensitive British thinkers in the past – with the result that the swing of the pendulum sometimes makes it appear an end in itself. These are mere truisms, which need stating only because the notion of the possibility of a valid examination of the ideas of earlier ages, unless it is steeped in a rich cultural, linguistic and historical context, has been increasingly called into question in our day. Even though the shades of Vico and Herder are invoked in support of this doctrine, the importance of past philosophers in the end resides in the fact that the issues which they raised are live issues still (or again), and, as in this case, have not perished with the vanished societies of Naples or Königsberg or Weimar, in which they were conceived.

What, then, it may be asked, are these time-defying notions? In the case of Vico, let me try to summarise those which appear to me the most arresting in the form of seven theses:

(1) That the nature of man is not, as has long been supposed, static and unalterable or even unaltered; that it does not so much as contain even a central kernel or essence, which remains identical through change; that men's own efforts to understand the world in

which they find themselves and to adapt it to their needs, physical and spiritual, continuously transform their worlds and themselves.

(2) That those who make or create something can understand it as mere observers of it cannot. Since men in some sense make their own history (though what this kind of making consists in is not made entirely clear), men understand it as they do not understand the world of external nature, which, since it is not made, but only observed and interpreted, by them, is not intelligible to them as their own experience and activity can be. Only God, because he has made nature, can understand it fully, through and through.

(3) That, therefore, men's knowledge of the external world which they can observe, describe, classify, reflect upon, and of which they can record the regularities in time and space, differs in principle from their knowledge of the world that they themselves create, and which obeys rules that they have themselves imposed on their own creations. Such, for example, is knowledge of mathematics – something that men have themselves invented – of which they therefore have an 'inside' view; or of language, which men, and not the forces of nature, have shaped; and, therefore, of all human activities, inasmuch as it is men who are makers, actors and observers in one. History, since it is concerned with human action, which is the story of effort, struggle, purposes, motives, hopes, fears, attitudes, can therefore be known in this superior – 'inside' – fashion, for which our knowledge of the external world cannot possibly be the paradigm – a matter about which the Cartesians, for whom natural knowledge is the model, must therefore be in error. This is the ground of the sharp division drawn by Vico between the natural sciences and the humanities, between self-understanding on the one hand, and the observation of the external world on the other, as well as between their respective goals, methods, and kinds and degrees of knowability. This dualism has continued to be the subject of hot dispute ever since.

(4) That there is a pervasive pattern which characterises all the activities of any given society: a common style reflected in the thought, the arts, the social institutions, the language, the ways of life and action of an entire society. This idea is tantamount to the concept of a culture; not necessarily of one culture, but of many; with the corollary that true understanding of human history cannot be achieved without the recognition of a succession of the phases of the culture of a given society or people. This further

entails that this succession is intelligible, and not merely causal, since the relationship of one phase of a culture or historical development to another is not that of mechanical cause and effect, but, being due to the purposive activity of men, designed to satisfy needs, desires, ambitions (the very realisation of which generates new needs and purposes), is intelligible to those who possess a sufficient degree of self-awareness, and occurs in an order which is neither fortuitous nor mechanically determined, but flows from elements in, and forms of, life, explicable solely in terms of human goal-directed activity. This social process and its order are intelligible to other men, members of later societies, since they are engaged in a similar enterprise which arms them with the means of interpreting the lives of their predecessors at a similar or different stage of spiritual and material development. The very notion of anachronism entails the possibility of this kind of historical understanding and ordering, since it requires a capacity for discriminating between what belongs and what cannot belong to a given stage of a civilisation and way of life; and this, in its turn, depends on an ability to enter imaginatively into the outlook and beliefs, explicit and implicit, of such societies – an enquiry that makes no sense if applied to the non-human world. For Vico the individual character of every society, culture, epoch is constituted by factors and elements which it may have in common with other periods and civilisations, but each particular pattern of which is distinguishable from all others; and, as a corollary of this, the concept of anachronism denotes lack of awareness of an intelligible, necessary order of succession which such civilisations obey. I doubt if anyone before Vico had a clear notion of culture or historical change in this sense.

(5) That the creations of man – laws, institutions, religions, rituals, works of art, language, song, rules of conduct and the like – are not artificial products created to please, or to exalt, or teach wisdom, nor weapons deliberately invented to manipulate or dominate men, or promote social stability or security, but are natural forms of self-expression, of communication with other human beings or with God. The myths and fables, the ceremonies and monuments of early man, according to the view prevalent in Vico's day, were absurd fantasies of helpless primitives, or deliberate inventions designed to delude the masses and secure their obedience to cunning and unscrupulous masters. This he regarded as a fundamental fallacy. Like the anthropomorphic

metaphors of early speech, myths and fables and ritual are for Vico so many natural ways of conveying a coherent view of the world as it was seen and interpreted by primitive men. From which it follows that the way to understand such men and their worlds is by trying to enter their minds, by finding out what they are at, by learning the rules and significance of their methods of expression – their myths, their songs, their dances, the form and idioms of their language, their marriage and funeral rites. To understand their history, one needs to understand what they lived by, which can be discovered only by those who have the key to what their language, art, ritual mean – a key which Vico's *New Science* was intended to provide.

(6) From which it follows (in effect a new type of aesthetics) that works of art must be understood, interpreted, evaluated, not in terms of timeless principles and standards valid for all men everywhere, but by a correct grasp of the purpose and therefore the peculiar use of symbols, especially of language, which belong uniquely to their own time and place, their own stage of social growth; that this alone can unravel the mysteries of cultures entirely different from one's own and hitherto dismissed either as barbarous confusions or as being too remote and exotic to deserve serious attention. This marks the beginning of comparative cultural history, indeed of a cluster of new historical disciplines: comparative anthropology and sociology, comparative law, linguistics, ethnology, religion, literature, the history of art, of ideas, of institutions, of civilisations – indeed, the entire field of knowledge of what came to be called the social sciences in the widest sense, conceived in historical, that is, genetic, terms.

(7) That, therefore, in addition to the traditional categories of knowledge – a priori/deductive, a posteriori/empirical, that provided by sense perception and that vouchsafed by revelation – there must now be added a new variety, the reconstructive imagination. This type of knowledge is yielded by 'entering' into the mental life of other cultures, into a variety of outlooks and ways of life which only the activity of *fantasia* – imagination – makes possible. *Fantasia* is for Vico a way of conceiving the process of social change and growth by correlating it with, indeed, viewing it as conveyed by, the parallel change or development of the symbolism by which men seek to express it; since the symbolic structures are themselves part and parcel of the reality which they symbolise, and alter with it. This method of discovery, which

begins with understanding the means of expression, and seeks to reach the vision of reality which they presuppose and articulate, is a kind of transcendental deduction (in the Kantian sense) of historical truth. It is a method of arriving not, as hitherto, at an unchanging reality via its changing appearances, but at a changing reality – men's history – through its systematically changing modes of expression.

Every one of these notions is a major advance in thought, any one of which by itself is sufficient to make the fortune of a philosopher. Vico's work lay unheeded, save among scholars in his native city, until that most indefatigable of transmitters of ideas, Victor Cousin, brought it to the attention of Jules Michelet. The effect on the great French historian was immediate and transforming, and it was he who first spread Vico's fame throughout the length and breadth of Europe.

Even though Michelet, at the end of his life, claimed that Vico was his only master, like every strongly original thinker he took from the *New Science* only that which fitted in with his own, already formed, conception of history. He derived from Vico a vision of men as moulders of their own destinies, engaged in a Promethean struggle to achieve their own moral and social freedom, wresting from nature the means to serve their own human goals, and, in the course of this, creating and destroying institutions in the perpetual struggle to overcome obstacles, social and individual, to the full realisation of the moral energies and creative genius of entire peoples and societies. What does not fit into Michelet's ardent populist vision, for example the notion of a divine providence which, unknown to them, shapes the ends of individuals and societies – Vico's version of the Invisible Hand, or the Cunning of Reason – Michelet, in effect, half translates into secular terms and half ignores, as he ignores Vico's Platonic moments, his theory of historical cycles, his anti-democratic bias, his admiration for devout, authoritarian, semi-primitive societies, which is the very antithesis of Michelet's passionate faith in popular liberty.

This is an instance of a recurring phenomenon – that the importance and influence of ideas do not invariably depend on the validity or value of the systems in which they occur. That Plato or Spinoza or Leibniz or Kant were thinkers of genius has seldom been denied even by those who reject the central tenets of their metaphysical systems, or look on them as deleterious; this is so because they recognise that these philosophers advanced ideas the depth and power of which have permanently altered the history of thought, or (which comes to the same) that they raised issues which have exercised the minds of thinkers ever since; and this remains true even when some of the most ambitious and celebrated of the systems of thought which initially gave rise to these issues have long lost whatever life they may have had and are looked upon as being, at best, of purely historical interest. So it is with the two thinkers discussed in this book. Vico certainly supposed himself to have discovered a new science: that is, general principles capable of yielding rules the correct application of which could, at least in principle, explain the order of the phases in the recurrent cycles of human history as completely as the triumphant natural sciences of his day could account for the regularities of the positions and movement of physical matter. I am not here concerned with weighing the justice of this claim against the claims of rival systems made by earlier and later thinkers. All I have attempted to do is to cast light on some of the building-blocks in this vast, sprawling, at times fantastic, baroque edifice: stones that are valuable on their own account, capable of being used in the construction of firmer, if more modest, structures. This holds of such novel notions as, for example (to recall them once again), Vico's distinction between the realm of nature, which obeys (knowable but not intelligible) laws, and the man-made, which is subject to (intelligible) rules; his theory of the function of myth and symbolism and above all of language; his conception of a central style which characterises and expresses (he does not say that it determines or renders coherent) the varied activities of societies or entire epochs, which in its turn suggests the notion of a variety of human cultures; together with the radical implications for aesthetics, anthropology, and, of course, the entire range of the historical sciences, of such an approach to human activity.

So also with Herder. He too tried to embrace the entire province of knowledge of his time: science and art, metaphysics and theory, epistemology and ethics, social life, history, anthropology, psychology, all that men were most deeply concerned with in the past and the present and (with far greater emphasis than Vico) the future. Like the English thinkers by whom he was deeply influenced, like Young and Percy and the Wartons and Sterne (and Lavater in Zürich), he was a divine and a man of letters, and, in an age of increasing specialisation, aimed at universality. He was a poet, a philosopher, a literary scholar and historian, an amateur philologist, an aesthetic theorist and critic, an eager student of the biological and physical sciences of his day: he wished to bring all the sciences of man and of his environment, his origins, his history into a single integrated whole. He regarded the frontiers between the human sciences as pedantic and artificial devices, irksome hindrances to self-understanding by human beings in all their illimitable variety and spiritual power, which the tidy categories of philosophers vainly sought to contain. In the course of this vast undertaking, for which he had neither the capacity nor the knowledge, he originated and gave life and substance to ideas some of which have entered permanently into the texture of European thought and feeling.

Among the concepts which Herder originated or infused with a new life are at least three central ideas, which have grown in strength and influence since they were launched: the idea that men, if they are to exercise their faculties fully, and so develop into all that they can be, need to belong to identifiable communal groups, each with its own outlook, style, traditions, historical memories and language; the idea that the spiritual activity of men – expressed in art and literature, religion and philosophy, laws and sciences, play and work – consists not in the creation of objects, of commodities or artefacts, the value of which resides in themselves, and is independent of their creators and their characters and their purposes, but in forms of communication with other men. The creative activity of men is to be conceived not as the production of objects for use or pleasure or instruction, additions to or improvements on the world of external nature, but as voices speaking, as expressions of individual visions of life, to be understood not by rational analysis, that is, dissection into constituent elements, nor by exhaustive classification under concepts, subsumption under general principles or laws, incorporation in logically coherent systems or the use of other technical devices, but only by *Einfühlen* – empathy – the gifts not of a judge, a compiler or an anatomist, but of an artist endowed with historical insight and imagination. 'Every court, every school, every profession, every closed corporation, every sect,' wrote Herder's mentor, Johann Georg Hamann, 'each has its own vocabulary', which can be grasped only with the passion of 'a friend, an intimate, a lover';[1] abstract formulae, general theories, scientific laws are keys that open no individual door. Only a combination of historical scholarship with a responsive, imaginative sensibility can find a path into the inner life, the vision of the world, the aspirations, values, ways of life of individuals or groups or entire civilisations. Finally, it was Herder who set in motion the idea that since each of these civilisations has its own outlook and way of thinking and feeling and acting, creates its own collective ideals in virtue of which it is a civilisation, it can be truly understood and judged only in terms of its own scale of values, its own rules of thought and action, and not of those of some other culture: least of all in terms of some universal, impersonal, absolute scale, such as the French *philosophes* seemed to think that they had at their disposal when they so arrogantly and blindly gave marks to all societies, past and present, praised or condemned this or that individual or civilisation or epoch, set some up as universal models and rejected others as barbarous or vicious or absurd. To judge, still more to mock at, the past according to one's own – or some other alien – lights must lead to grave distortion. The ancient Hebrews must not be judged by the standards of classical Greece, still less by those of Voltaire's Paris or of his imaginary Chinese mandarins; nor should Norsemen or Indians or Teutons be looked at through the spectacles of an Aristotle or a Boileau. He is as critical of Europocentrism as his enemy Voltaire. For him men are men, and have common traits at all times; but it is their differences that matter most, for it is the differences that make them what they are, make them themselves, it is in these that the individual genius of men and cultures is expressed.

The denial, at any rate in Herder's earlier writings, of absolute and universal values carries the implication, which with time has grown increasingly disturbing, that the goals and values pursued by various human cultures may not only differ, but may, in addition, not all be compatible with one another; that variety, and perhaps conflict, are not accidental, still less eliminable, attributes of the human condition, but, on the contrary, may be intrinsic properties of men as such. If this is so, then the notion of a single, unchanging, objective code of universal precepts – the simple, harmonious, ideal way of life to which, whether they know it or not, all men aspire (the notion which underlies the central current

[1] W ii 172.21, 171.15.

of the Western tradition of thought) – may turn out to be incoherent; for there appear to be many visions, many ways of living and thinking and feeling, each with its own 'centre of gravity',[1] self-validating, uncombinable, still less capable of being integrated into a seamless whole. It is worth remarking that, apart from this revolutionary corollary, which undermined the ancient notion of the moral unity of the human race, or, at least, of that of its rational members – the notion that variety is either inescapable, or valuable in itself, or both at once, was itself novel. Herder may not be its only begetter, but the idea that variety is preferable to uniformity, and not simply a form of human failure to arrive at the one true answer, and consequently a form of error or imperfection – the rejection of the traditional belief in the necessary harmony of values in a rational universe, whether as the reality beneath the appearances, or as the ideal presupposed by both reason and faith – this radical departure is altogether modern. The ancient world and the Middle Ages knew nothing of it.

These ideas – that all explanation, all understanding, indeed, all living, depend on a relationship to a given social whole and its unique past, and that it is incapable of being fitted into some repetitive, generalised pattern; the sharp contrast between qualitative as opposed to quantitative approaches; the notion that art is communication, a form of doing and being, not of making objects detachable from the maker; the notion that change and variety are intrinsic to human beings; that truth and goodness are not universal and immutable Platonic forms in a super-sensible, timeless, crystalline heaven, but many and changing; that the collision of equally compelling claims and goals may be unavoidable and incapable of rational resolution, so that some choices may be at once unavoidable and agonising – all these notions, which entered into many varieties of romanticism, relativism, nationalism, populism, and many brands of individualism, together with corresponding attacks upon the methods of the natural sciences and rational enquiry based on tested empirical evidence, have their fateful beginnings here. To ascribe some of these views to either of the thinkers treated in these pages would be false and unjust. Men are not responsible for the careers of their ideas: still less for the aberrations to which they lead.

Both Vico and Herder tended to overstate their central theses.

[1] v 509.

Such exaggeration is neither unusual nor necessarily to be deplored. Those who have discovered (or think they have discovered) new and important truths are liable to see the world in their light, and it needs a singular degree of intellectual control to retain a due sense of proportion and not be swept too far along the newly opened paths. Many original thinkers exaggerate greatly. Plato and the Stoics, Descartes, Spinoza, Hume, Kant, Rousseau, Hegel, Marx, Russell, Freud (not to mention later masters) claimed too much. Nor is it likely that their ideas would have broken through the resistance of received opinion or been accorded the attention that they deserved, if they had not. The moderation of an Aristotle or a Locke is the exception rather than the rule. Vico was not answering questions posed by earlier thinkers. His vision of men and their past involved him in conceiving, in some excitement (to which he owns), new categories and concepts, and his struggle to adapt traditional terms to convey the basic structure of the new discipline to his contemporaries resulted in sudden leaps of thought and a convoluted and obscure terminology. Herder often wrote with a rhapsodic intensity not conducive to clear reflection or expression. The vehement zeal with which both Vico and Herder thought and spoke inevitably blinded them to the great cardinal merits of the methods of the thinkers against whom they inveighed. In a radical conflict of beliefs and methods on this scale, both sides were bound to attack too violently and to reject too much. It is plain to us now that insight, no matter how brilliant and intuitive, and attempts to reconstruct the main lines of entire cultures by sheer imaginative genius, based on scattered erudition, are not sufficient. In the end it is only scrupulous examination of the evidence of the past, and the systematic self-critical piecing together of whatever can be empirically established, that can confirm one hypothesis and weaken or rule out others as implausible or absurd. History needs whatever it can obtain from any source or method of empirical knowledge. As antiquarian research, archaeology, epigraphy, palaeography, philology have altered historical writing in previous centuries, so quantitative methods, the accumulation and use of statistical information to support economic, sociological, psychological, anthropological generalisations, have added to, and transformed, our knowledge of the human past, and are doing so to an increasing extent. The use of chemical and biological techniques has added materially to the knowledge of the origins of men and the dating and identification of the monuments on which our knowledge is founded. Without reliable empirical evidence, the most richly imaginative efforts to recover the past must remain guesswork and breed fictions and romances. Nor is there any assignable limit to the influence upon historical studies of disciplines yet unborn. Nevertheless, without such inspired insights, the accumulated data remain dead: Baconian generalisations are not enough. The revolt against, on the one hand, the labours of antiquaries and compilers (Voltaire was among the first to cover them with ridicule), and the ideological dogmas of the Enlightenment on the other, transformed both literature and history.

Vico, even after Michelet, remained an esoteric interest. But the influence of Herder's writings, acknowledged and unacknowledged, direct or indirect, was wide and permanent. After him the feeling grew that human history was not a linear progression, but a succession of distinct and heterogeneous civilisations, some of which influenced each other, but which could, nevertheless, be seen to possess an inner unity, to be individual social wholes, intelligible in their own right and not primarily as so many steps to some other, more perfect, way of life. Such cultures could not be reconstructed fragment by fragment in accordance with mechanical rules supplied by a generalising science: their constituent elements could be grasped adequately only in relation to each other – this indeed was what was meant by speaking of a civilisation, a way of living and an expression of a society characterised by an identifiable pattern, a central style which informed, if not all, yet a great many of its activities, and so revealed, even in its internal tensions, its differences and conflicts, a certain degree of unity of feeling and purpose. This style or character was not something that could be abstracted from its concrete expressions or used as a reliable method of infallibly reconstructing missing facts and filling gaps in our empirical knowledge; it was not governed by discoverable laws, nor could it yield a formula defining some metaphysical essence from which the attributes or history of men were logically deducible. It was an intelligible, empirically recognisable, pattern, a network of relationships between human beings, a way of responding to their environment and one another, a form – some said a structure – of thought, feeling and action. This could be grasped only by the use of the imagination, by a capacity to conceive the life of an entire society, to 'feel oneself into'[1] its mode

[1] v 503.

of thought, speech, feeling; to visualise the gestures, to hear the voices, to trace the changing moods and attitudes and in this way to follow the fortunes of its members.

Both these thinkers perceived – Herder more vividly than Vico – that the task of integrating disparate data and interpretations of events, movements, situations, of synthesising such heterogeneous material into a coherent picture, demands gifts very different from those required for rational methods of investigation or formulation and verification of specific hypotheses: above all, the gift of breathing life into the dead bones in the burial grounds of the past, of a creative imagination. In the absence of sufficient empirical evidence, such accounts of total social experience may remain no more than historical romances; but unless one is able in the first place to imagine such worlds in concrete detail, there will be little enough that is worth verifying: without the initial intuitive vision of a world about which one wishes to learn, the data remain lifeless, the individuals mere names, at most stylised figures in a procession, a pageant of operatic characters clothed in historical garments, or at best idealised personages in a classical drama. The rational methods of reconstruction of the past, whether human or non-human – zoological, palaeontological, geological – lead to conclusions that are precise or vague, valid or invalid, accurate or inaccurate, correct or incorrect, and are so certified by the application of methods accepted by reputable experts in the relevant field. But such attributes as 'profound' and 'shallow', 'plausible' and 'implausible', 'living' and 'lifeless', 'authentic' and 'unreal', 'rounded' and 'flat' and the like are not often ascribed to the achievements of logic or epistemology or scientific method but are more often used to characterise the arts and works of scholarship, which require a capacity for insight, responsiveness, understanding of what men are and can be, of their inner lives, perception of the meaning and implications, and not only of the appearances, of their observable gestures. These are terms used to describe works of humane learning – histories, biographies, works of criticism and interpretation, some branches of philosophy, and, indeed, the more precise labours of the reconstruction of the monuments of the past – social, religious, literary – works of art, buildings, cities. It was the psychological gifts required for imaginative reconstruction of forms of life – ideally to read the symbols with which societies and civilisations express themselves as a graphologist reads handwriting – if not as they were, at least, as

they could have been, as well as the intellectual capacity for
weighing the empirical evidence for and against the authenticity of
such accounts, that were demanded by the new kind of history,
and so sharply divided its founders – Boeckh and Niebuhr,
Augustin Thierry and Guizot, Ranke and, above all, Burckhardt
and after him Dilthey – from even the best writers of the
Renaissance or the Enlightenment. 'Even a half-false historical
perspective is worth much more than none at all', wrote Burckhardt in a letter in 1859.[1] To have opened doors to this great
enlargement of the human spirit is the achievement of the two
thinkers with whom this book is concerned.

[1] Letter of 20 June 1859 to Wilhelm Vischer the younger.

THE PHILOSOPHICAL IDEAS
OF GIAMBATTISTA VICO

Singulière destinée que celle de cet homme! Lui qui fut si intuitif, il sort du tombeau lorsqu'il n'a plus rien à enseigner.

Pierre-Simon Ballanche[1]

Historici utiles, non qui facta crassius et genericas caussas narrant, sed qui ultimas factorum circumstantias persequuntur, et caussarum peculiares reserant.

Giambattista Vico[2]

I

VICO'S LIFE and fate provide perhaps the best of all known examples of what is too often dismissed as a romantic fiction – the story of a man of original genius, born before his time, forced to struggle in poverty and illness, misunderstood and largely neglected in his lifetime and (save among a handful of Neapolitan jurists) all but totally forgotten after his death. Finally, when after many years he is at last exhumed and acclaimed by an astonished nation as one of its greatest thinkers, it is only to be widely misrepresented and misinterpreted, and even today to be accorded less than his due, because the *anagnorisis* has come too late, and during the century that followed his death ideas similar to his were better expressed by others, while he is best remembered for the least original and valuable of his doctrines. It is true that Vico's style tends to be baroque, undisciplined and obscure; and the eighteenth century, which came close to taking the view that not to say things clearly is not to say them at all, buried him in a grave from which not even his devoted Italian commentators have fully succeeded in raising him. Yet his works are of an arresting novelty, a

---

[1] 'What a peculiar fate this man's is! He was so full of intuition, but he is coming back from the dead when he no longer has anything to teach us.' *Essais de palingénésie sociale*: vol. 3, p. 338, in *Oeuvres de M. Ballanche* (Paris and Geneva, 1830).

[2] 'The useful historians are not those who give general descriptions of facts and explain them by reference to general conditions, but those who go into the greatest detail and reveal the particular cause of each event.' DA 145/60.

half-abandoned quarry of fascinating, if ill-developed, ideas unique even in his own intellectually fertile age.

Vico's claim to originality will stand scrutiny from any point of vantage. His theories of the nature and development of the human mind, of culture, society and human history, are audacious and profound. He developed a novel theory of knowledge which in the hands of others played a decisive role. He distinguished for the first time a central type of human knowledge which had been misunderstood or neglected by previous thinkers. He was a bold innovator in the realms of natural law and jurisprudence, aesthetics and the philosophy of mathematics. Indeed his conception of mathematical reasoning was so revolutionary that full justice could scarcely have been done to it until the transformation effected by the logicians of the twentieth century, and it has not been fully recognised for what it is even now. More than this, Vico virtually invented a new field of social knowledge, which embraces social anthropology, the comparative and historical studies of philology, linguistics, ethnology, jurisprudence, literature, mythology, in effect the history of civilisation in the broadest sense. Finally, he put forward a cyclical view of human history, which, although it is significantly different from those of Plato, Aristotle, Polybius and their followers in the Italian Renaissance, and has had some influence on later thinkers, is probably the best-known and the least valuable among his achievements.

One can readily understand that in the case of a thinker so rich and so confused, and above all so genuinely seminal – the forerunner of so many of the boldest ideas of later, more celebrated, thinkers – there is a permanent temptation to read too much into him, especially to sense intimations, perceive embryonic forms and prefigured contours of notions dear to the interpreter himself. Michelet, Dilthey, Croce, Collingwood (and less certainly Herder and Hegel) are among his progeny, and some among them, notably Michelet and Croce, consciously or unconsciously tried to repay their debt by attributing too many of their own most characteristic ideas and attitudes, sometimes at the cost of patent anachronism, to Vico's writings. To attribute one's own opinions to an earlier thinker is doubtless a sincere form of admiration. It is one of the attributes of intellectual depth that very different minds fancy that they find their own reflection in it. But this characteristic is purchased at a price, and has rendered Vico a disservice. Neither the romantic humanist of Michelet's fervid imagination, nor the more plausibly drawn quasi-Hegelian metaphysician celebrated by Croce (still less Gentile's bold variation of this), nor Enzo Paci's proto-existentialist, nor Nicola Badaloni's naturalistic forerunner of Feuerbach, reveal enough of Vico's own original shape and colour. The devoted labours of the most scrupulous, scholarly and dedicated of the editors and glossators of Vico, Fausto Nicolini, provide a marvellous monument of lucid learning, but no more.[1] There is, as in the case of all authentic thinkers, no substitute for reading the original. This is no easy labour, but – here one can speak only from personal experience – the reward is great. Few intellectual pleasures are comparable to the discovery of a thinker of the first water.

Giovanni Battista Vico was born in 1668, the son of a bookseller in Naples. He died there in 1744. Apart from the few years which he spent in nearby Vatolla in Cilento, as a tutor to the sons of Domenico Rocca, Marchese di Vatolla, he never left Naples. All his life he had hoped to be appointed to the principal chair of jurisprudence in his native city, but succeeded only in holding various lower posts in the related field of 'rhetoric', ending with an inferior professorship which he held from 1699 until 1741. It provided him with a modest salary, and obliged him to deliver a number of inaugural lectures, some of which contain his most original ideas. He eked out his low income by accepting commissions from the rich and the grand to write Latin inscriptions, official eulogies and laudatory biographies of important persons. The best-known of these are his life of Antonio Caraffa, a Neapolitan *condottiere* in the service of the Emperor, and an account of the unsuccessful Macchia conspiracy in Naples. Caraffa's campaigns involved Vico in the study of inter-State relations, and it is probably this that caused him to read Grotius and other philosophical jurists. This had a decisive effect on his own ideas. The story of the Macchia was concerned with an attempt made at the turn of the century to replace Spanish by Austrian rule in Naples. The plot was uncovered and in 1701 the ringleaders were executed by the Spaniards. In 1702 Vico published an account of the conspiracy denouncing the participants as criminals and

[1] Neither the later Italian scholars, with Antonio Corsano and Paolo Rossi at their head, nor the admirable German critics Erich Auerbach and Karl Löwith, nor the English-speaking students of Vico, among whom Max Harold Fisch is the most distinguished, widely as their interpretations differ, can, for the most part, be charged with a tendency to transform Vico into a vehicle for their own ideas.

traitors. Five years later the Austrians acquired Naples and held it for the next twenty-seven years. In 1708 Vico issued a memorial volume which made no reference to the earlier work and celebrated the two chief conspirators as patriots and martyrs. In 1734 Naples was reoccupied by Spain. The new ruler, Charles de Bourbon, was duly offered humble congratulations by Vico at the head of a delegation sent by the University of Naples, and in the following year graciously appointed Vico historiographer royal. Political courage was no more characteristic of Vico than of Leibniz or a good many other scholars and philosophers of the age; nor did the political issues seem to be as clear, or as profoundly felt, as those of earlier or later times.

In 1692 Vico wrote a poem, in a conventional genre, on despair and the vanity of human wishes. None of these works are today of more than biographical interest. The poem (*Affetti di un dispera-to*)[1] expresses Lucretian-Epicurean sentiments which he was later exceedingly anxious to disclaim. It contains no trace of orthodox Christian belief, and constitutes important evidence of the preoccupations in the last decade of the century of Vico and his free-thinking friends, to whom he appears to have been closer than his autobiography would lead one to believe. The first work by him containing original ideas appeared in 1709, in the form of his last routine inaugural lecture in Latin, and attracted little attention. It was entitled 'On the Method of the Studies of our Time'[2] and contains important adumbrations of his later work. This was followed a year later by a major Latin treatise 'On the Oldest Wisdom of the Italians',[3] which attracted more attention. Both these works, one in the guise of an educational programme, the other of a linguistic and legal investigation of a fancifully conceived tradition of ancient Italian thought, advanced some of the boldest hypotheses in the philosophy of history. Some ten years later, in 1719, he published, also in Latin, an oration on Universal Law, and in the following two years an expansion of this called 'On the

---

[1] *Opere*, vol. 5, pp. 313–17.

[2] *De nostri temporis studiorum ratione*, delivered in 1708 and published by Mosca in Naples in the following year. There is an illuminating account of this work by Elio Gianturco, published as an introduction to his translation (see p. xii above).

[3] The full title is *De antiquissima italorum sapientia ex linguae latinae originibus eruenda*, 'On the Oldest Wisdom of the Italians Recoverable from the Origins of the Latin Language', commonly referred to as *De antiquissima*.

Single Principle of Universal Law and its Single Purpose',[1] the second part of which deals with specific topics in jurisprudence. This was almost certainly his bid for the First Chair of Jurisprudence at the university, which he long and passionately hoped for.

The election had been pre-arranged long before, and he was not appointed. He claimed, not without some bitterness, that this was a blessing in disguise, for it enabled him to devote himself freely to the new philosophical ideas which took possession of him. Four years later, in 1724, he completed a treatise refuting the views of some of the most admired thinkers of the age – the jurists Grotius, Selden and Pufendorf, the philosophers Hobbes, Spinoza, Locke and Bayle, the scholars Casaubon, Saumaise and Voss. His patron Cardinal Corsini, later Pope Clement XII, to whom it was dedicated, declined to provide the sum which he had promised for its publication. In despair, Vico sold his only valuable possession, a ring, but this covered only a quarter of the required amount. Thereupon Vico cut out the entire 'negative' part of the work – the attack on the natural-law theorists, contractualists, neo-Stoics, neo-Epicureans, Aristotelians, Cartesians – the most influential schools of the age – and retained only his own positive doctrine. The excised portion is lost. The book, shrunk to a quarter of its original size, was published a year later. This was his crowning masterpiece, the *New Science*. The first edition appeared in 1725; the second and altered version – virtually a new composition – in 1730, reprinted with additions in 1744, the year of his death.

It was also in 1725 that he wrote down an account of his own intellectual development. He composed it at the invitation of a rich Venetian dilettante, Count Gian Artico di Porcía, to whom the notion of inviting learned men to record the most important steps in their intellectual development may have been suggested by his friend the abbé Conti, a well-known man of letters. Conti was a friend and correspondent of a number of German scholars and intellectuals, one of whom, the great Leibniz, had written to their common friend, Louis Bourguet, expressing his regret that men who had made great discoveries often left no record of the steps by which they had arrived at them. Porcía invited the leading scholars and thinkers of Italy to contribute accounts of their mental development to be published in a single anthology. In this casual

---

[1] *De universi juris uno principio et fine uno*, 1720–2 (the first part of *Il diritto universale*).

fashion the art of intellectual autobiography was born. The editors expressed their delight with Vico's contribution, which, they were enlightened enough to realise, was a perfect model of the genre which they sought to establish. Indeed, to his extreme annoyance, they circulated it as a model to other contributors. Vico, who never ceased altering and correcting, made some additions to it later.

The *Autobiography* is a vivid and arresting record of the life of a man wholly preoccupied with philosophical issues. When Vico said that he was a solitary traveller in territory hitherto traversed by no one, this often repeated classical cliché for once expressed the literal truth. Vico knew that he had made discoveries unlike any that had been made before, and he knew that these discoveries were of cardinal importance. The violent intensity of his intellectual life, and its remoteness from the pathetic worries and humiliations of his lowly academic existence, were to some degree a compensation for his degraded status as a client of clerical and secular patrons. He lived in embittered poverty; he had little contact with the life round him; he was a cripple all his life as a result of a fall in childhood. His elder son became a criminal, one of his daughters was diseased from birth, all his devotion went to his younger son, for whom he managed to secure the succession to his chair. After his son, he loved his library best. Like Machiavelli, he escaped from his miseries into the world of books: Plato, Varro, Mucius Scaevola, Lucretius, Tacitus, Ulpian were more real to him than the writers of his own time, except, perhaps, Bacon, whom he adored, and Descartes, against whom he turned. All his life he lacked the most precious possessions of a scholar – tranquillity and leisure. He was a timid, obsequious, poverty- and anxiety-ridden scholar, who wrote too much and in haste, 'in the midst of the conversation of his friends and the cries of his children',[1] but he knew that he had made a major discovery and had opened a door to a world of which he alone was master, and the thought, so he tells us in his autobiography, made him happy and serene.[2]

---

[1] A 46/163.

[2] This was not as true as he wished, and, perhaps, believed, it to be. To the end of his life he longed for recognition, which had so signally been refused him in Naples. His letter of 9 January 1722 to the Protestant French editor of a learned journal is revealing in this regard. He begs this man of letters, Jean Leclerc, who had written him a laudatory letter, for the favour of a word in his publication, which would, he feels sure, make the name of Vico resound throughout Europe. *Opere*, vol. 5, p. 177.

One of his listeners described him as a lean man with a rolling eye, ferule in hand, who lectured with an intensity of eloquence which fascinated his students. He was much respected by his learned Italian contemporaries. The great historiographer Muratori procured his election to the Academy of Assorditi; the eminent jurist Gravina admired his learning. But it is clear that neither of these great lights of their age (Gravina, it is true, died before the publication of the *Scienza nuova*), nor even Conti, had any inkling that their admired friend possessed gifts of an order altogether different from their own. Certainly there is no evidence that any of his fellow scholars had begun to realise that Vico was a man of genius, and that his ideas about history and about natural law would one day render many of their own assumptions obsolete.

He had been taught by priests, and received a strictly traditional education in the, at that time, deeply clerical kingdom of Naples. But despite this almost exclusively medieval diet, scholastic philosophy left comparatively little trace upon his thought, and merely saddled him for life with a ponderous and pedantic manner of writing. His interest was excited by the new philosophy which had, half a century before, been initiated by Grotius and Descartes, and had been developed and applied by their followers with revolutionary results to the natural sciences and legal, political and metaphysical thought. Vico fully understood the aims and methods of this revolution. It liberated him and his entire generation from Aristotle and the schoolmen. He began by accepting its method, but then rebelled against it; indeed, he was the most original figure in what may be called the Counter-Reformation in the history of early modern philosophy. Vico was not interested in mathematics or in the natural sciences as such. Despite the efforts of Vincenzo Cuoco in his own century, and Fausto Nicolini in ours, to acclaim his geophysical and medical discoveries, Vico was remote from the scientific revolution of his time; his physics was the physics of Zeno, touched only remotely by imperfect acquaintance with Leibniz. He seems to have had no notion of what Galileo had achieved, and did not begin to grasp the effect of the new science upon the lives of men. He grew progressively more hostile to the assimilation of all knowledge to mathematical and physical models, and became preoccupied by problems of jurisprudence, humane learning and social psychology. Above all he grew more and more deeply convinced that earlier philosophy had failed to do justice to the methods and power of the sort of knowledge which he came to regard as central to human studies: in particular, the study of history. He conceived this study in the widest and most philosophical fashion – as being concerned with what it was for men to constitute a fully human society, more particularly, how men came to think, feel, act, live as they did. This sprang from his growing conviction that not a timeless analysis, but a genetic approach, that is, historical investigation, could alone discover and describe the relationships between various aspects of human experience and activity. Certainly no philosophy that failed to provide a method and criteria of truth for dealing with these matters could, in his view, have any claim to authority in the field of human knowledge.

The starting-point of Vico's revolt against Descartes was his conviction, articulated fully in 1708–9, that the Cartesian criteria of clear and distinct ideas could not profitably be applied outside the field of mathematics and natural science. The paradigm of true knowledge, according to the Cartesian school, consisted in beginning from truths so clear and so distinct that they could be contradicted only on pain of falling into absurdities; and in proceeding thence, by strict deductive rules, to conclusions whose truth was guaranteed by the unbreakable rules of deduction and transformation by which, as in mathematics, they were derived from their unassailable, eternally true, premisses. It was obvious to Vico, as indeed it had been to Descartes himself, that this model was inapplicable to the field of what today we call humane studies. Where in history, or in classical scholarship, or in literature, can we find strict definitions, rigorous proofs, concepts exhaustively analysed into their ultimate atomic constituents, demonstrated theorems, luminous and self-evident premisses leading with inexorable logic to unalterable conclusions? The application of such an a priori, deductive schema to any piece of narrative, or critical analysis of a work of art, or a historical or legal work or monument, or an account of the moral or intellectual development of an individual or a society, will not yield results. Descartes had seen this all too clearly, and had, in consequence, bluntly asserted that, while history, like travel, might do little harm as a casual source of entertainment, it was plainly not a branch of knowledge in which what had once been established did not need to be proved again, that is to say, in which scientific progress, universally recognised as such by rational thinkers, was possible. 'Memorable actions ... elevate the mind', he declared, and they might even 'help to form the judgement',[1] but otherwise they were of small value. Why study the chaotic amalgam of childish stories about the past, still less the passions and crimes of our dark beginnings, when reason can provide true and final answers to the problems which had puzzled our irrational ancestors? Valid knowledge is to be obtained only by the methods of the sciences, which Descartes and his followers contrasted with the unscientific hotch-potch of sense perception, rumour, myth, fable, travellers' tales, romances, poetry and idle speculation that in their view passed for history and worldly wisdom, but did not provide material amenable to scientific, that is, mathematical, treatment. Hence history and humane studies generally were relegated by Descartes to the province of miscellaneous information with which a serious man might while away an hour or two, but which was an unworthy object of a lifetime of study and meditation.[2] Vico was not prepared to accept this. His Catholic piety alone was sufficient to turn him against so positivist an approach, beside which must be set his passion for legal history and antiquarian learning as such. Yet the arguments which he uses against Descartes are neither theological nor rhetorical nor subjective. He became convinced that the notion of timeless truths, perfect and incorrigible, clothed in universally intelligible symbols which anyone, at any time, in any circumstances, might be fortunate enough to perceive in an instantaneous flash of illumination, was (with the sole exception of the truths of divine revelation) a chimera. Against this dogma of rationalism, he held that the validity of all true knowledge, even that of mathematics or logic, can be shown to be such only by understanding how it comes about, that is, its genetic or historical development. In order to demonstrate this, he attacked the claims

[1] *Oeuvres de Descartes*, ed. Charles Adam and Paul Tannery (Paris, 1897–1913) (hereafter *Oeuvres*), vol. 6, p. 5, lines 23–5.

[2] Descartes' view of humane learning may be gathered from such remarks as 'A decent man needs Greek or Latin no more than Swiss or Low-Breton, to know the history of the Roman Empire no more than of the smallest country in Europe' (*La Recherche de la vérité par la lumière naturelle*: *Oeuvres*, vol. 10, p. 503, lines 1–5), or the better-known passage in the *Discours de la méthode* on the unimportance of travel and the exaggerations of historians (*Oeuvres*, vol. 6, pp. 6–7); to which must be added the contemptuous remarks about the study of the classics in the first Article of his essay on 'The Passions of the Soul' (*Oeuvres*, vol. 11, pp. 327–8). It is against the *Discours*, with its, as it seemed to him, baseless claim to take all knowledge for its province, that Vico's polemic appears almost exclusively to be directed.

of the Cartesian school in the very field in which it felt itself strongest and most impregnable.

II

Descartes' new criterion of truth is that judgements claiming to be true must be seen to consist of clear and distinct 'ideas', ultimate constituents which are 'simple', that is, not further analysable. These ultimate atomic entities of thought are conceived as being connected with one another by 'necessary' logical links, that is, such that to attempt to sever them by contradicting their nexus would lead to self-contradiction, since each atom is logically bound to none but a particular set of other atoms, each set being logically an island, distinct or separate from other similar systems of interconnected atoms. The doctrine further holds that the structures of such systems, and of movements in, or by, them, can be clearly, that is, logically or mathematically, described. What cannot in principle be stated in such terms is automatically defined as less or more delusive. This applies notably to the unstable, melting data of the human senses – sights, sounds, smells, tastes – with their frequently vague outlines and indefinite, kaleidoscopically altering, hues or tones, and equally to that other realm of qualitative distinctions –'inner' psychical states, muscular sensations, states of feeling, dreams, images, memories, imprecise thoughts, wishes, purposes and the like. This must apply to attempts to examine historical data, however scrupulously and however narrow their compass, where the factual evidence may indeed be plentiful, but cannot be formulated in precise quantitative terms. True intellectual progress clearly depends, as the natural sciences have shown, on the reduction of the matter to be studied to clear and distinct, that is, mathematically expressible, concepts and judgements. Thus the devoted labours of antiquarians and historians to reconstruct, say, the events of the last years of the Roman Republic, can at best (as Descartes contemptuously remarked) furnish us with no more information than such as might have been possessed by Cicero's servant girl. Was this to be dignified by the name of science? Would anyone but an ignoramus or a bigot venture to deny that mathematical knowledge was the paradigm of all knowledge attainable by human beings, the collection of the clearest and most certain propositions thus far discovered by man's own efforts, the nearest approximation to infallible knowledge to which man had yet attained?

This is the triumphant thesis that Vico at first accepted and echoed, and then audaciously attacked. He rejected it after he had become convinced that whatever the splendours of the exact sciences, there was a sense in which we could know more about our own and other men's experiences – in which we acted as participants, indeed as authors, and not as mere observers – than we could ever know about non-human nature, which we could observe only from outside. It seemed to him clear that the external world must remain opaque to men in a sense (which he endeavoured to make clear) in which it could be said that their own thoughts, feelings, purposes and volitions were not opaque, but capable of being understood. This is the position which he set himself to defend in 1708, in his seventh Inaugural Lecture. The distinction he draws is between 'outer' and 'inner' knowledge, what later came to be distinguished as *Naturwissenschaft* and *Geisteswissenschaft*. It was the opening shot in a battle which from that moment has never ceased.

Vico concedes that mathematical knowledge is indeed wholly valid and its propositions are certain. But the reason for this is only too clear: 'We demonstrate geometry because we make it';[1] similarly, in the *New Science*, he says that geometry, 'when it constructs the world of quantity out of its elements, or contemplates that world, is creating it for itself'.[2] This is a particular application of a wider principle, that full knowledge can be knowledge only 'through causes', *per caussas* (in Vico's spelling);[3] according to this principle we can be said fully to know a thing if, and only if, we know why it is as it is, or how it came to be, or was made to be, what it is, and not merely that it is what it is, and has the attributes it has.

The view that knowledge *per caussas* is superior to any other is an old idea, frequently found in scholastic philosophy. Thus God knows the world because he has made it in ways and for reasons which he alone knows;[4] and we cannot know it in that full sense,

---

[1] 'Geometrica demonstramus, quia facimus.' DN 85/23.   [2] NS 349.

[3] Vico also uses the expression 'a caussis' in this sense: see DA 149–50/64–5.

[4] Indeed, for God, knowing and making are one act, as Augustine and Aquinas had taught: Aquinas, *Summa theologiae*, I. 14. 8, quoting Augustine, *De trinitate*, 15. 13. On this see Karl Löwith, ' "Verum et factum convertuntur": le premesse

because we have not made it – because we find it 'ready made' – it is given to us as a 'brute fact'. To the maker of a thing, particularly if (as in the case of God), as well as making the artefact, he has also made the material out of which he constructs a thing, and, in addition, has invented the rules in accordance with which he made it, nothing can in principle be opaque. He is responsible for it all, and has made it in accordance with his own will, out of stuff the reason for the existence and behaviour of which he knows, since he has created it for purposes of his own, which he alone (since he is the author) fully understands. This is the sense in which, for instance, the novelist can be said to be capable of fully understanding the characters of his novel, or the painter or composer the painting or the song. It is true that in the case of the writer or the composer not everything has been made by him – the words he uses, the sounds he employs, have not, for the most part, been invented by him, and to that extent there is something that is even for him 'brute fact' – a given medium which he is, within limits, free to choose, but to which, having chosen it, he must submit, without necessarily understanding the 'reasons for' its properties – without knowing it *per caussas* – and which he can alter only within certain limits. Only in the ideal case, where we make or design something out of literally nothing, can we be said fully to understand what we have made; for in that situation to create, and to know what and why we are creating, is a single act. This is how God creates. The nearer artistic creation approaches this limiting case – the greater the element of sheer creation and the smaller that of 'brute' matter obeying 'external' laws of its own – the more we can be said to understand *per caussas*, the more we truly know. This is virtually the case with algebra and arithmetic. The shapes of the symbols, auditory or visual, that we employ, are, it is true, made of sense-given material. But they are arbitrarily chosen, and are used as counters in a game that we ourselves have freely invented.

teologiche del principio di Vico e le loro conseguenze secolari', in A. Corsano and others, *Omaggio a Vico* (Naples, 1968), pp. 73–112, which seems to me far more convincing than Croce's account in his lecture on Vico's sources ('Le fonti della gnoseologia vichiana', read before the Accademia Pontaniana on 10 March 1912, published in the *Atti della Accademia Pontaniana* 42 (1912), Memoria No 6, and included as 'Appendix III: The Sources of Vico's Theory of Knowledge' in R. G. Collingwood's translation of Croce's important and influential book on the philosophy of Vico: Benedetto Croce, *The Philosophy of Giambattista Vico* (New York, 1964) [originally *La filosofia di Giambattista Vico* (Bari, 1911)]).

'Geometrica demonstramus, quia facimus.' Vico was certainly familiar with Hobbes's *De corpore*, in the beginning of which these words are contained. But he draws a further implication from it: 'Si physica demonstrare possemus, faceremus.'[1] If we could literally demonstrate the propositions of physics, we should be making it – that is, we should be creating its object, the material world. But we cannot do this. Only God can do so, for 'in him alone are the true forms of things after which nature is modelled',[2] and it is the quest for this reality that draws us towards God, who alone is the Truth and the Way. This is a form of Christian Platonism or Neoplatonism, and leads us back to the Renaissance doctrine that to know something is to become it: at any rate to dominate it. Thus Patrizi says that to know is to be united with what one knows,[3] and Campanella declares that to know is to become what is known.[4] There is a mystical play here on the notion of union – *coitus* – in *cognoscere*: 'co-knowing' is being made one with the thing known. This stems, perhaps, from the ancient metaphysical (and mystical) doctrine, of which Plato's *Symposium* contains the most memorable version, that in the beginning subject and object, man and nature, sensation and thought were one; then a great

---

[1] 'If we could demonstrate physics, we would make it.' DN 85/23.   [2] ibid.

[3] 'cognitio, nihil [est] aliud, quam Coitio quaedam cum suo cognobili.' *Panarchia*, book 15, 'De intellectu': fo. 31ᵛa in *Nova de universis philosophia* (Ferrara, 1591).

[4] Ernst Cassirer gives Campanella's formula as 'Cognoscere est fieri rem cognitam.' See his *Individuum und Kosmos in der Philosophie der Renaissance* (Leipzig/Berlin, 1927), pp. 178–9 – p. 169 in the English translation by Mario Domandi, *The Individual and the Cosmos in Renaissance Philosophy* (Oxford, 1963). In this passage Cassirer also cites other Neoplatonic formulae, sometimes inexactly and without a reference – as in the present instance, since these precise words appear to be a summary of Campanella's doctrine rather than a direct quotation. Examples of relevant exact quotations from Campanella are as follows: 'intelligimus alias res, quoniam intelligimus nos ipsos mutatos ab aliis rebus in ipsas' ('we understand other things because we understand ourselves when we have been changed by other things into those things': *Universalis philosophiae, seu Metaphysicarum rerum, iuxta propria dogmata, partes tres* (Paris, 1638), 1. 1. 8. 1, p. 60a [beware non-continuous pagination]); 'cognoscere est esse' ('to know is to be': ibid., 2. 6. 8. 1, p. 59); 'cognoscens est esse cogniti: vel fit' ('the knower is or becomes the being of the known': ibid., 2. 6. 8. 2, p. 60 [heading]); 'palam est, omnem cognitionem esse entitatem rei cognitae, in quam res cognoscens mutatur ... ergo ... cognoscere est esse' ('it is plain that all knowing is [the same as] the being of the thing known, into which the knower is changed ... therefore ... to know is to be': ibid., p. 61b). Ed.

catastrophe divided them; since when they everlastingly seek reunion – re-integration – which can be achieved in 're'-cognition. Hence the belief in magic as the acquisition of power by the subject over the object by re-entering it, immersing oneself in it, and so re-assimilating it to oneself, a notion which is at the heart of much Renaissance natural philosophy. This is the meaning of Pico della Mirandola's celebrated proposition in his *Apologia* that 'Magic is identical with wisdom.'[1] There is no doubt that there is something in Vico of this doctrine of perfect knowledge as identical with creation, but for him only God can know reality in this sense; men cannot intuit it, they cannot contemplate Platonic essences, at any rate so far as the external world – the world of nature – is concerned. He does not believe, with Leonardo, for example, that reason obviates the need for experience.[2] Far from it: experience – empirical knowledge, above all study of the monuments of the past – is everything. But, Janus-like, Vico faces both worlds; his anti-mathematical bias blends oddly with his genuine empiricism, and Meinecke's characterisation of him as basically a *Barockmensch*, despite the arresting modernity of his central doctrines, is not inapt: although it describes only the face turned to the past. However this may be, more important is his central doctrine, which takes him far, at times too far, beyond Hobbes's thesis – namely, that mathematical knowledge is, in principle, not identical with knowledge of the real world: not even with that of physics, no matter how susceptible to mathematical treatment this science has proved to be. For we cannot literally manufacture the physical world as he supposes that we can that of algebra and geometry.

In an age when mathematics was almost universally considered to be a form of factual knowledge about nature, the deepest, most revealing and certain of all the sciences, the object of metaphysical insight of a power denied to the grosser senses, the special glory of human reason, able to reveal the real attributes of things as against their often blurred and always misleading appearances, it was a momentous step to declare that mathematics is indeed most clear, most rigorous and wholly irrefutable, but only because it is the free creation of our own minds, that mathematical propositions are true only because we ourselves have made them. This is the meaning of

---

[1] 'Magia idem est quod sapientia': p. 170 in Pico's *Opera omnia* (Basle, [1557]).
[2] '[I]ntendi la ragione, e non ti bisogna sperienzia.' *Il codice atlantico*, fo. 147^v: p. 459 in *Il codice atlantico di Leonardo da Vinci* (Milan, 1894–1904).

Vico's famous formula, 'The true [*verum*] and the made [*factum*] are convertible.'[1] It may be doubted whether the eminent persons present on this occasion, for example the Viceroy of Naples, or Cardinal Grimani, who listened to Vico's enunciation of this

[1] ' "verum" et "factum" ... convertuntur.' This bold statement was first published in 1710 in the treatise allegedly concerned with the ancient wisdom of the Italians (see p. 24 above, note 3), hereafter referred to as *De antiquissima* (DA 131/45; cf. ibid. 132/47, 'the ancient sages of Italy considered the true and what is made convertible'). The question of whether the doctrine of the interchangeability of *verum* and *factum* has medieval roots has been much disputed. Benedetto Croce, in the lecture already referred to (p. 31 above, note 4), argues that it does not come from the Thomists or scholastic philosophy in general, and establishes a good case against the derivation from Ficino, Cardano, Scotus, or even Occam (in the version given to it by Sarpi), and others. These writers, and many others, had indeed remarked that what one creates one can fully know, but not the converse – that one can fully know only what one has created; the doctrine that perfect knowledge, whether rational or resting on faith, is confined to what one has oneself made, does not appear to be an orthodox scholastic doctrine. The one actual formulation of this doctrine before Vico, among the authors examined by Croce, seems to be that of Sanchez, whom, as Croce notes, Vico certainly read, since he quotes from his *Opera medica* of 1636 in a wholly different connection. But in Sanchez it seems to occur as a casual observation, with a sceptical intent common enough in sixteenth- and early seventeenth-century writers: since men have created so little, their real knowledge is very small. The revolutionary implications of this formula were for the first time drawn by Vico, when he set himself to distinguish what man has created and can know from what he cannot create, and consequently cannot know.

The relation of Vico's doctrine to Spinoza's doctrine of the relation of the *ordo et connexio idearum* to the *ordo et connexio rerum* – 'The order and connection of ideas is the same as the order and connection of things' (*Ethics*, part 2, proposition 7; cf. NS 238, 'The order of ideas must follow the order of institutions') – to which some commentators refer, is a good deal less plausible. There is more to be said for the parallel with the Renaissance doctrine of man as a microcosm of *natura naturans* – just as God alone understands the world he has created (which is identical with Nature), so man can understand in this 'divine', that is, perfect, sense, only the world he himself creates. He possesses a derived, but nevertheless genuine, capacity for creativity – a divine attribute. Moreover, in the unity – and the parallelism – which obtains between the necessary succession of the phases of a civilisation and the development of mental attributes and powers in the growing individual – Vico's *idée maîtresse* – the Renaissance notion of the relationship between the macrocosm and the microcosm is clearly central. The fullest development of this conception is, of course, to be found in Hegel's *Phenomenology*. It forms the basis of the historical theories of Marx, Comte and Croce, and bears directly on the phylogenesis–ontogenesis parallel in some versions of psychoanalytic theory. On Vico's possible sources see the next essay in this volume.

principle, were aware of the momentous nature of what was being said. In this they did not differ from most men of learning in their own time or later.

Algebra is an unshakeable deductive edifice, but it cannot give us factual information, any more than a game or a piece of fiction which we have made up can, as such, describe the world to us. Mathematics is not determined by reality outside itself, to which it has to conform, but only by our own fancy or creative imagination, which moulds the material (in this case, the symbols and rules) as it pleases. Once you try to apply mathematics to the world, for example in the way in which it is applied in the science of mechanics, the results are *pro tanto* less certain than those of pure mathematics, because there enters an element not freely created by us, namely the 'brute' matter of the external world, resistant to our minds, of which mechanics seeks to be the science. Then, in order of decreasing certainty, there come, according to Vico, physics, psychology, history.[1] Certainty increases in inverse ratio as the proportion of matter not made but merely found by us; the smaller the element of free manipulation imported by ourselves, the less certain our knowledge. *Mathesis* is a *scientia operatrix*: 'The criterion of the truth', he declares in *De antiquissima*, 'is to have made it.'[2] 'Demonstration is operation; truth is what has been made, and for this very reason we cannot demonstrate physics *a caussis* because the elements which compose nature are outside us.'[3] We can no more generate a pebble out of nothing than an entire universe. History, at this point, is still rather low in the table of the sciences headed by mathematics: physics, indeed, has been demoted – this is directed at the presumption of the Cartesians – but the humanities come lower still in terms of *verum*. This is Vico's semi-Cartesian position in middle life, in about 1710. The degree of knowability of any subject-matter is determined both by the degree of the stability and regularity of its 'elements', and of the 'clarity' or 'opaqueness' of the object of investigation: thus 'physica sunt opaca, nempe formata et finita'.[4] Hence we get an order of the sciences determined by the extent to

---

[1] DA 136/52.   [2] 'Veri criterium ... [est] ipse fecisse.' ibid.

[3] 'Demonstratio eadem ac operatio [est], et verum idem ac factum. Atque ob id ipsum physica a caussis probare non possumus, quia elementa rerum naturalium extra nos sunt.' DA 150/65.

[4] 'Physical facts are opaque, that is, formed and finite': DA 150/66. This is the central doctrine of *De antiquissima*.

which the mind is capable of penetrating them. Thus physics is more 'opaque' than mechanics, mechanics than geometry and arithmetic; morality is even less certain than physics, because it is concerned with unstable sentiments, something that is subject to the wayward waves of *libido*, irregular movements of the inner spirit tossed about by passions. History is to be found in this somewhat chaotic region, somewhere at the level of morality. In other words, physics has been demoted from its Cartesian pinnacle, but history has not been promoted yet; that radical move is still to come.[1] At this stage of his thought he has not moved from the deeply Cartesian position which he held eight years before, in 1702, when in his third Inaugural Oration he mocked his fellow humanists with the words: 'You boast, philologist, of knowing everything about the furniture and clothes of the Romans, of being more intimate with the streets, tribes and quarters of Rome, than with those of your own city. Why this pride? You know no more than did a potter, a cook, a cobbler, a summoner, an auctioneer in Rome.'[2] This is an echo of Descartes' gibe about the fact that historians of Rome can know at best no more than Cicero's servant-girl. Ten years later, however, in 1712, in the Second Reply to criticisms of *De antiquissima*, Vico complains that philological studies are regarded as useless nowadays 'on the authority of Descartes', and repeats the remark about the servant-girl, this time with obvious disapproval.[3]

If the only perfect knowledge is *per caussas* – the creator's own knowledge of his creature – what becomes of Descartes' crucial

[1] 'Scientiae minus certae, prout aliae aliis magis in materia corpulenta immerguntur: uti minus certa mechanice quam geometrica et arithmetica, quia considerat motum, sed machinarum ope: minus certa physice quam mechanice ... minus certa moralis quam physica' ('The more our sciences are immersed in bodily matter, the less certain they are: for instance, mechanics is less certain than geometry and arithmetic, because it deals with motion, but with the aid of machines; physics is less certain than mechanics ... morality is less certain than physics'). This is so because the 'motus animorum, qui penitissimi sunt' ('the motions of minds, which are very deeply hidden') are very unstable, whereas physics is concerned with 'motus interni corporum qui sunt a natura quae certa est' ('the internal motions of bodies, which are from nature, which is certain'). DA 136/52.
[2] 'Gloriaris, philologe, omnem rem vasariam, vestiariam, Romanorum nosse et magis Romae, quam tuae urbis vias, tribus, regiones callere. In quo superbis? Nihil aliud scis, quam figulus, coquus, sutor, viator, praeco Romanus.' IO 35–6/89.
[3] DA 274/183.

criterion of clear and distinct ideas? Vico boldly takes the war into the enemy's country. He declares that factual propositions can be exceedingly clear – in the sense of seeming wholly self-evident – and yet be false.[1] If there is only a single criterion of the truth or the validity of a proposition, namely, that such a proposition consists of or can be analysed into 'simple', indivisible ingredients, this would instantly rule out the greater part of our most common experience, that is, whatever is not susceptible to quantitative treatment. Such knowledge may not be of *verum* – of what can be logically demonstrated – but it is knowledge nevertheless, of *certum*, based on direct experience of the world, what is common to all men, everywhere, at all times – on which all empirical knowledge is based. Such 'certainty' may not be incorrigible, but it is what men necessarily live by: to relegate it to the sphere of mere opinion, as Descartes appears to do, is to imply that ideally men could live by true knowledge – *verum* – alone. Vico perceives that if his view of a priori knowledge is correct, this cannot possibly be so. For the only objects we can know through and through – in the sense required by Descartes – are what we have wholly created. Even geometry, on reflection, if it is interpreted as a metric of space (and not as pure algebra), remains only a tool leading to no more than tentative results; for we have not created physical space. If the only true knowledge is knowledge of necessary connections, then it is knowledge only of what obeys the rules that we have ourselves made: for nothing else can be known a priori.[2] We can, of necessity, wholly guarantee the validity only of what we have ourselves wholly invented: but this would plainly exclude the entire world of men and nature. We cannot know this a priori, it cannot be *verum* for us; yet we cannot begin to do without it, for it constitutes the basic data of all human experience. Only the Creator looking at, or rather 'within', himself, that is, at the Universe which is identical with his own self, can be said to have knowledge in this sense. Being author of all, he contemplates only the fruit of his own creative activity. Men can fully know only what they (being made in the image of God, and consequently creative within limits), in their turn, have made. But they are not

[1] Vico seems to suspect that Descartes' criterion of clarity and distinctness is, in the end, not logical but psychological, and therefore subjective and liable to error – see his letter to Esperti of 1726, *Opere*, vol. 5, pp. 201–3, at p. 202.

[2] It is, perhaps, this doctrine that led Jacobi and, later, Franz von Baader, to see Vico as a forerunner of Kant.

gods; they must begin with material not made by themselves, and so not fully knowable by them.

Hobbes, following Bacon, had said something along these lines:

Of arts, some are demonstrable, others indemonstrable; and demonstrable are those the construction of the subject whereof is in the power of the artist himself, who, in his demonstration, does no more but deduce the consequences of his own operation ... Geometry therefore is demonstrable, for the lines and figures from which we reason are drawn and described by ourselves; and civil philosophy is demonstrable, because we make the commonwealth ourselves. But because of natural bodies we know not the construction, but seek it from the effects, there lies no demonstration of what the causes be we seek for, but only of what they may be.[1]

Vico develops this by drawing a crucial distinction between the fullest and clearest knowledge in physics, and full demonstration, to which even proofs in physics are not equivalent. For 'the things which are proved in physics are those to which we can perform something similar, and ideas about natural things which are thought to have the most perfect clarity, and on which there is the completest consensus, are those to the support of which we can bring experiments by which we so far imitate nature'.[2] But experiment is not creation, yet it gives knowledge because by its means we recreate the processes of nature. What we can take to pieces and reassemble, we know – know the 'working of' – in a more genuine sense than that of which we, as it were, see only the surface and the outward changes. Yet to the extent to which we do not ourselves create physical matter or its laws, physics is not a demonstrative science and therefore not fully knowable. Only so far as it yields to experiment and is susceptible to mathematical treatment can it be, to that limited degree, called a science at all.

On this topic Vico is eloquent and unequivocal:

The rule and criterion of truth is to have made it. Hence the clear and distinct idea of the mind [i.e. the Cartesian criterion] not only cannot be the criterion of other truths, but it cannot be the criterion of the mind itself; for while the mind apprehends itself, it does not make

[1] *The English Works of Thomas Hobbes of Malmesbury*, ed. Sir William Molesworth (London, 1839–45), vol. 7, pp. 183–4.
[2] DA 136–7/52.

itself, and because it does not make itself, it is ignorant of the form or mode by which it apprehends itself.[1]

And, still more boldly: 'Those who try to prove that God exists a priori are guilty of impious curiosity. For to do that is tantamount to making oneself the god of God, thereby denying the God one seeks.'[2]

If I can be said to know beyond the possibility of error only what I myself have – or could have – created, only mathematics can be called knowledge. This is evidently regarded by Vico as too paradoxical. For it would follow that not only natural – that is, scientific – knowledge, can no longer be called knowledge, but metaphysics and theology, if they are not to be regarded as man-made fictions, fall too. We should be forced to rule out the greater part of what even Descartes regarded as valid knowledge. Vico is not a sceptic nor an irrationalist, and looks on this as a kind of *reductio ad absurdum*. Hence Descartes is dismissed, firstly because of the inadequacy of his (psychological) criteria of truth, and secondly for not realising that mathematics is rigorous only because it is arbitrary, that is, consists in the use of conventions freely adopted as in the playing of a game; and is not, as had hitherto been generally supposed, a set of innate and objective rules, or a discovery about the structure of the world. This theory of mathematics as the manipulation of counters lay unregarded until our own time, when it became a leading doctrine.[3] It must not be confused with the view that mathematical propositions are analytic or tautologous. Tautologies are statements, though they may not describe anything; inventions, like rules or moves in games, do not state at all. It is one thing to regard deductive

[1] DA 136/52.   [2] DA 150/65.

[3] I have, since writing this, discovered that Vico had at least one notable forerunner in this respect: Nicholas of Cusa, who sometime in the mid-fifteenth century boldly departed from Platonic orthodoxy and declared that mathematics was a purely human creation, which we know because we alone have made it. Nicholas of Cusa, *De coniecturis* I. 11 (so numbered in the edition by Josef Koch and Karl Bormann that comprises vol. 3 (Hamburg, 1972) of *Nicolai de Cusa opera omnia* (Leipzig and Hamburg, 1932–   ); earlier editions number the chapter I. 13). Honour where honour is due, although Cusanus did not, of course, apply his insight to historical knowledge or other humane studies. See on this *Early German Philosophy: Kant and his Predecessors* by Lewis White Beck (Cambridge, Mass., 1969), from the excellent pages of which I have gleaned this fact, not, in general, noticed by students of Vico (see pp. 67, 69–70). Beck does not mention Vico in this connection, and sees a parallel with Kant.

reasoning as giving us no new information (an ancient common-place), and quite a different one to say that it is, like music, an activity. Similarly, it is one thing to warn against confusing the causes of things with their definitions, or facts with symbols (which nominalists had done even before Occam), and much more startling to suppose, as Vico did, that formal sciences, like mathematics or logic, are not forms of discovery at all but of invention, so that if they are to be called true and false, it must be in a sense widely different from that in which these words are applied to statements.[1]

III

Vico's next large step was a thesis which undermined the accepted division of all knowledge into three kinds: metaphysical or theological, that is, based on rational intuition or faith or revelation; deductive, as in logic or grammar or mathematics; and perceptual, based on empirical observation, refined and extended by hypotheses, experiment, induction, and the other methods of the natural sciences. There exists, for him, yet another type of awareness, unlike a priori knowledge in that it is empirical, unlike deduction in that it yields new knowledge of facts, and unlike perception of the external world in that it informs us not merely of what exists or occurs, and in what spatial or temporal order, but also why what is, or occurs, is as it is – that is, in some sense *per caussas*. This species is self-knowledge: knowledge of activities of which we, the knowing subjects, are ourselves the authors, endowed with motives, purposes and a continuous social life, which we understand, as it were, from inside. Here and only here we are not passive observers looking on from the outside, as when we contemplate the external world, where all that we can see are events, or the 'surfaces' of things about the inner lives or goals of which – or whether, indeed, they have, or in principle could be said to have, goals or inner lives – we can only darkly speculate.

In the case of the external world the naturalists are right: all that we know is based on what the senses report. We can classify their

---

[1] Let me give an illustration. When Torricelli asserted that to say of a horse that it is rational is like uttering a mathematical contradiction, this might have seemed valid to an Aristotelian, perhaps even to a Cartesian. But for Vico it would constitute a confusion of two wholly distinct types of truth (and of nonsense), and therefore be an utterly misleading analogy.

contents into regular uniformities, apply mathematical techniques, decompose them into smaller parts, re-combine them, but the result of our investigations will be no more than a report of what stands in that spatial relation to what, or what follows, or is simultaneous with, what else. Yet to say that this is all we can know about human beings, and that the techniques of our ways of apprehending the external world are, therefore, all that we can use in learning about each other, would be a grave understatement, a denial of what we know to be true. In the case of human behaviour we can surely ask why men act as they do; ask not merely what mental states or events, for example feelings or volitions, are followed by what acts, but also why; not only whether, but also why, persons in this or that mental or emotional state are or are not likely to behave in a given fashion, what is, or what would be, rational or desirable or right for them to do, how and why they decide between various courses of action, and so on. In short, we judge human activity in terms of purposes, motives, acts of will, decisions, doubts, hesitations, thoughts, hopes, fears, desires and so forth; these are among the ways in which we distinguish human beings from the rest of nature. We expect to obtain answers, less or more satisfactory, to such questions. To conceive of non-human nature in such terms is irrational: a misapplication of categories, called anthropomorphism or animism, characteristic of primitive times, the ages of 'the Gods' or of 'the heroes', or, when it was used by poets in more sophisticated times, liable to be called the pathetic fallacy.

These things were affirmed by Vico before Herder and the romantics made them their own. There are adumbrations of this position in the Italian Renaissance, particularly among the Neoplatonists, and in French historiography in the sixteenth century, but they are no more than adumbrations. No one before Vico declared that if our knowledge is not demonstrative in the way in which mathematics (or divine omniscience) is so, neither is it that of perception or the natural sciences, based on the senses, as our knowledge of material objects or plants and animals must be. We can perceive and describe a table, a tree, an ant, accumulate information about their behaviour, establish laws such as those of physics, botany, entomology and so on, but all this, even at its fullest, will tell us only what it is to look like a table, a tree, an ant, or to move, or be causally affected, like one. What we still cannot tell is what it is like to *be* a table, a tree, an ant, in the sense in which we do know what it is not merely to look or behave like, but to be, a human being. If, following Descartes' rigorous rule, we allowed only that to be true knowledge which could be established by physics or other natural sciences, we should be confined to behaviourist tests, and this would result in the opposite fallacy to that of anthropomorphism, namely the uncritical assimilation of the human world to the non-human, the restriction of our knowledge to those characteristics of men which they share with the non-human world; and consequently the attempt to explain human behaviour in non-human terms, as some behaviourists and extreme materialists, both ancient and modern, inspired by the vision (or mirage) of a single, integrated, natural science of all there is, have urged us to do. It may be that a good deal more can be said in such purely 'physicalist' language than its opponents have, at times, thought possible; but certainly not enough. For we should find ourselves debarred by such self-imposed austerity from saying or thinking some of the most natural and indispensable things that men constantly say or think about other human beings. The reason is not far to seek: men can think of others only as being like themselves.

Just as we can say with assurance that we ourselves are not only bodies in space, acted upon by measurable natural forces, but that we think, choose, follow rules, make decisions – in other words, possess an inner life of which we are aware and which we can describe – so we take it for granted, and, if questioned, say that we are certain, that others possess a similar inner life, without which the notion of communication, or language, or of human society, as opposed to an aggregate of human bodies, becomes unintelligible. Anthropomorphism is the fallacy of attributing specifically human characteristics to non-human entities – gods or rivers or planets or abstract notions. It follows that there must exist a region in which anthropomorphism is valid, where these characteristics are not misapplied but correctly attributed, namely the world of men. To speak as if even men did not possess these attributes, or that they can be 'reduced' to characteristics shared with non-human entities, characteristics which alone can form the subject-matter of any reputable natural science, is to ignore the distinction between human beings and non-human nature, between material objects and mental or emotional life. Why has this knowledge been so strangely ignored in comparison with that of the external world? Because men, Vico declares, find it difficult to think of anything in other than bodily terms, inasmuch as bodies are the most familiar entities in the world of their common experience. Vico stresses over and over again how difficult it is to concentrate on, discriminate and describe mental activity. 'The human mind is naturally inclined by the senses to see itself externally in the body, and only with great difficulty does it come to understand itself by means of reflection.'[1] Hence there is a powerful tendency to describe mental phenomena in corporeal terms, which leads to crude materialism on the one hand, and fetishism and animism on the other.

The emphasis on this contrast, which runs through all Vico's thought, is, in effect, the original formulation of the familiar and much controverted distinction between the methods and goals of *Naturwissenschaft* and *Geisteswissenschaft* – natural science as against humane studies, *Wissen* and *Verstehen*. If some of the central categories of interpretation of human behaviour are in principle different from those used in explaining facts about animals or plants or things, this is a fact of cardinal importance. For it points to a type of knowledge which, in at least some respects, differs in kind from deduction, from sense perception as well as generalisations based upon it, and from scientific or immediate sense-based kinds of knowledge, as they are normally understood. Vico plainly regards such cognition as being superior to anything based on mere observation, since it is knowledge of what we ourselves have in some sense created and of which we consequently possess an intimate knowledge *per caussas* – 'from within' – a capacity with which men have been endowed from their earliest beginnings without consciously realising this: like Monsieur Jourdain, who did not know that he was speaking prose.

This distinction is not wholly absent from the thought of earlier Italian thinkers. In 1452 Gianozzo Manetti in his *De dignitate et excellentia hominis* proclaims: 'Ours, that is, human, because made by men, are what we gaze upon: all houses, all towns, all cities, all the buildings in the world ... Ours are paintings, ours are sculptures, ours are the arts, ours the sciences ... and all the inventions, ours all the varieties of different languages and of diverse letters...'[2] – ours, that is, as against those of nature. So,

[1] NS 236.
[2] 'Nostra namque, hoc est humana, sunt quoniam ab hominibus effecta quae cernuntur: omnes domus, omnia oppida, omnes urbes, omnia denique orbis terrarum aedificia... Nostrae sunt picturae, nostrae sculpturae; nostrae sunt artes,

too, Marsilio Ficino declares: 'We are not slaves of nature, we emulate her.'[1] And this is echoed by Pico, Bouelles, Bruno. The conception of man as an autonomous being, a creator and moulder of himself and the world, is a notion often found in the Renaissance and indeed both before it and in the sixteenth century in France. Vico's momentous step is to have combined this notion with the older idea of the schoolmen, that we can truly know only what we create;[2] and – the most audacious step of all – to apply this not only to the works of man in general, conceived in timeless fashion, the *urbes* and *artes* and *scientiae*, but to his history conceived as a collective, social experience extended through time; that is, not as a passive acceptance of 'ideas' showered upon men (as both Descartes and Locke in their different ways conceived human consciousness), but as a perpetual 'intentional' activity, a ceaseless employment of historically changing conceptions, categories, interpretations – mythical, symbolic, metaphysical, logical, empirical – an endless probing, questioning, ordering and moulding and goal-seeking, which characterise the restless human mind.

This is the revelation to the exposition of which Vico dedicated the second and most creative part of his long life. Descartes is the great deceiver, whose emphasis on knowledge of the external world as the paradigm of all knowledge has set philosophy on a false path. I know what it is to look like a tree, but I cannot know what it is to be a tree. But I do know what it is to be a mind, because I possess one, and create with it. 'Create the truth that you wish to cognise; and I, in cognising the truth that you have proposed to me, will "make" it in such a way that there will be no possibility of my doubting it, since I am the very one who has produced it.'[3] Vico is here speaking of 'scientific' – in this context, mathematical – ideas. But what he says applies to all human invention. Men 'create' in doing or knowing or desiring; in this they are active, they do not simply record passively. Because, by action, they 'create', or mentally live through the creations of others, they have a more

---

nostrae scientiae ... omnes adinventiones, nostrae omnia diversarum linguarum ac variarum litterarum genera.' Book 2, [paragraph 20]: p. 77, line 18, in the edition by Elizabeth R. Leonard (Padua, 1975).

[1] 'non servi [sumus] naturae, sed aemuli.' *Theologia platonica* 13. 3: p. 295 in Ficino's *Opera* (Basle, [1576]).

[2] On the superior knowledge of those who play an active, as opposed to a passive, role in a process, see p. 130 below.

[3] *Opere*, vol. 1, p. 258; translation by Gianturco, DN xliii.

direct and intimate acquaintance with action than with the natural data that they merely observe outside themselves. This is Vico's reason for believing that human studies, inasmuch as they are concerned with both the content and the form of the entire field of men's activity – arts and sciences, custom and law, indeed every form of life and human relationship, expressed as they are in monuments, in rites, in forms of symbolism and articulation, rudimentary and developed, emotional and reflective, abstract and concrete, collective and individual – that this great realm is intelligible to men, who are its authors, in a way in which nothing else can be. It is the nearest approach attainable by his creatures to divine knowledge, which only the Creator of all things has of all things.

The truly revolutionary move is the application of the *verum/factum* principle to the study of history. Vico probably found a clue to this in Hobbes.[1] But Hobbes' statement that 'civil philosophy is demonstrable, because we make the commonwealth ourselves'[2] seems to refer to conscious plans and arrangements: constitutions or blueprints, and other constructions of human minds; like geometrical figures, for example, that are fully intelligible or 'demonstrable' because they are literally invented. Vico transformed this notion and gave it immensely greater scope and depth (and increased its dangerously speculative character) by extending it to the growth in time of the collective or social consciousness of mankind, particularly at its pre-rational and semi-conscious levels, to the dreams and myths and images that have dominated men's thoughts and feelings from his earliest beginnings. Vico stated this bold thesis, of which he seems to be the only true begetter, in a famous passage in the *New Science*:

... in the night of thick darkness enveloping the earliest antiquity, so remote from ourselves, there shines the eternal and never failing light of a truth beyond all question: that the world of civil society has certainly been made by men, and that its principles are therefore to be found within the modifications of our own human mind. Whoever reflects on this cannot but marvel that the philosophers should have bent all their energies to the study of the world of nature, which, since God made it, he alone knows: and that they should have neglected the

[1] Did Vico read Hobbes in the original? M. H. Fisch argues that he knew at any rate his Latin works: A 211 (note 39).
[2] loc. cit. (p. 39 above, note 1).

study of the world of nations, or civil world, which, since men had made it, men could come to know.[1]

By 'modifications' he appears to mean what we should mean by the stages of the growth, or of the range or direction, of human thought, imagination, will, feeling, into which any man equipped with sufficient *fantasia* (as well as knowledge acquired by rational methods) can 'enter'. Vico nowhere, so far as I know, fully or exactly explains the way in which men understand other men – 'know their minds', grasp their goals, outlooks, ways of thinking, feeling, acting. He does not account for our knowledge of other selves – individual or collective, living or dead – by invoking the language of empathy, or analogical reasoning, or intuition, or participation in the unity of the World Spirit. That has been left to his interpreters. He rests his case on his conviction that what men have made, other men, because their minds are those of men, can always, in principle, 'enter into'.[2]

This is the proclamation of the autonomy of historical studies and of their superiority over those of nature. The first adumbration of this step occurs in the *Diritto universale* of 1720–2. Vico's views have undergone a radical shift. History is promoted from the comparatively lowly place it still occupied in his hierarchy of types of knowledge in 1709–10 – the period of *De nostri* and *De antiquissima* – and, because it is seen to be a form of self-knowledge, has now risen above the place assigned to natural science. Vico cannot claim for it the certainty of mathematics: but it has in it something of the 'divine' pleasure which that creative discipline, not trammelled by 'opaque' facts, provides. It is the queen of all the studies that are concerned with reality, with knowledge of what there is in the world.

Since it is their minds that are so harnessed, men can grasp what they and other men are at; for they know what a mind is, what a

[1] NS 331.

[2] But see p. 52 below, note 1. This view can be developed in many directions, of which the Absolute Idealism of Hegel and of his Italian disciples, Croce and Gentile (and the peculiar variant advocated by their English follower, R. G. Collingwood), is only one, deeply metaphysical, form, for which some authority may be sought in Vico's text (see, e.g., p. 97 below, note 2), not in my view with great plausibility. The influence of Vico's central principle on the German philosopher Wilhelm Dilthey and on the French historian Jules Michelet, and, less directly, on social anthropologists, philologists and historians of culture, has, as a rule, taken more empirical and less speculative forms.

plan and a purpose are, whether one's own or another's. Above all, men know what it is to be a man – not merely a solitary individual, but a man in society, in reciprocal relations, co-operating consciously, with other similar men. Such self-knowledge, because it is knowledge *per caussas* – knowing why, and not merely knowing that, or knowing how – is the nearest that man can attain to divine knowledge. If ever I can understand myself at all, even though I may do it imperfectly, and could learn to do it better (as a trained critic must have learned, if he sees more in a work of art, 'knows why', better than I do), I am no longer merely recording or classifying or deducing from external data.

This kind of knowing is what German thinkers later distinguished as understanding. It is different from knowing facts, however systematically and scientifically. Understanding other men's motives or acts, however imperfectly or corrigibly, is a state of mind or activity in principle different from learning about, or knowledge of, the external world. We observe, we learn facts about, but we cannot understand, stones or the death-watch beetle. Since I did not create my own personality – my psychological characteristics or the contents of my mind – I cannot be said to know myself through and through, as I can know mathematics, which I, or other men, have created; or as my Creator can know me. On the other hand, mathematics, compounded as it is of fictions, of counters made by men, and played according to man-made rules, cannot give knowledge of reality. Because I have not made myself, self-knowledge is less 'transparent' than mathematics or logic (or, one might add, chess or heraldry or fiction); but because I, or other men, are not mere passive spectators but actors, and understand, 'enter into', the purposes, states of mind or will, of which actions are the expression, such knowledge, because its principles, being *modificazioni* of the human *mente*, are common to men in widely different cultures, is more 'transparent', nearer to mathematical knowledge *per caussas*, than mere contemplation of the successions and compresences of things in nature can ever be. Such historical insight thus seems to stand half-way between the deductive or formal *scienza* of pure artefacts, and the scientific, inductive or experimental, perceptual *coscienza* of given, irremovable, opaque, 'brute' nature. I understand the human past, the experience of my society or of other societies – 'what Alcibiades did and suffered'[1] – in a sense in which, in principle, I cannot

---

[1] Aristotle's illustration of the subject-matter of history. *Poetics* 1451^{b}11.

understand the history of stones or trees or animals. For this reason stones, trees, animals have a knowable past, but no history. Historical knowledge is not mere knowledge of past events, but only of events so far as they enter into human activity, and are an element in the biography of an individual or a group.[1] They are intelligible only to creatures who know what it is like to be a man. Whatever has been made by men, or thought, willed, imagined by sentient beings, because they follow certain rules, obey certain principles (which can be discerned and formulated), and only that (even though God is the ultimate source of it all), can be grasped by the similarly rule-guided imaginations of other men.

How, otherwise, could communication occur? How are sentences spoken to one man by another, or any other mode of direct expression, understood? Not by inductive reasoning. Knowledge of other human beings is supplemented, rendered less or more probable, systematised, corrected, justified by scientific method, but is not gained by it. For Vico, such knowledge is the result of a human capacity for imaginative understanding. The task of historians cannot be performed without this faculty, and their success will, in part, depend on how richly endowed with it they are, and how well they use it. Just as I can attempt to comprehend what the man who is at this moment speaking to me seeks to convey, which involves some understanding of his outlook, his social milieu – his past, the likelihood of this or that kind of behaviour on his part – so, too, must I be able to grasp (if I try hard enough, and possess the kind of genius needed) what it must have been like to have been a primitive man: for example, not to have lived in an organised society, or (harder still) to have been without language. This, Vico freely acknowledges, may require a 'great effort'.[2] It is almost, but not quite, impossible to work back from the present, think away society and civilisation, and imagine what it must have been like to be a primitive savage wandering in the 'great forest of the earth',[3] scarcely able to communicate, with a vocabulary of gestures or pictures much smaller even than that of a modern child. We cannot hope to recover it all. It is 'beyond our power to enter the vast imagination of those first men'.[4] Yet (Vico

---

[1] This is at the root of Hegel's celebrated distinction of *an sich* and *für sich*. But see p. 52 below, note 1.

[2] NS 338.   [3] NS *passim*, e.g. 13, 195, 301, 369, 736, 1097.

[4] NS 378; see also 338. On this see pp. 64–5 below.

comes back to this obstinately and repeatedly) history has, after all, been made by men, and therefore in the end it must always be penetrable by other men, as that which is not made by men – rocks, trees and animals – is not. The very same imaginative faculty which makes it possible for me to conceive the feelings, thoughts, acts of human beings of my time, but distant from me in space, or of different habits or language or mentality, ultimately makes it possible for me to understand remote cultures too.

How in practice is this to be done? How can I grasp what was thought or willed by the aggressive brutes described by Hobbes, or the helpless simpletons of Grotius, or Pufendorf's waifs and strays,[1] or the other stock figures of the theorists of the state of nature? Vico had been deeply influenced in his youth by Lucretius' account of human origins; he had had an Epicurean and a Cartesian phase, and his Catholic orthodoxy has been strongly doubted; but it was a genuinely devout Christian who wrote the *Scienza nuova*. Consequently it may be that Vico's belief in an omnipresent creative spirit – God, who made him and in whom he lived, the central fire of which he was a spark – led him to the metaphysical belief that a man could have a direct relationship in some non-empirical fashion with spiritual activity in times and places other than his own. For, as has often been remarked, it is some sort of pantheism or panpsychism, rather than orthodox Catholicism, that is constantly suggested by his language. But whether or not Vico was in any degree a pantheist or, as Croce and his disciples hold, an Absolute Idealist, and whatever the psychological roots of his beliefs, his view of historical knowledge does not, in fact, require such transcendentalist assumptions. All that he demands is a vivid capacity for imaginative reconstruction, for conceiving the *modificazioni* of the human mind, for knowing what human beings could, and what they could not, have done or thought. One can grasp what it is like to be a savage, or at least believe, whether correctly or not, that one can succeed in doing this, without mystical or non-empirical presuppositions. When, for example, Vico argues that it cannot be true that the Romans borrowed the Twelve Tables (the original Roman code of laws) from the Athens of Solon's day (as Roman tradition maintained), he is asserting not that he positively knows that they did not in fact do so – he does not claim to know the past by a direct act of metaphysical

[1] NS1, synopsis: *Opere*, vol. 3, p. 5; cf. NS 338, 553.

clairvoyance – only that the Romans could not have done so, because such barbarians as the Romans must, to judge by the evidence, at that time have been could scarcely have known where Athens was, or that it possessed the kind of culture which had something specific to give Rome, or the nature or value of Solon's activities. He knows, too, that even if one makes the absurd assumption that the prehistoric Romans somehow divined all this, they could scarcely have translated the Attic words into the most idiomatic Latin, without a trace of Greek influence upon it, using such a purely Latin word as *auctoritas*, for example, for which no Greek equivalent existed.

When Vico argues that the Romans could not have done these things, that the story is intrinsically too implausible, his argument rests not so much on an empirical accumulation of evidence about human behaviour in many places and situations, from which such conclusions can be drawn by normal scientific reasoning (although, no doubt, this too is necessary), as upon some more immediate apprehension of what it is to be civilised and how this differs from being barbarian, on some acquaintance with the stages of the growth of self-consciousness in individuals or societies, based, in its turn, on some notion of what constitutes a man, some awareness of the way and the time order in which the interplay of natural and spiritual factors is likely to give birth to different human faculties, or modes of feeling or expression, and to the evolution of various concepts and categories, and the institutions, habits and 'styles of life' bound up with them, at various times and in various conditions. Unless we possess some knowledge of what in fact occurred, gained by orderly, that is, scientific or 'common-sense', methods of acquiring information, such general notions will lack content – indeed could not arise at all. But neither factual information nor reasoning power is enough.[1] Without the grasp

---

[1] He fully recognises that deductive techniques are indispensable for examining and criticising sources, but he is, as might be expected, apprehensive of the scepticism which such destructive critics of the Scriptures as Spinoza and *Père* Simon thereby breed. (On the relationship to Spinoza, see the interesting article by Arnaldo Momigliano entitled 'Vico's *Scienza Nuova*: Roman "Bestioni" and Roman "Eroi"' in *History and Theory* 5 (1966), 3–23.) He supposes that the power of *fantasia*, imaginative insight, was an antidote to this subversive and, in his day, fast growing intellectual fashion. He was, ironically enough, accused of this very vice by orthodox Catholic critics not long after his death. See p. 99 below.

of what it is to possess a mind, what it is like to respond to stimuli, and how this differs from following rules or pursuing a policy, from love or hate, worship or recognition of authority, of what it is to be imaginative or critical, childlike or mature, unworldly or possessive, religious or atheistic, a master or a servant – without this understanding, acquaintance with empirical facts will be of little avail. Only sentient beings can have this basic understanding, and only of creatures similar to themselves – angels of angels, men of men. We begin with this capacity for understanding. We may possess it only in embryo, but we could not even begin, and should not be recognisably human, without it. Possession of its rudiments is intrinsic to being a man.[1]

[1] On this, however, see 'Vico's Science' by Leon Pompa, *History and Theory* 10 (1971), 49–83. In this well-argued, though to me not altogether convincing, exposition, which seeks to demonstrate that Vico's 'science' is truly scientific, Pompa advances the view that by *modificazioni* (one of the crucial terms on the interpretation of which a very great deal turns) Vico means not individual but social 'purposes, necessities, utilities; those of the social world', and treats *mente* as a kind of general social consciousness governed by the laws on which the new science is founded. This may well be correct; Vico discusses the purpose of societies and classes and scarcely at all of 'world-historical' individuals. But this interpretation still seems to me to leave exceedingly obscure the exact way in which Vico supposes that men of a later age can 'enter' – only, he tells us, with the utmost difficulty – the remote social 'purposes, necessities' etc. of earlier, barbarous times. The laws that determine the successive stages of the *corsi e ricorsi* are too few and too general to make it possible to reconstruct specific social or cultural phenomena: the scientific method employed in the natural sciences is excluded inasmuch as it yields only 'external' knowledge, whereas we have an 'inside' view of the acts and works of man. If the method is not connected with the capacity for intercommunication whereby men are enabled to understand and misunderstand one another, both within the same culture and historically, across stretches of time and varieties of culture – Dilthey's *Verstehen* – then what does Vico mean? His *fantasia* – capacity for imaginatively 'entering' worlds different from our own, or perhaps even any experience that differs from the most familiar – may be fallible, and, in any case, is not a sufficient condition for arriving at historical truth, which needs verification by the ordinary methods of research; but may it not be a necessary condition, since without it we should not be capable of even so much as conceiving what it is that we are looking for – a possible world, the 'portrait' of a society or an age – and not a mere collection of data or propositions? Doubtless we cannot understand ourselves save by understanding others, or our own present state save by becoming aware of whence we came and how; but equally we cannot understand others save in terms of their relation to ourselves and our world, nor the human past unless we trace it backwards from our present. If this is correct, is Vico entitled to speak of a 'science', even as the term was understood in his own time? But Pompa may not wish to press the

A sense of historical perspective – for that is Vico's new and revolutionary discovery – cannot, unaided by empirical data, 'intuit' what actually occurred; it can at best rule out what could not have occurred. It works with such vague basic concepts as change, causality, growth, the pattern of a culture, time sequence, anachronism – concepts by which we order the data, attribute characteristics and perceive irreversible relationships. When we say that the social (or economic, or religious) condition of England in the fifteenth century could not have been what it was if the events which constitute, say, the history of the fourteenth and thirteenth centuries in England had not taken place; and therefore that someone who knows, no matter how minutely, the history only of the twelfth century could not understand, or account for, what took place in England in the fifteenth; or if we say that it is wholly impossible for *Hamlet*, or anything like it, to have been composed in the kind of society which inhabited Outer Mongolia in the third century AD, and look on any theory which rests on the opposite assumption as too absurd to be worth a moment's notice; these 'could nots' and this 'impossible' are categories of the historical sense, of the sense of what goes with what, and of what is incompatible with it. The recognition of an irreversible process of infancy, youth, maturity, old age, final decline in the lives of societies, no less than of individual men, and of what types of language or ritual or economic relations belong to each stage of social growth, is something, it seemed to Vico, that the philosophers or jurists of his own and of other times did not sufficiently possess or understand, otherwise they would not have credited early man with their own sophisticated mental processes.[1] This

appropriateness of this term – in which case there may not be much disagreement between us. On this entire topic see also the excellent discussion in Peter Winch, *The Idea of a Social Science and its Relation to Philosophy* (London and New York, 1958; 2nd ed., London, 1990).

[1] Pompa, in the article cited in the previous note, has taken me to task for supposing that according to Vico the capacity to think historically was the condition of any thinking whatever about ourselves, involving as it does such basic concepts as coherence and implausibility, since if this were so, he could scarcely have charged modern scholars with the very kind of unhistorical thinking which he denounces as a cause of anachronism and misinterpretation. But neither Vico nor I seem to me to be guilty of this fallacy: a man's sense of what is and what is not likely or even thinkable within a particular society need not rest on what fits into his own world; only the general category or notion of coherence is required. The data needed for grasping the activities of a given society are to be

blindness vitiated their work and made it necessary to reconstruct the entire science of man from the foundations. He meant by this science the study of all that pertained to men as such, as contrasted with that which they shared with the non-human world, such as their bodies, or the physical properties of the physical matter by which their lives were sustained.

The theorists whom he singled out for attack were those who seemed to him to have perpetrated unhistorical anachronisms: like the upholders of theories of natural law or social contract, who credited primitive men with some of the civilised attributes of their own 'magnificent' age;[1] and those rationalists like Descartes and Spinoza, or utilitarians like Hobbes and Locke, or 'Epicureans' like Gassendi, who, however deeply they differed from one another, all assumed the existence of a fixed, unchanging human nature, common to all men, everywhere, at all times, a fully developed moral and psychological structure from which rights, obligations, laws, flowing from universal goals, identical for all men, could be logically deduced. Vico attacks the great jurists Grotius, Selden, Pufendorf, whose gifts and erudition he admired, and to whose notions of social laws (especially Grotius') he acknowledged a profound debt, for their blindness to the idea of development, *nascimento*, coming to birth, from which *natura* is derived, whereby one generation, or culture, grows into another. Blind to this, they cannot see the organic interconnection which unites the various fields of activity which belong to any one particular stage of social growth. Above all, he charges them with ignoring the cardinal truth that all valid explanation is necessarily and essentially

discovered by the methods of ordinary empirical research: observation, hypothesis, confirmation etc. To interpret the data correctly, however, the historian needs the aid of the set of principles of what Vico claims to be his new science, which indicates by means of universally applicable and intelligible 'laws' the necessary succession of stages that each culture must go through. This discovery seems to be founded on an analogy with the irreversible pattern of individual lives or of the short span of the more or less immediate past of a man's own society. We cannot think of our own lives (he seems to assume) or of the immediate past of our own societies, or of those sufficiently close to them in space and time, save in historical terms – as structured processes, some formed by our own lives, others formed by the social patterns out of which we emerge. The fault of the scholars who perpetrate anachronisms is not to apply this (evidently given or inescapable) notion of a fixed order – e.g. of the primitive stage succeeded by the mature, the mature by the decadent – to the remoter past. I owe this highly plausible interpretation of Vico's thesis to Pompa, to whom I gladly acknowledge this debt.

[1] NS 123.

genetic, in terms either of human purposes, which change with changing circumstances, or of the alteration of circumstances by these purposes themselves, that is, by human action, or the interplay of purposes and 'blind' circumstances or environment, which often leads to consequences unintended by men.

The central idea at the heart of Vico's thought is that, in the individual and society alike, phase follows phase not haphazardly (as the Epicureans thought), nor in a sequence of mechanical causes or effects (as the Stoics taught), but as stages in the pursuit of an intelligible purpose – man's effort to understand himself and his world, to realise his capacities in it. History for him is the orderly procession (guided by Providence, working through men's capacities) of ever deepening types of apprehension of the world, of ways of feeling, acting, expressing, each of which grows out of, and supersedes, its predecessor. To each type or culture necessarily belong some characteristics not found in any other. So begins the conception of the 'phenomenology' of human experience and activity, of men's history and life as determined by their own, at first unconscious, then progressively more conscious, creative moulding, that is, mastery of nature both living and dead. In the forms given it by Hegel and Marx and their followers, this idea dominates the modern world. It is for this that Marx praised him. Of this view of men and history, for better and for worse, Vico is the pioneer.

How are we to discover how we came to be what we are, why we think and act as we do, and what we truly need or want? Only by the study of our own development. The ancient analogy between the individual and society, microcosm and macrocosm, ontogenesis and phylogenesis, dominates Vico's thought as much as that of the Renaissance. The task is to uncover the actual story of how and, above all, why cultures come to be, rise and fall. This is what the new science is to tell us: how is this to be achieved? We have the means within our grasp. They have not been used only because men have not realised their marvellous potentialities.[1] The key lies in the past experience of the human race, which, from its earliest origins, may be read in its mythology, its language, its

---

[1] Bodin and Bacon had both noted that fables and myths provided evidence of the beliefs and social structure of primitive peoples, but did not develop this insight with anything resembling the breadth and depth of Vico. Nevertheless, he is probably more indebted to them and others, e.g. Jean Leclerc and, perhaps, Lafitau and the Chevalier Ramsay, in this respect than he chooses to acknowledge.

social and religious institutions. In particular it may be perceived in the evidences still extant of earlier forms of life, discoverable in ancient monuments and the accounts of the early customs and institutions of peoples, as well as their occasional survival – living or fossilised – in isolated places, among backward or simple folk, especially in the poetry, the magical rites, the legal structure of primitive societies. To suppose this process to be intelligible is to find an order in the apparent chaos – an Ariadne's thread that will not merely lead us out of the labyrinth, but will explain its complexities. This Vico affects to find in the Platonic idea of man as he should be – not in Plato's static ideal pattern, but in a dynamic principle of 'growth', a principle of movement, itself immutable, which governs human evolution. The unfolding – the succession of states – is a process; but the pattern is always the same. Vico expands this Platonic truth by saying that the intelligible 'substance' is one, although the 'modes' of its development are diverse.[1]

This single, unvarying, central truth, apprehended with varying degrees of clarity and fullness in its many 'modes' or appearances – from the *certum* of insufficiently developed societies to the *verum* of high cultures, from concrete imagery of poetry that is plunged in the senses to metaphysical soaring towards abstractions[2] – is to be grasped by the use of systematic comparisons between the beginnings and last phases of ancient and modern nations. It is this method that, by abstracting what is common to various phases of culture – what Vico calls 'induction' – reveals the unalterable inner pattern, the Platonic law, that not only shapes our world, but, since 'the rise, development, maturity, decline and fall' is a universal principle, is eternally valid for all possible societies.[3] This marks the birth of full-fledged modern historicism – a doctrine that in its empirical form has stimulated and enriched, and in its dogmatic, metaphysical form, inhibited and distorted, the historical imagination.

The work of Providence, Vico's anticipation of Hegel's 'cunning of reason',[4] obeys (or imposes) this Platonic pattern. It is

---

[1] NS 1096. See the excellent exposition of Vico's Platonism by Werner Stark, the best and most convincing known to me: 'Giambattista Vico's Sociology of Knowledge', in Giorgio Tagliacozzo and Hayden V. White (eds), *Giambattista Vico: An International Symposium* (Baltimore, [1969]), pp. 297–307.

[2] NS 821.   [3] NS 349, 348.

[4] Georg Wilhelm Friedrich Hegel, *Sämtliche Werke*, ed. Hermann Glockner (Stuttgart, 1927–51), vol. 5, p. 226; vol. 6, p. 127; vol. 8, p. 420; vol. 11, p. 63.

Providence that turns men's instincts and purposes to the creation of institutions which do indeed minister to their true ends on earth, but which, primitive and vicious savages that they are, they are in no condition to conceive, let alone aim at; and Providence is identified with this Platonic pattern, the laws that govern the *storia ideale eterna*[1] of the peoples. Seen in retrospect, men, or, at any rate, Vico, can discover how the vicious desires of the *ferini* (on which Tacitus, who paints 'man as he is',[2] is regarded by him as the supreme expert) have been turned to the profit of justice and truth, the seeds of which, buried by sin, nevertheless live on in the most degraded savages.[3] Above all we must not search for the nature of man as some unaltering static 'core' within the flux of experience, but perceive it in the flux itself – the 'coming into being' of institutions 'at certain times and in certain guises'.[4] All that can be gathered about the past and present of the moral, religious, aesthetic outlook of human groups, or their social, economic, linguistic habits as they gradually alter and grow; in short, all that comparative mythology, philosophy, jurisprudence, anthropology, ethnology, sociology and the other sciences of man duly came to investigate, falls into this province. But one must have eyes to see and ears to hear. Small wonder if Vico found difficulty in conveying to his contemporaries a vision so transforming and so universal.

IV

Men make their own history, that is, they shape their own lives, both deliberately and without conscious intention, in response to physical environment and to unintended, 'providential' changes in their own natures. To understand their present condition, to be able to answer the most urgent problems which trouble men, political, moral, social, legal, religious, is to understand how these men came to be in a situation where alone these problems have arisen in this or that specific shape. Why, for example, should we obey our constituted superiors? All kinds of conflicting answers have been given; each, in the end, appeals to a specific model of

---

[1] See p. 86 below, note 1.   [2] A 138.
[3] See Alain Pons, 'Nature et histoire chez Vico', *Études philosophiques*, New Series, 16 No 1 (January–March 1961), 39–53.
[4] NS 147.

what a human being is, usually a figment compounded from characteristics which the theorist has met in his own limited and transient world, or those which he needs for his theory, or both together. But do these abstractions, whether the natural man of Grotius, or Hobbes's ruthless egoist, or Spinoza's free and rational mind, correspond to anything actual or possible? Natural-law theorists, social contract theorists, utilitarians, individualists, materialists and rationalists of various types have, according to Vico, gone hopelessly astray because they do not understand the systematically developing and altering succession of outlooks and motives dictated by the changing needs of human nature, a nature which is a *nascimento* – a process; for him human nature, in the course of seeking to satisfy its needs, cannot help transforming itself, and so constantly generates new characteristics, new needs, new categories of thought and action. The leading theorists of the age – lawyers and philosophers – are blind to this because they do not understand the nature of history or society or the individual soul. They love to speak of 'the matchless wisdom of the ancients',[1] as if early men could conceivably have known more than their descendants, who have inherited all the discoveries and inventions of the past and improved upon them; or, more absurdly still, as if these early men were fully rational beings, or lived (or could have lived) in a world similar to our own, or faced the kind of problems that necessarily belong to our own unique phase of historical growth. If we do not study origins, we shall never know to what problems the thought or behaviour of our ancestors was a continuous response; and since their response ultimately shaped not only them but us, too, we shall not understand ourselves unless we trace our own growth to its roots. 'Doctrines must take their beginning from that of the matters of which they treat.'[2] Then, and then only, shall we understand how men came to be what they are, and how the problems which torment us have come to be problems for us at all.

This is the whole doctrine of historicism in embryo. Knowledge of genetic psychology, of the history of social consciousness, the retracing of our steps, light cast upon the path that we have traversed – these alone can settle the controversies of the dogmatic jurists and political thinkers. Problems are intelligible – and soluble – only within their own socio-historical context. It is plainly

[1] NS 128.   [2] NS 314; cf. 338, 394.

ridiculous to assume, in the teeth of all historical evidence, that in early, barbarous societies there sprang forth, fully armed like Athena from the head of Zeus, poets and lawgivers, beings of vast knowledge and consummate wisdom who owed nothing to the primitives among whom they were bred but, possessing esoteric sources of information and intellectual and moral attributes and insight undreamt of by the societies of their time, proceeded to dispense eternal laws and timeless wisdom to their peoples. Yet, Vico asks, is not this precisely what is attributed to Lycurgus, Draco, Homer, Solon and all the mythological sages of antiquity?[1] Are we seriously to suppose that the 'first men, stupid, insensate and horrible beasts',[2] the impious progeny of Noah, wandering in the great forest of the earth – that these creatures found not the slightest difficulty in conceiving a set of eternal, unalterable, universal principles ('quod ubique, quod semper, quod ab omnibus creditum est')[3] binding on all men at all times, and laying down once and for all both what men do, and what they ought to do: principles concerning which the most profound philosophers and the most learned jurists notoriously do not agree, but which, nevertheless, are said to be engraved on the hearts of all men from all eternity?[4] It was a stroke of genius to deny, as Vico did in the face of the highest authorities of his time, and of Aristotle, Seneca and the central Western tradition, the existence of an unaltering human nature whose properties and goals are knowable a priori.

It has been argued that although such models of human nature

---

[1] Yet, of course, it is precisely this that he supposes to have been the case with the Jews, to whom the truth was directly revealed by God. Vico cautiously leaves the case of sacred history largely undiscussed; he is mainly concerned to deny that the principles of natural law, or any other esoteric knowledge, were to be found among the primitive Gentile peoples – hence his denial that the pagans derived natural law from the Jews and corrupted it, as maintained by Huet, Bochart, Witsius and others; or that hieroglyphs concealed secret Christian truths, as asserted by Athanasius Kircher. So far as God shaped the lives of the pagans, he did so by purely naturalistic means. On this see Arnaldo Momigliano, 'La nuova storia romana di G. B. Vico', *Rivista storica italiana* 77 (1965), 773–90, at 779–81.

[2] 'primi uomini, stupidi, insensati ed orribili bestioni'. NS 374.

[3] 'What is believed everywhere, always, by all.' Vincent of Lérins, *Commonitorium* 2. 3.

[4] This was not wholly fair, since these thinkers did not maintain that all men were necessarily able to formulate explicitly the principles they were following – although they could always, in theory, have done so. Nor does Vico concede that savages followed these principles even unconsciously.

may be historically or psychologically unreal, yet they may have value as analytic fictions (like the atom or the economic man) in terms of which a science can be built – entities which may, indeed, be imaginary or idealised, but, despite this, perform an indispensable function by constituting standards or types in terms of deviation from which natural objects can be measured or classified. Vico's reply to this is contained in his criticism of the theories of natural law and of the social contract, which is designed to show that to leave out history is to render the model of man too remote from reality to be of use. When, in addition, the plasticity of men, and especially their capacity for transforming themselves by their own creative activity, is omitted from the model, it becomes a caricature and, if applied to reality, leads only to errors and absurdities. Vico argues that the theory of the social contract, for example, which dominated his own age, takes it for granted that the original solitary wanderers who came out of the woods to make a compact to live together already understood what a compact was. But he points out that this is patently absurd; for such men could not have understood so complex a notion – or even used it – unless they were already living in society governed by rules, since only within such a social whole could the concept of a compact or promise – an elaborate piece of social machinery or convention – have originated or been understood. Men could not have invented social organisation by means of a promise given by all to all, or by all to one man – democratic or monarchical – for if the social nexus – rules, conventions, compacts and all – had not already existed, the notion of a promise would have meant nothing to them. To found the State on a promise, and not the other way about, is thus a logical absurdity.

This demonstrates not merely that the institution called the social contract cannot have been the historical origin of later social habits, but that it is useless even as an analytical device to explain why today we have come to behave (or to think it right to behave) as we do: why we do not rebel, why we condemn resistance to authority, pay debts, think it right to serve in the army, allow ourselves to be taxed, and so on.[1] Moreover, to say that although

[1] Something similar, but not identical, is to be found in Hume's later objections to the view that political arrangements rest on a contract (that is, a solemn promise), when he argues that whatever explains the sacredness of promises (in his opinion, social utility) is by itself sufficient to account for those social institutions which promises are brought in to explain and justify.

no contract was ever in fact made, yet we now behave (as Hobbes or Rousseau maintained) exactly as if such a contract, overt or tacit, existed, is to ignore or misinterpret the fact that human beliefs, conduct, character, experience are today what they are not in obedience to a historical fiction, but only because they once were what they were, that is, as a stage in a continuous evolution in time. It follows that no one can understand either how or why men act as they do without knowing by what steps they came to be what they are. A static model like the social contract omits sociological and psychological facts – the survival of the past into the present, the influence of tradition, of inherited habits and the shapes they assume. It ignores or distorts the true view of society as something compounded out of many interlaced, altering strands of conscious, semi-conscious and buried memories, of individual and collective reactions and sentiments, of patterns of social life which we speak of as the character of a family, a tribe, a nation, a historical period, the roots of which are all but lost, yet to some degree still remain traceable in the opaque and tantalising past. Only those who have the imagination and knowledge to trace this process to its origins, and so reconstruct it, can understand its effects in the present or assess its value and prospects. Implausible myths like the contract, or obedience to universal reason, or calculation of rational self-interest, placed at the centre of their systems by Hobbes and Spinoza, are, for Vico, merely the refuge of ignorance. If we understand what we come out of, the perplexing problems of why we are as we are – and whether it is desirable or right to continue to be so – will be nearer solution. Whatever accounts for our character and institutions will also account for our values, which themselves belong to, and are effective and intelligible at, only their own specific stage in human history. The notion of absolute standards, moral, aesthetic, social, in terms of which the entire human past is largely a story of mistakes, crimes, deception – the very cornerstone of the outlook of the Enlightenment – is the absurd corollary of the fallacious belief in a fixed, ultimate, unchanging human nature. But Vico is not primarily concerned with morality, or value judgements. Like Spinoza – the adversary often in his thoughts[1] – he seems content to understand. He does, of course, in fact make moral judgements,

---

[1] See Arnaldo Momigliano, op. cit. (p. 59 above, note 1), esp. p. 781. Also his 'Vico's *Scienza Nuova*' (see p. 51 above, note 1).

and in them unhesitatingly takes for granted the validity of the values embodied in his own faith and civilisation; but this is quite consistent with his 'historicist', conservative thesis. He does, at times, remind himself that Christian values are timeless and absolute; but for the most part he forgets this, and speaks as if necessarily *autres temps, autres moeurs*.

If knowledge of the past is so vital to our understanding of ourselves, what methods are we to use to obtain it? The evidence lies scattered about us, yet historians have steadily ignored it, and tell us stories which, besides contradicting one another, must often appear inherently implausible to anyone who has grasped in what ways human beings in fact develop. Yet the remedy lies at hand. There are, Vico declares, three incorruptible sources of true historical knowledge of man: language, mythology, antiquities; these cannot lie. He develops this thesis with learning, imagination and audacity.

V

Men embody their feelings, attitudes and thoughts in symbols. These symbols are natural means of self-expression; they are not forged for the purpose of misleading or entertaining future generations. Consequently they are dependable evidence of the minds and outlooks of which they are the vehicles, if only we knew how to read it. Language is not a deliberate invention on the part of men who think thoughts, and then look around for means of articulating them. Ideas and the symbols in which they are expressed are not, even in thought, separable. We do not merely speak or write in symbols, we think and can think only in symbols, whether words or images; the two are one.[1] From words and the way they are used we can infer the mental processes, the attitudes and outlooks of their users, for 'minds [*ingenia*] are formed by the character of language, not language by the minds of those who speak it'.[2]

[1] cf. Joseph de Maistre's remark, still novel enough when it was made a hundred years later, that 'la pensée et la parole ne sont que deux magnifiques synonymes': *Oeuvres complètes de J. de Maistre* (Lyon/Paris, 1884–7), vol. 4, p. 119. This probably derives from Vico, of whose works Maistre was one of the few readers in his day, and not from Hamann or Herder, whose views reached Paris (and Piedmont) somewhat later.

[2] DN 95/40.

This is an observation of great suggestiveness: men are born into traditions of speech and writing which form minds as much as minds form them. Although probably merely occasioned by a famous controversy, in Vico's own day, about the superiority of French as against Italian literary style claimed by the abbé de Bouhours and others, this insight embodies a point of central importance – the denial of the very possibility of an unaltering, logically perfect language, constructed to reflect the basic structure of language – the famous revolutionary thesis adumbrated by Leibniz and developed in modern times by Russell and some of his disciples. For Vico there is no such structure, at any rate in the human world, no world of perfect, unaltering essences. What kind of words have human beings used to express their relation to the world, to each other, and to their own past selves? Vico speaks of what he calls the 'poetical' cast of mind – poetical language, poetical law, poetical morals, poetical logic and so on. By 'poetical' he means – what, following the Germans, we tend to attribute to the people or 'folk' – modes of expression used by the unsophisticated mass of the people in the early years of the human race, not by the children of its old age – self-conscious men of letters, experts or sages. The earliest human beings, primitive savages, in order to communicate, used natural signs and gestures: what Vico calls 'mute acts'[1] – the designating of some one actual thing to stand for or signify other things that it resembles, or of a pictorial representation of something to stand for a whole class of entities which it resembles. This, for example, is done by hieroglyphs or ideograms, which, Vico surmises, were once in use everywhere, but have survived only in Egypt and China (and among the Indians of the New World), because the civilisations of these countries have long been insulated from the main stream of human culture. For this reason he believed that writing preceded speech. Such objects, signs, pictures or gestures can refer not merely to material objects, but to what we should now call mental qualities as well, for which there have emerged as yet no separate terms, so that, in view of what Vico (mistakenly) supposed to be the extreme poverty of primitive language, these few gestures or pictures are obliged to stand for abstract notions too. This is so because in early times 'words are carried over from bodies and from the properties of bodies to signify the institutions of the mind and spirit'.[2] This

---

[1] NS 32; cf. 401, 434. [2] NS 237.

evolutionary view has proved more fruitful than the better-known theories which dominated the earlier eighteenth century, for example Condillac's contractual-utilitarian theory, which bases language on agreed conventions, or the opposing view which traced language to the imitation of sounds in nature, or Süssmilch's doctrine of the divine origin of language, or the emotive theory of Rousseau and others.

The next stage in the ascent of humanity is marked by the use of metaphors, similes, images and the like, which characterises the language that we now call poetical (in the normal sense, not in Vico's). Primitive men, Vico tells us, do not denote things each by its own 'natural' name (Adam did, indeed, give each thing its own unique name, but the Flood obliterated the high civilisation that he founded) but by 'physical substances endowed with life'.[1] Fables and myths, or rather the characters who occur in them, are 'imaginative universals'[2] – attempts to refer to whole classes of entities without, as yet, the aid of proper general terms (for the capacity for abstraction is not, at this stage, sufficiently developed), and therefore by means of some magnificently conceived example of the class (not yet clearly conceived as a class) which stands both for itself and for the entire class. Thus 'Jove' is at one and the same time the name of the sky, of the father of the Gods and ruler of the universe, and of the source of thunder, terror and duty – he is both the embodiment and the wielder of all the compulsive forces before which men must, at their peril, bow down. 'Hercules' is the name of a heroic individual, the performer of vast and beneficent labours, but also of the class of all the heroes of all the various mythologies: hence every people worships its own Hercules. 'Neptune' refers to a trident-carrying divinity, but also to all the seas of the world; 'Cybele' symbolises the earth and at the same time a woman, mother of the giants.[3] Vico calls this 'credible impossibility',[4] which he regards as the 'proper material' of 'poetry'. Such images may later come to seem logical monstrosities, yet Vico is convinced

---

[1] NS 401. This is Vico's way of preserving orthodox Christian doctrine, and avoiding the Epicurean-evolutionist heresy for which the Inquisition, in the last years of the seventeenth century, had inflicted terrible punishment on some of his Neapolitan friends and contemporaries. Yet, although he may have feared charges of heresy, there is no reason for thinking that he is necessarily insincere in this or any other affirmation.

[2] See NS 209, 381, 403, 933.   [3] NS 402, 549.

[4] 'l'impossibile credibile': NS 383.

that this is not mere confusion: these are categories in which early men thought. He warns us that unless we make a gigantic effort to enter into this type of mentality, we shall never penetrate into the remote world of our ancestors, which alone holds the key to our own. 'It is impossible that bodies should be minds, yet it was believed that the thundering sky was Jove.'[1] The sky is a huge and terror-inspiring person – Jove. This is what Virgil means when he says 'omnia plena Jovis'.[2] We think in abstractions, but they were immersed in the senses. For this reason 'It is . . . beyond our power to enter into the vast imagination of those first men, whose minds were not in the least abstract, refined or spiritualised, because they were entirely immersed in the senses, buffeted by the passions, buried in the body.' Nevertheless, we must do what we can to 'enter into' these vast imaginations ('entrare nella vasta immagin-ativa di que' primi uomini').[3] We must 'descend to' in order to 'comprehend' these 'savage natures' which identify causes with persons.[4] Sometimes they even said that they saw these divine beings,[5] for instance Jove, and believed that he 'commanded by signs, that such signs were real words, and that nature was the language of Jove'.[6] Hence sprang divination, 'the science of the language of the Gods', which the Greeks called theology; and not the Greeks only, but later mystics and indeed Vico's younger contemporaries, Berkeley and Hamann. At the same time 'they make of all nature a vast animate body which feels passions and effects',[7] they personify nature as a 'mistress', as 'Sympathetic Nature', something that we could surely no longer comprehend;[8] yet this is the world we must seek to 'enter', to 'descend to', to 'comprehend', if we are to grasp what early societies were like. Vico claimed as his cardinal achievement this anthropological approach: 'To discover the way in which this . . . arose in the Gentile world, we encountered exasperating difficulties which have cost us the research of a good twenty years . . . to descend from these human and refined natures of ours to those quite wild and savage natures, which we cannot at all imagine and can compre-hend only with great effort.'[9] This we must do not by looking for evidence outside our minds, but as metaphysics does, which looks 'within the modifications of the mind of him who meditates it'[10]

[1] ibid.
[2] Virgil, *Eclogues* 3. 60; cf. Aratus, *Phainomena* 2–4; quoted with the wrong word-order in NS 379.
[3] NS 378. [4] NS 338, 375. [5] NS 375. [6] NS 379. [7] NS 377.
[8] NS 378. [9] NS 338. [10] NS 374.

– that is, by a species of self-analysis, by tracing the phases of the development of one's own individual mind from childhood to maturity.

We normally distinguish between the literal and the metaphorical use of language. To be literal is to call things by their appropriate names, and describe them in plain, simple terms; to use metaphor is a sophisticated or poetical way of embellishing or heightening such plain usage for the sake of giving pleasure, or of creating vivid imaginative effects, or of demonstrating verbal ingenuity; this is usually considered the product of conscious elaboration which could, with enough effort, always be translated back into the plain or literal sense of which it is merely an artificially heightened expression. Metaphor and simile, even allegory, are not, for Vico, deliberate artifices. They are natural ways of expressing a vision of life different from ours. Men once thought, according to him, in images rather than concepts, and 'attributed senses and passions ... to bodies as vast as sky, sea and earth'.[1] What is for us a less or more conscious use of rhetorical devices was their sole means of ordering, connecting and conveying what they sensed, observed, remembered, imagined, hoped, feared, worshipped – in short their entire experience. This is what Vico calls 'poetic logic',[2] the pattern of language and thought in the age of heroes. The metaphorical use precedes – and must precede – the 'literal' use of words, as poetry must come before prose, as song is earlier than spoken speech; 'the sources of all poetic locutions are two: poverty of language and need to explain and be understood'.[3] Early man, animist and anthropomorphist, thought in terms of what we now call metaphor as naturally and inevitably as we now think in 'literal' phrases. Hence a great deal of what now passes for literal speech incorporates dead metaphors, the origins of which are so little remembered that they are no longer felt – even faintly – as such. Since the changing structure of a language 'tells us the histories of the institutions signified by the words',[4] we can glean from it something of how their world looked to our ancestors. Because primitive men cannot abstract, 'metaphor makes up the great body of the language among all nations'[5] at that time. Vico supposed that such men used similes, images and metaphors much as people, to this day, use flags, or uniforms, or Fascist salutes – to convey something directly; this is a

---

[1] NS 402.   [2] NS 400 ff.   [3] NS 34.   [4] NS 354.   [5] NS 444.

use of signs which it would today seem unnatural to call either metaphorical or literal. Vico maintains that when a primitive man said 'the blood boils in my heart',[1] where we should say 'I am angry', his 'metaphorical' phrase is a uniquely valuable evidence of the way in which such a man thought, perceived and felt. What he felt when he spoke of blood boiling seemed to him – and indeed was – more directly related to his perception of water in a heated cauldron than our sensation of anger would seem to us today. The marvellous images, the immortal phrases coined by early poets are, according to Vico, due not to conscious flights of fancy, but to the fact that the imaginations of such men and their capacity for direct sensation were so much stronger than ours as to be different in kind, while their capacity for precise analogies and scientific observation was far less developed. Hence, if we are to understand their world, we must try to project ourselves into minds very remote from our own and endowed with these unfamiliar powers. A world in which men naturally talk of the lip of a cup, the teeth of a rake, the mouth of a river, a neck of land, handfuls of one thing, the heart of another, veins of minerals, bowels of the earth, murmuring waves, whistling winds, smiling skies, groaning tables and weeping willows[2] – such a world must be deeply and systematically different from any in which such phrases are felt, even remotely, to be metaphorical, as contrasted with so-called literal speech. This is one of Vico's most revolutionary discoveries.

According to Vico, words, like ideas, are directly determined by things – the concrete circumstances in which men live – and are therefore the most reliable evidence for them. As so often, he illustrates his most original and important perceptions with highly fanciful examples: he points to the fact that life in 'the forests' is earlier in date than life in 'huts', earlier still than the civilisation of villages, cities or academies.[3] This seems to him borne out by linguistic evidence: thus Latin, which Vico regards as a very ancient language, springs from life connected with forests; to demonstrate this he devotes one of his many essays in genetic etymology to grouping together words like 'lex' (acorn), 'ilex', 'aquilex', 'legumen' and 'legere' as typical 'sylvan' words drawn from life in the woods, which then come to be used to denote quite different

[1] NS 460, 935.
[2] NS 405. Vico's examples are drawn from metaphors taken from the human body.
[3] NS 239.

activities, states and objects.[1] Language, again, 'tells us the history of the institutions signified by the words',[2] beginning with the original meanings of words in the earliest of all periods, and illustrating historical change by its modifications in – and in response to – the successive phases of civilisation. Language reflects these phases: 'First the forests, then the huts, thence the villages, next the cities, finally the academies.'[3]

Like many thinkers, Vico is fascinated by the magic of the number three. Humanity has passed through three stages.[4] First comes the 'divine' period dominated by 'the senses', when the 'poetic' language was that of 'natural symbols', hieroglyphs or ideograms – 'mute' signs. Thunder and other natural phenomena are a language in which the gods speak: so are the entrails of animals or the flights of birds, symbols which the experts – priests or augurs – can read. The next period – the 'heroic' – is dominated by oligarchies of 'heroes', of which language rich in simile and metaphor – created by an imagination still directly related to nature – is characteristic. Finally comes the 'human' period in which *ragione* (reason) and language as we now know it, that of purely conventional signs invented and altered at will – 'a language of which [the people] are absolute lords'[5] – predominate. Vico tries to be more specific still. He says that first came onomatopoeic monosyllables, then polysyllables, followed by interjections, pronouns, prepositions, nouns and finally verbs. This is not accidental, but springs from the fact that the concepts of 'before' and 'after', and of movement, which verbs convey, necessarily came later than the apprehension of things – lumps of material stuff – objects denoted by nouns, which in their turn came later than the sense of personal identity, or the states conveyed by primitive cries. He

---

[1] 'For example, *lex*. First it must have meant a collection of acorns. Thence, we believe, is derived *ilex* ... the oak (and certainly *aquilex* means the collector of waters); for the oak produces the acorns by which the swine are drawn together. *Lex* was next a collection of vegetables, from which the latter were called *legumina*. Later on, at a time when vulgar letters had not yet been invented for writing down the laws, *lex* by a necessity of civil nature must have meant a collection of citizens, or the public parliament; so that the presence of the people was the *lex*, or "law", that solemnised [their] wills ... Finally, collecting letters, and making ... a sheaf of them for each word, was called *legere*, reading.' NS 240.

[2] NS 354.   [3] NS 239.

[4] Comte's law of the three phases – the theological, metaphysical and positive – is clearly influenced by Vico's ages of Gods, heroes and men, a notion, he tells us (NS 173), that had 'come down to us' from 'Egyptian antiquity'.

[5] NS 32.

provides equally fanciful arguments for the view that the earliest forms of verbs must have been in the imperative.

But these fantasies should not obscure Vico's central and vastly suggestive notion that the development of the morphology of a symbolic system is one with the growth of the culture of which it is the central organ. Moreover, he believes that since men are everywhere men, it follows that although there are as many languages as types of custom and outlook, yet 'There must in the nature of human institutions be a mental language common to all nations, which uniformly grasps the essence of things feasible in human social life and expresses it with as many diverse modifications as these same things have diverse aspects.'[1] This unifying factor, which makes history the story of the development of a single species – mankind – seems to Vico demonstrated by the similarity of proverbs in many tongues, and he thinks a dictionary could be composed of basic ideas (voci mentali) common to all peoples, although each of these cultures might perhaps have evolved at a different tempo in different environments. Such central ideas (or words – for he insists that it is a mistake to try to distinguish the two) are 'gods', 'family', 'heroes', 'auspices', 'paternal power', 'sacrifices', 'rights' (to a piece of land), 'command', 'authority', 'conquest', 'courage', 'fame'. These are, as it were, basic terms or ideas which all human beings must have conceived and lived by at some time or other; from their evolution the story of the societies in which they were current can, according to Vico, be reconstructed.[2] This is perhaps too simple and bold a programme, but it has in it the seeds of what, under the impact of German historicism, ultimately revolutionised the writing of history. That day, however, was not yet. Vico went a considerable way towards it with his new method, which he applied with brilliant effect to the issue over which a famous war was fought in his day, of whether the wisdom of the ancients was superior to that of the moderns.

Vico notes the deep, recurrent, nostalgic human tendency

[1] NS 161.

[2] Enzo Paci in his study of Vico – Ingens sylva: saggio sulla filosofia di G. B. Vico ([Milan], 1949) – draws attention to the parallel between Vico's conception of deep, recurrent themes in the history of the collective human consciousness (and its subliminal regions) and the great myths of the German romantics Schelling, Novalis and, above all, Richard Wagner. Fafner and Fasolt, Siegmund and Sieglinde do indeed, as Paci remarks, belong to the grim, early world of Vico's orribili bestioni and giganti; Vico would have understood Wagner's cosmic myths.

(revived in his day by Bacon and the natural-law theorists) to assume that once upon a time there existed a marvellous science which, owing to our sins or ill luck, we have lost, a science which can, perhaps, be recovered from ancient monuments that might have preserved something of it.[1] This underlies the conviction that ancient myths must enshrine some profound lesson for our own time, inasmuch as they embody the pure knowledge possessed by our antediluvian ancestors, governed, as they surely were, by an élite of sages, whose poems, oracles and maxims – the ancient lays and legends of the tribe – contain esoteric truths long lost or forgotten, or distorted by their degenerate descendants. Vico's outright rejection of this almost universal belief is one of his many claims to originality. History reveals no golden age to him. He gets over the difficulty presented by his orthodox Christian faith by explaining that the Flood has obliterated all earlier culture, including that of the Garden of Eden.[2] After it men were once again brutish, solitary savages wandering in 'the great forest of the earth'. Ancient poetry does indeed require wise minds to interpret it, but it is not a path to forgotten eternal truths: it is a window into a crude and barbarous world, into laws and customs remote from our own; 'ancient jurisprudence was a severe poetry'.[3] *Genres* that we distinguish now, prose and verse, law and history, are still one and undivided. Roman law 'was a serious poem'.[4] 'Poetical' is Vico's term for 'primitive', formalised, social imagery which tells us how men saw themselves and their social relationships at the time when it was created; 'poetical' law is the language 'natural' to that specific moment of evolution, and is full of animism and fetishism. This is so because 'the human mind ... makes itself the rule of the universe in respect of everything it does not know' and 'When men are ignorant of the natural causes producing things,

[1] A century later, Joseph de Maistre defended against the *philosophes* the special status which the Church accorded to Latin (which he too thought a very ancient language) on the ground that it was the matchless repository of the accumulated wisdom of the human race.

[2] It is worth noting that a century earlier Jean Bodin, whose works Vico certainly knew well, had rejected the idea of a golden age on much the same grounds, e.g. in his *Methodus* (1566): see *Oeuvres philosophiques de Jean Bodin*, ed. Pierre Mesnard (Paris, 1951), p. 226, col. 1 (translated into French on pp. 427–8).

[3] NS 1037.

[4] ibid. For Vico's view that the Twelve Tables were the Roman equivalent of customary laws to be found in the Homeric poems see NS 154, 156, 904.

and cannot even explain them by analogy with similar things, they attribute their own nature to them. The vulgar, for example, say the magnet loves the iron.'[1] For Vico this is not a consciously exaggerated or deliberately fanciful use of words, but the natural language of a particular stage of evolution, symptomatic of a particular type of immature apprehension that occupies its own unique and unalterable place in a recurrent, intelligible pattern of the development of the human spirit.

His sensitiveness to words and the philosophical significance of their use can be very modern. So, for example, he notes what has only in our day been analysed and classified as the 'performative' function of words,[2] namely the fact that words themselves need not merely describe or attract attention to something outside themselves, but may themselves be acts or intrinsic elements in action, as, for example, in the part that they play in legal transfers, or religious ceremonial. That words are not invariably used to describe, or command, or threaten or ejaculate or convey images or emotions, but can themselves be a form of action, is certainly a new and important idea, whenever it may first have been enunciated. Vico declares that, just as peasants still think that their rights, say to a piece of land, lie in the actual words of the contract – because words themselves have a compulsive power – so in primitive societies such important acts as the manumission of slaves, or taking possession of a property, or retaliation for an injury, were acts performed by means of words which themselves had the force of the original acts. Agamemnon and Jephtha (who belonged to the age of 'the gods') sacrificed their daughters because the very action of uttering the oaths had the force of natural causality, and the words directly altered (and were recognised as acts which could not but alter) the *status quo* simply in virtue of having been spoken. For Vico a society where words can function in this way must see, feel, think, act in ways unlike those of any society in which words are not so employed, but are used, let us suppose, only to describe, or explain, or express, or pray, or command, or play certain verbal games, and the like.

Whether this – or any other among Vico's many specific hypotheses – is correct or not is less important than what he did

[1] NS 181, 180.
[2] By J. L. Austin. Something of this kind was adumbrated by Hobbes, and later by Hume, but its full significance was brought out only in our own time.

achieve. Much of his genetic etymology and philology is clearly faulty or naïve or fantastic. But it is equally clear that he was, so far as I know, the first to grasp the seminal and revolutionary truth that linguistic forms are one of the keys to the mind of those who use words, and indeed to the entire mental, social and cultural life of societies. He saw much more clearly than anyone before him, even the great Valla (a century and a half earlier) and his disciples, that a particular type of locution, the use and structure of language, has a necessary, 'organic' connection with particular types of political and social structure, of religion, of law, of economic life, of morality, of theology, of military organisation and so on. He was convinced that this 'organic' connection can always be traced between all the various aspects of the activity of the selfsame men; that these interconnections, which in their totality form ways of life or cultures, do not follow each other in a haphazard order, but in a pattern, so that each phase flows out of, and is at once a development of, and a revolt against, its predecessor; moreover, that the pattern is intelligible, inasmuch as it flows from the nature – interpreted as *nascimento* – of man, from those developing faculties which alone make men human and go through an objective universal order of stages of growth in the lives of individuals and societies, a process which can be not merely recorded, but understood. It can be understood because (although he was perhaps not the first thinker to perceive this) men are conscious of their own powers, types of motives, reactions, social relationships, as participants, and not as spectators – from, as it were, within; and, so he believed, can see in their own experience not only the workings of their own purposes, but glimpse those of their Maker. Providence, he declares, shapes our lives, at times against our conscious purposes; but it is our desires, our goals, our motives, our acts through which it works its will. In this sense at least, it is we who make our own history. This is analogous to Hegel's view of human passions as the dynamic forces used by the cunning of reason, and Marx's conception of class interest as the engine of progress.[1] The proper study of man is his own evolving character and the pattern of cultures in which it is made concrete. He can understand what he has, in some sense, himself created in a different and profounder way than the 'external' nature which is his environment and his raw material. The study of language is one

[1] On this see pp. 136–8 below.

of the paths to this kind of self-knowledge. These were ideas of exceptional originality and fertility.

The second great door to the recovery of the past is mythology. Mythology is neither, as was held by neo-classical theorists in the Renaissance, the picturesque invention of the poets seeking to stimulate our imagination, nor, as rationalists maintained, lying fables spread by unscrupulous priests or other self-interested charlatans to deceive or lull the ignorant masses. Nor are myths, as the euhemerists declared, confused memories of extraordinary men, promoted by popular imagination to divine or heroic status. Myths, according to Vico, are systematic ways of seeing, understanding and reacting to the world, intelligible fully perhaps only to their creators and users, the early generations of men: 'in the fables the nations have in a rough way and in the language of the human senses described the beginnings of this world of sciences, which the specialised studies of scholars have since clarified for us by reasoning and generalisation'.[1] Mythologies are 'civil histories of the first peoples, who were everywhere naturally poets',[2] that is to say, they are natural modes of expression for those who felt, thought, spoke in ways which we can now grasp only with the greatest effort of the imagination.

How can we fully enter, Vico asks, into a world in which it was normal to see the sky as incarnate Jove (for what can such phrases as 'Jovis omnia plena' mean to us? how can Jupiter be at once the father of the gods and also the whole of heaven?)[3] and nature as an immense woman or 'a vast animate body which feels passions and effects'.[4] We are reminded again that for us it is almost impossible to think and feel in 'corporeal' categories, 'to enter into the vast imagination of those first men'.[5] The gods of the ancient peoples – of the Greeks and Romans, for instance – are not devils (as the early Christian theologians taught), nor are their attributes and histories poetic constructions, deliberate products of a long period of elaboration created for aesthetic contemplation, but the 'poetic' (that is, generated by the *Volksgeist*) creations of early human consciousness, now dead, fossilised, and ready for dissection and analysis by experts. Myths are the concrete mode of expression of the collective imagination of early mankind, and for modern critics the richest of all sources of knowledge of the physical and mental habits and the social ways of life of their

[1] NS 779.   [2] NS 352 (see pp. 66–7 above).
[3] See p. 65 above, notes 1 and 2.   [4] NS 377.   [5] NS 378.

creators. Fables are true histories of customs.[1] Homer in particular
is a rich treasure-house of information about the Hellenic past.[2]
Fables are 'the first histories of the Gentile nations', hence
mythology is 'the first science to be learned'.[3] They reflect the
realities of the time in which they were born. So, for example, the
relationships of the gods must be understood in terms of the
primitive society of which they are symbolic: to be shocked by
their 'immorality', or to be amused by it, or to look upon them as
material for poetical treatment, as was done by Greek or Roman
poets, philosophers and critics, rests on a misinterpretation of the
Olympian religion by later, sophisticated writers, lacking in
historical sense, who misunderstood the past by applying their
own social and moral categories to worlds remote from their own.
As for the allegorical fancies of modern writers, they bear no
relation to genuine myths – indeed they stand at the farthest
possible remove from them.

Where there are laws of development, there must be the
possibility of a systematic science. Armed with his new principles,
Vico tries to reconstruct long lost worlds out of the myths of
which the grammarians who preserved them did not begin to grasp
the 'true' meaning. What kind of society, he asks again and again,
could have given rise to this or that fable or image? He is the father
of the economic interpretation of ancient legends, which, striking
enough in his own day, at times foreshadows the approach of later
anthropological, particularly Marxist, writers. The story of Theseus
and Ariadne, for example, is, according to him, primarily concerned with early seafaring life. The Minotaur represents the pirates
who abduct Athenians in ships, for the bull is a characteristic
ancient emblem on a ship's prow, and piracy was held in high
honour both by the Greeks and the ancient Germans. Ariadne is

---

[1] NS 7.   [2] ibid.

[3] NS 51. Only of the 'Gentile peoples', because the history of the Jews, who
had been made rational by divine revelation (NS1 317 ff. [book 3, chapter 18]), has
been directly revealed by God in the Scriptures, and does not need archaeological
reconstruction. Vico plainly tried to avoid giving examples from the 'sacred
history' of the Jews to illustrate his thesis. For obvious reasons he deliberately
averted his gaze from this rich treasure of myth and fact, yet his eye occasionally
and perhaps inevitably strays towards it. The notion that fables and legends are
evidences of the *moeurs* of the past and that the 'first historians were poets' is to
be found in French historiography in the sixteenth century, e.g. in Bodin and La
Popelinière, as well as in Bacon (see pp. 156 ff. below).

the art of seafaring, her thread is navigation, the labyrinth is the Aegean Sea. Alternatively, the Minotaur, when he is not the embodiment of piracy, is a half-caste child – a foreigner come to Crete – indicating that immigration from the mainland was prevalent at the time.

No myth is safe from Vico's zeal: every legend is so much grist for his socio-economic mill. Cadmus is primitive man, and his slaying of the serpent is intended to convey the notion of the clearing of the vast forest. He sows the serpent's teeth in the ground – the teeth are in reality the teeth of the plough. The stones he casts about him are the hard clods of earth which the nobility – the oligarchy of the heroes – retain against the land-hungry serfs; the furrows are the orders of feudal society; the armed men who spring up from the teeth are heroes, but they fight not each other as the myth relates (at this point Vico, like many a higher critic or the less restrained followers of Freud and Jung, feels impelled to 'correct' the evidence), but attack robbers – the still unsettled vagabonds who threaten the lives of the settled agricultural folk. The wounding of Mars by Minerva is the defeat of the plebeians by the patricians. Minerva, who conspired against Jupiter, is the nobility that bands together against tyrants, and so on. The notion of early class war preoccupied Vico. C. E. Vaughan[1] has compiled a useful catalogue of some of Vico's symbols for the rebellious plebeians for their rights against the aristocracy. It includes the Sirens, the Sphinx, Marsyas, Circe, Ixion, Tantalus, Midas, Phaethon, Antaeus, Orpheus torn limb from limb by the Maenads, Vulcan hurled down by Jupiter, and Penelope's suitors. All these he takes to be memories, symbols and later rationalisations of traumatic collective experiences – the critical turning-points (and the wounds sustained in the course of them) in the lives of entire societies.

Pegasus, on the other hand, has quite a different, and a logically more interesting, function: *prima facie*, Vico tells us, he might be taken to represent the invention of riding; but one can delve deeper. Since in early times universal notions had not been attained, complex ideas were represented by means of spatial combinations of the relevant characteristics, resulting in physical monsters. In the case of Pegasus, wings represent the sky, and the

---

[1] In 'The Eclipse of Contract: Vico, Montesquieu', in his *Studies in the History of Political Philosophy before and after Rousseau*, vol. 1, *From Hobbes to Hume* (Manchester/London etc., 1925), at p. 232, note 4.

sky represents the birds the flight of which yields the all-important auspices. Therefore wings plus a horse is equivalent to the horse-riding nobility with the right of taking auspices and, on the strength of that, in authority over the people. Myths represent powers, institutions, radical changes in the social order; hence, according to Vico, nothing can be more absurd than to try to fit an obviously mythological creature like, say, the lawgiver Draco, the symbol of authority, a serpent found in China and Egypt as well as among the Greeks, or, for that matter, Minos or Hercules or Aeneas, into the real chronology of history. Gods, heroes, mortals are each a myth and symbol. The descent of Aeneas to Avernus is a symbol of sowing. Pythagoras and Solon turn out to be pure myths – Solon, for example, simply represents the aspirations of the Athenian lower class for equal rights. Apollo[1] symbolises historically successive human and social functions – first he is the hunter, then a tree-trunk wielder, then an inventor and a rider, and always the immortal, long-haired youth (for these are all social habits or ideals at various moments of history). Three-quarters of a century before Wolf and his school, Vico saw in Homer not an individual who wrote the *Iliad* and the *Odyssey*, but the national genius of the Greek people itself, as it articulates its vision of its own experience over the centuries.[2] Seven Greek cities vied for the honour of being the birthplace of Homer, not because he was born in one of them, but because he was born in none – 'the Greek peoples were themselves Homer',[3] he is the creative poetic imagination of all the Greeks, the symbol of the 'many centuries' which divided the *Iliad*, written by a poet of North-Eastern Greece who sings of 'pride, wrath and lust for vengeance ... Achilles, the hero of violence' from the *Odyssey*, written by a man of the South-West, who celebrates 'the luxury of Alcinous ... the joys of Calypso ... the songs of the Sirens' and 'Ulysses, the hero of wisdom'.[4] The Homeric poems are what certain classical scholars at the beginning of our own century used to call a 'floating mass of *epos*'.

VI

Some of Vico's ideas are patently extravagant, but some are of the greatest pregnancy. The notion that there are abiding symbols in

[1] NS 533–8.   [2] NS 873.   [3] NS 875.   [4] NS 879–881; cf. 789, 904.

the imagination – in the semi-conscious mental processes of individuals and groups (some of which evolve at a different pace from others) – that certain images persistently recur in the history of mankind, such as salvation and resurrection, cataclysm and rebirth; that myths and magic and formal ritual may be a natural – indeed, the only historically possible – way of describing their experience on the part of human beings at a given stage of linguistic, and *eo ipso* of social and psychological, development; that attitudes, beliefs, cultures are products of a given stage of social change, indeed of class structure and class warfare, and could not have arisen at any other stage (a hypothesis which in its Hegelian and Marxist forms led to the modern schools of the sociology of knowledge and of culture) – these ideas, derived for the most part from other authors and schools of thought, have affected our own views both of men and of the writing of history. The light cast since Vico's day by comparative mythology, philology, anthropology, archaeology, art history, by all the interrelated studies of human antiquities pursued under the influence of contending theories and systems, of Hegel, Marx, Comte, Durkheim, Weber, Freud; the very idea of using empirical methods to find order and meaning beneath the vast variety of social experience in its historical movement; the notion that there stretches a gulf, or at least a great distance, between us and the early centuries of man, so that a powerful, but not impossible, leap of the imagination must be made by anyone who seeks to explain to himself that remote world; these transforming conceptions ferment in what Michelet admiringly called 'the little pandemonium of the *New Science*'.[1] Vico is the author of the idea that language, myths, antiquities directly reflect the various fashions in which social or economic or spiritual problems or realities were refracted in the minds of our ancestors; so that what may appear as profound theological conflicts or impassable social taboos are not what mechanically-minded thinkers have taken them to be – by-products of material processes, biological, psychological, economic, and so on – although they may be that too, but, primarily, 'distorted' or primitive ways of recognising social facts and of reacting to them. He is the author of the view that a rite or symbol or object of worship, from fetishism to modern nationalism, is most correctly interpreted as an expression of resistance to some social pressure,

---

[1] Preface to *Histoire romaine*: Jules Michelet, *Oeuvres complètes*, ed. Paul Viallaneix (Paris, 1971–   ) (hereafter *Oeuvres*), vol. 2, pp. 340–1.

or joy in procreation, or admiration for power, or craving for unity or security or victory over a rival group (what later theorists were to call ideologies), which may take diverse forms, mythological, metaphysical, aesthetic – different types of spectacles through which reality is apprehended and acted upon. He was the first to conceive the notion that in this fashion it was possible to achieve a kind of window into the past – an 'inside' view – to reconstruct, not simply a formal procession of the famous men of the past, clad in their stock attributes, doing great deeds or suffering some fearful fate, but the style of entire societies which struggled and thought, worshipped, rationalised and deluded themselves, put their faith in magical devices and occult powers, and felt, believed, created in a fashion which may be strange to us, and yet not wholly unintelligible. All these astonishingly bold hypotheses Vico conceived and applied in a world which was then, and for many years, acutely hostile to this 'psychologising', anti-Cartesian, anti-'physicalist', approach.[1] It is scarcely credible that Vico could have achieved all this in the intellectual solitude and squalor of the conventional, timid and narrow society which he accepted completely, and in which he lived out his long, oppressed, unhonoured life.

The principles of the new method can now be re-stated more fully. The search for the truth is for the most part a genetic and self-analysing enquiry. Wherever man is more than a mere spectator, wherever he takes part as an actor, that is, outside the province of the natural sciences, of the objective laws of which he is an observer, and of mathematics, which he invents, and which cannot, therefore, by itself yield information about the real world, he is examining the activity of his own spirit in its interaction with the external world. This activity shapes and leaves unmistakable evidence of itself in human institutions – the chief amongst which are language, customs, religious rites, legends, myths, moral and legal systems, literature, the arts – everything that together constitutes a culture or way of life. Examination at first hand of surviving monuments is a direct door into the human past, and casts a steadier light both on what men were and did, and on their reasons and motives for it, than the stories of later chroniclers and historians, many of whom lacked knowledge and, above all, historical imagination, and were often guilty of anachronisms,

[1] See the first section of the next essay (pp. 122–8 below).

crude and shallow psychology, undisciplined fancy, and innocent or corrupt personal bias. Men must write history afresh in the light of the new critical principles, using as material the long familiar data, but subjecting them to questions of a novel kind: what kind of men can have talked, written, worshipped, governed themselves, created as these men did? What must the natures and lives of such men have been, and what kind of social experiences must have shaped them, to have generated the successive stages through which they developed?[1] Can a fixed order or pattern of such stages be shown to follow by causal or metaphysical necessity from the changing natures of these men, or, it may be, of all men and societies as such? If there are such patterns, are they linear and non-repetitive or cyclical and recurrent? All 'vulgar' traditions must have 'grounds of truth', that is, some direct vision of the world of which they are incarnations, 'preserved by entire peoples over long periods of time': the function of Vico's new science was 'to recover these grounds'.[2] This was the programme, and the *New Science*, especially in the second, recast, version of 1730, was Vico's attempt to realise it.

It was clear to him that, whatever the correct solution of the problem of development, the fashionable theories of his time were false. It is not conceivable that men have reached their latest state as a result of a single, collective act of will, starting from 'the ferine wanderings of Thomas Hobbes's licentious and violent men, of Hugo Grotius' solitary, weak and needy simpletons, of Samuel Pufendorf's vagrants cast into this world without divine care or help'.[3] Nor does Spinoza's psychology begin to explain men as they are, or as they ever could have been or have come to be. Self-interest is not, and could never have been, the mainspring of action: passion, duty, tradition, a sense of human or national solidarity; shame, conscience, awe, the sense of a divine presence – these cannot be reduced to 'modifications'[4] of the rational egoism of a nation of shopkeepers, 'hucksters'[5] often deflected by irrational passions or frustrated by ignorance, which Vico declares to be Spinoza's caricature of men; and Locke is no better. The true route to the past is through the popular traditions which 'must have had

[1] More than half a century later the German metaphysician F. H. Jacobi perceived in this the embryo of Kant's transcendental method; and indeed the analogy is not absurd.

[2] NS 149, 150.   [3] loc. cit. (p. 50 above, note 1).   [4] cf. e.g. pp. 46–7 above.

[5] NS 335.

public grounds of truth'.[1] But these evidences have been inevitably distorted by the mere passage of time, by the human tendency to forget and breed fictions, by the vanity – *boria* – of nations and scholars,[2] above all by changes in language which cause words to mean something different in one age from what they meant in another. Nevertheless, there are laws of social development on which the *New Science* rests; moreover, group memories persist, something lingers, and if we set about it in the right way (because we are men, and there is a spiritual affinity between us all, so that what one generation did or suffered, another can 'enter into', and comprehend as part of its own autobiography), and make that immense effort of imagination of which Vico never tires of talking, we can get a glimpse of what the world looked like to remote barbarian, or even remoter savage, eyes. He thinks that what survives of the earliest age of men clearly shows that the origins of men were crude and barbarous. These monuments of the past have been falsely interpreted by the scholars of our own 'enlightened, cultivated and magnificent times', who talk nonsense about 'the matchless wisdom of the ancients',[3] ascribe their own knowledge to the past, suffer from cultural and national arrogance and self-centredness, and, above all, like to think that what interests them, and what they know, must have existed and been known from the beginning of time.

VII

The nature of men, as of everything, can be discovered by asking the question 'What comes into being, at what time, in what fashion?'[4] Men began not in Rousseau's state of innocence, unspoilt by institutions, but as semi-bestial giants – 'stupid, insensate and horrible beasts'[5] – filled with fears, lusts and frightful (*spaventose*) superstitions.[6] A peal of thunder from the heavens was a voice that spoke to them, raging at them, or warning them, or thundering commands. They were shocked by such natural terrors into seeking hiding-places; shame and fear of some superhuman power caused them to drag their women with them into the caves to which they fled, and so out of *pudore* and lust, privacy and matrimony began. What Vico calls their forms of early

---

[1] NS 149.   [2] NS 124–8.   [3] NS 123, 128, 384.   [4] See NS 147.
[5] NS 374; cf. 243, 296, 338, 547, 644.   [6] e.g. NS 503–4.

prowess (*virtù*) were disfigured by horrible rites and bestial cruelty.[1] He conceives these men as being like the Cyclops Polyphemus in the *Odyssey*, fathers of primitive families, despotic, savage, violent, ferocious, able to survive only by means of the most terrifying discipline, by enforcing absolute obedience. Nature for these men was filled with frightening powers; ritual and rigid forms of institutional behaviour – self-protective devices – were there from the start: they slaughtered their children to appease the unseen rulers (the Phoenician Moloch is Vico's example), a practice of which, among the 'gentiles', Ennius had spoken with horror.[2] Brutal as the exercise by the fathers of their absolute power might be, it was, nevertheless, modified by an embryonic sense of shame and awe: this is the root of religious feeling, the means used by Providence to raise men from their wild beginnings; not self-interest, which could never have sufficiently checked their savage egotism. Without such feeling, they would not have been human: without shame and awe there can be no self-control or self-direction, and without these not even the minimum of civilisation, still less liberty under the law of a later day, could ever have arisen.[3] These men knew nothing of beauty; even now, Vico remarks, peasants are remote from any such concept.

These owners of the original homesteads were subject to attack by the still lawless, 'natural' men – savage vagabonds roaming the earth. To resist these marauders, they joined with each other, and the first organised groups created the first embryonic settlements. Some among the nomads themselves, in terror of stronger creatures, sought protection in these primitive stockades against the violent vagabonds with their 'infamous promiscuity',[4] and so arose the first class of servants and slaves, and with it a class structure and, in due course, class war. It is not true (as, for instance, Bodin had supposed a century earlier) that the earliest form of political life was kingship: that is a typical blunder, Vico declares, probably based on an unhistorical etymology – the word

[1] NS 516.

[2] 'et Poenei solitei sos sacruficare puellos' ('and the Phoenicians were accustomed to sacrifice their own children'). Ennius, *Annals* 237, cited at NS 517.

[3] 'In this fashion the first theological poets created the first divine fable, the greatest they ever created: that of Jove': Jupiter *optimus maximus*, the strongest and greatest, terrible but also *Soter* – saviour, for he did not destroy them – and *Stator* – stabiliser, for he provided them with ritual, institutions, social structure. NS 379.

[4] NS 1099.

'kings' used by Homer and the early writers in their time plainly meant not individuals but ruling groups. The earliest societies were small oligarchic 'republics', groups of fathers living together, chained by iron laws – the necessary condition of survival – ruling over womenfolk, children, clients and slaves. This is the age of the gods: of the 'mute' signs and hieroglyphs. At first the rulers were prudent and temperate,[1] then the laws were abused by them, the slaves revolted, demanded recognition, and forced a compromise.[2] This marked the creation of the first civil order with defined rights for both classes, patricians and plebeians, noblemen and their clients (Vico's imagination is throughout obsessed by the history of Rome). This is the heroic age.

The beliefs of an age – what, before Herder had invented the *Volksseele*, Vico had called the 'common sense' of a society, that is, 'judgement without reflection, shared by an entire class, an entire people, an entire nation, or the entire human race'[3] is embodied most vividly in its literary monuments. The 'heroic' age is faithfully reflected in the early poetry with its pride, avarice, cruelty,[4] qualities typical of every ruling aristocracy, and of the culture which it generates. The laws were cruel, because men cannot be governed in any other fashion at this 'heroic' stage of their development (the Homeric age, and the beginnings of feudalism in the West, are, for him, parallel cases of this phase). These rules, and the social order which embodied them, came into being because men cannot at this stage survive without them. But they would have lacked the absolute authority – the power to cause unruly savages to prostrate themselves before them – if they had been conceived as issuing from mere individual human wills.

Primitive men are bound by rules more rigid than those of advanced societies, and can advance only if the rules seem to them made not by themselves, but to be objective and absolute, carrying the authority of some vast external sanction – nature, God, or something too mysterious and terrible to mention. These unconscious creations of men's minds, which are inevitable at a certain stage of social growth, must, no less inevitably, at this level of mental development, present themselves as external entities, demanding absolute obedience – issuing rules on pain of terrible penalties. This is the first formulation of the celebrated theory of

---

[1] ibid.   [2] NS 1100.   [3] NS 142.   [4] NS 38.

reification, one of the forms of alienation, *Entfremdung*, a cornerstone of Hegel's philosophy of history and of Marx's sociology, whereby men are for long ages governed by rigid beliefs, unseen divinities, laws and institutions created, indeed, by men, but deriving their authority from the delusion that they are objective, timeless and unalterable like the laws of physical nature. Vico's notion of history makes use of this concept long before Feuerbach. Men fear death, and collectively invent gods stronger than death. They crave for laws, and so invent objective entities called laws, justice, the divine will, to maintain and protect their form of life. Rites that inspire terror are created, albeit unconsciously, to preserve the tribe against dangers and enemies, external and internal. Yet all this is man's own creation, and man can come to understand it, however imperfectly, because (though he is fulfilling a plan not of his but of God's devising) he alone made it. That is what makes history penetrable to him in the very sense in which nature remains for ever opaque.

The institutions of the heroic age – the framework of 'divine', imprescriptible laws, a cruel discipline imposed within it by the rulers on their subjects – dominate the second phase of social evolution. Nor must words mislead us. The liberties for which these men fought were liberties for themselves against usurpers and despots, not liberty for their servants or dependents, whom they ruthlessly punished and exterminated. It is later ages, Vico points out, which have grossly misinterpreted such words as 'liberty' and 'people' as they occur in 'heroic' writings, and have given them a democratic meaning, thereby showing a lack of the sense of history. In due course the plebeians became dissatisfied with their inferior status, founded upon the metaphysical assumption of the inherent inequality of their natures, which debarred them from such rights of their masters as inheritance, landownership, legal marriage, legal succession and the like. Once again there arose mounting social pressure, sometimes erupting into violent battles for civil or religious rights. Plutocracy and rewards for merit succeeded oligarchy, and this in its turn broke down before demands for popular sovereignty by the majority of the unprivileged. The rich grew too secure, and were defeated by the populace. The rule of democratic justice set in, with its accompaniment of free discussion, legal arguments, prose, rationalism, science. Freedom of speech inevitably breeds unrestricted questioning of accepted values, that is, philosophy and criticism, and in the end undermines the accepted structure of society. Individualism grows to excess, dissolves the ties that unite the mass of the people, now no longer clamped together by the terror of inexorable, supernatural laws. This leads to scepticism, destruction of piety and unifying faith, and the disintegration of the tightly knit 'organic' State. The process ends either in anarchy, or (Vico is a deeply anti-democratic thinker) in 'the unchecked liberty of the free peoples, which is the worst of all tyrannies'.[1] Civic virtue melts away, and is replaced by *anomie* and arbitrary violence. This disease duly breeds its own drastic remedy: it is repressed either by a strong individual who dominates his society, and restores order and morality (as Augustus did in Rome), or by conquest at the hands of a fresher and more vigorous society, at an earlier, more primitive stage of its development. But sometimes the rot has gone too deep, and the members of the decadent society collapse into a kind of second barbarism, the 'barbarism' not of youth or of 'sense', but of 'reflection' – a kind of senility and impotence, when each man lives in his own egotistic, anxiety-ridden world, unable to communicate or co-operate with his fellows. This is the situation in which men, although they still physically throng together, 'live like wilds beasts in a deep solitude of spirit and will, scarcely any two able to agree since each follows his own pleasure or caprice'.[2] The human beings dehumanised by what, in a remarkable phrase, he calls 'the barbarism of reflection' (*la barbarie della riflessione*) – 'a base savagery, under soft words and embraces'[3] – finally succumb to their own weakness and corruption. Society falls to pieces; frightful wars, both internecine and with foreign foes, destroy its members, civilisation collapses, men scatter, cities fall; over their ruins forests rise again. Thereby one cycle completes itself, and a new one begins.

Once again there is the reign of simplicity, brutality, and the Cyclopean 'fathers'. Among the relics of a dead culture, now overgrown with new virgin woods, men once more become 'religious, truthful and faithful'.[4] Religion once more takes its proper place as the sole truly cohesive force of society. It was so in Rome after barbarians overran it, and the new cycle opened, with its inevitable succession of the three stages of civilisation: first came the Cyclopean Frankish 'kings' with primitive forts built against

[1] NS 1102.   [2] NS 1106.   [3] ibid.   [4] ibid.

wandering barbarians, blind authority, protection sought by the weak from the strong, the beginnings of feudalism. Then came the second 'heroic' period, symbolised by crests and coats of arms, heraldic emblems that are the natural symbolism of this phase of culture, wrongly interpreted by later generations as conscious artifice. The second cycle is not a precise replica of the first, if only because it contains memories of its predecessor. Besides, it is Christian.[1] The movement is, as it were, a spiral rather than circular. Nevertheless, the correspondences are striking. Medieval society, like the heroic age of the classical world, was dominated by priests, and in due course generated its own great poet, the wielder of the new 'heroic' Italian language – Dante, the Homer of the second lap of human culture. The place of the gods of Olympus is now taken by the Christian saints. Even the public ritual repeats itself: in Homeric times, when a city was besieged, the gods of the city were solemnly adjured to leave it before it was finally sacked and destroyed; so now the saints were invited to leave the doomed towns by conquering Christian armies. This oligarchical order in its turn has been (by Vico's time) succeeded by a plutocracy, and will, no doubt, be succeeded by democracy, individualism, scepticism, atheism and, in due course, dictatorship or conquest. Once again a period of high civilisation will be followed by a decline and fall, and, after that, the inevitable primeval forest. These are the famous *corsi e ricorsi* that are Vico's form of the cyclical pattern of the succession of civilisations, perhaps the most celebrated of all his doctrines. It is not the least among the misfortunes of this singularly unlucky writer that he should be best known to posterity for the least interesting, plausible and original of his views.

VIII

The notion that human history moves in cycles was an old and, in Vico's day, widely discussed one. Plato, Aristotle, Polybius and their followers, particularly during the Renaissance,[2] had advanced similar hypotheses. What is novel is Vico's notion of what later came to be called the phenomenology of the human

---

[1] Yet even so, they seem, unlike pre-Christian Jews, doomed to traverse the stages of the *storia ideale eterna* of the Gentiles. Vico seems to offer no explanation of this anomaly, strange in a Christian writer.

[2] Machiavelli is the best known among them.

spirit. He sees the history of mankind as 'an *ideal eternal history* traversed in time by the history of every nation in its rise, development, maturity, decline and fall'.[1] This is the *idée maîtresse* of his whole thought. He means by it a pattern of development which human society, wherever it is found, must obey. Indeed this pattern, like a Platonic Idea, is what makes human nature human: it is not a necessity imposed on men's souls or bodies from outside – from above by a deity, or from below by material nature. It is the principle of growth, in terms of which nature herself, *natura* as *nascimento* – birth and growth – is defined. Human nature is to be defined dynamically, in terms of the ascent of man from 'crude' beginnings to our own 'magnificent times',[2] and, who knows, to what sublimer heights as yet unscaled.

For Vico, human beings are not Cartesian substances, or static entities definable in terms of their Aristotelian entelechies or essences, whose development consists in the emergence, one by one, of properties which have lain hidden within them eternally, from the beginning, and then gradually come into being, become 'unfolded' and revealed, like the leaves of a book or the feathers of a peacock's tail. In Vico's conception man is not distinguishable from the actual process of his development – at once physical, moral, intellectual, spiritual, and, equally, social, political, artistic. For him the nature of men is intelligible solely in terms of men's relations with the external world and with other men, interaction with whom in the realisation of ends which they cannot but strive to fulfil (and which can be realised only by society as a whole, and not by individuals alone) is the history of mankind. This 'ideal eternal history' is the single, universal pattern which all societies, in their rise and fall, are bound sooner or later to fulfil. Particular societies traverse this path in different ways and at varying *tempi*. The advance of one may be observed at the same date as, and be affected by, the collapse of another. But the stages of the journey are set in an unalterable order, for each arises out of the needs created by the completion of the potentialities of its predecessor. The potentialities to be realised do not coexist from all eternity, for

---

[1] 'una *storia ideale eterna*, sopra la quale corron in tempo le storie di tutte le nazioni ne' loro sorgimenti, progressi, stati, decadenze e fini': NS 349; cf. 245, 393. Elsewhere he speaks of 'un diritto eterno che corre in tempo' ('an eternal law which traverses time'): NS1 49.

[2] NS 123.

each possibility of development is literally conditioned only by the fulfilment of its predecessor. There is an objective order among them; one faculty, capacity, outlook, way of feeling, acting cannot arise until and unless it has been called into existence by needs created by the changes which its antecedent has brought about. This growth of mental life of men is for Vico the growth of the institutional life of society. When a society is young, vigorous, disciplined, it is 'poetical', then 'heroic' and governed by myths and blind dogma. When it has been undermined by critical rationalism, then philosophy, democracy and the sciences transform social organisation too. The path is fixed by the structure of 'the mind',[1] and is the same for all men and all societies (at any rate 'Gentile' societies), for it alone is what makes them human. Before Hegel and Saint-Simon, Vico defined human nature as an activity, and necessarily a social one.

This progression is not conceived as a causal process, in mechanistic terms. Vico is a Christian teleologist no less than Augustine or Bossuet. He believes that mankind pursues purposes which God has once and for all set before it. But, unlike Bossuet, Vico believes that this purpose has not been directly disclosed to all men, only to the 'philosophical' Jews, to whom the goals of man have been revealed by Moses and the prophets. They alone do not seem subjected to the cosmic wheel. The 'ideal eternal history', the unalterable pattern, is the history of the 'Gentiles'. Its content as opposed to its general structure – its temporal order – cannot, although it is metaphysically necessitated, be known in advance of the facts. But neither is it an empirical hypothesis, or mere conjecture. It is eternally true, events cannot falsify it: in Leibniz's language it is a *vérité*, not *de fait* but *de la raison*. How do we grasp it? Vico never clearly tells us: but there is little doubt that he supposed that, once we had immersed ourselves in the concrete historical evidence, we should perceive the pattern as an a priori truth, scientifically *per caussas*, as the thinkers of Vico's time in general supposed the central principles of the sciences to be known, as Descartes or Spinoza, or Leibniz or Newton, conceived of the laws of nature; save that Vico believed the laws of social

---

[1] *Mente* is not a clear concept in the *New Science*: it is most often the mind of individuals, but sometimes seems to be a collective entity, not unlike the similarly ambiguous *Geist* in German Idealist thought. This, as might be expected, has generated conflicting interpretations of Vico's metaphysical views – Hegelian, Catholic, Marxist, existentialist, empiricist, and combinations of these; nor is the end in sight.

development to be more certain than those of the external world, indeed the most certain form of knowledge of the world that was open to men. Indeed he blames Grotius, for example (and could have criticised Bodin), for offering principles which are not 'necessary', but merely 'probable and veri-similar',[1] whereas the 'true constituents [or 'elements'] of history'[2] can be established with absolute certainty – in the manner of Plato rather than Bacon. Are these 'elements' the categories, the basic relationships, presupposed by historical thinking – an application of Kant's transcendental logic *avant la lettre*, as Jacobi thought?[3] Whether his certainty is of a metaphysical-Leibnizian or a critical-Kantian sort, it seems to be this that permits him to call his discoveries a new 'science': something which has been discovered once and for all beyond corrigibility, the preordained timetable of human history.[4] Even so, man cannot attain to the perfect knowledge which only the author of the entire cosmic drama can possess. But although it is, of necessity, finite, such historical knowledge is yet superior to all other human knowledge; since the comprehension by the actors of the parts that, in some sense, their own acting creates, will, if they understand the regular and recurrent structure of the ends and methods of social activity, be superior in kind to the knowledge possessed by spectators, however perceptive they may be. In history we are the actors; in the natural sciences mere spectators.[5] This is the doctrine, above others, on which Vico's claim to immortality must rest. For upon it rests the crucial distinction between *Geisteswissenschaft* and *Naturwissenschaft*. The battle over this distinction has continued unabated until well into our own day.

IX

In reading Vico it is constantly necessary to sift the chaff from the grain. This is not an easy task. All his philosophical works, and the *Scienza nuova* in particular, are an amalgam of sense and nonsense, an ill-assorted mass of ideas, some lucid and arresting, others

---

[1] 'probabiles verisimilesque': DU 32.

[2] 'veri elementi della storia': NS1 208.

[3] This, if I do not misunderstand him, is also Pompa's view, op. cit. (p. 52 above, note 1).

[4] NS 348.

[5] For a sixteenth-century anticipation of this (in Baudouin's *De institutione historiae universae*) see p. 161 below, note 4.

shapeless or obscure, bold and novel thoughts cluttered with trivial fragments of a dead scholastic tradition, all jostling each other in the chaos of his astonishingly fertile, but badly ordered and overburdened, mind. He is at once obsessed by a single vision of mankind and its history, strictly obeying laws of social development which he is the first to discover, and overwhelmed by too much detail, too many implications of the central thesis, large and small, clamouring for expression at the same time. He seeks desperately to fit everything into the framework of his central pattern, but the new ideas prove too heterogeneous, too rich and too self-contained to fall into the scheme provided for them; they fly apart and pursue their own paths through the mass of superfluous and, at times, wildly irrelevant matter with which their author's digressive and intuitive mind is at all times clogged; nevertheless their intrinsic force and uniqueness somehow break through. Add to this Vico's lack of literary talent, his struggle and frequent failure to create adequate terms to convey so much that was novel and wholly out of tune with the spirit of his times, an ill-disciplined imagination which has tempted so many later writers to read their own very different thoughts into the luxuriant jungle of his mind, the haste and clumsiness with which his masterpiece was knocked together (or, rather, painfully extracted out of the larger, unpublished work) in the intervals from ill health and menial hackwork, then endlessly corrected and recorrected, added to and altered, under an incessant pressure of an inexhaustible supply of examples, allusions, parallels, associations, which he could not organise, circling round the same central notions by which he was obsessed; if all this is taken into account some of the shortcomings of the *New Science* and its lack of readers are not difficult to account for. Nevertheless it remains a work of genius.

I shall not attempt to assess the plausibility of Vico's specific schema of human history. His obsession with triads, which influenced later thinkers; his parallels between the patterns of rise, apogee and fall of civilisations, the first in a series of fanciful constructions which culminate in the morphologies of history of Saint-Simon, Fourier, Comte, Ballanche, Spengler, Sorokin, Toynbee; his peculiar interpretations of Greek, and especially Roman, history and philology (which is his paradigm), and much else of this kind, seem of remote interest now. Indeed, his more specific reconstructions of the past carry little conviction in the light of subsequent research. Vico's merit lies not in the discovery of new facts, but in asking new questions, throwing out new suggestions, and establishing new categories the grasp of which has altered our ideas of what kind of facts are important for the understanding of history, and why. That the vocabulary of savages was poorer in nouns than ours may be false; that language changes or evolves may have become, by Vico's day, a truism; but that to each type of society belongs its own peculiar structure of myth (or language, or artistic creation, or economic habits) expressive of its own unique outlook is an idea of major importance. That every society must inevitably pass through the same stages of oligarchy, slavery, serfdom, tenancy and 'Quiritarian' ownership as in Rome is not true. But the notion that social institutions evolve under the pressure of conflicts between classes which arise out of property relationships is one of the great transforming hypotheses of our age. Vico perceived a revolutionary truth when he asserted, before Herder or Hegel or Marx, that to each stage of social change there correspond its own types of law, government, religion, art, myth, language, manners; that fables, epic poems, legal codes, histories express institutional processes and structures which are parts of the structure, and not of the 'superstructure' (in Marxist terms); that together they form a single pattern of which each element conditions and reflects the others; and that this pattern is the life of a society.[1] He said something scarcely less important when he asserted that social history was in large measure (not wholly – that is a later, Marxist, dogma) the struggle of the 'have nots' for rights and powers – economic rights of possessing the soil, moral rights in the form of claims to legal status, particularly marriage and inheritance, originally confined to the patricians and gradually won by the plebeians after a series of bloody insurrections, political rights to a share in the government of the State, for example the right of taking auspices, which give the right to guide its destinies. Moreover, he looked for the evidences and reflections of such social struggles in new places, in what had hitherto been the preserve of antiquaries remote from political or social problems, for example in the story of the successful pressure of the 'under-privileged' minor divinities, *di minorum gentium*, for full citizenship of Olympus, where the *di majorum*, the gods of the major Roman *gentes*, had hitherto enjoyed undisputed supremacy.

[1] He is, however, careful to point out that customs change slowly (NS 249), and consequently the new forms of life tend to 'retain for some time the impression of their previous customs' (NS 1004).

The 'organic' interconnection of these, not *prima facie* connected, spheres of human action (which today few would question) is due to the fact, so Vico tells us, that men's lives are governed not by change, as Epicurus and his disciples Hobbes and Machiavelli held, nor by fate, as the Stoics, Zeno and Spinoza believed[1] – for this would make history incapable of rational explication – but by the divine spark in man, his effort to get away from brute nature, towards 'humanity' or 'civilisation'. Conscience, shame, a sense of the numinous or divine authority, of law, of responsibility, whence spring their sense of rights, of the minimum that they need to lead a life in which their faculties can obtain adequate scope; these are the universal human goals to which (under the concealed impulsion of Providence) men's 'divine' craving to realise themselves urges them. Laws and customs are the social products which respond to changing social needs. They are not the embodiment of infallible rules which individual sages, lifted above the stream of history, conceive in the fullness of their perfection, and lay down as immutable codes for all men, at all times, in all places. For men evolve: there can be no timeless minds or timeless laws of this kind.

Civilisations start from crude beginnings, 'corporeal imagination', 'frightful religions'.[2] Out of its dark, confused origins (of which Schelling was later to make so much), humanity moves forward slowly and painfully, and reaches maturity, usually after turmoil, struggle, cruel oppression and bitter conflict. Must this price always be paid? Vico's entire doctrine rests on the affirmation that it must. He cites those who think otherwise. Lucretius, the greatest disciple of Epicurus, held the influence of religion responsible for most of the crimes and miseries of mankind. Earlier still, Polybius had declared that 'if there were philosophers in the world there would be no need of religions'.[3] This implies that if wise and rational teachers had existed, they could, at any time, have saved humanity from its follies and sins and agonies, so that it was simply a piece of bad luck for the human race that at critical

---

[1] NS 342. 'Cicero was indeed right when he told the Epicurean Atticus that he could not discuss laws with him unless he first granted the existence of divine providence.' NS 335. Grotius and Pufendorf ignored it in their hypotheses, Selden took it for granted; but the Roman jurists really established it. See NS 310, 350, 394–7.

[2] e.g. NS 376, 379.   [3] NS 179, 1043 (Vico's paraphrase of Polybius 6. 56. 10).

junctures no sages arose, or made themselves heard – a view strongly implied by Voltaire and other thinkers of the Enlightenment who rejected appeals to the inscrutable will of God made by theists who gloried in the blindness of their faith. Vico had read Lucretius' magnificent poem with veneration, and borrowed from it (especially from the fifth book, even if he concealed this later), and he owed still more to Polybius. Moreover, he admired Stoicism, especially the Roman Stoics. And he was a pious if peculiar Christian. But these views he rejected totally and with passion. The notion that men could have been rational, virtuous, wise from the beginning – that savagery and barbarism could, but for the intervention of forces beyond human control, have been avoided; that religious obscurantism and the fear and ignorance which led to it were either disastrous accidents, which need never have occurred, or unintelligible mysteries – this seemed to him blindness to man's nature as a historically evolving entity, failure to understand what it is to be a man. For Vico, men are what they are in virtue of their development according to an intelligible sequence through stages which explain each other. Man cannot spring fully armed like Athena from the head of Zeus. Rationality is painfully acquired. Just as individuals cannot be conceived of as fully rational until they have attained to a certain level of maturity – until they have gone through, and, in due course, grown out of, earlier modes of experience, the outlook of infants, children, savages, the worlds of immediate sense and imagination; so a society of men for Vico, as for Pascal (who described mankind as being like a single centuries-old man), cannot attain to, for example, civil equality or monotheism or republican virtue until it has gone through the phases which must necessarily precede this culmination, until it has exhausted these simpler forms of life – authoritarian, magical, animistic, polytheistic – of which the full flowering of a culture is at once the fulfilment and the destruction. Polybius' error thus consists, for Vico, in the neglect of history as an essential category, which underlies his fallacious assumption that philosophic wisdom could have occurred in any social milieu at any time, that it was a mere accident that it took so long to arrive, leaving the field open to its calamitous rival, religion; and no less fortuitous that when philosophy (or science) did finally speak its truths, they should have been so little followed, and become so soon forgotten in the long, sterile night of the Middle Ages. Vico attributes this lack of the true sense of history to Polybius; but he could equally well have cited Descartes[1] or Grotius or Spinoza or Voltaire.

The analogy between the individual and society, microcosm and macrocosm, is at least as old as Plato. But the notion of movement towards *humanitas* owes more to Stoicism and the Renaissance humanists. So Marsilio Ficino says that boys are more cruel than men, the dull than the intelligent, madmen than the sane, because they have less *humanitas*, are less fully human: brutality is a form of immaturity. This doctrine is common to Vico and the Enlightenment. But whereas for the *philosophes* the stages represent merely imperfections to be transcended, for Vico they also possess marvellous 'poetic' properties which are lost in the process of civilisation. No *Iliad*, no *Divine Comedy* can be created in our own 'magnificent times', but only during the 'heroic' phase to which the avarice, cruelty, arrogance of the rulers are intrinsic. This is Vico's phenomenology: there is no real bridge between his thought and that of the progressive intelligentsia of his time. What was for them the beginning of liberation by reason was for him the beginning of the disintegration of the social texture.

The doctrine that he attacked lay at the heart of the teaching of the Enlightenment both in Vico's own day and in the two centuries that followed. What Descartes cautiously implied, the radicals of the eighteenth century proclaimed boldly and clearly: that every form of belief and practice that was not founded on a rational basis, such as religious or non-rational or subjective thought or feeling, is so much gratuitous deviation from the one, eternal, timeless truth. The follies, vices, crimes and miseries of mankind are, on this view, principally due to the (largely unexplained) failure to appear, when they were most needed, of teachers of sufficient knowledge, virtue and authority over men to set humanity on the right path and break, once and for all, the sway of the fools and impostors who have hitherto wrought havoc with men's lives. In so far as Vico, with his doctrine of the *storia ideale eterna* in which human nature transforms both itself and its environment, denied precisely this possibility, such optimistic reformers as Helvétius, Holbach,

---

[1] Sparta's greatness was attributed by Descartes to the fact that its laws, 'having been originated by a single individual, all tended to a single goal': *Discourse on Method* (*Oeuvres*, vol. 6, p. 12, lines 20–5). A century earlier, Machiavelli paid a similar tribute to Lycurgus. Vico, for whom Lycurgus is a social myth, regards such individualism as being characteristic of Descartes' blindness to the nature of man and history.

Condorcet (and their followers in the nineteenth and twentieth centuries) would, if they had read them, have found in Vico's writings all that they most passionately rejected: historicism, that is, belief in the unique character and indispensability, and, above all, validity at its own stage of development, of each of the phases through which mankind has passed and will pass; belief in an immaterial soul, with its own immanent laws of growth, modified by external factors but not subject to mechanical causation; belief that men understand themselves and their own works in a sense different from, and superior to, that in which they know the external world; the view that history is a humane study in some sense in which physics is not; finally, the belief that the goals of men are set by Providence, and that their past and future are strictly governed by it, and much else of the same sort that they would have found wholly repugnant. In this sense Vico was a reactionary, a counter-revolutionary figure, opposed to the central stream of the Enlightenment. His hostility to Descartes, Spinoza, Locke, and to all attempts to apply the concepts and methods of the natural sciences to what is human in human affairs – which seemed to him tantamount to dehumanising men – anticipated the positions of Hamann and Herder and Burke, and the romantic movement. 'The listener to his lectures should have been a Francesco de Sanctis, or a Georg Hegel, or a Barthold Niebuhr, who ... would continue the renewal [rinnovamento] of criticism, philosophy, history that he had begun.'[1] This may account to some extent for the neglect to which his work was instinctively consigned by generations dominated by the advance of the natural sciences.

X

Nevertheless there is another and a profounder sense in which Vico (like Montesquieu) was more of an empiricist than his materialist and utilitarian adversaries. For while it is true that he believed that man's nature and potentialities, and the laws which govern him, had been bestowed on him by his Creator to enable him to fulfil goals chosen for, and not by, him, he also believed that we could not know the Creator's ultimate purpose as the Creator knew it;

[1] Fausto Nicolini, preface to his edition of Vico's Opere (Milan/Naples, 1953), p. x.

and moreover he believed that only one way was open to us of discovering what this nature and these potentialities and laws were – that of historical reconstruction. We must pay minute attention to historical facts – to the story of men's daily lives and activities on earth, which alone revealed the pattern that determined what men were, had been and might have been, could and would be. Unlike Leibniz (whose doctrine of development his own at times seems to resemble), Vico says nothing to imply that an intellect of sufficient penetration could, by mere insight into the structure (the 'essence') of any given human soul, or any 'spirit of the age', deduce a priori what it is bound to be and do – and so be enabled in principle to calculate the entire past, present and future of all men without recourse to empirical evidence. Nor, like the majority of the jurists of the seventeenth century, and the *philosophes* of the eighteenth, did he hold that a relatively simple set of psychological laws was sufficient for the analysis of the characters and acts of men. Vico worked on the opposite assumption, that only empirical knowledge, at times abstruse and peculiar, of what actually occurred, and exceptional imaginative power brought to bear upon it, reveal the working of the 'eternal' pattern that shapes the characteristics of human beings, the laws that are responsible for those parallels and correspondences of psychological and social structure that are found between societies or individuals remote from one another in space and time, race and outlook – correspondences in virtue of which, despite their differences, these societies nevertheless constitute links in one great, winding, rising and falling stair. Each step in this spiral or cyclical structure leads to the next in an intelligible fashion – for they are all necessitated by the development of one and the same entity – the creative human *mente* guided by Providence. This 'mind', which for Vico appears to be, at times, simply men interacting in pursuing their needs and utilities, guided by Providence, can by memory, imagination, intelligence, the new method based on Vico's conception of a science of history, understand its own past states as stages towards its single ultimate, never fully realised goal – the realisation of its capacities, as they come into being, each in its own due season, each in response to the demands created by the operation of its predecessor, each generating outlooks, institutions, forms of life, cultures, an 'organic' interweaving of diverse activities and states of mind or feeling, physical and spiritual, religious and legal, political and economic, spontaneous and self-conscious, stimulated by fear or interest, love or shame, awe and the sense of right, by desire for order or knowledge or freedom or fame or power or pleasure. The totality of these activities and states is the history of mankind.

For this reason, to condemn an activity because it offends against our present-day morality is for him an approach both arrogant and shallow. The savage religions with all their horrors fulfilled an indispensable function in their own day, of binding (Vico suggests that the very word 'religion' stems from this) a chaotic multitude into a disciplined whole. Moreover (to this he returns again and again), many human acts have unintended consequences of vast utility and importance. Like many thinkers before and after him, Vico interprets this as evidence for a supreme purpose concealed from human eyes, transcending individual purposes – the hidden hand of a divine Providence without which the movement of history cannot be grasped, and which resembles Hegel's 'cunning of reason'.[1] There are 'institutions by which, without human discernment or counsel, and often against the designs of men, Providence has ordered this great city of the human race'.[2] Legislation out of 'ferocity, avarice and ambition' creates 'the military, merchants and governing classes' and by this means arise 'the strength, riches and wisdom of commonwealths'; and so 'out of these three great vices, which could certainly destroy all mankind on the face of the earth', legislation 'makes civil happiness'.[3]

Something of this kind had been said by Hobbes and Mandeville, and would be said again by Helvétius and Adam Smith and Bentham. Legislation can turn private vices into public virtues by dangling rewards and punishments judiciously before men. Their egoistic instincts can be canalised by education and laws into doing public good. But this is not what Vico means. When he explains how lust and fear lead to marriage and the family, or the violence of patrons to their clients leads to revolt and so to the establishment of cities; how the oppression of the plebeians ends in its opposite, laws and liberty; how the risings of the people bring about monarchy; while the corruption of peoples by their rulers leads to the opposite of the rulers' purpose, namely conquest by stronger and purer peoples from without; how self-destructive

---

[1] loc. cit. (p. 56 above, note 4).   [2] NS 342.   [3] NS 132.

decadence leads to solitude and savagery,[1] and then, by a miracle, to the resurrection of the phoenix out of its ashes and the new cycle of human history, what Vico means is something closer to the ideas of Herder and after him Schelling and Hegel. He believes, like them, that there exists a cosmic, purposive tendency which moulds men's passions and desires into institutions and forms of social life in an intelligible pattern, and consequently that this cannot be done, as the utilitarians thought, by the conscious control of intelligent experts who know how to canalise human weaknesses either for the society's advantage, or for their own selfish ends.[2]

[1] The primary cause of this is the destruction of religion, which, for Vico, is the social cement and 'shield of princes' without which there is 'no shield of defence ... nor basis of support, nor even a form by which [peoples] may exist in the world at all'. NS 1109.

[2] This is asserted in the magnificent peroration with which the *Scienza nuova* virtually ends: 'It is true that men have themselves made this world of nations (and we took this as the first incontestable principle of our science, since we despaired of finding it from philosophers and philologists), but this world without doubt has issued from a mind often diverse, at times quite contrary, and always superior to the particular ends that men had proposed to themselves; which narrow ends, made means to serve wider ends, it has always employed to preserve the human race upon this earth. Men mean to gratify their bestial lust and abandon their offspring, and they inaugurate the chastity of marriage from which the families arise. The fathers mean to exercise without restraint their paternal power over their clients, and they subject them to the civil powers from which the cities arise. The reigning orders of nobles mean to abuse their lordly freedom over the plebeians, and they are obliged to submit to the laws which establish popular liberty. The free people mean to shake off the yokes of their laws, and they become subject to monarchs. The monarchs mean to strengthen their own positions by debasing their subjects with all the vices of dissoluteness, and they dispose them to endure slavery at the hands of stronger nations. The nations mean to dissolve themselves, and their remnants flee for safety to the wilderness, whence, like the phoenix, they rise again. That which did all this was mind, for men did it with intelligence; it was not fate, for they did it by choice; not chance, for the results of their always so acting are perpetually the same.' NS 1108.

It is difficult to believe that neither Hamann, nor his far more influential disciple Herder, did more than glance at Vico's philosophy of history, and that they did even this well after they had composed their own; or that the sole link between Vico and the early Herder (whose central views possess an uncanny resemblance to those of the *New Science*) is Vico's disciple Cesarotti, with whose commentaries on Homer Herder was acquainted, with, perhaps, a memory of a vague mention by Thomasius. Yet it may well be the case; there is as yet little evidence worthy of the name for any other conclusion. The effect of one thinker upon others is, at times, anything but direct; and the origins and rise of the new conception of society and social evolution, which reached its apogee in the

ultimately came to concede, Duni's attempts to defend Vico's self-proclaimed orthodoxy are totally unconvincing. His modern editor, Fausto Nicolini, has little difficulty in disposing of most modern writers (the most learned and interesting is Franco Amerio) who wished to annex Vico to the ranks of orthodox Catholic theorists.[1]

Although Vico makes a point of distinguishing *bestioni* from the 'scempi di Grozio', the 'abbandonati di Puffendorfio' and the 'violenti di Obbes',[2] there is no relevant difference between them; Vico protests too much about this, as indeed he does his piety and devotion to the precepts of the Church. Perhaps, as Corsano thinks, he was afraid of the Roman Inquisition in Naples, which, although not as savage as that of Spain which it replaced, did punish some of his free-thinking friends and silenced others, so that Vico would, for all his genuine piety, have had reason to be as frightened as Descartes had been in 1619 by the terrible fate of Vanini. Nicolini thinks that this is exaggerated, for the victims of the Neapolitan inquisition were few, obscure and not deprived of their lives. Croce's image of a poverty-stricken schoolmaster nervously genuflecting to avoid disgrace or censorship, anxious to be counted a devout member of his Church even though his views were suspiciously non-conformist, is probably correct. Vico 'fait d'étonnants efforts pour croire qu'il est encore croyant', wrote Michelet in 1854,[3] and this echoes his remark in 1831 that Vico's thought is 'plus hardie peut-être que l'auteur lui-même ne l'a soupçonné ... Heureusement, le livre était dédié à Clément

---

una bestia (Venice, 1768), reprinted by Croce as *Difesa dell'autorità della sacra scrittura contro Giambattista Vico* (Bari, 1936). There were attacks on similar lines by Damiano Romano in 1736, Cosimo Mei in 1754, Donato Rogadeo in 1780, etc. For the bibliography of anti-Vichismo, see Benedetto Croce and Fausto Nicolini's magnificent *Bibliografia vichiana* (Naples, 1947–8) and Paolo Rossi, 'Giambattista Vico', in Walter Binni (ed.), *I classici italiani nella storia della critica*, vol. 2, 2nd ed. (Florence, 1961).

[1] See Fausto Nicolini's *La religiosità di Giambattista Vico: quattro saggi* (Bari, 1949), particularly the introduction.

[2] NS 553; cf. p. 50, note 1, and p. 79, note 3, above.

[3] 'Makes an amazing effort to believe that he is still a believer.' From 'Ma liberté, Virgile, Vico', a draft of 1854 for a chapter of *Le Banquet: Oeuvres*, vol. 16, p. 658. This remark is preceded by the following: 'Vico shows how the gods are made and unmade ... It is man who makes [them]. He ceaselessly creates himself, he manufactures his earth and his heaven. Thus is the mystery revealed. The revelation is so bold that Vico is himself afraid of it.'

XII.'[1] Moreover, Vico's use of critical methods first applied by Spinoza and *Père* Simon, the fathers of higher criticism, is obvious enough. Vico loathed Spinoza, but did not escape the influence of his method; he applies it only to pagan antiquities, but he applies it.

Stranger psychological contradictions could be found. There is no reason, for example, to think that Machiavelli, who had moved further in an obviously anti-Christian direction, was insincere when he wrote his canticles of penitence[2] or when he made his last confession when he was dying. Hobbes, too, probably regarded himself as a Christian. The attempt to defend Vico after his death on Averroist lines – on the ground that his philosophical views belonged to a different realm from his religious or theological convictions, and that therefore there was no possibility of collision between them – whether or not it is philosophically defensible, undoubtedly reflects what has been psychologically true of men who remain fervently orthodox in their own minds, and passionately desire to remain loyal members of their Church or party or nation, while professing dissident views. There is no doubt that during the entire second part of his life – his most creative years – Vico lived in the most intimate intercourse with priests and monks, and looked to them for sympathy, help, advice, protection. His dislike of materialism, atheism, natural science and his ignorance of the major scientific advances of his own century are patent. He was a faithful and fervent ally of 'spiritualism' and religion as such. Indeed, the cornerstone of his reconstruction of the life of primitive men is the belief that religion, however primitive and delusive, alone creates and preserves the social bond, alone humanises and disciplines savage men. Without Providence there is no progress; it may work through the human faculties (hence we can, to a limited degree, discover its methods), but without the divine plan we should still be wandering in the 'great forest' of the early world; religion alone – shame before the thundering God in Heaven, a feeling of awe implanted by the true God – is the first and most powerful of the ways used by Providence to turn our vices into means of our preservation and improvement. The weakening of the feeling of awe, of piety, of religious authority, spells the doom of the entire social texture and leads to that second

---

[1] 'Bolder, perhaps, than the author himself suspected . . . Fortunately the book was dedicated to Clement XII.' Preface to *Histoire Romaine*: ibid., vol. 2, p. 341.

[2] Although their authenticity has been questioned.

barbarism described in a famous passage of the *New Science* (remarkable enough to be quoted more than once), when men, though physically thronging together, 'live like wild beasts in a deep solitude of spirit and will, scarcely any two being able to agree since each follows his own pleasure or caprice'.[1] Religion is not for him, as for Comte or even Saint-Simon, simply a social cement whose value lies in its utility: it is what makes men men; its loss degrades and dehumanises. Unorthodox Vico plainly was; heretical perhaps; but unswervingly religious.

Despite these deviations and contradictions, Vico's central schema is not obscured. It remains, in its essentials, a theory of history founded on a metaphysical conception of men's nature as driven on by its own inner purposes, with a vitalistic sociology which can be held as fervently by an atheist as by a Christian. 'The world of civil society has certainly been made by men', and 'its principles are therefore to be found within the modifications of our own human mind'.[2] This is what counts. It is this humanist doctrine, neither mechanistic nor determinist, but also not transcendental, that made the doctrine of this 'reactionary', less than a century after his death, acceptable to the secular defenders of French or Italian nationalism, who could not have held an uncompromisingly theocratic and authoritarian doctrine like those, for example, of Bossuet or Maistre (or even Burke). This is so because Vico's arguments for the finger of God in history are, in the end, no more than contentions that attitudes, purposes and forces are never wholly man-made or planned, and in particular that some of the most beneficent, permanent and universal human institutions are not the result of men's conscious intentions. But all that this shows is that even if men largely create their own history, they do not do so alone, and do not create themselves. An atheist is left free to assume that the co-author of men's lives is an impersonal, and indeed purposeless and inanimate, nature, the laws of which are wholly discoverable by the material sciences. Vico would doubtless have rejected this; it is Providence that shapes our lives, and it is therefore presumptuous for men to claim wholly to understand its ways, but they are its instruments and of one spiritual substance with it, and therefore able to understand what they themselves create.

The 'ideal eternal history', the laws that govern 'the history of

[1] NS 1106.   [2] NS 331.

every nation in its rise, development, maturity, decline and fall',[1] seem based on a polyphonic simile, in which each group of instruments (each nation, each culture) plays its own tune, the structure of which corresponds to the identical, or at least similar, tunes played in other keys and at other *tempi* by other groups of instruments – other nations and cultures, elsewhere, at other times.[2] Obscurities and problems remain. In Vico men can retrace the cycles of *sorgimenti, progressi, stati, decadenze e fini* because men have 'made' them; consequently they can recover them by sufficiently powerful intellectual-imaginative effort. How is this done? Can men do this because they are in communion with, live in, 'una mente eterna ed infinita che penetra tutto e presentisce tutto';[3] because they are a part of a universal spirit which entitles Croce to speak of Vico, if not as a pantheist, at least as an Absolute Idealist? But then, what are we to make of his insistence on a personal God, the transcendent deity of orthodox Catholic Christianity? Or can men do this because 'the world of civil society has certainly been made by men', and 'its principles are therefore to be found in the modifications of our own human mind'[4] by the *verum/factum* principle, and, therefore, not in the modifications of the divine mind, to claim to 'penetrate' which would be absurd and blasphemous? Again, if the criterion of truth is 'to have made it', and we claim to know our past, what becomes of divine intervention? When Vico speaks of 'our human mind', 'our understanding', 'a certain human mind of nations', 'our human thought', 'our spirit'[5] and so on, do such phrases refer to what is common to all individual minds, or to some 'collective' mind, like Jung's collective unconscious, but with pantheistic implications?

[1] cf. p. 86 above, note 1.

[2] It is a Leibnizian image, not a harmonic one (which could have been intelligible only some decades later), like that which dominates, for example, Hegel's organicism, where the significance of individual sounds – particular ingredients in the development of world history – may not be intelligible save in conjunction with the other 'sounds', which, taken by themselves, at times may seem ugly, or meaningless, and acquire meaning and value only when 'heard' as elements in, and from the standpoint of, the organic whole.

[3] 'An eternal and infinite mind that penetrates and foresees everything.' NS1 45.

[4] NS 331.

[5] These terms of Vico's – 'nostra mente umana', 'nostro intendere', 'una certa mente umana delle nazioni', 'nostro umano pensiero', 'nostra anima' – are listed in *The Historical Theory of Giambattista Vico* by Thomas Berry (Catholic University of America Ph.D. thesis: Washington, DC, 1949), p. 76.

Or is the use of the term *nostro* merely metaphorical or distributive? Or again, do the *gentes* create law? Are they rational precisely to the degree to which, and because, they have created it themselves and understand it, as they would not if it had been imposed upon them by an inscrutable Providence?

Vico is a rich, suggestive and original, but scarcely a clear or coherent, thinker. One is tempted once again to quote Bizet's celebrated comment on Berlioz that he 'had genius without any talent'.[1] The tension between Vico's theism and his humanistic historicism, between his conception of the cunning of Providence, and his constant emphasis on the creative and self-transforming labours of men, is not resolved in the *New Science*; to call it dialectical is only to conceal this fact by the use of a portentous term; Vico's Catholic interpreters lay stress on the former, Michelet and humanist thinkers on the latter, strain in his thought. It is certainly the humanist vision that seems to evoke his more ardent words. There is (for human beings) 'a divine pleasure' in seeing the great cosmic ideas working themselves out;[2] divine because we see our own creative activity. 'History cannot be more certain than when he who creates the things also narrates them.'[3] And then, in a curious, obscure, but arresting and characteristic passage, he adds: 'By means of their logic [the founders of Gentile humanity] invented languages; by morals, created heroes; by economics, founded families, and by politics, cities ... by the particular physics of man, in a certain sense created themselves.'[4] What is this 'certain sense'? Vico does not explain. What men are and believe, they have themselves made; if not individually, then collectively. If the whole human race could speak as one man, it could perhaps remember all and understand all, and say all there is to be said. Because men have not each individually created the whole of human history, they cannot know the truth as the mathematician knows it about his invented entities; but because the subject-matter of history is not fictional but real, the *New Science*, even if it is less translucent than mathematics, tells the truth about the real world, as geometry, or arithmetic, or algebra, cannot.

History, mythology, literature, law – these are among the studies that teach men what they are and what they were, why they must be what they are, what they could be, how 'the nature of peoples is

---

[1] Undated letter (June 1871) to Léonie Halévy: p. 322 in *Lettres de Georges Bizet: Impressions de Rome (1857–1860); La Commune (1871)* (Paris, 1907).
[2] NS 345.   [3] NS 349.   [4] NS 367.

first crude, then severe, then benign, then delicate, finally dissol-ute';[1] which stage in this cycle they have reached, where they are on the great stair of history, and what courses it is therefore best for them to pursue. Hegelianism, Marxism, Comtian positivism, the Catholic theories of 'palingenesis', to some degree social psychol-ogy influenced by Freud and his disciples, are attempts to elaborate and apply in very differing fashions the phenomenology of the *New Science*, whereby men seek, as it were, to psychoanalyse their own childhood and adolescence, and found predictions upon this evidence.

So caught was Vico by the novelty and the power of his new ideas that he troubled too little to collect adequate evidence for his conclusions. By the end of the seventeenth century there came into being a plethora of travellers' tales and accounts of exotic peoples, upon which Montesquieu and many social and moral theorists in the eighteenth century drew avidly. Vico touched upon them, and mentioned them here and there, but on the whole made little use of them. Those whose minds are dominated by a powerful and revolutionary vision, which has transformed their view of the world, are sometimes averse from careful attention to empirical facts. Vico's outlook and his methods were unlike those of the inductive sciences; he was a philosopher and a jurist, he thought in terms of general ideas buttressed by occasional examples, but not of detailed evidence for carefully tested hypotheses.[2] He seems blind to the decisive impact of the natural sciences on Western culture. Perhaps this, too, helped to bring about the oblivion into which his work sank after his death. In an age in which the physical sciences achieved unparalleled progress, Vico's audacious claim in the *De antiquissima* that physics cannot define things *ex vero*, whereas (as he later believed) history comes closer to this; his fierce opposition to atomism, 'Epicureanism', utilitarianism – all the mechanical models which dominated the social and political

---

[1] NS 242. Enzo Paci, op. cit. (p. 69 above, note 2), thinks that Vico conceived man's ascent as a struggle of the 'bestial' with the 'heroic'. Certainly Vico does not idealise the remote past – or, indeed, any other period.

[2] The reader should be warned that M. H. Fisch does not agree with this, and regards the *New Science* as proceeding by induction and by hypothesis: *Giambattista Vico* (see p. 56 above, note 1), p. 423. I must own that I see little sign of this in the texts; moreover, it would contradict one of Vico's central theses – the unbridgeable gulf between the methods of natural science and historical disciplines.

thought of this time – stand out as a monument of (at times perverse) originality and independence.

XI

Vico had no doubt that he had discovered the central truth about philosophy and history; nevertheless he thought of himself primarily as a jurist, and his own greatest effort is directed against the application of the fallacies of Descartes and Grotius to the domain of law. The doctrine which he attacks with all his might is that of the great schools of natural law. His main charge against the famous masters of the seventeenth century, Grotius, Selden, Pufendorf (and, for that matter, the medieval Christian theorists too, although he tactfully does not say so), is that they all assume a fixed, universal human nature, from the needs of which it is possible to deduce a single set of principles of conduct, identical everywhere, for everyone, at all times, and constituting therefore the perennial basis of all human laws, whatever special modifications and adjustments might be required by changing times and circumstances. For Vico there is no static nucleus, no unalterable minimum of this kind. 'The nature of institutions is nothing but their coming into being [*nascimento*] at certain times and in certain guises.'[1] Nature is change, growth, the interplay of forces that perpetually transform one another; only the pattern of this flow is constant, not its substance, only the most general form of the laws which it obeys, not their content. True natural law is not 'the natural law of the philosophers',[2] not a set of universal rules, however general, however few, however old, but the emergence of new laws as expressions, in the social sphere, of each new way of life as it arises. Thus, for example, 'civil equity' is not a timeless and universal principle, latent in the souls of all men as such, but established by those whom Ulpian calls 'those few who ... have come to know what things are necessary for the conservation of human society'.[3] No doubt each society is governed by some one set of rules, about which all, or at least most, of its members must be in broad agreement; but these are not objective truths waiting to be discovered by a lawgiver of genius, and then 'received' by lesser men, or entire nations, bound by his vision of reality; they are

[1] NS 147.   [2] NS 313.   [3] NS 320.

produced by the fact that in a given set of circumstances human beings are liable to believe, express themselves, live, think and act in common ways. The 'common sense' – by which Vico means something like the collective social outlook – 'of each people or nation so regulates social life and human acts that they accord with whatever the whole of a people or nation feels in common'.[1] It harmonises the various laws of a nation 'without one nation following the example of another'.[2] This is Vico's concept of true natural law, the natural law of the nations, not of the philosophers.[3] There are, no doubt, some institutions which all men have in common – for instance, some form of religion; some form of marriage; some form of burial. These, Vico notes, are to be found in all societies. But he evidently does not think these a sufficient basis for a static universal law, since these forms vary widely from people to people, from age to age. It is impossible to abstract what is common to all the phases of a continuous dynamic process of change, as it is impossible to abstract what is common to all shapes, or all colours, or all human faces or lives, and pronounce that to be the basic or natural shape, or colour, the basic or natural human face or life. That is why it is idle to seek to abstract common unaltering beliefs and call them natural law.

What then is the natural law of the nations, *ius naturale gentium*? Vico characteristically explains that if by 'nature' is meant the monotonous repetition of causes and effects, that is precisely what men resist and transcend. The generations of birds learn nothing new, but merely do again and again what their ancestors have done before them, eternally. This is the mechanical 'nature' from which men can free themselves, which they must shun. *Naturale* for men means, not fixed, but (again from *nascimento*) 'growing into society', and *gentium* means whatever is generated by the societies of human beings themselves (each generation bearing its successor on its shoulders), not by an élite of sages dictating from above, or speaking in the name of objective order – 'ipsis rebus dictantibus' ('the things themselves speaking'),[4] as the older theorists liked to say. Each society has its own 'civil law' appropriate to its stage of culture. But the nations in their 'poetical' or 'heroic' phase, incapable as yet of general ideas,

---

[1] NS1 46.   [2] NS 311; cf. 142, 145–6.   [3] See NS 332; cf. 135.
[4] This phrase appears to originate in Justinian's *Digest* at 1. 2. 2. 11. 2, a passage (mis)quoted at NS 584, 1007. Ed.

unable to conceive their own slow evolution, tend to embody their
sense of their own past in a myth – the god or the legendary
legislator who gave them all their laws in one great creative act –
Lycurgus, Draco, Solon, the great founders and fathers of their
peoples, symbols of an entire society. But to see a myth for what it
is, one must penetrate to the truth behind it.[1] Laws are the
embodiment of a gradual and collective response on the part of an
entire society. So, too, ancient poetry (Vico's principal example is
the Homeric poems) is the greatest 'treasure house'[2] of the laws
and customs of the Greeks, of their view of life, in which the
Hellenic nation, whatever origin it attributed to them, rightly saw
an incarnation of its traditional values, the historical reasons for
which, having as yet little self-consciousness, it could not know;
and, since only God is omniscient, could never know completely.
Such traditional wisdom tends to be questioned as self-consciousness and self-criticism grow. Thus their lowly status is accepted by
plebeians so long as they do not question its metaphysical basis –
the objective inferiority of their natures to that of the 'superior'
patricians. Once critical reason causes them to question this dogma,
then doubt it, and finally reject it, the path is open to rebellion,
which in its turn is symbolised by the Roman myth of the
Secession and by the institution of the Tribunate. Myths give way
to metaphor, metaphor to conventional use of language, which
coincides with philosophy, democracy, the growing use of prose
and the growing self-consciousness and artificiality of poetry as a
deliberate aesthetic exercise. Natural law and positive law alike
cease to be expressed in the 'serious poem'[3] of ancient Roman
jurisprudence. The evolution of law (and the entire story of the
progress of humanity) can be traced best of all 'philologically', by
looking at the transformation of the language in which the
successive legal codes are expressed.

Vico's intellectual courage – even if it is the only kind of courage
he possessed – was very great. It was a very bold undertaking to
attack the ancient conception of natural law as being something
universal, absolute, objective, a set of eternal truths in the light of

---

[1] Yet, if Homer or Lycurgus could be explained away in this fashion, could
not, his Catholic critics asked with justified suspicion, Moses, the prophets, the
founder of the Church himself, be similarly dissolved? cf. p. 100 above, note 3,
and A 63.

[2] cf. NS 156, 904.   [3] NS 1037.

which Europe had lived for two millennia. It was especially audacious to do so in the century the greatest jurists of which had laid it down that these laws were as certain as those of mathematics and could not be altered even by God himself; and to substitute for this the notion of natural law as a set of rules covering all the vast variety of social experience, organised not by its deducibility from a single set of timeless axioms, but by its relation to the fundamental – not perhaps wholly immutable – categories in which human beings in fact think and act. Right and wrong, property and justice, equality and liberty, the relations of master and servant, authority and punishment – these are evolving notions between each successive phase of which there will be a kind of family resemblance, as in a row of portraits of the ancestors of modern society, from which it is senseless to attempt, by subtracting all the differences, to discover a central nucleus – the original family as it were, and declare that this featureless entity is the eternal face of mankind.

XII

Where the natural law theorists are abstract, Vico is concrete; where they invented fictions, the natural man, or the state of nature, he remained uncompromisingly committed to what he called history, a history which may not have been accurate, but which was time-bound through and through. Where they distinguished morals from politics, he regarded these as one organic evolutionary process, connected with every other self-expression of human beings in society. Where the natural lawyers were individualists, he grasped the social nature of man – in the sense that he thought that the majority of human activities would not be intelligible if one attempted to describe them as the acts of solitary Robinson Crusoes. For Vico, men acted as they did because their membership of social groups, and their sense of this relationship, was as basic and as decisive as their desire for food, or shelter, or procreation, as their lusts and sense of shame, their search for authority and truth, and everything else that makes men what they are. Where the lawyers were exact, clear, formal, rationalistic, utilitarian, he remained religious, vague, intuitive, disordered, and painfully obscure.

His theory of truth and certainty is equally *sui generis*.[1] He

---

[1] On this entire topic see the next essay.

attacked the mathematical model of Descartes as leaving out the richest and most important part of human experience – everything that is not in the realm of natural science – daily life, history, human laws and institutions, the modes of human self-expression. Two hundred years before our time he conceived of mathematics as the invention of fictions, as an art or game like chess, not as a descriptive procedure, or system of tautologies. He conceived of aesthetics, which he called 'poetics', as being concerned with a basic activity of men seeking not to give pleasure or embellish truths,[1] but to express a vision of the world, an activity that could be studied on a level with law or politics. He saw language and mythology as a free creation of the human spirit, and one providing more dependable data for human history than conscious records, and conceived history itself, not as almost everyone else did in his time, and had done during two millennia since Herodotus, either as 'philosophy teaching by examples',[2] or as a recital of past glories, or as the discovery of mechanical, recurrent causes and effects, or of what actually happened at specific moments, or as rendering justice to the dead, or as providing entertainment – but as the story and explanation of successive stages of social organisation and consciousness. He exposed the inadequacy of utilitarianism before Kant, and of the atomistic view of society before Rousseau and Hegel. He distinguished the canons of certainty and judgement from those of both validity and demonstrable truth, discovery from invention, making from recording, the nature of principles, rules, laws from that of propositions, the categories of cognition from those of the will, and anticipated ideas developed in the nineteenth century, and still more in the twentieth, by legal and moral philosophers and

[1] Horace's almost universally accepted maxim – 'aut prodesse volunt aut delectare poetae' ('poets want either to be useful or to give pleasure', *Ars poetica* 333) – is precisely what he denies. He anticipated Herder's conception of artistic creation as self-expression, not the purveying of beautiful objects the value of which is independent of their creators, that is, as communication, not as manufacture; he is in this respect a direct forerunner of the romantic critics.

[2] [Henry St John, Viscount] Bolingbroke, *Letters on the Study and Use of History*, letter 2: vol. 2, p. 177, in *The Works of Lord Bolingbroke* (London, 1844). Bolingbroke says that he thinks he read the remark in Dionysius of Halicarnassus, and he is right (see *Ars rhetorica* 11. 2), except that the *Ars rhetorica* is no longer attributed to Dionysius. Pseudo-Dionysius attributes his version – 'History is philosophy from examples' – to Thucydides, but it is in fact a creative paraphrase of what Thucydides says at 1. 22. 3. Ed.

philosophical sociologists. He is the true founder of the German historical school in his rejection of natural law and emphasis on human plasticity and the interpretation of all the aspects of social life. He preceded Hegel and the social psychologists in pointing out that the direction of a society may be very different from the sum of the conscious intentions of its members, so that one can speak of a society seeking this or that goal even if its members, or a majority of them, are, as individuals, consciously striving for something else. He perceived the formative part played by myths, archetypal images and symbolic structures before Hamann or Schelling, Nietzsche or Durkheim, or the founders of psychoanalysis. He, if any man, is the creator of the great realm that comprises the comparative studies of mythology, anthropology, historical archaeology, philology, as well as linguistics, historical criticism of the arts, above all history itself conceived as the development of cultures. He spoke before Saint-Simon of the central historical role played by class war, his doctrine of the new barbarism that must succeed civilisation anticipates those of Herzen and Sorel, his notion of heroic values foreshadows that of Nietzsche. Above all he traced the frontier, disputed ever since, between the natural sciences and the human – between *Naturwissenschaft* and *Geisteswissenschaft* – the first proceeding by hypothesis and confirmation, inductively and deductively, arguing for and from generalisations and idealised models derived from the uniformities of the compresences and successions of phenomena; the second seeking to describe human experience as concretely as possible, and therefore to emphasise variety, differences, change, motives and goals, individuality rather than uniformity or indifference to time, or unaltering repetitive patterns. He was, that is, the first modern thinker to grasp the fundamental difference between scientific and historical analysis – the X-ray and the portrait – between the method which consists in perceiving and abstracting what is identical or similar in a large number of different cases, in order to establish some law or model from which new knowledge can be obtained by applying it to the unknown future or past; and, as distinct from this, the method whose task it is to uncover not the common kernel of dissimilar cases, but, on the contrary, the individual character of each – that which makes each action or event or person, or society or school of art or work of literature, what it is, uniquely; and does so by placing the human beings with whom it deals in their own specific time and environment, their own moral, intellectual, historical and social 'context', by means, and by reference to standards, more refined than, but not necessarily different in principle from, those used in the normal processes of life by men in their intercourse with one another. He described as useful only those historians who present facts in all their individual concreteness, and not those who deal in wholesale generalisations, as philosophers are bound to do. There is something of this in Bacon, but Vico takes it further.[1] He was the first thinker to ask himself about – and deny – the possibility of assimilating the methods of history (and life) to those of the natural sciences; and vice versa. The controversy over this issue is, if anything, more alive in our day than in his own.

XIII

Did anyone read Vico? Does anyone do so now? Eminent *dilettanti* like the abbé Conti and Count Porcía in Venice, who commissioned his autobiography (then a relatively new genre lacking its modern name),[2] realised that he was something more than a locally well-known polymath. His patron, Cardinal Corsini, when he was elected to the papacy, did not altogether forget him. But he remained, on the whole, out of account. He was at best looked upon as an eccentric writer with flashes of talent, but of interest only to specialists. Conti recommended his *New Science* to Montesquieu when the latter visited Venice, but despite Croce's assertion to the contrary, there is no solid evidence that Montesquieu ever read it, or even that he had acquired it for his library.[3] Vico's reputation, despite Leclerc's encouragement, remained largely Neapolitan, that of a remarkable local scholar, the friend of Gravina and Muratori, of interest to students of Italian learning. After his death, portions of his work were made accessible at various dates by Pagano, Cesarotti, Genovesi and Galiani. The *abate* Galiani, a nephew of one of Vico's ecclesiastical patrons, was a brilliant and original talker and writer, a diplomat, an

---

[1] See the second epigraph on p. 21 above.

[2] Father Carlo Lodoli, censor of publications, coined a name for it derived from Greek: the genre he called 'Periautografia', its authors 'Periautografi'. See D[on] Angelo Calogerà, 'Prefazione', *Raccolta d'opuscoli scientifici, e filologici* 1 (1728), p. xviii.

[3] On Montesquieu and Vico, see the account given by Robert Shackleton in *Montesquieu: A Critical Biography* (London, 1961), pp. 114–16.

economist, and a friend and ally of Holbach and Helvétius, who evidently thought he could pay his queer compatriot no higher compliment than to describe him as a forerunner of Montesquieu. 'Vico', he once said, 'was bold enough to try to ford the dark river of metaphysics; he was drowned, but he provided a bridge for more fortunate thinkers who wanted to cross after him.'[1]

In 1787 the Neapolitan lawyer Filangieri gave a copy of the *New Science* to Goethe, who glanced at it and sent it to Jacobi. Goethe wrote later:

[Filangieri] introduced me to the work of an older writer, whose profound wisdom is so refreshing and edifying to all Italians of this generation who are friends of justice. His name is Giambattista Vico, and they rank him above Montesquieu. From a cursory reading of the book, which was presented to me as if it were sacred writ, it seems to me to contain sibylline visions of the Good and the Just which will or should come true in the future, prophecies based on a profound study of life and tradition. It is wonderful for a people to have such a spiritual patriarch [*Altervater*]: one day *Hamann* will be a similar bible for the Germans.[2]

As anyone can tell who has the smallest acquaintance with the doctrines of the *New Science*, Goethe's remarks bear little relation to the text. He evidently did not bother to read the 'sibylline' book.[3] In this respect, however, he does not seem to have differed much from other Germans whose acquaintance with Vico's work is usually cited by the scholars. J. G. Hamann (the *Altervater* referred to by Goethe), who had ordered the book in 1777,

---

[1] Quoted in 'Galiani, ses amis et son temps', an introductory essay to L'Abbé F. Galiani, *Correspondance*, ed. Lucien Perey and Gaston Maugras ([Paris], 1881), vol. 1, p. xxxvi. Galiani claimed, however, that at least one French writer had used Vico's ideas without acknowledgment. Francesco Predari, who edited the *Scienza nuova* a century later, says in his introduction that Hume, de Brosses, d'Alembert, Helvétius, Bentham and others borrowed from Vico. This appears to be pure fantasy. *La Scienza Nuova di Giambattista Vico*, ed. Francesco Predari (Turin, 1852), pp. xxx–xxxi.

[2] *Italienische Reise*, 5 March 1787: vol. 31, pp. 27–8, in *Goethes Werke* (Weimar, 1887–1919). Quoted here from the translation by W. H. Auden and Elizabeth Mayer: J. W. Goethe, *Italian Journey* (London, 1962), pp. 182–3.

[3] Friedrich Meinecke in his *Die Entstehung des Historismus* (Munich and Berlin, 1936) – translated by J. G. Anderson as *Historism: The Rise of a New Historical Outlook* (London, 1972) – slides over this somewhat disingenuously, evidently out of piety towards the venerated figure of Goethe.

evidently under the illusion that it dealt with the new economics –
for what other new science was there? – in a letter to his young
friend Herder said that the introduction to the *New Science* seemed
to him a 'very long-winded explanation of the allegorical frontis-
piece, whereon *Metaphysics* and a *statue* of *Homer* are the main
figures, the rest being *hieroglyphs*'.[1] Twenty years later Herder
looked at the *New Science* himself, and after comparing Vico with
'Bacon, Harrington, Milton, Sidney, Locke, Ferguson, [Adam]
Smith, Millar' decided that Vico 'was looking for the common
principles [*gemeinschaftliche Grundsätze*] of physics, ethics, law,
the law of nations . . . for the principle of the humanity of nations
(*dell'umanità delle nazioni*), which he found in Providence and
Wisdom'.[2] This was certainly an advance on Goethe, but a
somewhat modest one.

Yet the parallels with Herder's ideas are very striking; indeed, it
is difficult to think that Herder is not, at times, consciously
echoing Vico's theses. Yet Herder is not known to have seen the
New Science before 1797, long after his own major ideas had been
given to the world. Even if Hamann had told him something about
Vico twenty years before (of which, so far as is known, there is no
evidence), this still, at the earliest, came a few years after the
publication of his most Vichian views. Five years after receiving it
from Goethe, Jacobi read the book, and both he and Baader
thought that it anticipated Kant's transcendental method, a
judgement which tells us more about the historicist interpretation
of Kant than about the central ideas common to him and Vico. The
famous classical scholar F. A. Wolf, whose own revolutionary
'dissolution' of Homer into a succession of multiple storytellers
had been published in 1795, some ten years later had his attention
drawn to the fact of Vico's formulation of a similar hypothesis
almost a century before. He was not pleased; and in 1807
mentioned Vico's theory casually and irritably in an attempt to
minimise the fact of its existence. Nor did the great Niebuhr
welcome the suggestion that his own epoch-making transformation
of Roman history could be found in a developed and articulate
form in the pages of a forgotten Italian jurist, either when Orelli
tactlessly pointed this out to him, or, some years later, when the
poet Leopardi (so we are told by Ranieri) insisted quite spontaneously on bringing this to his attention in Rome in 1816.

[1] Letter of 21–2 December 1777: B iii 394.3.
[2] *Briefe zu Beförderung der Humanität*, letter 115 (1797): xviii 245–6.

Savigny, the greatest figure in the historical school of jurisprudence, was somewhat more generous, even while he felt it
necessary to defend his great compatriot and friend from suspicion
of plagiarism:

Vico, with his profound genius [he wrote], stood alone among his
contemporaries, a stranger in his own country, overlooked or derided,
although now the attempt is made to claim him as a national
possession. Among such unfavourable circumstances his spirit could
not come to full fruition. It is true that one finds in him scattered
thoughts on Roman history resembling *Niebuhr's*. But these ideas are
like flashes of lightning in a dark night, by which the traveller is led
further astray rather than brought back to his path. No one could
profit from them who had not already found the truth in his own way.
Niebuhr in particular learned to know him only late and through
others.[1]

The real rise in Vico's fortunes began when the Neapolitan
patriot Vincenzo Cuoco, seeking to defend the abortive liberal
revolution of 1799 which had been made in his native city against
French invasion, went to Vico as an original source of anti-Jacobin,
gradualist, moderate nationalism, and used him as a text for his
own homilies to the French on the difficulty of translating
institutions from one society to another, inasmuch as each obeys
its own specific 'organic' laws. Cuoco's propaganda had a good
deal of success: Chateaubriand, Joseph de Maistre, Ballanche and
other counter-revolutionary writers duly discovered in Vico a kind
of Italian Burke. Sixty years after his death Vico was resurrected
and celebrated by the publicists of the Restoration as a major link
in the great chain of secular Italian political thought which began
with Marsilio and Machiavelli. Gioberti and Manzoni carried his
fame abroad. Gianelli wrote about him very intelligently, but
remained unread.[2] Lomonaco, Salfi, Prati tried to establish a
reputation for him in France, and Pietro de Angelis persuaded the
omnivorous philosophical *vulgarisateur* Victor Cousin of his
importance. Cousin sent de Angelis to his colleague the historian
Jules Michelet, who realised, the first man to do so, that he had

[1] Friedrich Carl von Savigny, *Vermischte Schriften* (Berlin, 1850), vol. 4, pp.
217–18. This historical account owes a great deal to the discussion of this topic by
M. H. Fisch in his most valuable introduction to his and Bergin's translation of
Vico's autobiography. This translation of Savigny's remarks will be found at A 70.

[2] See the account of Paolo Rossi, op. cit. (p. 99 above, note 3).

come upon a work of genius. He was immensely excited by the *New Science*, and felt, he wrote in 1824, like Dante led by Virgil into an unearthly world: '1824. Vico. Effort, infernal shades, grandeur, the golden bough.'[1] He declared that Vico had totally transformed his ideas – for the first time he understood that history was the account of the spiritual self-creation of peoples in the unending struggle of men against nature. Michelet became a fervent, effective and lifelong apostle of Vico in the artistic and intellectual circles of Paris. His abridged translation of the *New Science*, romanticised but exceedingly readable, appeared in Paris in 1827, and a translation of selected texts from Vico in 1835. He induced his friend Edgar Quinet, who at that time was preparing a French translation of Herder, to read Vico too. A more ponderous but somewhat more accurate French version appeared under the name of the celebrated Princess Belgiojoso nine years later; it may well be the work of Quinet.

Michelet was the true rediscoverer of Vico, and himself the only man of genius among his disciples. In 1869 he could still write, 'I had no master but Vico. His principle of living force, of *humanity creating itself*, made both my book and my teaching.'[2] His ardent advocacy created a new image of Vico as a forerunner of romanticism and humanist nationalism, and, for a while, his name enjoyed celebrity in Paris and its intellectual dependencies: Balzac and Flaubert, for example, both mention him as a famous thinker. The more sober estimates of him by earlier French writers such as Chastellux, Degérando, Fauriel were swept away by the torrent of Michelet's eloquence:

> In the vast system of the founder of the metaphysics of history, there already exist, at least in germ, all the labours of modern scholarship. Like Wolf, he said that the *Iliad* was the work of a people, its learned work and last expression, after many centuries of inspired poetry. Like Creuzer and Görres he interpreted the heroic and divine figures of primitive history as ideas and symbols. Before Montesquieu and Gans he showed how law springs from the customs of a people and

---

[1] Quoted without reference by M. H. Fisch at A 76. The nearest I have yet found to this is in Jules Michelet, *Journal: Tome IV (1868–1874)*, ed. Claude Digeon (Paris, 1976), p. 110 (entry for 3 April 1869): 'Ma jeunesse dévorée par ces élans: / 1824: Vico et la ténébr. grand.' Ed.

[2] Preface of 1869 to his celebrated *L'Histoire de France*: *Oeuvres*, vol. 4, p. 14; translation from A 79.

represents faithfully every step of its history. What Niebuhr was to find by vast research, Vico divined; he restored patrician Rome and made its *curiae* and *gentes* live again. Certainly, if Pythagoras recalled that in a previous life he had fought beneath the walls of Troy, these illustrious Germans might have remembered that they had all formerly lived in Vico. All the giants of criticism are already contained, with room to spare, in the little pandemonium of the *New Science*.[1]

Yet, despite this and Comte's cooler, but equally firm, admiration, interest in Vico declined; the book, even in Michelet's version, was no longer read. Taine took some interest in him, to no avail. Vico remained a name in encyclopaedias and the more comprehensive histories of philosophy.

In England his fame was spread by the Italian exiles, the greatest of whom, Ugo Foscolo and Mazzini, were his devoted admirers. Coleridge quoted him with enthusiasm in 1816. But in spite of the interest taken in him by Thomas Arnold (who understood him and paid him a tremendous tribute) and by F. D. Maurice; despite the fact that he had secured a place beside Herder in the Positivist Calendar, and was duly celebrated by Bridges and Grote and the English Comtians; despite Robert Flint's admirable Victorian monograph, his influence remained negligible. He was shown to be the founder of the philosophy of history, but like other intellectual pioneers he remained in England a figure of interest only to specialists.

In Germany he was taken a little more seriously: the *Scienza nuova* was translated in 1822 and edited in 1854. The Hegelian radical Eduard Gans in 1837 pronounced him to be one of Hegel's forerunners. Marx recommended him to Lassalle and saw him as the father of the history of human technology. A German monograph – greatly inferior to Flint's book – appeared in 1881. Windelband and representatives of other philosophical schools showed some faint interest in him. But it was not until the devoted editorial labours of Fausto Nicolini in Vico's native city, which sprang from the passionate advocacy and brilliant monograph of his compatriot Benedetto Croce, and the interest which this stimulated in England and especially America,[2] that he began to

---

[1] Preface to *Histoire romaine*: ibid., vol. 2, pp. 340–1; translation from A 78.

[2] The labours of Bergin and Fisch, and especially the introductions to the *New Science* and the *Autobiography*, to which this study owes a great deal, are examples of philosophical scholarship at its most illuminating.

come into his own. Yet the formidable difficulties presented by the tangled forest of Vico's thought and style have not been diminished by the mere passage of time. Gentile and Collingwood developed his doctrines. Pareto and Georges Sorel, Joyce and Yeats and Edmund Wilson testified to his genius. It has made little difference. He is constantly rediscovered and as constantly laid aside. He remains unreadable and unread.

XIV

There is a particular danger that attends the fate of rich and profound but inexact and obscure thinkers, namely that their admirers tend to read too much into them, and turn them insensibly in the direction of their own thoughts. Michelet took from Vico what he needed for his own vision of history, but there is more of Michelet than of Vico in his magnificent version. If Flint cannot be accused of imposing his own personality on Vico, that is only because he had no philosophical personality to impose. Among his modern disciples neither Croce nor Collingwood escaped, or wished to escape, this temptation. Not only his book on Vico but much of Croce's own philosophy is a development of Vico in a Hegelian direction, which the latter could scarcely have understood. Croce paid his debt to Vico almost too generously: for he put into Vico's thought more than he derived from it. Vico's authentic features are at times concealed by the metamorphosis which Croce, like all original thinkers, inevitably produces; he built a noble monument to Vico, but transformed him into an Absolute Idealist. Sorel (and perhaps Trotsky and Gramsci) saw him as a proto-Marxist. He has been represented as a pragmatist, a Catholic apologist, a Neapolitan patriot, a forerunner of Fascism, an existentialist, and much else. Gentile carried Vico's doctrine to extravagant lengths, intelligible only in the light of the speculative flights of late neo-Hegelianism. As for Collingwood, his most gifted English disciple, his fruitful notion of the 'absolute presuppositions' of every culture,[1] those basic categories and concepts of an age or culture which determine the shape of its mental activity and render its problems uniquely different from those of all other cultures, that does indeed derive from Vico, and perhaps from him

---

[1] R. G. Collingwood, *An Essay on Metaphysics* (Oxford, 1940), *passim*, esp. chapter 5.

alone. But when Collingwood adds to this notion the far more questionable one of a capacity to transport ourselves into the minds of persons or periods historically remote from us, a transcendental, timeless flight across the barrier of time, culminating in the metaphysical act of penetrating into the mind of Julius Caesar, or, let us say, the Puritan movement, or the Gothic Revival, he goes beyond his master. Vico speaks of the need to make the appalling effort of trying to adjust one's vision to the archaic world – the need to see it through deeply unfamiliar spectacles – but this is very different from the quasi-mystical act of literal self-identification with another mind and age of which Collingwood evidently thought himself capable.

It may be that, finding in Vico so much that became fully articulate only in the nineteenth or twentieth century, I, too, am guilty of precisely the same fault. Yet I find it hard to persuade myself that this is so. Premature anticipations of the ideas of one age in another happen seldom, but they happen. A thinker whose most original ideas are misunderstood or ignored by his contemporaries is not a mere romantic myth. In the heyday of the age of science, when the last feeble defenders of the old scholasticism were finally routed by the new enlightenment, Vico preached distinctions fully intelligible to neither side. He distinguished between, on the one hand, observation, measurement, deductive reasoning, the construction of idealised models, fictional entities, and their application to the opaque outlines of the real world – the 'external' knowledge systematised by the natural sciences – and, on the other, the perception of the relations of elements in man-made patterns to each other and to the wholes to which they belong: of means to ends, of the purposes and outlooks of individuals to the activities of groups and generations. Above all he casts light on what it is for a wide variety of gestures, words, acts, ceremonies, rules to be an expression of one and the same style, characteristic of a class, a nation, an age, a civilisation. Furthermore, he identified what it is to understand this, to detect it, to trace it in detail, with the aid of the scientific methods of scholarship, and the way in which such human self-investigation must affect one's fundamental beliefs. In the course of explaining this Vico distinguished differences of quality from those of quantity, of nuance from measurable forms, and, above all, between knowledge of factors at work in the continuous growth in time of persons, groups, institutions, and knowledge of the causal, repetitive uniformities of co-existence or succession. He discriminated, in effect, between the sense of understanding in which a scholar may be said to understand a text when, for example, he emends it successfully, or as a man may understand a friend, an artistic movement, or a political atmosphere, a sense not capable of precise analysis, and related to skills which can be trained and sharpened and which make use of rules and laws, but which cannot be systematised or taught to the competent but insensitive or ungifted; and the techniques involved in inductive or experimental or deductive procedures – something which can be communicated and taught to any rational being. He did not, like Dilthey, categorise this contrast, but he used it in contrasting knowledge of man with knowledge of objects. He believed that a man could understand himself, and therefore others, and therefore what they were at, and how the world looked or felt to himself or them, and why, as he could not understand things or plants or animals of which he could perceive only the behaviour. Above all he had a sense of how various elements were blended in social existence – the pattern which Burke and Herder, Schelling and Hegel, Tocqueville and Burckhardt, Dilthey and Max Weber attempted to convey – a capacity for perceiving the way in which the 'senseless factor' in history interacts with conscious motives and purposes to produce unintended consequences – a quasi-aesthetic capacity for discrimination, integration and association, needed by historians, critics, novelists more than the capacity for abstraction, generalisation and dissociation of ideas indispensable to original discoveries in the natural sciences. The discovery and proclamation of this great dividing line seemed to Vico's critics and commentators during the last hundred years to be his major achievement.

No doubt Vico exaggerated. Pioneers are apt to do this in moments of creative excitement, particularly when, like Vico, they are largely self-taught and live in self-constructed private worlds. Moreover, few new truths have ever won their way against the resistance of established ideas save by being overstated. Plato, the Stoics, Descartes, Spinoza, Hume, Kant, Hegel all overstated their case, and might not have obtained a hearing if they had not. Vico belongs to this company (even if he is not a major figure in it), for his ideas are those of a man of original genius. He may well have hoped to be clear: his four intellectual heroes, Plato and Tacitus, Bacon and Grotius, possessed this enviable gift. He did not succeed, and his ideas often remain tantalisingly dark. Nor did he invent, as he supposed, a new science based on the discovery of inescapable cycles in the life of societies; this idea proved a will-o'-the-wisp, as it has to other imaginative thinkers before and after him. Like Columbus, like his own *orribili bestioni* whose desires lead to unsought for consequences, he came upon an unknown country: the study of the human past as a form of collective self-understanding.

It may be that, as with other original thinkers, future generations will think our verdict unduly limited by the experience of our own time, and (like James Joyce, whose later work was filled with allusions to Vico) will single out other aspects of his writings for the attention of the students of ideas.

VICO'S THEORY OF KNOWLEDGE
AND ITS SOURCES

I

ONE OF the central theses of the *New Science*, which goes back to *De nostri* of 1708 and *De antiquissima* of 1710, is the distinction between truth and certainty, *verum* and *certum*. Yet neither in these works, nor anywhere else, does Vico make this radical distinction thoroughly clear. As so often in his writings, too many novel and inchoate ideas are simultaneously and feverishly struggling for expression, in language painfully ill-adapted for this purpose. This flood of clear and confused insights, antiquarian memories and constant diversions, gives his style, especially in the *New Science*, a rhapsodic, sometimes volcanic, force, but does not make for lucid exposition. Nevertheless an arresting new doctrine does emerge. This has not always been conceded by those who minimised its originality, either from lack of understanding, or out of national pride, or ideological antipathy, or jealous concern for the reputation of some other thinker.[1] Yet his contribution to philosophical thought is of the first order, if only because he distinguished and cast new light on the notion of historical understanding.

According to Vico we begin with *certum*, acquaintance with and beliefs about particular matters of fact – a pre-condition of all thought and action – and are capable of attaining to *verum*, knowledge of universal truths. He does not make clear whether a transition from one to the other can, even in principle, ever be

---

[1] See pp. 112–13 above. The latest example of this is the assertion by George Huppert in his *The Idea of Perfect History: Historical Erudition and Historical Philosophy in Renaissance France* (Urbana etc., 1970) (hereafter Huppert) that Vico was a mere 'straggler in the history of ideas, echoing Bodin, not announcing Hegel' (p. 166). This argues a degree of blindness both to Vico's positive achievement, and to crucial differences between his ideas on history and those of Bodin. (On this see p. 156 below.) Fortunately this glancing gibe is a mere footnote to Huppert's main thesis, and does not significantly diminish the value of his interesting and informative book.

achieved, or indeed how it is to be attempted. Yet without general truths there cannot be a science, so that if the *New Science* is to justify its title, it must consist of a logically connected system of true general propositions about facts and events in time. How is this to be achieved? *Verum* for Vico is a priori truth, truth such as is reached, for example, in mathematical reasoning, where, starting from axioms, every step is demonstrably and irrefutably proved; but this is accomplished (in the case of human thought) only at the cost of being left with artificial constructions, logical figments with no necessary relation to the outside world. By the 'verum est ipsum factum'[1] criterion of 1710 we can logically guarantee only what we ourselves make: this alone is *verum*; of that alone there can, in the strict sense, exist a *scienza*. But if the structure of this *verum* is designed by us, how can it claim to reflect or describe 'scientifically', that is, demonstratively and irrefutably, anything outside itself – the character of the external world?

Vico accepts this startling conclusion. The truth is what is made: and because mathematics is 'operatrix' ('productive')[2] it is a science. We do not create things in space, hence physics is not, for us, *verum*; it is so, he says (following Augustine), only for God, 'quia Deus primus Factor'.[3] The notion that there can be such a thing as creation out of nothing is, of course, a Judaeo-Christian idea; it is not Greek.[4] For Pythagoras the cosmos, the symmetries of nature, its mathematical structure, are built into the nature of things. This is equally objective for Plato: the demiurge in the *Timaeus* creates the world according to a plan of which he is not, however, the author; the plan is given from eternity. The notion of cosmic harmony had at least in part been known to the thinkers and artists of the golden age of Greece; it could be rediscovered, and the world be made beautiful and rational in its light – this is the central vision of the Renaissance. In a less mystical form it inspired the Enlightenment, too, in particular the physiocrats and the believers in the 'invisible hand'[5] or the 'cunning of

---

[1] 'The true is precisely what is made.' DA 131/46.   [2] DA 133/48.

[3] 'Because God is the first Maker.' DA 132/46.

[4] On this see Karl Löwith, 'Geschichte und Natur in Vicos "Scienza nuova"', *Quaderni contemporanei* 2 (n.d. [1969?]), 135–69, at 137–9.

[5] Adam Smith: *The Theory of Moral Sentiments* 4. 1. 10, p. 184 in the Glasgow Edition (Oxford, 1976); *An Enquiry into the Nature and Causes of the Wealth of Nations* 4. 2. 9, p. 456 in the same edition (Oxford, 1976); cf. *Essays on Philosophical Subjects*, 'History of Astronomy' 3. 2, p. 49 in the same edition (Oxford, 1980).

reason',[1] which will always prevail in the end. Löwith[2] rightly points out that this was not so for Vico, who believed in divine creation *ex nihilo*.

Since physics deals with objects in nature which men do not create, Vico's first move, in 1708–10, was to degrade physics from the eminence on which Descartes had placed it to the level of other studies of that which men find but have not made; it now ranks above, but is classified with, history, literature and so on, of which we can have no *scientia*, only *conscientia* – where we cannot attain to more than *certum*, that is, *de facto* truths, the kind of knowledge on which ordinary rational action rests. The reason for this is clear. Once you demand that your thought should correspond with something outside itself and independent of it – with reality – you can no longer guarantee *verum*, which must be wholly in your control; you can speak at best of certainty, self-evidence, what later came to be called a sense of reality, which Vico correctly regards as something different from logically demonstrated truths. He does not use these terms, but the distinction is one between the truths of metaphysics or logic on the one hand, and those of ordinary observation or perception (including introspection) on the other. Certainty (which Vico at times also calls 'authority') is the light by which in fact we live our lives. It is not primarily inductive knowledge (in Bacon's sense, with which Vico at times mistakenly identifies it), but is rather our grasp of the basic data of direct experience, from which scientific hypotheses start, and to which they return for confirmation. Vico's illustrations of 'certainty' come not from the external world of sense perception, but from a sphere in which his chief interest lies, namely social relationships – 'the human necessities or utilities of social life'.[3] We are born into a culture (which for him is a social process) – a network of institutions which springs from the claims of such necessities and utilities, forms of communal life which evolve in time, in which we live and think and have our being. Language is such an institution: 'languages create minds [*ingenia*], not minds language'[4] he said in *De nostri*, and although the context suggests that this passage probably refers to his preference for the tradition of Italian imaginative writing over the drier, more cerebral and anti-metaphorical French style, the phrase is characteristic of what

[1] See p. 56 above, note 4.   [2] loc. cit. (p. 123 above, note 4).   [3] NS 347.
[4] DN 95/40.

today would be called his socio-linguistic approach. We are able to conceive or express only that which our particular culture makes possible, and only by the means provided by the social structure of that culture because it has the properties it has, and represents the particular stage of social growth in an identifiable process or pattern of development. Thus we move from the culture of 'mute' signs[1] – the ideograms and hieroglyphs of the 'age of the gods' – to the 'heroic' language of poetic metaphor and simile, and so, step by step, to the more literal and precise prose utterances of the lawcourts and philosophical criticism that belong to democratic life. One cannot generate a timeless universal symbolism, any more than one can invent a timeless, universal way of life which a rational being could pursue whenever and wherever he happened to be. One is what one is, in a specific historical context; no one can escape the particular categories, social and psychological, mental and emotional, that obtain in given times and places, and are subject to the laws of development. Nature is growth. This is the world of the (evolving) *sensus communis* of a society, the 'judgement without reflection, shared by an entire class, an entire people, an entire nation, or the entire human race'.[2]

Such judgements embody not demonstrable truths, but (presumably) contingent ones. The fact that we cannot do without them is, for us at any rate, a contingent fact. If we would know the world as God, its Creator, knows it, then the *certum*, which is contingent, would be transformed into *verum*, which is a priori.[3]

Yet our knowledge of our own ideas and volitions, individual and social, including past experience – both that which men have individually and that which they share with others – is not simply given us as a brute fact: we can understand ourselves as we cannot understand stocks and stones. Men are finite and fallible creatures and so cannot understand even their own mental processes wholly. To understand other men, and what they were and the worlds they 'created', is to recognise – imaginatively grasp – their experience within the potentialities of our own human consciousness: '*dentro le modificazioni della nostra medesima mente umana*'.[4] What is

---

[1] See p. 63 above, note 1.   [2] NS 142.

[3] Leibniz formulated a similar doctrine about the relation of necessary (rational) truths to contingent (factual) truths. For God alone all truths are necessary. But this dichotomy leaves no room for what is peculiar to Vico – understanding of institutions, relationships, purposes, outlooks, which shape human behaviour and are neither wholly contingent nor deducible a priori.

[4] '*Within the modifications of our own human minds*': NS 331.

wholly unlike ourselves we cannot hope to understand. We can understand only that which is potentially our own, which men can be or become without ceasing to be men. This is why it is not utterly impossible, although agonisingly difficult, to enter into the outlook – the thoughts, feelings, fears, hopes, ambitions, imaginative experience – of beings very different and remote from us, like our first ancestors, the 'horrible' *bestioni*, Polyphemus in his cave. To grasp motives, intentions, to understand, however imperfectly, why men act and live as they do, is to have knowledge *per caussas*, and therefore, however incomplete, is superior to, more godlike than,[1] mere 'knowing that' – the awareness 'from without' which provides the data of the natural sciences, or of the ordinary knowledge of the external world – and is equally superior to 'knowledge how', the acquisition or possession of a skill or method.

Experiment does, no doubt, help to understand nature, as Hobbes pointed out. But merely to take a thing apart and put it together again is not to understand it through and through, as Vico holds that we understand the 'inner' movements of our own spirit, since the ultimate constituents of matter which in experiments we rearrange at will are still not ours – are *extra nos*.[2] Knowledge *per caussas* is that of a creator when he understands his own creatures, as an artist understands his work of art, and, at times, his own creative activity. Even the Neoplatonists of the Renaissance – Marsilio Ficino, Pico, Landino – did not suppose that the poet did more than create a world of his own parallel to that of God, and, in this, were followed by Tasso (misquoted by Shelley in *The Defence of Poetry*), Philip Sidney, Donne, Dennis, Shaftesbury and the eighteenth-century forerunners of romanticism.

Vico goes further. He supposes not merely that the poets create artificial worlds, but that all men during the early 'poetical' stage of culture can conceive of the real world only 'in this fashion', that the creative imagination plays a dominant role in the normal consciousness of this stage of development, so that song is the natural mode of expression before speech, poetry before prose, written

---

[1] cf. 'ad Dei instar' ('on the model of God'), DA 135/51.

[2] 'For God reads all the elements of things whether inner or outer, because he contains and disposes of them in order, whereas the human mind, because it is limited and external to everything else that is not itself . . . can indeed think about reality, but it can not understand it fully.' DA 132/46.

symbols before spoken; and this, he holds, constitutes a vision of reality which is more primitive than, but not necessarily superior or inferior to, that which follows it – more barbarous, but not less valuable than (if not spiritually, then at least aesthetically), and superior, perhaps, in sheer power and spontaneous vitality to, its more civilised successors.

This was, indeed, to swim against the current. The seventeenth century is a time in which the very use of metaphor was widely suspect, especially in the centres of progressive thought, in France, in England, in Holland, inasmuch as this kind of luxuriant imagery was associated with a pre-scientific or anti-scientific frame of mind. Metaphor was connected with the false world of ancient super-stition, dreams, myths, terrors with which lurid, barbarous imaginations peopled the world, causing error and irrationalism and persecution.[1] Thomas Sprat, one of the founders of the Royal Society, declared that eloquence, with its 'specious *Tropes* and *Figures*' should be 'banish'd out of all *civil Societies*, as a thing fatal to Peace and good Manners'; the Royal Society should avoid 'mists and uncertainties', and return to 'a close, naked, natural way of speaking . . . bringing all things as near the Mathematical plainness, as they can'.[2] So, too, Hobbes banished metaphor from all writings aimed at the rigorous search for truth.[3] Locke, Hume and Adam Smith say much the same, although Hume allows that rigid adherence to 'geometrical truth and exactness' might have an 'insipid and disagreeable' effect upon the reader.[4] It enters into the celebrated controversy between the champions of the French and Italian styles which broke out towards the end of the seventeenth century, played a dominant role in France in the eighteenth century (particularly between the champions of the French and Italian styles in opera), and was almost as violent as the battle between the Ancients and the Moderns. Among the merits for

[1] M. H. Abrams, *The Mirror and the Lamp: Romantic Theory and the Critical Tradition* (New York, 1953), p. 285.

[2] Tho. Sprat, *The History of the Royal-Society of London, for the Improving of Natural Knowledge* (London, 1667), pp. 111–13.

[3] *Leviathan*, chapter 4, 'Of Speech': pp. 26 and 31 in Richard Tuck's edition (Cambridge, 1991).

[4] 'Of the Standard of Taste': p. 236 in David Hume, *Essays: Moral, Political and Literary* (London, 1963). M. H. Abrams, op. cit. (note 1 above), chapter 10, gives a great many other examples of, and references to, this highly prevalent 'Cartesian' attitude.

which the great French masters – Racine, Molière, Boileau – are most highly praised is their freedom from metaphor, hyperbole, the vagaries of fancy. One of the best-known leaders of the French school of criticism in the *grand siècle*, *Père* Bouhours, thinks that fiction, metaphor, similes, and the like, can be permitted only when, 'like transparent veils', they do not really hide what they purport to cover; that the only possible reason for tropes is the pleasure which such permissible lies may give.[1]

But for Vico metaphor and the like constitute a fundamental category through which at a given stage of development men cannot help viewing reality – which is for them reality itself, neither mere embellishment, nor a repository of secret wisdom, nor the creation of a world parallel to the real world, nor an addition to, or distortion of, reality, harmless or dangerous, deliberate or involuntary: but is the natural, inevitably transient, but, at the time of its birth or growth, the only possible, way of perceiving, interpreting, explaining that is open to men of that particular place and time, at that particular stage of their culture. Such ways of speech, he supposes, only later become artificial or decorative, because men have by then forgotten how they came into being and the purposes for which they were originally used. Such myths and their modes of expression, however faulty they may seem to the theologians or philosophers of our own sophisticated times (and to those of earlier 'classical' periods too), were, in their own day, appropriate and coherent. To understand the metaphors of the 'heroic' age – the world of ballads, lays, epics – one must transport oneself by the imagination, and therefore reconstruct, with learned care and insight, the vision of which they formed an organic, inalienable part.

The times were not propitious for this conception of man, society, history; less so, perhaps, than even the preceding century. Even though the roots of this doctrine are far older, it was not until Herder that this kind of historicism began to bind its spell on European thought in general. In spite of his habit of presenting his works to as many of the learned and influential critics of his day in Italy and abroad as he could reach, Vico failed to elicit the recognition which he felt that the originality of his discovery deserved. The tide was flowing too strongly against him.

---

[1] [Dominique Bouhours], *La Manière de bien penser dans les ouvrages d'esprit: dialogues* (Paris, 1687), dialogue 1, esp. pp. 10–17; the quoted phrase is to be found on p. 17.

II

In this connection, it may be useful to attempt to indicate the main features of Vico's epistemology. He seems to distinguish four types of knowledge: (a) *Scienza*: knowledge which yields *verum*, truth a priori, which one can have only of one's own artefacts or fictions – logical, mathematical, poetical, artistic. It is in this sense that God alone fully knows the world which he has created. (b) *Coscienza*: the 'external' knowledge of matters of fact common to all men, the *certum* that one has of the 'outer' behaviour of whatever entities compose the external world of events, men, things. (c) The kind of knowledge which Vico's admired master Plato claimed to possess: of patterns, eternal truths and principles (Vico throughout takes for granted revelation as a source of knowledge, for example, for the Jews and, *a fortiori*, for the Fathers of the Church). Presumably this is how we can discern the unaltering pattern of the *storia ideale eterna*, which is the history of the 'Gentile' nations. But how, without grace or revelation, men can acquire this kind of profane metaphysical insight Vico does not make clear: it is certainly not inductive or merely probable in Bodin's or Bacon's sense; Grotius is blamed precisely for supposing that it was. Perhaps it is connected with (d) the 'inner' or historical knowledge to which Vico gives no special name, the 'intentional' awareness which human beings have as actors, not mere observers from outside, of their own activities, of their own efforts, purposes, direction, outlook, values, attitudes, both present and past, familiar and exceedingly remote, and of the institutions which embody and, in their turn, determine them. This is certainly what he calls knowledge *per caussas* – obtained by attending to the *modificazioni* of our *mente* – and leads to knowledge of what men or societies or cultures are *at*, that is, not merely of what happens to them, or of how they react or behave as causal agents or patients, but of those internal relationships and interconnections between thought and action, observation, theory, motivation, practice, which is precisely what observation of the external world, of mere compresences and successions, fails to give us. In the world of things we see only similarities, conjunctions, regularities, successions or their absence; these can be summarised under laws and necessities in a Cartesian or Newtonian system; but this yields no knowledge of why things and events are as they are; for no one but the Creator of this world knows what it is *at* or for. This distinction between the 'inside' and 'outside' views, between mechanical cause and purpose, between understanding and knowledge, the human and the natural sciences, was to be made much of by later thinkers like Herder, Maine de Biran, Fichte, Schelling, Dilthey, Croce and, to some degree, Max Weber, and duly exposed them to the criticism of those who detected in this distinction anti-empirical, anti-scientific, obscurantist implications.

Vico was a deeply metaphysical thinker, but in this instance what he meant was, I think, no more than the difference between active participation in something and passive observation of it. To know what it is to do something – what Vico called *operatio* – is to understand human motives, purposes, ideals in their relations with the environment and the material on which men are at work, as well as the relationships that individuals have with other goal-pursuing, motivated, active beings – which seemed to him to be different from the mere contemplation of a succession of mental and/or physical stages, and the systematic classification of them and their behaviour in uniform patterns that enable men to predict and manipulate. When Vico speaks of knowledge 'through causes', he means by 'cause' not a mere correlation of the uniformities of either characteristics or events, but the active and deliberate making or doing of something by someone (individual or collective: the life of institutions is for him a collective activity).[1] His sense of causing and making is that in which we speak of a man or a class or a movement or an idea as causing a change of mind in a man (or a group), or as causing or making a revolution. The emphasis upon this distinction – between activity and the passive registration of experience, between the senseless factors of history and the motivated – has played a major role in philosophical theories of action, of history, of mind and of moral and social life.

Nature, events in time, do not, for Vico, depend on what men make of them. He explicitly acknowledges the role of inductive and deductive techniques in the researches of scholars, above all in the sifting by scientific historians of fact from fiction. But this is not for him the same as the use of imaginative understanding, *fantasia*. A capacity for such critical scholarship, as practised, for example, by his friend the great Muratori, indispensable as it is, is

[1] He does not distinguish, as Aristotle did, between 'doing' and 'making'; nor, for his purposes, was this necessary.

only the most refined and solid establishing of *certum*, not in principle different from the natural sciences. But selection, classification, above all, interpretation, of the material – these (as Erich Auerbach points out in one of his excellent studies of Vico) are our own: ultimately subjective, dependent on our own experience, our own investigation of the *modificazioni* of our own minds. The sounds may be independent of the hearer, but different cultures will listen to, and select, different patterns from the selfsame sounds; and all the melodies, harmonies and rhythms are equally genuine and real.

Vico virtually invented the concept of the understanding – of what Dilthey and others call *Verstehen*. Others before him, philologists or historians or jurists, may have had inklings of it; Vico brings it to light. No one after reading him will suppose that the sense in which we are said to understand a feeling, a gesture, a work of art, a man's character; an entire civilisation or a single joke; the sense in which a man can be said to know what it is to be poor, to be jealous, to be a lover, a convert, a traitor, a banker, a revolutionary, an exile, is (to say the least) the same sense as that in which we know that one tree is taller than another, or that Hitler wrote *Mein Kampf*, or how one text differs from another, or what neutrons are; nor is it like knowing the differential calculus, or how to spell, or play the violin, or get to Mars, or what an imaginary number is, or what prevents us from moving faster than light. It is much more like the kind of awareness that is fed and developed by varied activities and experience of how things look in different situations, how the world appears, through what concepts and categories, to individuals or groups in different social or emotional conditions. It is this kind of knowledge that is spoken of in such terms as plausible or absurd, realistic or idealistic, perceptive or blind; that makes it intelligible to describe the works of historians and social theorists, artists and men of action, not merely as well-informed, or skilful, or lucid, or misled, or ignorant, but also as wise or stupid, interesting or dull, shallow or profound – concepts which cannot be applied to knowledge in either of the two senses discussed in our time by Gilbert Ryle: 'knowing that' and 'knowing how'. This is what Vico called *fantasia*: man's unique capacity for imaginative insight and reconstruction.

There is another way of approaching this distinction. *Certum* presides over the realm of facts as we perceive and deal with them. *Verum* – for human beings – presides over the realm of what men make: for example, rules, norms, standards, laws, including those which shape 'the facts' themselves. These are categories of the will, of action, of creative imagination; the products they generate individually or collectively are not discovered a posteriori – by, for example, psychologists or anthropologists – as so many objects leading an existence independent of their creators – but can be known in advance, at any rate to those who make them, like (to take only the products of conscious purpose) decisions, or agreed conventions, or codes of law, or anything else that men invent and live by, which therefore have no logical claim to 'correspond' to any 'outer' structure of things. It is only when such human arrangements are mistakenly assimilated to objects or laws of nature that hypostatisation – what Hegelians and Marxists call 'reification' – arises, and with it 'false consciousness' and the self-alienation of men from the world they have themselves had a hand in creating. The distinction is, of course, not absolute: 'facts' are not hard pellets of experience, independent of the concepts and categories by which they are discriminated, classified, perceived, interpreted, indeed shaped. Nevertheless, the distinction made by Kant or James or their modern followers, or thinkers influenced by Hegel or Marx or the psychologists or anthropologists or linguists of our own century, still stands. We perceive and act in terms of responses to our questionings, which themselves are conditioned by our institutional life, but we do not generate the answers freely, 'out of the whole cloth'.[1] The answers to our questions are not arbitrarily invented by us, but their shape is determined by the nature of the questions: selection is a creative art. In this respect Vico is the ancestor of those romantic voluntarists, idealists, pragmatists and existentialists who stress the role played in men's experience by their own transforming acts, individual or collective; or, indeed, of those who, if they are metaphysically inclined, go beyond him and virtually identify the world with such activities; and *per contra*, he is opposed to the claims of rigorous determinists, positivists, philosophical realists and materialists, or psychologists, sociologists and philosophers of science with a mechanistic bias, and the like.

As early as 1700 Vico declared in his third Inaugural Lecture that 'Unus homo est quod vult, fit quod lubet.'[2] This overweening

[1] See p. 99 above, note 2.

[2] 'Man alone is whatever he chooses to be. He becomes whatever he desires to become.' IO 27/74.

belief in the individual's freedom to take on any shape or semblance (which is substantially modified in the *New Science*) is in line with Renaissance voluntarism, of which the most famous expression is Pico della Mirandola's great discourse on the dignity of man. Nevertheless, Vico came to think that an objective science of the cultural development of men is possible, based on the uniformity of the *voci mentali* – the basic symbols or notions that are common to all nations, that embody the great 'natural', non-arbitrary, institutional human regularities – the analogous responses of human groups, remote in time and space, to similar conditions, inasmuch as they spring from similar needs. His examples are the ideas of gods, marriage and burial rites, as well as family, auspices, sacrifices, paternal authority, and so on. It is the ubiquity and uniformity of the 'maxims of vulgar wisdom'[1] that embody these responses that make generalisations about the growth of a single human culture possible. But before one can generalise and use abstract terms for such notions or institutions, recognition of them, acquaintance with them – as particular, concrete phenomena at particular times and in particular places – is indispensable. The history of culture is, for Vico, the development of human creatures from unorganised savage, ferine sensations to the beginnings of critical self-consciousness and organisation – from sensuous perceptions of objects to experience 'with a troubled and agitated spirit'[2] – and so to calm thought, by way of images, myths and symbols appropriate to each stage. This conception can be criticised as too exclusively anthropocentric and too social, ignoring as it does irreducibly natural – physical and biological – causal factors, not to speak of psychological ones as well. This bias may well spring from Vico's over-violent reaction against Cartesian mechanistic and atomistic notions. His desire to move from *certum* towards something which, if not fully *verum*, is an approach towards it – from brute fact to intelligible purposive conduct, clearly dominates his thought.

Can the gap between *certum* and *verum* be bridged, at any rate for finite creatures? Can we ascend from knowledge of what we do not make, to the a priori knowledge that we have of mathematics, and God has of all there is and could be? Is this possible, even in principle? Vico does not make this clear. He holds that we rise above mere external observation, as in physics, to the degree to

[1] NS 161.   [2] NS 218.

which we can reproduce natural processes and objects artificially, as in the laboratory. Hobbes and, indeed, Bacon had supposed as much.[1]

But then is everything in our own historical development created by ourselves? Are there no 'elementa rerum naturalium extra nos'[2] – our bodies, indeed the whole of physical and biological nature – which play as essential a part in human activities as ideas, relations, feelings? If we cannot 'make' all these – nor all our mental states either (not to speak of the unintended consequences of our actions on which Vico lays such stress, inasmuch as they are for him evidences of the 'providential' nature of history) – why is Vico's new discipline dignified with the name of *scienza*, a term originally annexed only to *verum*, to a priori knowledge, the free creation of a *scientia operatrix*?

The answer is, I think, twofold: it lies in the interplay of what Vico symbolised as the 'Platonic' and the 'Tacitean' – the general and the particular, the eternal and the temporal, the necessary and the contingent, the ideal and the actual.[3] Some would call this relationship 'dialectical'. Whether Vico could have begun to understand this term in its Hegelian or post-Hegelian sense, I do not know. However this may be, the empirical or Tacitean aspect

[1] C. F. von Weizsäcker, in his comments on *De nostri* – see his afterword to Gian Battista Vico, *De nostri temporis studiorum ratione/Vom Wesen und Weg der geistigen Bildung* (Godesberg, 1947), esp. p. 162 – anxiously wonders whether the distinction, crucial in Vico, between observation from outside and knowledge of our own artefacts, is not approaching vanishing-point with the achievements of modern technology, and the startling increase in the rate at which man's capacity for modifying, reproducing and creating new entities is growing at present. This leads him to gloomy reflections about our misuse of our newly found powers. While the scientific and technological picture has radically altered since Vico's day, and one can sympathise with and, indeed, share von Weizsäcker's social and moral concern, his theoretical point seems to me to rest on a plain mistake. So long as we remain unable to create *ex nihilo*, and are limited by uniformities of nature that we appear unable to alter and upon the continued existence of which the very possibility of technology rests, Vico's distinction stands. To identify it with the diminishing differences between various kinds and degrees of empirical knowledge of 'the given', or of growing skill in operating on it, is a mere confusion. So long as we merely transform the 'given', which we cannot make, knowledge remains, to that degree, in Vico's sense, *ab extra*, that is, what he calls *cogitatio*, and not 'internal', not his *intelligentia*. Hannah Arendt's similar reflections seem to me to rest on no better ground: see her *Between Past and Future: Six Exercises in Political Thought* (London, 1961), pp. 57–8.

[2] 'Elements of natural things external to us.' DA 150/65.   [3] A 26/138–9.

emerges in Vico's conception of historical knowledge as consisting in the understanding by *fantasia* of particular men's particular activities – for example, of what specific groups of human beings in the past intended, wanted, felt, of how they reacted to the world, much of which, of course, they had not made; acting not only deliberately in pursuit of conscious purposes and according to ideas formulated in their heads, but also unconsciously or instinctively, or out of habit, or in ways which they did not themselves fully (or at all) comprehend, no matter how they might have explained their behaviour to themselves (or others) when reflecting upon it.

Vico (influenced perhaps by 'magical' theories of becoming one with the object, widespread in the Renaissance) is one of the true fathers of the doctrine of the unity of theory and practice which was afterwards developed so richly in various directions by Hegel and his disciples, and, in various new directions, by Marx, Nietzsche and Freud. He believed that in principle we could re-enact in our minds – 'enter' into by sympathetic imagination – what a class, a society, perhaps (though he gives no example) individuals were at; what such beings wanted, worked for, were after; what forwarded, what frustrated them in their search to satisfy their needs; the demands of social necessities and utilities in this or that situation; how they were affected by their own creations, cultural and historical. He supposes that we can, by a species of imaginative insight, turn every *an sich* (to use Hegelian language) – an entity observed from outside by the agent (even if it is his own state of mind or body) – into a *für sich*, an element in, assimilated to, his purposive, 'spiritual' activity. If we fail to effect this transformation, even after Vico has pointed the way, this can (for him) be only for lack of sufficient imaginative power – reconstructive *fantasia* undistorted by anachronistic analogies fed by reading into the past the writer's own nationalistic or philosophical ideas – a faculty with which some men (Lucretius, Tacitus, Bacon) were more generously endowed than others; and of which, evidently, no mortals have enough. But such deficiencies are not obstacles of principle, that is, logical or metaphysical, but empirical – of 'brute' fact. How many men have enough reconstructive genius to recapture the light of perennial human needs in their systematic evolution, the entire past of their society or class? In principle, given adequate powers of *fantasia*, plus the 'laws' which Vico supposes himself to have discovered – the laws of his 'ideal eternal history' of the nations – any stage of human history can be mentally resurrected. Men 'make themselves', and men can therefore re-experience the process in imagination. The *fantasia* which creates myths and rites in which primitive conceptions of the world are acted out is the faculty that generates our sense of the past. Vico comes perilously close to implying – if he does not actually state – that our historical consciousness, even in our sophisticated, self-conscious, civilised condition, may be no more than the vision which belongs to the particular stage that we have reached: itself a kind of myth, the myth of the civilised; in other words, the view that all history is mythological – not an account required to correspond to a structure of fact independent of it, but something which human imagination creates as a pattern demanded by the needs of practice, by men's need to domesticate themselves in the world.

This, if pushed to its logical culmination, would destroy, at least in principle, all distinction between history as a rational discipline and mythical thinking. But Vico, unlike some modern irrationalist thinkers,[1] does not make this move. This implication of the *storia ideale eterna*, developed by Schelling and Nietzsche, does an injustice to Vico's sense of the realities of human development, in contrast with patriotic and other fantasies about it. Yet the danger always remains. It is not this kind of synthesis of Plato's vision of man as he should be, and Tacitus' view of the imperfect creature that he is, that is to be found in the *New Science*. The relations of *verum* and *certum* are somewhat differently treated. Vico does undoubtedly hold that there exists a fixed pattern or order in the growth of human societies – of, in theory, only the 'Gentile' peoples – although he sometimes forgets to add this proviso, and speaks as if the *corsi* and *ricorsi* govern the whole of mankind. This story – the succession from dark, rude beginnings to youth, maturity, decline, collapse which characterises every cycle (apparently without end) – is, in its structure, a *storia ideale eterna*, a Platonic pattern, *verum*, in principle knowable a priori. It is not a hypothesis which could be falsified or weakened, or an inductive generalisation, resting on empirical evidence which is never perfectly known and could be interpreted in different ways. The structure of the *storia ideale*, fashioned and guided by Providence, is an eternal truth, a major discovery, and Vico's claim to

[1] e.g. the use made of Vico's ideas by N. O. Brown in his later works; and by James Joyce, especially in *Finnegans Wake*.

immortality as the founder of a new science based on the uncovering of the true theodicy.

How do we come to know it? Not, it is clear, because we have made it. We do, in some sense, make our own cultures, but not the laws which they – that is, we – obey; these are the work of God. They may be rules for their divine inventor, but they are inexorable laws for us. We did not, even in some half-conscious or 'poetical' way, plan them: they are a *verum*, and no more a *factum* made by us than the laws of physics. Their operation is due to divine Providence, but for which we should never have risen above the beasts. Indeed the original sense of awe, the primeval terror inspired by thunder which caused the *bestioni* to feel shame about promiscuity beneath the open sky and drove them into caves, was created by Providence, working through man but not originated by him. Nor did man create the mysterious machinery which transforms human vices into forces making for social solidarity, morality and civilisation. The doctrine of the universal, unalterable, eternal, cyclical character of the stages of man's history – its Ideal Form – has Pythagorean, Platonic, Neoplatonic and Renaissance roots; it is wholly *verum*; but it is difficult to see, since it is not the content of an identifiable human purpose, however occult, how it can be grasped as such by men. Yet Vico knows it: and knows that he knows it, and claims it as a major discovery. This is the Platonic strain in his thought and a link with Hegelian and pantheist doctrines. The relationship between what men 'make' and the laws and categories which govern their operations, like the related tension between value and fact, human purpose and the nature of things, freedom and determinism, action and 'the given', seems (to me at least) to have been made no clearer by Vico than by the post-Kantian idealists and Marxists who also struggled with this problem. I envy those more fortunate thinkers who have found in one of the great metaphysical systems final solutions to these ancient puzzles.

Providence is the author of the cosmic drama; but, according to Vico, the actors can understand their parts – *are* their parts – and can, in principle, achieve self-understanding. As for the nature of the relation between God's creation and men's self-creation, between what is given or determined by powers beyond human control or understanding, and what men can mould – this our author, either from excess of prudence, or because of sheer failure to think it through, does not tell us. What is clear is that he believed that men and societies grow and alter in response not only to natural factors but also to their own goal-pursuing activities and goal-understanding capacities, and that consequently there is no unaltering and unalterable human nature, nor has it any fixed, timeless goals. In the excellent words of M. H. Fisch, 'Vico shares with the Marxists and existentialists the negative view that there is no human essence to be found in individuals as such, and with the Marxists the positive view that the essence of humanity is the ensemble of social relations, or the developing system of institutions.'[1] Whether, and if so how far, Vico's thesis is tenable is another matter. But there can be little doubt of its remarkable originality.

THE SOURCES

III

When an idea of genuine audacity and power is met in the history of thought, the question of its sources is bound to present itself to historical scholars. There is always a peculiar danger that attends any such enterprise. The assumption that no idea can ever be wholly original – that it must always be traceable to earlier notions, of which, even if it is not a mechanical compound, it must at least be a development or peculiar synthesis analysable into its original ingredients – seems to entail the odd proposition that nothing can ever be said literally for the first time: that there can be no such thing as wholly novel invention in this world. This unacceptable paradox seems to spring from the crude application of something like a theory of the conservation of matter – a kind of vulgar atomism – to the realms of art and thought; as if all thinking begins with a collection of Cartesian or Lockean 'simple ideas', uncreated units present from the beginning, out of the combinations or modifications or, at best, 'development' of which all other ideas arise.

It is true that the very notion of historical scholarship, and particularly of the history of culture, seems to imply the notion of the continuity of civilisation, of a developing, complex interplay of personal and impersonal factors, of which men's lives consist. From this it is, at times, held to follow that no matter how

[1] NS p. xxxix (J4).

audacious a leap of genius a given work of art or thought may seem to embody, it is what it is wholly because of its antecedents, and is intelligible only in terms of its context, its roots, its milieu – the 'trends' and 'currents' which bring it into being and shape its path. This method, applied rigorously, threatens to melt the individuality of any human achievement into impersonal factors, and so lead to a kind of historicist depersonalisation. In a sense no one did more for this doctrine than Vico himself, who virtually dissolved the 'essences' of men and their natures into the historical process of their generation. Even if one takes care to avoid either of two extremes – the Scylla of analysing a work away into its sources (or the process of its creation), or the Charybdis of insisting that only the end result matters, only the beauty of the flower or the pleasure given by the fruit, to which knowledge of its roots is irrelevant – even if one takes a middle course, and draws a distinction between the value of the flower and its coming to be, while at the same time maintaining that knowledge of its roots is indispensable to the full understanding of what it is (and that it is this, indeed, that constitutes the ultimate and only justification of learning as such), this principle will prove to have been more difficult to apply to Vico than to the majority of other thinkers of the first importance. For his major discoveries have seemed to his interpreters to derive from no obvious sources, and have often been represented as a brilliant illustration of that very act of inspired creation out of nothing, so dear to the champions of extreme romanticism for whom even historicism seemed too much of a concession to the hated doctrines of classicism and Mimesis. But can this ever really be? Has Vico no intellectual parentage, no true anticipators? Are his most revolutionary ideas generated *ex nihilo*?

Erich Auerbach, in his comparison of Herder with Vico,[1] says that whereas Herder's ideas were clearly influenced by Shaftesbury and Rousseau, by Ossian and German patriotism, by reaction against Voltaire and by the new biology, Vico cannot be explained, and he leaves the matter there. Efforts have been made, of course, to trace the genesis of his views. M. H. Fisch[2] lays emphasis on the vast impetus to historiography given by the Reformation, both as a result of the coming into the open of books and manuscripts

---

[1] 'Vico and Aesthetic Historicism', in *Scenes from the Drama of European Literature* (New York, 1959).

[2] In his introduction to Vico's *Autobiography*, by far the best and most succinct account to date [1976] in English of Vico's intellectual genealogy: see A 20–31.

hitherto locked in monastic repositories, and through the recognition on the part of the Roman Church of the need to fight historical attacks upon herself with historical weapons; and he speaks also of the stimulus given to historical writing by the national pride (Vico's *boria*) of the new nation States; and mentions the influence of Bacon's propaganda against abstraction and in favour of concrete data. While this is true and important and casts light on the rise of interest in history in the seventeenth century and the analysis of documents by Bollandists, Maurists and secular scholars, particularly in England, this is not, by itself, sufficient to account for the roots of Vico's most original theses. Nor does it do this even if we add the influence of the growing new literature of travel, stimulated by the discovery of new worlds, in the East and in the West. Vico mentions such sources a good deal less than might be expected. He does occasionally refer to the customs of exotic and barbarian people to illustrate his theses,[1] but their part in his work, even as illustrations, is comparatively minor. Much original and illuminating work has, of course, been done by historians of ideas, particularly Italian scholars, headed by Benedetto Croce (the true rediscoverer of Vico for our time) and the indefatigable Fausto Nicolini, to trace the origin of individual doctrines in Vico's work. Thus Karl Löwith[2] asserts, against Croce,[3] the dominant influence of Aquinas and Thomism on the *verum/factum* doctrine. This doctrine ultimately stems from the Augustinian dogma that God by knowing creates, that for him knowing and creating are one, a doctrine that goes back to the conception of the divine Logos; God alone knows all because he creates all; man, because he is made in God's image, has a limited power of creation, and therefore full knowledge only of what he himself creates and of nothing else. Whether one accepts the derivation of Vico's view from orthodox Catholic doctrine by Löwith (which seems to me convincing) or Croce's counterargument against this (in support of which he cites the nineteenth-century theologian Jaime Balmes), it seems clear that the *verum/factum* doctrine is medieval and Christian and, by Vico's time, a

---

[1] On Vico's references to the ancient Germans and Scythians, and modern Hungarians and Saxons, as examples of transition from 'heroic' to 'human' culture see Giuseppe Giarrizzo, 'La politica di Vico', *Quaderni contemporanei* 2 (n.d. [1969?]), 63–133, at 114–17.

[2] op. cit. (p. 31 above, note 4).   [3] op. cit. (ibid.).

theological commonplace. The application of this principle by him is another and far more interesting matter.

Again, the great edition of Vico's works to which Nicolini devoted his long life, and which he surrounded with a small flotilla of other works of interpretation of various aspects of Vico's life and work, remains a model of illuminating *Kulturgeschichte*. Taken in conjunction with the monographs of Corsano and Fassò, Paolo Rossi and Paci, Badaloni and Gianturco, Amerio and Cantelli, Vaughan and Fisch, Whittaker and Adams (to mention only contemporary scholars), it gives us a great deal of information about the influence upon Vico of writers ancient and modern: Polybius and Lucretius, Campanella, Ficino and the Neoplatonist schools, Sanchez and Bodin, Bacon and Hobbes, Grotius, Pufendorf, Selden, Descartes, Bayle, Leclerc, and the scholars of his native city, Cornelio, Aulisio, di Capua and many others. All this is valuable: it does much to explain Vico's ideas about the ascent of man and his 'ferine' origins, and in particular his views of myth and ritual as practical tools in man's attempts to dominate his environment, as well as his notions of the relations of law to politics and morals, and a multitude of other conceptions, theories and allusions scattered in what Michelet called the 'little pandemonium of the *New Science*'.[1] But it does rather less towards the solution of the question of the sources, or at least anticipations, of Vico's two dominant doctrines: the conviction (which grew evidently during the 'silent' years in Naples between the *De antiquissima* of 1710 and the *Diritto universale* of 1720–2) that the *verum/factum* formula could be applied to human history conceived in its widest sense, to all that men have done and made and suffered; and, arising out of it, the very conception of culture as a category of historical thought, and indeed of thought in general.

The transforming idea which links both these doctrines is surely Vico's greatest single claim to immortality. Whence did it originate? Where else do we find the notion of *verum/factum* as the master key to the understanding of history? Or the doctrine of the existence of a variety of autonomous cultures, entire ways of life, each with its own outlook and values flowing out of one another, which are not a mere succession of efforts, attended by varying success, to achieve the same universal goals – the very notion, indeed, of a culture as the central style of ways of life, of the entire range of feeling and thought and action of human communities?

[1] loc. cit. (p. 117 above, note 1).

None of the writers for whom Vico expresses admiration, however deeply some of them were concerned with something wider than the mere sequence of important events, or dominant personalities and their acts, conceived explicitly of a culture as a total expression of an individual society, a central style which pervades and connects the different activities of its members – its literature and religion, its politics and its arts, its language and its legal, military, economic institutions, its class structure and its *mores*. None among them, neither Plato nor Polybius, neither Varro nor the *quattro autori*, spoke of a unifying pattern, at once individual and developing (as Meinecke expresses it), which lies at the heart of a given society's peculiar structure (so that its constituents tend to reflect one another to some degree) and thus serves to distinguish it as an identifiable and, above all, intelligible whole among the many similar evolving structures or cultures of which human history consists. Is it possible to trace the origins of this view and method in the vast variety of texts, ancient and modern, which Vico consumed so voraciously? Or was his vision spontaneously generated in his own fervid imagination?

It is natural enough to look for the answer in Vico's own social and intellectual milieu – the kingdom of Naples in the seventeenth century. This is the path pursued by Nicolini[1] and Corsano,[2] whose reconstructions of the social, political and religious life of the kingdom are models of lucid and imaginative learning. The most recent [1976] and perhaps the most ambitious attempt along these lines is that of Nicola Badaloni.[3] He finds the answer in the history of scientific ideas in Naples, especially those of Bishop Caramuel and the Society of the *investiganti*. He speaks of the neo-Pythagoreanism of the Renaissance; of the single dynamic principle, dear to it, that activates all things, as expounded by such men as Severino and Della Porta, who held that men and animals ultimately differ only in degree; of Bartoli and Cornelio, who believed in the unity of mind and nature; of Porzio, who saw man as the ripest fruit of nature, of the single great indwelling *spiritus*; of Borelli's and Caramuel's stress on the role of experiment and

---

[1] Especially in *La giovinezza di Giambattista Vico (1668–1700): saggio biografico*, 2nd ed. (Bari, 1932), and *Uomini di spada di chiesa di toga di studio ai tempi di Giambattista Vico* (Milan, 1942).

[2] Antonio Corsano, *Umanesimo e religione in G. B. Vico* (Bari, 1935), and *Giambattista Vico* (Bari, 1956).

[3] Nicola Badaloni, *Introduzione a G. B. Vico* (Milan, 1961).

hypothesis, on the empirically probable as against the a priori, mathematically demonstrable, character attributed by the dominant Cartesianism to all scientific knowledge. Badaloni lays particular stress on Borelli's theories of *vis percussionis* and of *conatus*, the heart of the vitalistic natural philosophy of his day.

There is, of course, a good deal in Vico to which all this is relevant. Vico, too, formulated a physical theory. He believed in 'metaphysical points'[1] of which *conatus* was the attribute – points which in some fashion 'mediate'[2] between God and material bodies – and he attributes this theory to Zeno (it is not clear which of the two Greek philosophers of that name is meant: perhaps he did not distinguish between them). In *De antiquissima* he speaks of the *motus* 'quo flamma ardet, planta adolescit, bestia per prata lascivit'[3] – a *motus* and *conatus* which evidently make the world go round – and this may well derive from the thinkers whom Badaloni's formidable learning resurrects. But this Renaissance metaphysics, Neoplatonic and vitalistic, which influenced Leibniz, too, is not what is most original or important in Vico. Whether, and how deeply, he read in the works cited by Badaloni is less significant than the fact that all these *conatus* and *motus*, whether they came from Borelli or Leibniz or Della Porta, are not accessible to human insight; we do not understand their workings *per caussas*. All this is part of Vico's doctrine of the external world, of which we attain to *coscienza* which cannot get beyond the *certum* – an object of knowledge which is opaque to our intellect in the crucial and contrasting sense in which human volitions, thoughts, actions are held by him not to be, in this respect, opaque. Vico does not, so far as I know, anywhere say that there is any continuity between the metaphysical points and their *conatus* on the one hand, and human activity on the other. Philosophers of nature before him, Paracelsus, perhaps, and Campanella, and after them Herder, Schelling, the romantics, did believe, as against both Descartes and Kant, in precisely such continuity, and it forms the heart of their doctrines. So, in their own fashion, did Hamann and Goethe and Coleridge. Badaloni's early Neapolitan scientists may well be among the ancestors of these writers. But Vico's claim to originality lies in the exact opposite: not in identifying, but in

---

[1] DA 152 ff./68 ff. (chapter 4, section 2).   [2] DA 152/68, 156/74.
[3] The motion 'by which fire burns, plants grow, and animals frolic in the meadows'. DA 166/83.

distinguishing between, on the one hand, natural processes which are more or less inscrutable, and, on the other, human activity which we can 'enter'. So far from deriving his ideas from these monistic forerunners of Schelling, Ravaisson, Bergson, Teilhard de Chardin and all the modern adherents of various kinds of *Naturphilosophie*, Vico opposed them. It is true that Caramuel and the other early scientific writers cited by Badaloni were anti-Aristotelian and anti-Cartesian; that they were admirers of Bacon; that this is true, too, of Vico. And it may be that the emphasis of the *investiganti* on experimentalism and the concrete, like Campanella's (and of course Bacon's) recourse to the senses and the imagination, and their antipathy to the abstract and the a priori, had their effect on him. Moreover, Vico's views on physics are not wholly without interest, as anything may be that relates to men of genius; but they remain peripheral to his thought, as Descartes' physics, or Kant's racial theories, are to theirs. When Badaloni draws a parallel between Aulisio's theory of biblical mythology (for example, his identification of Moses with Mercury, in the spirit of Spinoza and *Père* Simon) or Grimaldi's notions about *verum* and *certum* and Vico's corresponding doctrines, or draws our attention to Leonardo di Capua's theory of myths, or of the relation of theory to practice, he makes novel, useful and interesting additions to our knowledge of Vico. But his central thesis – that Vico's cardinal doctrines are traceable to Caramuel and the *investiganti* – is not helped thereby.[1]

Caramuel and his followers were concerned to show that the true path to natural, and perhaps all factual, knowledge (other than theology) lay through experience and not through a priori reasoning. Such knowledge could arrive at no more than high

---

[1] All this quite apart from the question of how much Vico actually knew of the work of Bishop Caramuel and the *investiganti*. Paolo Rossi is surely right in speaking of Vico's cosmology as 'gnostico-cabalistica', derived from the hermetic and Neoplatonic mystical tradition stretching back to the *Timaeus* (Introduction to his edition of Vico's *Opere* (Milan, 1959), p. 26). To insist on a place for Vico, who seemed unaware of the great intellectual revolution of his century, in the history of natural science seems misplaced piety. The more arresting fact, noted by H. P. Adams in *The Life and Writings of Giambattista Vico* (London, 1935), p. 131, that for him myths are imaginative reconstructions not so much of nature as of social life – are in fact a kind of mythologised politics – gives him an honoured place in the history of sociology, and makes him, with his emphasis on class war as a central factor in history, a genuine forerunner of Saint-Simon and Marx – a very different matter.

probability: a priori certainty was a snare and a delusion; in this respect they stood close to Bacon. But Vico's central point – and his ultimate claim to genius – rests on the proposition that historical knowledge is, in fact, capable of much more than this: if not of greater truth, then of truth of another and a superior character which the natural sciences cannot hope to reach. 'The whole of Vico's philosophy should be interpreted', says Badaloni, 'as a transfer to the level of civil [that is, social and political] philosophy of the experimental method of the *investiganti*, and of the metaphysics of *mens*',[1] now no longer applied to the natural world, but (he goes on to say) 'taken as Socrates had already taken it, from Heaven to earth'. If this were so, then all that Vico would be saying is that history and social science should be satisfied with the probable – a commonplace which few before him questioned. To say that natural science was not an a priori discipline in method and conclusions was, if not revolutionary, at any rate a bold rejection of the prevailing Cartesian doctrine and, at the same time, was to resist a powerful tradition of Aristotelian scholasticism, if not Aristotle himself. To say this of history was simply to reiterate what not only Descartes but virtually all philosophy and, indeed, common sense had maintained since time immemorial: that real certainty was not attainable in human affairs. Whoever did not believe this? To reduce Vico to this platitude is indeed to relegate him to the level of a very minor empiricist.

Vico, whatever else he was, was not a monist, as Caramuel and his allies evidently were. He became a dualist: this, indeed, was his cardinal move. He did not draw a line at the point at which Descartes drew it – between mind and matter, or between a priori knowledge of the real world and a posteriori perception of the world of the senses, with its unreliable secondary qualities. Vico drew such a line, but he drew it elsewhere: between activity and passivity, between, on the one hand, *mens* in human affairs, incarnated in human beings, guided, indeed determined, by God and Providence, but themselves creative agents, who have constructed the civil or political-historical world; and, on the other, *mens* in nature, which God, whose instrument it is, can understand, but which to men, who have not made it, is opaque and

---

[1] op. cit. (p. 142 above, note 3), p. 291. 'Nel suo complesso infatti la filosofia del Vico deve essere interpretata come un aggiornamento sul piano della filosofia civile del metodo sperimentale degli investiganti, e della metafisica della *mens*.'

inscrutable. This gulf is, in its own way, as wide as any that Descartes conceived – although it stretches across a different part of the metaphysical map. The development which is at the centre of Vico's vision – his phenomenology of the spirit – does not bridge this gulf: it does not move from nature to mind, nor from the contingent to the logically necessary (as that of Leibniz does), nor (as in late Idealism) from the *an sich* of things to the *für sich* of persons. Badaloni's interpretation of Vico's *verum/factum* formula is part of his general – to me unconvincing – thesis. It is, he says, intended to curtail the sole domination of *mens*: mind – the minds of men – must take account of nature, that is, of *factum*: there must be interplay between them. There can presumably be no such interplay between *mens* and *verum*, because *verum* is intrinsic to *mens*: created by it, indeed. But in that case neither can there be any 'interaction' between *mens* and *factum*, since Vico explicitly says that *factum* and *verum* are literally interchangeable:[1] what God has made by men's agency is ours already; what he has made outside it is impenetrable to men. 'The rule and criterion of truth is to have made it,' he said in 1710:[2] this, and nothing else, is what *verum et factum convertuntur* means. The break is that between what men's minds 'make', and what they do not make but find or act upon: the former is, or can be, transparent to mind; the latter resists it.

For Vico (it is necessary to say once again) nature remains opaque. He attacks the new scientific ideas precisely because they acclaim scientific method (which can deal only with 'externals') as the open sesame to all problems.[3] Paolo Rossi seems to me to come much nearer the mark in supposing that Vico was a conservative, not to say a reactionary, intellectually as well as personally close to the Jesuits, for instance in his anti-mechanism and, perhaps, his ambivalent attitude to freedom of the will.[4] Despite Vico's fascination with the growth of civilisation, the whole of his doctrine, in particular his emphasis upon the objective order – the eternal law which governs the cycles of the *storia ideale delle leggi eterne*, has a conservative tendency; for it seems to entail that one cannot force the pace, break with the past, create a lasting rational order rapidly, in the manner attempted by, for example, Vico's contemporary Peter the Great. This is the spirit of Hooker,

---

[1] cf. p. 35 above, note 1.   [2] DA 136/52; cf. p. 40 above, note 1.
[3] NS 331.   [4] op. cit. (p. 144 above, note 1), p. 22.

Matthew Hale, Montesquieu, Burke, Hegel, even Joseph de Maistre.[1] Whatever the correct interpretation of Vico's position, to turn the father of a profoundly theological historicism into a champion of scientific rationalism, a militant social progressive, an ally of the Royal Society, of Voltaire, the *philosophes*, ultimately of Engels and the dialectics of nature, is to run counter to the most obvious facts. Enzo Paci[2] may go too far in representing Vico as looking on nature with existentialist eyes, as the wild, terrifying, primeval forest of the savage, panic-stricken *orribili bestioni*, a vision which, he suggests, irrupts even into Vico's elaborate, baroque world in the form, for example, of the rough and barbarous soldier Antonio Caraffa, whose biography he had written. But Paci is fundamentally right in stressing that at the heart of Vico's thought is the contrast between two worlds: the recalcitrant external world which we can manipulate only within limits set by Providence, and the world of men, which their creative spirit 'makes', with its recurrent images, mysteries and symbols that haunt men's collective consciousness, the man-made world of which we are true citizens, the stream of history in which alone we are at home.

Badaloni's book is an erudite and richly informative account of seventeenth-century Neapolitan science; but, whatever else it does, it does not provide a convincing answer to the question of the sources of the central doctrines of the only Vico who matters – the author of the *Scienza nuova*. Are there no obvious bridges between its radical break with tradition and earlier thought? Did historicism come, fully fledged, without antecedents, out of the head of an isolated Italian antiquary into the world of Newton, Locke, Voltaire? Before conceding that this was indeed so, I should like to advance, somewhat tentatively, at least a partial answer to a problem to which men of far greater learning have thus far not succeeded in providing a satisfactory solution.

IV

Since Vico's main claim to fame rests on his views about the nature and methods of historical knowledge and its relations or absence of relations with the methods of the natural sciences, that is, in the

---

[1] See Elio Gianturco, *Joseph de Maistre and Giambattista Vico: Italian Roots of de Maistre's Political Culture* (Columbia University Ph.D. thesis, 1937).

[2] In his most original study of Vico, *Ingens sylva* (see p. 69 above, note 2).

field of theory and methodology, and not upon his achievements as a historian or a jurist, it is in the fields of philosophy, theology and scientific theory that scholars have tended to look for the sources of his ideas. Yet he was, above all, a legal scholar preoccupied with the history of jurisprudence, more especially the history of Roman law, which is the central paradigm of his *storia ideale eterna*, and to which he constantly returns. He was immersed in the study of legal antiquities far more deeply than in metaphysics or even theology; there is no branch of learning or disputation with which he was more familiar; it is in this field that he so desperately wished to make his name and obtain the coveted post that was so unjustly and dishonourably denied him. Yet this is a direction which has not perhaps been investigated sufficiently.

What was it that first planted in his mind the notion of the diversity of cultures? Attention has often been drawn to the familiar fact that the discovery of new and strange societies in the New World provided new evidence for the well-known contentions of Greek Sophists about the variety of customs and the relativity of values. Yet this commonplace needs to be treated with caution. Travellers' tales about American Indians or the peoples of the Far East were just as widely used to prop up the doctrine of the universality of natural law, whether classical or Christian, Catholic or Protestant, since it was this universal human code that was believed to have survived in an uncorrupt form among these primitive and remote societies, uncontaminated by contact with (and untouched by the sources of) degenerate European morals. This was part of the humanist tendency to look for the uniform and the universal, to rediscover the basic structure of moral and social, as of physical and metaphysical, reality that had been forgotten or perverted during the long night of the Middle Ages. Those who wished to stress the relativity of attitudes and values did not need these discoveries; examples from modern civilisation had for a long time lain close at hand; Pascal did not need to go beyond Europe to point his celebrated moral that what was orthodox on this side of the Pyrenees was heretical on the other.

Vico does indeed adduce examples from remote societies – Spanish America, Siam, the Celts – but C. E. Vaughan, who has counted these examples, says that there are not more than a dozen of them;[1] this contrasts sharply with, say, Montesquieu's, Lafitau's, Voltaire's, even Bodin's far richer use of such material. What

[1] op. cit. (p. 75 above, note 1), p. 227.

engages Vico's thought is ancient Rome, and after Rome, Greece – the classical hunting-ground of the theorists of natural law – and he draws a moral that is precisely opposite to that of the natural lawyers: that man's nature is to be conceived in social terms, not individual; those of movement and change, not fixity and rest; to be sought in history, not in a timeless metaphysics. Vico's conception goes well beyond the rise, or rebirth, of historical consciousness whose roots are described by M. H. Fisch.[1] To say that historical knowledge differs from scientific is one thing: but Vico's thesis that historical knowledge is better founded than scientific is quite another and much bolder. The labours of pious Bollandists and Maurists, of Mabillon or Montfaucon, of Leibniz or Muratori, increased interest in origins, and in history as a repository of examples of virtue and vice, success or failure, useful for giving guidance to later generations; or as a witness to the truth of the Scriptures or of revelation; or as a monument to the achievements of a nation, a Church, a movement; or to the validity or the corruption of a tradition, especially that of the Roman Church. It became, in this way, the favoured field on which Papalists and reformers, Jesuits and Jansenists, fought their battles. These motives for the study of history during the Renaissance and the Reformation do much to account for the new fascination that historical studies had for humanists and churchmen, and the contempt for them on the part of the new, science-oriented, Cartesian positivists. But this is a far cry from *verum/factum* – the sharp contrast between our capacity to understand man-made artefacts as against nature, which God, who made it, can alone fully know.

The history of early modern jurisprudence lay closer to Vico's dominant interests. Here, it may be, the long-sought-for clue may at last be found.

V

One of the best known episodes in the later history of this subject is the great controversy among Roman lawyers and their critics which rose to a climax in the sixteenth century, stimulated by political at least as much as by purely scholarly considerations. One of the central motives behind the labours of the Renaissance

[1] See p. 139 above, note 2.

jurists and their disciples, particularly in France, was the conviction that eternal and universal truths, of inestimable value for the conduct of men everywhere, had been known to the great Greek and Roman thinkers, and could, with sufficient effort, be recovered. They believed that this *restauratio* could be achieved once the distortions, confusions, interpolations and incrustations of Byzantine and medieval editors and interpreters, from Justinian's editor Tribonian to the medieval Accursians and Bartolists and their successors (sadly affected as these last were held to be by the anti-pagan bias of the traditions of the Church), were identified and removed, and the original texts disinterred, reconstructed and understood. In part, the work of restoration was stimulated by sheer love of learning, by intellectual curiosity, by desire to rescue the truth from ignorance, error and deliberate perversion, and by pure admiration for the classical world, free from any utilitarian or ethical purpose. But together with such disinterested motives, there clearly were at work theological and political passions too: Protestant, anti-papal, anti-medieval, and, particularly in France, Gallican and nationalist. Nevertheless, it remains true that the dominant impulse was that of the Platonic and humanist faith that, in the light of the newly discovered standards of ideal truth and ideal beauty, gifted and energetic men, unaffected by the condemnation of this world by the *tristes docteurs*, and liberated from the tyranny of a superstitious and obscurantist priesthood, could once again develop the rich potentialities of human nature, and build a life worthy of their new-found knowledge and creative genius. The timeless principles in the light of which Roman law was built – whether *jus naturale* or *jus gentium* or *jus civile* – would, once the ground was cleared of the accumulated rubbish of centuries, be the basis of a new life, both social and individual, which rational men, from whose eyes the medieval scales had fallen, would establish in accordance with the unalterable laws of nature, which were identical with those of human reason as they were formulated by the great philosophers and jurists. Yet this very preoccupation with the restoring of classical texts led to two unexpected consequences that were at once interesting and paradoxical.[1]

[1] My main source of information on this subject is *The Ancient Constitution and the Feudal Law: A Study of English Historical Thought in the Seventeenth Century* by J. G. A. Pocock (Cambridge etc., 1957), especially the introductory chapter. This seems to me much the most original and illuminating, as well as the best written, treatment of this topic to be found anywhere at present. Pocock

In the first place, the very process of faithful reconstruction of any form of human communication requires a correct understanding of the meaning of what is said. This, in its turn, entails knowledge of the character and intentions of those whose language is being studied, and especially of the social structure within which such communication takes place – the milieu, the period and above all the specific conventions which govern both words and lives within it, for it is only in the context of a particular society, at a particular period in its development, that the significance and use of the terms used – legal, moral, religious, literary – can be understood. Hence every investigation of any aspect of human civilisation necessarily carries the student beyond the specific object examined – from legal formulae to the habits and purposes

mentions Vico in passing, but does not seek to connect his doctrines specifically with the startling implications of the controversies which he describes and analyses. Other discussions that I have found exceptionally valuable on the sources of the new historical consciousness in the sixteenth century, particularly in France, are to be found in (I cite them in alphabetical order of author): Arthur B. Ferguson, 'Bishop Pecock', *Studies in the Renaissance* 13 (1966), 147–66; Julian H. Franklin, *Jean Bodin and the Sixteenth-Century Revolution in the Methodology of Law and History* (New York and London, 1963); Eugenio Garin, *Italian Humanism: Philosophy and Civic Life in the Renaissance* (1947), trans. Peter Munz (Oxford, 1965); George Huppert, *The Idea of Perfect History* (see p. 122 above, note 1); Donald R. Kelley, (a) '*Historia Integra*: François Baudouin and his Conception of History', *Journal of the History of Ideas* 25 (1964), 35–57; (b) 'Guillaume Budé and the First Historical School of Law', *American Historical Review* 72 (1967), 807–34; (c) ' "Fides historiae": Charles Dumoulin and the Gallican View of History', *Traditio* 22 (1966), 347–402; (d) 'Legal Humanism and the Sense of History', *Studies in the Renaissance* 13 (1966), 184–99; and especially (e) the important and excellent *Foundations of Modern Historical Scholarship: Language, Law, and History in the French Renaissance* (New York and London, 1970), in which a good deal of the foregoing, but by no means all, is summarised, used and discussed, and which throws new light on the origins of historical and cultural history, to be found nowhere else; Frank E. Manuel, *Shapes of Philosophical History* (London, 1965), chapter 3; Arnaldo Momigliano, (a) 'Ancient History and the Antiquarian', *Journal of the Warburg and Courtauld Institutes* 13 (1950), 285–315; (b) 'La nuova storia romana di G. B. Vico' (see p. 59 above, note 1); (c) 'Vico's *Scienza Nuova*: Roman "Bestioni" and Roman "Eroi" ' (see p. 51 above, note 1); Franco Simone, (a) 'Introduzione ad una storia della storiografia letteraria francese', *Studi francesi* 8 (1964), 442–56; (b) 'La coscienza storica del rinascimento francese e il suo significato culturale', *Convivium* 22 (1954), 156–70.

Works listed in this note are cited hereafter only by the author's name (with the addition, where relevant, of a distinguishing letter): e.g. Kelley's *Foundations* . . . is cited as Kelley (e).

of the men whom the laws govern, from liturgical phrases to the religious rites and beliefs and cosmology in terms of which alone the functions of the words, and of the documents that embody them, can be correctly interpreted. This in its turn may require an investigation of origins – of the genesis and evolution of customs, laws, ideas, institutions, and the role played by legal or theological language in them. Hence the work of resurrecting any monument of antiquity, however uninterested in wider aspects of the past, as such, the restorer may be, involves him, willy-nilly, in some social history, or historical sociology or anthropology. The need for reconstruction has, consequently, acted as a powerful stimulus, not only to historical studies, but to a historicist attitude: to looking for the answers to legal or theological or political questions in social growth, in the interplay of a variety of social factors in determining the part which this or that set of symbols, or enactment, or institution played in the lives of a particular group of men – men whose ends and way of life were (to quote the *New Science*) 'such and not otherwise' because they came into being 'at certain times and in certain guises'.[1]

The mounting enthusiasm for the study of monuments and institutions was perhaps not totally unconnected with the rise of profound scepticism about the reliability of narrative history itself.[2] Critics like Cornelius Agrippa in the beginning, and Patrizi in the middle, of the sixteenth century, delivered the most vehement attacks on the reliability of narrative historians since Plutarch's onslaught on Herodotus. The historians and chroniclers were accused of inferiority of mind,[3] ignorance, irrational or

[1] NS 147.

[2] One of the best accounts in English of 'Pyrrhonism' and of the 'historicist' reaction against it, and in particular of the political uses of the attacks on the notion of natural law by the champions of custom-based, traditionalist and regionalist diversity, is to be found in Franklin. This valuable study of anti-universalism and anti-rationalism before Montesquieu and Burke casts a good deal of doubt on conventional accounts of political thought in the sixteenth century.

[3] This charge was revived three centuries later by Henry Thomas Buckle, who declared that history had not advanced as far as the sciences for the simple reason that historians were mentally not as well-endowed as scientists, since the best intellects in modern times had been attracted to the pursuit of the natural sciences. Once some really able people could be induced to occupy themselves with history, it would not be long before it was transformed into a properly organised natural science.

corrupt motives such as vanity, fanaticism, personal, political and religious jealousies and hatreds, patriotic exaggeration, venality, lack of coherent purpose or method and the like, all of which from the very beginning had caused constant and violent disagreements among them which there was no possible means of resolving. The attack, at times, went a good deal further – some of the assailants maintained that history was, in principle, incapable of arriving at truth or even verisimilitude, for all history was, in the end, founded on the evidence of eye-witnesses, or at least contemporaries; these were either themselves involved in the events described, or they were not. In the former case they were liable to be partisan; in the latter they got their data at second hand, and even then not the most secret, and sometimes most important, information, and consequently could never know the real springs of action of those involved, the crucial factors known only to participants, and liable to be used by them to feed historians with tendentious information, or to bribe them, in pursuit of personal ambition, or for the sake of a cause, or out of spite, or desire for glory, or for money, or from countless similar motives. Consequently, if historians were well informed, they were likely to be biased, if impartial, to be ignorant or misled. The horns of this devastating dilemma have, in one form or another, loomed before serious historians ever since. Nor was this all. A century later such philosophical opponents as Descartes and his followers, attacking from another quarter, maintained that without axioms, definitions, deductive rules, intellectual rigour, history could not, in any case, be a source of systematic knowledge.[1]

Caught in this pincer movement, narrative history, indeed history itself, might have been hard put to it to maintain its claims, were it not for new weapons against such scepticism provided by the new masters of 'philology'. Gifted scholars and critics, literary, antiquarian and legal, began to arrive at their conclusions by careful scientific techniques, using neither the materials nor the methods of the older narrative historians, but basing themselves on monuments – literary documents, inscriptions, coins, medals, monuments of art and architecture,[2] laws, rites, continuing or remembered traditions – 'objective' entities, *realia*, which, it was maintained, could not be corrupt or unscrupulous or tell lies.

[1] See pp. 28–30 above, especially p. 29, note 2.   [2] See Momigliano (*a*).

Thus the very desire to recover timeless verities, which had been forgotten or perverted, resulted in bringing into being a new dimension of historical understanding founded on a revival of antiquarian scholarship, accompanied by a new respect for a Varro or a Scaevola as against even the greatest narrative historians of the ancient world.

The truths so reconstructed were perhaps more general than those which the narrative historians claimed to report, but also seemed more solidly based, and to possess wider significance. When Patrizi maintained that monuments no less than stories could, in fact, be made to fit into almost any pattern, that out of such bricks any edifice could be built, what he was saying was not, indeed, absurd, but certainly exaggerated; the tests of internal coherence in the reconstruction, say, of the constitution of Periclean Athens, or of private law in the Rome of Ulpian or Gaius, could in principle be made as rigorous as the methods of medicine or geography. The emphasis laid by philologists and 'grammarians' on empirical evidence – concrete examples of the application of the general rules which Bacon and Campanella stressed so strongly – became the cornerstones of the new method. Thus the route to the genuine past, it was now believed, lay via 'philology'. Valla (and Dumoulin and Cusanus) demonstrated this in the course of exposing the forged Donation of Constantine; the great historical jurists – Budé, Cujas, Alciati – and their disciples used the new method to clear away the medieval rubble and Byzantine carelessness which, in their view, concealed the authentic texts of the great Roman lawyers.

One of the great battle-fronts was that between the upholders and critics, both Gallican and Protestant, of the authority of the Vatican: all sides appealed to tradition. This itself, as M. H. Fisch has pointed out,[1] gave a great fillip to historical studies. But what is more relevant to the formation of Vico's views is the fact that the appeals to the past largely took the form of examination of etymology and monuments, as well as documents and narrative history. The great Gallican controversialist, Charles Dumoulin, the disciple of Valla and the one-time friend of Calvin, appealed to linguistic usage in interpreting the true tradition in his defence of the claims of the French monarchy against Roman universalism. In the same spirit the defender of Roman orthodoxy, Raymond Le Roux, takes Dumoulin to task for being over-literal: words change

[1] A 20–1.

meanings; lawyers who deal with facts and not with mere words should not fall into the error of attaching static meanings to words; central terms change meanings at different times and in different states.[1] But the same principle could be used with equal effect by the opponents of Rome: language and monuments can be used not only to expose clerical anachronisms and forgeries, but to reconstruct the structure of past societies in terms of which alone the significance of this or that sentence in the Digest or Ulpian can be understood.[2] So François Baudouin demanded knowledge of universal history on the part of anyone claiming true mastery of the law; to understand the tradition of the Church one must understand the Commonwealth 'in whose bosom, as it were, [the Church] is nourished';[3] all history and all jurisprudence should ideally be united in one single *corpus*.[4] Law and history are one and indivisible.[5] It is by adhering to this principle that Budé and Cujas, Alciati and Le Douaren and their disciples succeeded in purging the texts of Roman law from the distortions and blunders of medieval 'barbarians' – Bartolists and Accursians. Indeed it was only by using such methods that the unhistorical lumping together of Roman texts of different dates by Justinian's editor Tribonian – the *bête noire* of the new school of French jurists – could be exposed, and the chronology and therefore the significance and relationships of the texts properly established. Had not Valla already declared that it is 'ab institutione' or 'ab artifice' that the historical meaning of the crucial terms can be revealed?[6] This is equally the doctrine of François Hotman, and of his master Cujas. Even the papalist Le Roy declares that 'languages, like all things human, have a beginning, progress, perfection, corruption, end'.[7]

---

[1] See Kelley (c). Kelley's works (listed on p. 150 above, note 1) are an invaluable historical guide to this movement of thought.

[2] See Kelley (d), *passim*.

[3] Fr. Balduinus, *De institutione historiae universae, et eius cum iurisprudentia coniunctione, προλεγομένων libri ii* (Paris, 1561), p. 30.

[4] ibid., p. 129.

[5] '... unius corporis indivisae partes aut membra divelli neque possunt neque debent' ('the undivided parts or limbs of a single body neither can nor ought to be pulled apart'): ibid., p. 104. On Baudouin see Kelley (e), pp. 129–141. The very title of his work (see note 3 above) is telling enough.

[6] *Dialecticae disputationes* 1. 14: p. 676 in *Laurentii Vallae opera* (Basel, 1540) [photographically reproduced as vol. 1 of Laurentius Valla, *Opera omnia* (Turin, 1962)].

[7] Loys Le Roy, *De la vicissitude ou varieté des choses en l'univers ...* (Paris, 1576), p. 22.

This is the very language of the *storia ideale eterna*. The hunt for anachronisms in medieval or Byzantine compilations goes back to the fifteenth century,[1] but becomes more systematic in the course of the legal and religious controversies in the sixteenth, particularly in France. The heightened sense of changing styles, and consequently of the stream of history and the evolution of ways of life, in the Christian West, which these styles reflect, is certainly a new door to the past: the marriage of 'philology' and law is the contribution of the *mos gallicus* to historical understanding. Bodin, a century before Vico, looked on myths and popular legends as evidence for social beliefs and structures. Vico's conception is larger and more profound: he discriminated what was, from what was not, compatible with this or that stage in the evolution of an entire culture, not merely with this or that linguistic usage or legal or constitutional set of rules; these last were for him themselves aspects of a single unitary pattern that was exhibited in all the manifestations of a particular civilisation. Nevertheless, there is a similarity of approach, both basic and in detail, between the historical jurists, especially Hotman and Baudouin, and Vico. Distrust of narrative history, antipathy to timeless principles, whether those of natural law or, later, Cartesianism, faith in 'philology' as a kind of rudimentary anthropology and social psychology are held in common: they are equally remote from Augustine and Aquinas, Sanchez and the other accepted forerunners of the Neapolitan philosopher.[2]

---

[1] This is well described by Ferguson.

[2] There are other anticipations of Vico's doctrines: Budé and Le Roy had spoken of life cycles of civilisation, from the poetry and primitive beliefs of its childhood to an adolescence of scholarship and eloquence, ending in decline and corruption. (See Kelley (*e*), pp. 64, 83.) The French sixteenth-century historiographer La Popelinière also said as much, and spoke of the poets as the first historians (ibid., pp. 140–1). The succession fable–folklore–truth is to be found in Christophe Milieu, Le Roy, Polydore Vergil etc. (ibid., p. 304), and Pasquier 'had a sense of the interconnectedness of cultural phenomena' (ibid., p. 309; cf. Huppert, pp. 65, 158). Kelley, so far as I know, is the first scholar to perceive these important links. He tells us that 'Vico was not so much the creator of a "new science" as the preserver of an old science, the science of philology. In this sense, he did not so much found historicism as inherit it' (Kelley (*e*), p. 7). This seems to me an underestimate of Vico's achievement. The programme of the complete re-creation of a strange and barbarous past by a great and painful effort of the imagination, which seeks to enter into 'la vasta immaginativa di que' primi uomini' ('the vast imagination of those first men', NS 378), the discovery of a path to an entire world of the 'orribili bestioni' (NS 374) as they and their 'heroic'

Vico does not discuss Budé or Dumoulin or Hotman in this connection. But the names of 'Cuiacio', 'Bodino', 'Ottomano', 'Salmasio' occur not infrequently in his pages: the hypothesis that Vico, or indeed any other legal scholar whose life was spent on the study of historical jurisprudence, knew nothing of, or paid no attention to, these great quarrels, seems improbable. Vico, if anyone, must have had it borne in upon him that the doors to antiquity had been opened, not by historians, but by 'philologists', the masters of classical learning and especially of Roman law. It would not be absurd to say that the history, indeed the very concept, of culture began in the heat of argument, especially in France, about the credentials of texts or traditions, argument which, however academic in manner and method, sprang from social, political and economic conflicts. Vico's doctrine appears as a bold and transforming development of methods invented by and for the polemics about where true – valid – authority for political action by the contending parties could be found. At the same time, the case must not be overstated; there is, so far as is known, no positive mention in Vico's works of these great controversies; and this total silence does need some explanation. The anti-papalists were, of course, dissidents and heretics – and to acknowledge a direct debt to them or to mention them with too much fervour would not have been either altogether safe in the Neapolitan kingdom of Vico's day, or likely to commend itself to Vico's friends and patrons, especially the clerical circles with which he was closely bound up all his life, and which he evidently found congenial. He does of course speak with favour of Grotius, Selden, Pufendorf, Bacon – Protestants all – but he rejects the central doctrines of at least three among them; nor did any of them conduct political and theological warfare against the authority of the Vatican in the sense in which this was done during the wars of

successors conveyed it in rites and poetry and laws, viewed not as a more primitive version of, or step towards, our own more civilised society, but as a cruel, frightening but powerful and self-contained civilisation, with its own inner coherence and its own peculiar values and creations, such as the Homeric poems, which we cannot hope to match – this is surely a conception far beyond the perspective of even the boldest Renaissance philologists, jurists and men of letters. Vico's originality seems to me to be one not of degree but of kind. Even his wildest flights of anthropological etymology – as well as his far-reaching economic interpretations of cultural symbols – seem well outside the intellectual region of the kind of philological fancies or legal muddles which Valla or Budé exposed or put right.

religion in sixteenth-century France. Moreover, like many another discoverer of original truths, he was not, perhaps, too anxious to acknowledge intellectual debts of so direct a kind. Nevertheless we cannot say, in the present state of knowledge, that there is positive evidence that Vico derived some of his central notions from the historical jurists: only that it is exceedingly unlikely that he did not do so; for this is the world that he knew best.

The second paradox has been mentioned already. One of the original motives for labouring to restore the texts of Gaius or Papinian was the belief that they contained the clearest statement of those universal rules of conduct to which all men aspire by nature, no matter how barbarous or deeply perverted they may be, so that contemplation of the principles of Roman law should give any man a sense of homecoming, of return out of the long night of the Middle Ages to the rule of reason and the light of day. But what was gradually discovered was a way of life that seemed remote or, at the very least, unfamiliar to these seekers for the single true tradition. The more faithfully the despised medieval accumulation was removed, the stranger the classical world appeared: if anything, it was the alleged monkish distortions that gave it such affinity to the ideas of later ages as it once seemed to have. This was not what had been expected by neo-Stoics, neo-Aristotelians, or Platonists and Neoplatonists of the Renaissance. But it was grist to the mills of those who wished to protect local or corporate liberties and privileges against the encroachment of the great centralising powers – whether papal or royal. Legal historians have often remarked on François Hotman's unceasing effort, while ostensibly wholly engaged on learned labours intended to establish the true meaning of Roman law, to emphasise the unbridgeable differences between it – and, indeed, the rules of *jus naturale*, too – and the ancient customs of France, which followed an authentic, native, 'Franco-Gallic' tradition; from which it followed that Roman law, whether 'municipal' or international, was not relevant to the French State. Hotman's and his allies' insistence on the gulf that divided Roman law from the 'immemorial' native Franco-German traditions was part of their defence of feudal, or local, or national rights against the champions of uniformity, centralisation and all those who appealed to timeless and universal truths to support claims to overriding authority.

This great argument, stemming as it did from many sources – early consciousness of nationhood, the zeal of reformers, Gallicans and other dissenters against the Roman hierarchy, the claims of estates and provincial *parlements* and corporations against the central executive: from every movement or outlook that found it advantageous to underline differences between places, times, ways of life – was eagerly seized upon by the defenders of local custom, ancient ways, individual traditions that varied from place to place with roots too remote and tangled to be rationalised and fitted into any universal system. This great political and theological conflict, one of the great ideological battles which has continued into our day, as often as not clothed itself in legal forms, appeals to precedents and historical institutions the path to which was built by embattled jurists and grammarians. In the effort to diminish the authority of Roman law, to undermine the notion that civil law, even if it was not always, at least always strove to be, the application of natural law to particular situations, Hotman speaks of 'les saisons et mutations des moeurs & conditions d'un peuple',[1] which divide it from other people's, and indeed even from its own past; the French have their own *complexions* and *humeurs*.[2] What have they to do with the laws of a society long dead and originating in another country? What have the lists of 'natural law' maxims enunciated by Gratian or his predecessors, obedient mouthpieces of the Vatican, or spokesmen for an ancient civilisation born in far-away Athens and flourishing in an only slightly less distant Rome, what have they to do with our own peculiar, unique, Frankish, that is, in the end, Germanic, or 'Franco-Gallic', individuality or 'complexion'? In his *Anti-Tribonianus* (which Vico cites in another connection),[3] Hotman uses this appeal to historical continuity in resisting royal claims as against the customary law of the Frankish conquerors of Gaul, or against other codes which had developed out of the needs and traditions of the varied associations of men of whom the King's realm consists. The Romans had a *respublica*, not a monarchy: the administration of France 'has nothing in common with' that of

---

[1] 'The seasons and mutations of the manners and conditions of a people.' 'L'Antitribonian ou Discours ... sur l'estude des loix', end of chapter 2: p. 9 in *Opuscules françoises des Hotmans* (Paris, 1616).

[2] See Kelley (*d*), p. 195. Kelley adduces the similar remarks of Le Caron, Dumoulin, Pierre Ayrault and other adherents of the doctrines of territorialism and national autonomy.

[3] See Croce and Nicolini, op. cit. (p. 99 above, note 3), p. 51, and, for the echoes of this controversy in Gibbon, pp. 376–7.

Rome, said Étienne Pasquier.[1] The argument from the 'irrelev-
ance' of what the Romans did to modern situations became a
powerful weapon in the hands of the defenders of the prerogatives
of various estates – Montesquieu's later defence of such *corps
intermédiaires*, and his anti-centralist pluralism, drew sustenance
from the sharp contrasts between the variety of systems, each valid
for its own day. Hence flowed relativism, historicism, political
pluralism, and, more particularly, suspicion of abstraction, of tidy
general schemas, whether a priori or naturalistic, advocated by no
matter whom – Aristotle, Seneca, Ulpian, the Digest, Aquinas,
Descartes, Locke, the *philosophes*. Hence, above all, ever since
Lorenzo Valla and the new 'philology', the appeal to the concrete
and the particular in specific times and places.

Nor is the new path to the past confined to historical lawyers.
The *mos gallicus* captured history proper as well. Étienne Pasquier
looks on laws as custom recorded in writing, and since society and
its language and habits alter, there is need of constant readjustment.
One can reconstruct the past not by attending to narrative history,
so much as by renewed study of acts of *parlements*, juridical
records, papal bulls, poems, coins, statues; historians tend to be
subjective, a 'je ne sçay quoy de passion'[2] is apt to affect them,
especially if religion is at issue.[3] Pasquier's distaste for Roman law
and architecture throws the dissimilarity between the Roman past
and the French tradition into sharp relief: this is surely the direct
result of the doctrines taught in the schools of Bourges, Valence,
Toulouse, Turin. Vignier, who treats Homer and the Bible in the
same detached fashion as he does coins and inscriptions, shows no
respect for the 'immemorial wisdom of the ancients'. La Popelinière is concerned to achieve an understanding of ancient ways of
life, 'les moeurs, & en général la Police des Grecs',[4] for example,

---

[1] Undated letter to Adrien Turnèbe: vol. 2, col. 293 C, in *Les Oeuvres
d'Estienne Pasquier* (Amsterdam, 1723). See Huppert for a good many instances
of this kind of expression, and all that it implies, in Hotman, Pasquier, La
Popelinière and others in France in the sixteenth century.

[2] Pasquier, 'Pour-parler du prince' (1560): ibid., vol. 1, col. 1034 C.

[3] Huppert's pioneering study of the rise of the new history contains valuable
information on the alliance between jurists and historians in this respect.

[4] 'The manners of the Greeks, and in general the nature of their society.' [La
Popelinière] in *L'Idée de l'histoire accomplie*: this work was published with two
others as *L'Histoire des histoires, avec L'Idée de l'histoire accomplie, plus Le
Dessein de l'histoire des françois...* (Paris, 1599); the pagination starts afresh at
the beginning of the second work, but not at the beginning of the third; this

by examining the 'coustumes & façons de faire'[1] of a people, their 'forme de vivre';[2] the path to this lies through their songs, dances, sagas, linguistic usage – for (in Pasquier's words) 'nostre langage symbolise ordinairement avec nos moeurs'.[3] He is correspondingly sceptical about the credentials of ancient historians – these must be checked with what one knows of their country, religion, sources, their patrons, what charges they are concerned to ward off, and what degree of consistency they display. Even so, like Bodin, he thinks that their conclusions can never be more than probable: the mere fact of disagreements between historians ensures this.

Vico, of course, thinks he can do better, and attain to a degree of certainty beyond mere probability by the use of his reconstructive *fantasia*; for him humane studies – 'philology' – can claim superiority over the natural sciences: understanding of a world men have created is not governed by laws of sciences concerned with the opaque external world. Whether or not he is mistaken in this, it is important to realise that in this important respect he differs in principle both from Bodin and from the Neapolitan 'probabilists' (to whom Badaloni vainly seeks to attach him); *scienza* for him is of the eternally true; indeed he reproaches Grotius precisely for supposing that historical propositions of which the *New Science* is the *scienza* can never be more than probable. Nevertheless, it is difficult to believe that his historical method, and indeed his entire schema of development, is wholly independent of the doctrines of these French jurists, 'grammarians' and historians: the arm of coincidence can scarcely stretch quite so far. What is altogether his own is the notion of history as the continuous self-transformation of man and of human institutions in the course of man's struggle to overcome human and natural obstacles, which, because it is the activity of men, and the consequence of human structures, can be understood by men, understood as nature cannot be. This is his own:[4] it is this original doctrine that inspired Michelet and Croce

passage is to be found on p. 93 of *L'Idèe*. For La Popelinière see Huppert, chapter 8.

[1] 'Customs and way of life.' ibid., p. 95.

[2] *Le Dessein* (see p. 160 above, note 4), p. 352.

[3] 'Our language is usually in harmony with our way of life.' Undated letter to Claude de Kerquifinen: op. cit. (p. 160 above, note 1), vol. 2, col. 45 B.

[4] It is true that Baudouin, in the opening and closing paragraphs (pp. 1, 214) of *De institutione historiae universae* (see p. 155 above, note 3), pointed out that in history man has the advantage of being a performer as well as a spectator and

and gained the admiration of both Marx and Dilthey.[1]

In England this movement took the form of Coke's sense of the common law, and Matthew Hale's doctrine that law was born not made, and those other forerunners (such as Hume and Boling-broke) of Burke, who reacted against the cut and dried 'rigidities of ordered reason' and 'towards the customary, the native, the feudal and the barbarous ... the primitive, the inarticulate and the mutable'.[2] In the seventeenth century this movement spread to Sweden, the Netherlands and Sicily as well as England, and, provided with an ideological defence by Burke and Herder, ultimately led to the legal romanticism of Savigny and the German historical school.

If this account is anywhere near correct, it follows that the late Renaissance gave birth to two seminal ideas. The first is that history – the restoration of the past – consists not merely in reporting a string of events or deeds, or providing portraits of the great human actors and their lives, or even supplying the social, economic, demographic and 'cultural' facts and connections, together with comments upon styles of art, which Voltaire, for instance, was among the first to select, discuss and evaluate; but also in understanding the historical stream as a whole, in terms of which alone that which is studied – a law, a religion, a policy, or the acts or fortunes of individuals or nations – makes sense; and that the surest path to such understanding lies through 'philology', if only because monuments and institutions – language, customs, laws, coinage, art, popular beliefs – unlike historians, may be misinterpreted, but cannot lie.

The second is that the high civilisations of the past are a good

critic, as he is of nature; and Kelley acutely notes the parallel with Vico, and adds the names of Croce and Troeltsch. But this, although remarkable enough, is, at most, like Manetti's contrast (see p. 44 above) of what is man-made ('ours') and what is not, the merest embryo of Vico's bold new doctrine, as sketched above.

[1] Huppert's blind spot about Vico causes him to say (p. 167) that Michelet and the Germans mistakenly pay homage to Vico only because they did not know his sources. Although my knowledge of fifteenth-century historiography is based on secondary sources, such as his own very informative book, I find it hard to believe that the revolutionary notion of the self-transforming nature of man, or of language, myth and symbolic rites as modes of experience and interpretation of reality, have been lying quiet and unperceived in the pages of Pasquier or La Popelinière, or even Baudouin.

[2] Pocock, p. 15. So began what Maitland once called 'a Gothic revival' in jurisprudence. 'English Law and the Renaissance' (1901): p. 146 in *Selected Historical Essays of F. W. Maitland*, ed. Helen M. Cam (Cambridge, 1957).

deal less like our own 'glorious age' than the proponents of natural law assumed; that they were the expressions of societies sufficiently similar to ours not to be totally unintelligible, but different enough not to be authoritative for us, with their own independent structures and patterns of development; and have been found fascinating by later ages precisely because they are remote, and incorporate values different from, perhaps superior to, but at any rate not compatible with, our own. This seems to me the authentic beginning of the idea of culture as a complete pattern of living, which can be studied not merely as the arts and skills and ideas of a community can be investigated, each in separation from the others,[1] but as a central style, exhibited equally by law and poetry, myths and forms of family life, economic structure and spiritual activities – all the diverse provinces of the behaviour of a society, a tradition, an age, which form an interrelated unity, a single pattern of development which, even if it cannot be precisely defined or even described, is sufficiently individual to enable us to recognise certain possibilities as incompatible with it – as being un-Greek, or un-Roman, or un-French, or un-medieval. This is La Popelinière's 'façons de faire'[2] of a society, in virtue of which we attribute them to that society and no other. In short, we are in at the emergence of the concept of the uniqueness and individuality of an age, an outlook, a civilisation.

In its extreme form belief in an inexorable *Zeitgeist* which shapes all the phenomena of an age or a culture led to the dogmatic imposition of a priori straitjackets, idealist or materialist, on accounts of the past: inconvenient facts were eliminated or glossed over if they did not fit the theory. Even such scrupulous writers as Max Weber and Huizinga are occasionally guilty of this, not to speak of fanatical schematisers like Spengler or Pokrovsky. Nevertheless the notion of a single central style which permeates an epoch has, by providing pointers to connections and similarities between phenomena in disparate regions of human activity, transformed the art of attribution and created the discipline of cultural history.

No doubt the discovery of the native cultures in Asia or America increased awareness of the diversity of customs and attitudes. But the revelation of a Roman culture which was remoter than had

[1] As, for example, despite his claims and the claims made for him by some of his interpreters, was done by Voltaire.

[2] See p. 161 above, note 1.

been supposed before was, in one sense, more important still. The societies of American Indians or Siamese could be represented as primitive versions of our own civilisation: admired by some as shaped by man's true nature before his corruption and decadence, dismissed by others as immature, rudimentary and barbarous. Even the admired Chinese were conceded by Voltaire to be a case of arrested development. Rome was a different matter: it was the very paradigm of a fully developed civilisation, not merely a step towards our own, nor a falling away from it. Some preferred the Republic, others the Augustan age or that of the Antonines: in either case these ages were represented as the acme of cultivation. Voltaire thought, and the Enlightenment followed him, that Periclean Athens or Augustan Rome or Florence during the Renaissance, or France under Louis XIV, were peaks of a single range of ascending human progress. Yet if Rome and Greece at their best were not at all like the modern – post-Renaissance – West, it followed that more than one equally authentic, equally developed culture was possible, and that such cultures could be widely heterogeneous, could, indeed, be incomparable and incommensurable. This entailed genuine pluralism, and an explicit refutation of the belief that man everywhere, at all times, possessed an identical nature which, in its quest for self-fulfilment, sought after the same ends, and that this, indeed, was precisely what constituted man's human essence. Yet this could not be so if different cultures had their own ideals, their own irreducible peculiarities. 'Nothing', said Leonardo Bruni, a fifteenth-century humanist, in a celebrated sentence, 'is said in Greek that cannot be said in Latin.'[1] This is precisely what Vico denied[2] and sought to refute in his works: everything is uniquely what it is; there are similarities, echoes, parallels, but no central identity that makes translation from one milieu to another wholly possible (or, as Herder would later add, desirable). If the concepts of natural law or of a permanent human nature were to be retained, they would have to become far more flexible and elastic. Such modification is

[1] '... nihil Graece dictum est, quod Latine dici non possit'. 'De interpretatione recta' (c.1420): p. 95 in *Leonardi Bruni Aretino humanistisch-philosophische Schriften*, ed. Hans Baron (Leipzig and Berlin, 1928).

[2] So, but with a good deal less emphasis, did Leibniz in 'Ermahnung an die Teutsche, ihren Verstand und Sprache besser zu üben...' (early 1680s): see pp. 307 ff. in Paul Pietsch, *Leibniz und die deutsche Sprache* [*Wissenschaftliche Beihefte zur Zeitschrift des allgemeinen deutschen Sprachvereins*, series 4, Nos 29–30 (1907–8)]; also *Nouveaux Essais*, book 3, chapter 9.

compatible neither with strict Thomism, nor with the doctrines of Descartes or Spinoza or Voltaire. The notion that there exist eternal and unalterable truths, laws, rules of conduct which entail ends of life which any man might, in theory, have recognised in any time and in any place, and the discovery and pursuit of which is the sole and sufficient goal of all human behaviour, is the central principle of the Enlightenment. Its rejection, with its appeal for a far wider psychological imagination, marks a decisive turning-point in the history of Western thought.

My thesis, although I offer it tentatively, is that these two notions – of understanding through 'philology' and of the succession (or simultaneous existence) of equally authentic, yet autonomous, cultures which cannot be assimilated to one another – do more to explain the origins of Vico's conception of what cultures are and how we can come to know them, than the philosophical or theological or scientific ideas more commonly investigated by those in search of his sources. It seems to me *prima facie* more probable that legal, historical and literary scholarship were the regions closest to his lifelong interests.[1]

Nothing, needless to say, is thereby taken away from his claim to originality. The application of *verum/factum* to history remains indefeasibly his own. It is the fusion of this far older Christian doctrine with the Renaissance notion of the interrelation of different aspects of the spiritual activities of different societies that underlies Vico's distinction between nature and culture, between events and acts. This, in its turn, distinguishes what is history from what is not: what can and what cannot be 'entered' by the human mind. This mind is, as often as not, incarnated in institutions and traditions and the *sensus communis* of entire nations or all mankind, as, guided by divine Providence, it seeks to understand itself and its past in the many guises which it has assumed in its unceasing effort to explain and master itself and the external world. It was this synthesis that transformed the scattered insights of jurists or antiquaries, or the historians influenced by them, into a powerful and fruitful historical method.[2] After everything that is

[1] For the extent of Vico's legal learning, see Giuseppe Giarrizzo, op. cit. (p. 140 above, note 1), where we are assured that it stretched 'from Vulteius to Godefroy, from Cujas to Hotman' (p. 113). Moreover Huppert tells us (p. 167) that the French historical writers of the sixteenth century were widely read.

[2] Why has this probability, even if it cannot be demonstrated by references in Vico's works to actual names (as if ideas do not travel without labels, and men

absurd, ephemeral, confused, pedantic, trivial in Vico's work has been forgotten, what remains is the new conception of what men are. He dissolves the concept of a static human nature – the unaltering kernel, 'quod ubique, quod semper, quod ab omnibus creditum est'[1] – and replaces it with a pattern of systematic change. Historical insight for him is a form of men's awareness of themselves as purposive beings whose modes of thought, feeling and action alter in response to new needs and activities, which generate new institutions, entire new civilisations, that incarnate men's nature. Men are able to understand these civilisations, no matter how remote from their own, in a fashion different from that in which they can know the external world, because they are largely man-made. From this stems the notion of cultural style, which in its turn led to such notions as the *Zeitgeist* and the *Volksgeist* and groups of related ideas, vague and treacherous concepts much misused by metaphysicians who have treated them as a queer species of independent causal forces. Nevertheless, this notion points to an easily neglected truth: that all classification, selection, interpretation is in the end subjective, that is, does not correspond with, or fit into, 'objective' grooves in the external world, as the great mathematically minded realists had supposed; and therefore (even though Vico himself claimed objective validity for his schema) that, in Burckhardt's famous words, 'the outlines of a cultural period may present a different picture to every beholder'.[2]

cannot be influenced by Marx or Freud unless they mention them by name), found no echo in the Italian commentators – from Duni and Cuoco to Croce, Corsano, above all Nicolini, who devoted his long and honourable life to reconstructing every detail of Vico's life and thought and intellectual descent? Why is it assumed that Vico cannot have had forerunners outside Italy and the Roman Empire? Why should a host of minor schoolmen and provincial, not to say local, Neapolitan writers be (reasonably enough) thought worthy of mention as possible sources of his ideas, when the great luminaries in a field that was peculiarly close to Vico's interest, men of European fame and influence, are not once so much as referred to in this connection? Can this be because they are Frenchmen, and the war between the two great styles of thought and writing, in which Vico himself took part, is not over yet? Is this a case of that nationalistic *boria* against which Vico protests as an obstacle to the discovery of truth in history? Whatever the explanation, the fact itself remains exceedingly puzzling.

[1] loc. cit. (p. 59 above, note 3).

[2] Jacob Burckhardt, *Die Cultur der Renaissance in Italien: ein Versuch* (Basel, 1860), p. 1.

Over everything in Vico towers the *idée maîtresse* that what we call the nature of institutions is their history, 'nothing but their coming into being at certain times and in certain guises. Whenever the time and guise are thus and so, such and not otherwise are the institutions that come into being.'[1] The world of primitives is literally a different world from that of the sophisticated, as the world of the rich differs from that of the poor, or the world of believers from that of unbelievers; it follows that no single language is ever wholly translatable without residue into any other, for each categorises reality in different ways. These ideas, which broke with the tradition that began with the Greeks and ended with the Enlightenment, have profoundly altered men's outlook. It is this transformation, among others, that makes it difficult, if not impossible, for those whom it has affected to return to the conceptions of human nature and the real world held by Descartes or Spinoza or Voltaire or Gibbon, or, for that matter, Russell or Carnap in our own day; or to the conventional conception of the function of history (offered, for example, by Leibniz) as satisfying curiosity about origins, disclosing the uniformity of nature, doing justice to men of worth, offering support to revelation, and teaching useful lessons by means of examples. Vico attacked this view all his life; with much obscurity and confusion, but always vehemently, and with scattered insights of widely varying value, but, at times, of arresting genius. The controversy in which he played a major role has not ended; but at least the lines are today more clearly drawn.

[1] NS 147.

HERDER AND THE ENLIGHTENMENT

We live in a world we ourselves create.[1]

I

HERDER'S FAME rests on the fact that he is the father of the related notions of nationalism, historicism and the *Volksgeist*, one of the leaders of the romantic revolt against classicism, rationalism and faith in the omnipotence of scientific method – in short, the most formidable of the adversaries of the French *philosophes* and their German disciples. Whereas they – or at least the best known among them, d'Alembert, Helvétius, Holbach and, with qualifications, Voltaire and Diderot, Wolff and Reimarus – believed that reality was ordered in terms of universal, timeless, objective, unalterable laws which rational investigation could discover, Herder maintained that every activity, situation, historical period or civilisation possessed a unique character of its own; so that the attempt to reduce such phenomena to combinations of uniform elements, and to describe or analyse them in terms of universal rules, tended to obliterate precisely those crucial differences which constituted the specific quality of the object under study, whether in nature or in history. To the notions of universal laws, absolute principles, final truths, eternal models and standards in ethics or aesthetics, physics or mathematics, he opposed a radical distinction between the method appropriate to the study of physical nature and that called for by the changing and developing spirit of man. He is credited with having put new life into the notion of social patterns, social growth, the vital importance of considering qualitative as well as quantitative factors – the impalpable and the imponderable, which the concepts of natural science ignore or deny. Preoccupied with the mysteries of the creative process, whether in individuals or groups, he launched (so we are told) a general attack on rationalism with its tendency to generalise,

[1] viii 252.

abstract, assimilate the dissimilar, unify the disparate; and, above all, on its avowed purpose, to create a corpus of systematic knowledge which in principle would be capable of answering all intelligible questions – the idea of a unified science of all there is. In the course of this propaganda against rationalism, scientific method and the universal authority of intelligible laws, he is held to have stimulated the growth of particularism, nationalism and literary, religious and political irrationalism, and thereby to have played a major role in transforming human thought and action in the generation that followed.

This account, which is to be found in some of the best-known monographs on Herder's thought, is broadly true, but oversimplified. His views did have a profound and revolutionary effect upon later thought and practice. He has been praised by some as the champion of faith against reason, poetical and historical imagination against the mechanical application of rules, insight against logic, life against death; by others he has been classed with confused, or retrograde, or irrationalist thinkers who misunderstood what they had learned from the Enlightenment, and fed the stream of German chauvinism and obscurantism; still others have sought to find common ground between him and Comte, or Darwin, or Wagner, or modern sociologists.

It is not my purpose in this study to pronounce directly upon these questions, although I am inclined to think that the extent of his acquaintance with, and fidelity to, the natural sciences of his day has often been seriously underestimated. He was fascinated and influenced by the findings of the sciences no less than Goethe, and, like him, thought that false general inferences were often drawn from them. Herder was, all his life, a sharp and remorseless critic of the Encyclopaedists, but he accepted, indeed he acclaimed, the scientific theories on which they based their social and ethical doctrines; he merely thought that these conclusions could not follow from the newly established laws of physics or biology, since they plainly contradicted what any sensitive observer, since the beginning of social self-consciousness, knew to be true of human experience and activity.[1] But it is not Herder's attitude to the natural science of his day that I propose to discuss. I wish to

[1] On this see the excellent studies by H. B. Nisbet, *Herder and the Philosophy and History of Science* (Cambridge, 1970), and by G. A. Wells, *Herder and After: A Study of the Development of Sociology* (The Hague, 1959).

confine myself, so far as possible (and at times it is not), to what is truly original in Herder's views, and by no means to all of this: in particular I shall try to examine three cardinal ideas in the rich welter of his thought, ideas which have had great influence for two centuries and are novel, important and interesting in themselves. These ideas, which go against the main stream of the thought of his time, I have called *populism*, *expressionism* and *pluralism*.[1]

Let me begin by conceding the most obvious of Herder's debts to other thinkers.[2] Herder's thesis that the proper subject of the historical sciences is the life of communities and not the exploits of individuals – statesmen, soldiers, kings, dynasties, adventurers and other famous men – had been stated by Voltaire and Hume and Montesquieu, by Schlözer and Gatterer, and before them by French writers on history in the sixteenth and early seventeenth centuries, and with incomparable imagination and originality by Vico. There is, so far as I know, no conclusive evidence that Herder had read Vico's *Scienza nuova* until at least twenty years after his own theory of history had been formed; but if he had not read Vico he had heard of him, and probably read Wegelin, and Cesarotti's Homeric commentaries. Moreover, the idea that great poets expressed the mind and experience of their societies, and were their truest spokesmen, was widespread during Herder's formative years. Shaftesbury celebrated artists as the inspired voices of their times, von Muralt, Bodmer and Breitinger in

---

[1] I shall necessarily have to omit much else that is relevant and interesting: for example, Herder's dominant influence on romanticism, vitalism and existentialism, and, above all, on social psychology, which he all but founded; as well as the use made of his imprecise, often inconsistent, but always many-faceted and stimulating thought by such writers as the Schlegels and Jakob Grimm (especially in their philological excursions), Savigny (who applied to law Herder's notion of organic national growth), Görres (whose nationalism is rooted in, even if it distorts, Herder's vision), Hegel (whose concepts of becoming and of the growth and personality of impersonal institutions begin their lives in Herder's pages), as well as historical geographers, social anthropologists, philosophers of language and of history, and historical writers in the nineteenth and twentieth centuries. My principal reason for choosing the three ideas on which I intend to concentrate is that they are conceptions of the first order of originality and historical importance, the origins and properties of which have not received sufficient notice. My purpose is to do justice to Herder's originality rather than his influence.

[2] The best discussion of this topic known to me occurs in Max Rouché's excellent introduction to his edition and French translation of Herder's *Auch eine Philosophie der Geschichte* (Paris, n.d.), pp. 92–105.

Switzerland placed Shakespeare and Milton and the old German Minnesingers far above the idols of the French Enlightenment. Bodmer corresponded on these topics with Vico's devoted admirer, Count Pietro Calepio;[1] the battle between literary historicism and the neo-classicism of Paris and its German followers was in full swing in Herder's youth. This may perhaps be sufficient to account for the striking resemblance between the views of Vico and Herder, and obviate the long and desperate search for more direct lines. In any case the notion of cultural patterns was far from new in his day, as the ironical title of his early *Yet Another Philosophy of History* was meant to emphasise. The case for it had been presented effectively, if in somewhat general terms, by his arch-enemy Voltaire in the celebrated *Essai sur les moeurs* and elsewhere.

So, too, the notion that the variety of civilisations is, to a large degree, determined by differences of physical and geographical factors – referred to by the general name of 'climate' – had become, since Montesquieu, a commonplace. It occurs, before Montesquieu, in the thought of Bodin, Saint-Evremond, the abbé Dubos and their followers.

As for the dangers of cultural arrogance – the tendency to judge ancient societies in terms of modern values – this had been made a central issue by Herder's older contemporary Lessing (even though Lessing may well have been influenced by him). Nor had anyone written more pungently than Voltaire against the European habit of dismissing as inferior remote civilisations, such as that of China, which he had extolled in order to expose the ridiculous vanity, exclusiveness and fanaticism of the 'barbarous' Judaeo-Christian outlook that recognised no values besides its own. The fact that Herder turned this weapon against Voltaire himself, and accused him of a narrowly *dix-huitième* and Parisian point of view, does not alter the fact that the head and source of all opposition to Europocentrism was the Patriarch himself. Voltaire had praised ancient Egypt, and Winckelmann the Greeks; Boulainvilliers had spoken of the superiority of the Northern nations, and so had Mallet in his celebrated history of Denmark; Beat Ludwig von Muralt in his *Letters on the English and the French* had, as early as 1725, drawn a contrast between the independent spirit of the Swiss and English, particularly English writers, and the conventional

[1] There is an illuminating discussion of this in Carlo Antoni's *Lo storicismo* (Turin, 1957).

mannerisms of the French; Hurd, Millar and, after them, Justus Möser sang the praises of medieval Europe at the very height of the contemptuous dismissal of the Dark Ages by Voltaire and the *Encyclopédie*. They were, it is true, a minority, and, while Justus Möser's paeans to the free life of the ancient Saxons before they were so brutally civilised by Charlemagne may have been influenced by Herder, they were not created by him.

There was new emphasis on cultural differences, and protest against the authority of timeless general laws and rules. The notorious lack of historical sense that made Racine and Corneille represent classical or exotic oriental personages in the clothes and with the manners of the courtiers of Louis XIV was adversely commented on by Dubos and successfully satirised by Saint-Evremond. At the other end of the scale, some German pietists, Arnold and Zinzendorf among others, laid great stress on the proposition that every religion had a unique insight peculiar to itself, and Arnold based on this belief a bold and passionate plea for toleration of deviations from Lutheran orthodoxy, and even of heresies and unbelief.

The notion of the spirit of a nation or a culture had been central not only to Vico and Montesquieu, but to the famous publicist Friedrich Karl von Moser, whom Herder read and knew, to Bodmer and Breitinger, to Hamann and to Zimmermann. Bolingbroke had spoken of the division of men into nationalities as being deeply rooted in Nature herself. By the middle of the century there were plenty of Celtomaniacs and Gothomaniacs – notably Irishmen and Scotsmen who, even without the aid of Ossian, praised the virtues of Gaelic or Germanic tribes and represented them as being morally and socially superior not only to ancient Greeks or Romans, but still more to the decadent civilisation of modern Latin and Mediterranean peoples. Rousseau's celebrated letter to the Poles, advising them to resist forcible assimilation by Russia by stubbornly clinging to their national customs and characteristics, unacceptable as this was to the cosmopolitanism of his time, exhibits the same spirit.

As for the notion of society as an organism, with which Burke and Herder made such play, it was by this time very old indeed. The use of organic metaphors is at least as old as Aristotle; nobody had used them more lavishly than medieval writers; they are the heart and centre of John of Salisbury's political tracts, and are a weapon consciously used by Hooker and Pascal against the new scientific-mechanical conceptions. There was certainly nothing novel in this notion; it represents, on the contrary, if anything, a deliberate return to older views of social life. This is no less true of Burke, who was equally prone to the use of analogies drawn from the new biological sciences; I know of no evidence that Burke had read or heard of Justus Möser's or Herder's ideas.

Differences of ideals – of what made men and societies happy – had been illustrated vividly by Adam Ferguson in his highly original *Essay on the History of Civil Society*, which Herder had read.[1]

In his general explanation of events in naturalistic terms, whether geophysical or biological, Herder adopted the normal approach of the followers of Locke, Helvétius and the Encyclopaedists, and indeed of the entire Enlightenment. Unlike his teacher Hamann, Herder was decisively influenced by the findings of natural science; he gave them a vitalistic interpretation, though not the mystical or theosophical one favoured by Hemsterhuis, Lavater and other 'intuitivists'.

The ancient notion of a single great cosmic force of nature, embodied in finite, dynamic centres, had been given new life by Leibniz and was common to all his disciples.

So, too, the idea of a divine plan realised in human history had passed in uninterrupted succession from the Old Testament and its Jewish interpreters to the Christian Fathers, and then to the classical formulation of Bossuet.

Parallels between primitive peoples remote from one another in time and space – Homeric Greeks and early Romans on the one hand, and Red Indians or Germanic tribes on the other – had been put forward by Fontenelle and by the French Jesuit, *Père* Lafitau; the protagonists of this approach in the early years of the century, especially English writers such as Blackwell and the Wartons, owed much to these speculations. It had become part and parcel of Homeric scholarship, which flourished both in England and, under the impulsion of Vico, in Italy. Certainly Cesarotti had perceived the wider implications of this kind of approach to literature for comparative philology and anthropology; and when Diderot in the *Encyclopédie*, in the course of a general article devoted to Greek

[1] Harold Laski's description of Ferguson as a 'pinchbeck Montesquieu' throws light only on the quality of Laski's critical judgement, in this instance probably a mere echo of Leslie Stephen. Harold J. Laski, *Political Thought in England: From Locke to Bentham* (New York and London, 1920), p. 174.

philosophy, dismissed Homer as 'a theologian, philosopher and poet', quoting the view of a 'well-known man' that he was unlikely to be read much in the future,[1] this was a characteristically partisan *boutade*, in the spirit of Descartes and Pierre Bayle, against reverence for the past and dreary erudition, a belated echo of the battle of the ancients and the moderns. Nor was the Bible itself, which Vico had not dared to touch, left unmolested. Philosophical and historical criticism of the text, which had begun with Spinoza and *Père* Simon in the previous century, had been carried on cautiously – despite some opposition from Christian orthodoxy, both Catholic and Protestant – with strict regard to the rules of secular scholarship. Astruc in France, Lowth in England, and after them Michaelis in Germany (and Denmark), treated the Bible as a monument of oriental literature composed at various dates. Everyone knows of Gibbon's debt to Mosheim's coldly secular treatment of early Christian ecclesiastical history. Herder, who was not a trained researcher, had plenty to lean upon.

The same is true of Herder's linguistic patriotism. The defence of the German language had been vigorously taken up by Martin Opitz in the early years of the seventeenth century, and had since then formed part of the conscious programme of theologians, men of letters, and philosophers. Mencke, Horneck, Moscherosch, Logau and Gryphius are names that may not mean a great deal to English readers today; but in the two centuries that followed the Reformation they fought with stubbornness and success under Luther's banner against both Latin and French; and more famous men, Pufendorf and Leibniz, Thomasius and Wolff, Hamann and Lessing, were also engaged in this campaign that had begun long before. Once again, Herder began with something that had by that time become established as a traditional German attitude.

As for the famous reversal of values – the triumph of the concrete over the abstract; the sharp turn towards the immediate, the given, the experienced, and, above all, away from abstractions, theories, generalisations and stylised patterns; and the restoration of quality to its old status above quantity, and of the immediate data of the senses to their primacy over the primary qualities of physics – it is in this cause that Hamann made his name. It formed

---

[1] Diderot in the *Encyclopédie*, s.v. 'Grecs (philosophie des)', p. 908, col. 1. Diderot does at least protest that the view he quotes 'shows a lack of philosophy and taste', and the *Encyclopédie* also contains articles on the *Iliad* and the *Odyssey*.

the basis of Lavater's 'physiognomical' researches; it was at least as old as Shaftesbury; it is pertinent to the works of the young Burke.

The reaction against the reorganisation of knowledge and society by the application of rationalist and scientific principles was in full swing by the time Herder came upon the scene. Rousseau had struck against it in 1750 with his first *Discourse*. Seven years later his moralising and reactionary letter to d'Alembert denouncing the stage had marked a total break with the party of the *philosophes*, as both sides swiftly recognised. In Germany this mood was strongly reinforced by the inward-looking tradition of the pietist movement. The human solidarity and mutual respect of these small groups, inspired by their burning Protestant faith; their belief in the unadorned truth, in the power of goodness, in the inner light; their contempt for outward forms; their rigid sense of duty and discipline; their perpetual self-examination; their obsession with the presence of evil, which at times took hysterical or sadistic forms and generated a good deal of unctuous hypocrisy; and above all their preoccupation with the life of the spirit, which alone liberated men from the bonds of the flesh and of nature – all these strains are very strong in those who were brought up in this stern atmosphere, and particularly in the East Prussians, Knutzen, Hamann, Herder, Kant. Although a great intellectual gulf divides Kant from Herder, they share a common element: a craving for spiritual self-determination as against half-conscious drifting along the streams of uncriticised dogma (whether theological or scientific), for moral independence (whether of individuals or groups), and above all for moral salvation.

If Herder had done no more than create a genuine synthesis out of these attitudes and doctrines, and built with them, if not a system, at any rate a coherent *Weltanschauung* destined to have a decisive influence on the literature and thought of his country, this alone would have been a high enough achievement to earn for him a unique place in the history of civilisation. Invention is not everything. If one were called upon to show what is strictly original in the individual doctrines of Locke or Rousseau, Bentham or Marx, Aquinas, or even Hegel, one could, without much difficulty, trace virtually all their doctrines to antecedent 'sources'. Yet this does not derogate from the originality and genius of these thinkers. 'Small change for a napoleon is not a napoleon.' It is not, however, my purpose to evaluate the work of Herder as a whole, but only to consider certain authentically *sui generis* doctrines which he originated; to discuss them not only for the sake of historical justice, but also as views that are peculiarly relevant and interesting in our own time. Herder's final claim need not rest upon what was, if I am right, most original in his thought. For his vast general influence has sometimes, paradoxically, served to overshadow that which he, virtually alone, launched upon the world.

II

Let me return to the three topics of this study, namely:

1 *Populism*: the belief in the value of belonging to a group or a culture, which, for Herder at least, is not political, and is indeed, to some degree, anti-political, different from, and even opposed to, nationalism.

2 *Expressionism*:[1] the doctrine that human activity in general, and art in particular, express the entire personality of the individual or the group, and are intelligible only to the degree to which they do so. Still more specifically, expressionism claims that all the works of men are above all voices speaking, are not objects detached from their makers, are part of a living process of communication between persons and not independently existing entities, beautiful or ugly, interesting or boring, upon which external observers may direct the cool and dispassionate gaze with which scientists – or anyone not given to pantheism or mysticism – look on objects in nature. This is connected with the further notions that every form of human self-expression is in some sense artistic, and that self-expression is part of the essence of human beings as such; which in turn entail such distinctions as those between integral and divided, or committed and uncommitted (that is, unfulfilled), lives; and thence lead to the concept of various hindrances, human and non-human, to the self-realisation which is the richest and most harmonious form of self-expression that all creatures, whether or not they are aware of it, live for.

3 *Pluralism*: the belief not merely in the multiplicity, but in the incommensurability, of the values of different cultures and societies, and, in addition, in the incompatibility of equally valid ideals,

---

[1] I use this term in its widest, most generic sense, with no specific reference to the expressionist painters, writers and composers of the early decades of the twentieth century.

together with the implied revolutionary corollary that the classical notions of an ideal man and of an ideal society are intrinsically incoherent and meaningless.

Each of these three theses is relatively novel; all are incompatible with the central moral, historical and aesthetic doctrines of the Enlightenment. They are not independent of each other. Everything in the illimitable, varied and exceedingly rich panorama which Herder's works present is interwoven. Indeed, the notion of unity in difference, still more that of differences in unity, the tension of the one and the many, is his obsessive *idée maîtresse*. Hence the recurrence through all his discussions of a constant theme: the 'organic' oneness of personality with the form of life that it leads, the empirical and metaphysical unity of the physical and the mental, of intellect, will, feeling, imagination, language, action – distinctions and classifications that he regarded as at best superficial, at worst profoundly misleading. Hence the stress on the unity of thought and feeling, of theory and practice, of the public and the private, and his single-minded, life-long and heroic effort to see the universe as a single process.

The celebrated words with which he opens his most famous and ambitious work, *Ideas about the Philosophy of History of Mankind* – 'Our earth is a star among stars'[1] – are very characteristic. There follow chapters on geology, climate, mineral, vegetable and animal life, and lessons in physical geography, until, at last, man is reached. There is a corresponding attempt to link all the arts and all the sciences, to represent religious, artistic, social, political, economic, biological, philosophical experience as facets of one activity; and since the pattern is one, fact and value are not divided (*pace* Hume and Kant, with whose works Herder was only too familiar). To understand a thing was, for him, to see how it could be viewed as it was viewed, assessed as it was assessed, valued as it was valued, in a given context, by a particular culture or tradition. To grasp what a belief, a piece of ritual, a myth, a poem or a linguistic usage meant to a Homeric Greek, a Livonian peasant, an ancient Hebrew, an American Indian, what part it played in his life, was for Herder to be able not merely to give a scientific or common-sense explanation, but to give a reason for or justification of the activity in question, or at least to go a long way towards this. For to explain

[1] xiii 13.

human experiences or attitudes is to be able to transpose oneself by sympathetic imagination into the situation of the human beings who are to be 'explained'; and this amounts to understanding and communicating the coherence of a particular way of life, feeling, action; and thereby the validity of the given act or action, the part it plays in the life and outlook which are 'natural' in the situation. Explanation and justification, reference to causes and to purposes, to the visible and the invisible, statements of fact and their assessment in terms of the historical standards of value relevant to them, melt into one another, and seem to Herder to belong to a single type, and not several types, of thinking. Herder is one of the originators of the secular doctrine of the unity of fact and value, theory and practice, 'is' and 'ought', intellectual judgement and emotional commitment, thought and action.

The sharpest critics of Herder have always conceded the power and breadth of his imagination. He did have an astonishing capacity for conceiving a great variety of actual and possible societies in the past and the present, and an unexampled warmth of sympathy for them all. He was inspired by the possibility of reconstructing forms of life as such, and he delighted in bringing out their individual shape, the fullness of human experience embodied in them: the odder, the more extraordinary a culture or an individual, the better pleased he was. He can hardly condemn anything that displays colour or uniqueness: Indians, Americans and Persians, Greece and Palestine, Arminius and Machiavelli, Shakespeare and Savonarola seem to him equally fascinating. He deeply hates the forces that make for uniformity, for the assimilation, whether in life or in the books of historians, of one culture or way of life to another. He conscientiously looks for uniformities, but what fascinates him is the exception. He condemns the erection of walls between one genus and another; but he seeks for the greatest possible number of distinctions of species within a genus, and of individuals within the species. Hamann had preached to him the need to preserve sensitiveness to specific historical and cultural phenomena, to avoid becoming deadened by the passion for classification and generalisation demanded by networks of tidy concepts, a fatal tendency which he attributed to the natural sciences and their slaves, the Frenchmen who wished to transform everything by the application of scientific method. Like Hamann, Herder preserved his childlike impressionability – his capacity to react spontaneously to the jagged, irregular, not always describable data provided by the senses, by imagination, by religious revelation, by history, by art. He did not hasten to refer them to their appropriate cases in the museum of concepts; he was penetrated through and through by the new spirit of empiricism, of the sacredness of facts. Not so much as Hamann, but more than even Lessing and Diderot, and incomparably more than such official materialists and 'sensualists' as Condillac or Helvétius, Herder avoided the temptation to reduce the heterogeneous flow of experience to homogeneous units, to label them and fit them into theoretical frameworks in order to be able to predict and control them. The notorious luxuriance and formlessness of his ideas is due at least as much to his sense of the complexity of the facts themselves as to a naturally rhapsodical and turbid mind. As a writer he is exuberant and disordered, but not obscure or vague. Even at his most rapt he is not somnambulistic or self-intoxicated; he does not, even in his most lyrical moments, fly from the facts to an ideal heaven, like the German metaphysical poets of his time, Gleim or Uz or Klopstock or even Goethe on occasions. Great scientists and philosophers have often made their impact by violently exaggerating their original insights. But Herder cannot let go of what he sees, feels, hears, learns. His sense of the texture of reality is concrete, while his analytical powers are feeble. The three original theses which form the subject of this study display this again and again, and have consequently often been a source of irritation to tidier, clearer, logically more gifted thinkers.

III

Let me begin with Herder's populism, or his idea of what it is to belong to a group. Everyone seems agreed that Herder began as a typical, almost routine, defender of the great ideas of eighteenth-century enlightenment, that is, as a humanitarian, a cosmopolitan and a pacifist. Later, so it seems to be assumed, he moved towards a more reactionary position, the subordination of reason and intellect to nationalism, Gallophobia, intuition, uncritical faith and belief in tradition. Was this not, after all, the evolution in some degree of other thinkers of his and the succeeding generation in Germany? Almost without exception, they began by welcoming the French Revolution rapturously, planting trees of liberty, and denouncing as obsolete and brutally oppressive the rule of the three hundred German princes, until, horrified by the Terror and

wounded by the military humiliation of Germany by the armies of
Revolutionary France and, still more, those of Napoleon, they
turned into patriots, reactionaries and romantic irrationalists. Was
not this the path pursued by Fichte (above all Fichte), Görres,
Novalis and the Schlegels, Schleiermacher and Tieck, Gentz and
Schelling, and to some degree even by the great libertarian Schiller?
Were not Goethe and Humboldt (and Georg Forster, though he
died before the reaction set in) almost alone in their unswerving
fidelity to reason, toleration and the unity of mankind, in their
freedom from nationalism, and, in common with Kant and Hegel, in
their loathing for all forms of collective emotional afflatus? Is it not
reasonable to assume that this process of retreat from reason took
place in Herder too? True, he died before the most crushing defeats
had been inflicted by Napoleon on the German armies and princes;
yet was it not the case that Herder began as a cosmopolitan and
ended as a nationalist? Here too, then, so it would seem, wounded
national pride, and perhaps age and the cooling of youthful
Utopianism, had had their inescapable effect. Yet this view seems
to me untenable. Whatever may have been the evolution of Fichte
or Friedrich Schlegel, Herder's form of nationalism remained
unaltered throughout his life. His national feeling was not political
and never became so, nor did he abandon or modify the peculiar
brand of universalism with which he had begun, whether or not
the two tendencies were consistent (the least of his concerns),
throughout his long and voluminous intellectual activity.

As early as 1765, in an address composed in Riga (where at the
age of twenty-one he occupied the post of a Lutheran preacher in
that officially Russian city) in answer to the question 'Have we still
a republic and a fatherland like the Ancients?',[1] Herder declared
that this was no longer the case. In Greece the strength and the
glory of the *polis* were the supreme goals of all free men. Religion,
morals, tradition – every aspect of human activity stemmed from,
and was directed to, maintaining the city, and any danger to it was
a danger to all that these men were and lived by; if it fell,
everything fell with it. But then, he went on to say, Christianity
came and the horizons of mankind became immeasurably wider.
Christianity, he explained, is a universal religion: it embraces all
men and all peoples; it transcends all local and temporary loyalties
in the worship of what is universal and eternal.

[1] i 13–28.

This thesis was highly characteristic of the Christian humanism of the German *Aufklärung*, and, despite all that has been said to the contrary, Herder never abandoned this point of view. His central belief was expressed towards the end of his life in words similar to those of his early writings: 'To brag of one's country is the stupidest form of boastfulness . . . What is a nation? A great wild garden full of bad plants and good'; vices and follies mingle with virtues and merit. What Don Quixote will break a lance for this Dulcinea?[1] Patriotism was one thing, nationalism another: an innocent attachment to family, language, one's own city, one's own country, its traditions, is not to be condemned. But he goes on to say that aggressive nationalism is detestable in all its manifestations, and wars are mere crimes.[2] This is so because all large wars are essentially civil wars, since men are brothers, and wars are a form of abominable fratricide. 'One fatherland ranged against another in bloody battle is the worst barbarism in the human vocabulary.'[3] A year later he adds: 'We can be nobler heroes than Achilles, loftier patriots than Horatius Cocles.'[4] These views can scarcely be due merely to the fact, by which they are sometimes explained, that political nationalism would have been too unrealistic an outlook in a feeble and divided country governed by several hundred hereditary despots; so that even to look for it there demonstrates a lack of historical sense. Yet the Italians, who were no less divided and politically impotent, had developed a distinct craving for political unification which dated back at least to Machiavelli, even though the prevailing social and political conditions in Italy were not so very unlike those of eighteenth-century Germany.

Herder's attitude is clearly the normal enlightened attitude of his time; the point, however, is that he did not abandon it. He believed in kinship, social solidarity, *Volkstum*, nationhood, but to the end of his life he detested and denounced every form of centralisation, coercion and conquest, which were embodied and symbolised both for him, and for his teacher Hamann, in the accursed State. Nature creates nations, not States.[5] The State is an instrument of happiness for a group, not for men as such.[6] There is nothing against which he thunders more eloquently than imperialism – the crushing of one community by another, the elimination of local cultures

---

[1] xvii 211.   [2] See xvii 230 ff.   [3] xvii 319.   [4] xviii 86.
[5] xiii 339–41, 375.   [6] xiii 340.

trampled under the jackboot of some conqueror. He vies with Justus Möser in his tenderness towards long-lived traditions and institutions embodied in particular forms of life that have created unity and continuity in a human community. He cares nothing for *virtù* in the Renaissance sense of the term. Alexander the Great, Julius Caesar, Charlemagne are not heroes for him. The basis of the State is conquest, the history of States is the history of violence, a bloodstained story of aggression. The state is Ixion's wheel and calls for meaningless self-immolation. Why should hundreds suffer hunger and cold to satisfy the whim of a crowned madman, or the dreams bred by the fancy of a *philosophe*?[1]

This may be directed specifically at Frederick the Great and his French advisers, but the import of it is universal. All rule of men over fellow men is unnatural. True human relations are those of father and son, husband and wife, sons, brothers, friends, men; these terms express natural relations which make people happy. All that the State has given us is contradictions and conquests, and, perhaps worst of all, dehumanisation.[2] What pleasure is there in being 'a blind cog in a machine'?[3] God has divided the world by mountains and oceans in order to prevent some fearful Nimrod from conquering the whole. The *Ideen* anticipate socialist historians in representing the history of conquerors as the history of man-hunters. Despite his vow to look with a sympathetic, or at least impartial, eye upon all cultures and all nations, he cannot bring himself to forgive Rome for crushing the cultures of the peoples it had conquered, not even that of Carthage. There may be merit in efficiency and unity, but it is for him more than offset by the tragedy of the destruction; that is, by the evil of the barbarous disregard of so many spontaneous, natural forms of human self-expression: 'Whom nature separated by language, customs, character, let no man artificially join together by chemistry.'[4] This is what the Romans tried to do and how the whole Roman Empire was held together. And its 'Holy' successor was no better – it was

---

[1] ibid.
[2] e.g. xiii 341: 'Millions of people on the globe live without States ... Father and mother, man and wife, child and brother, friend and man – these are natural relationships through which we become happy; what the State can give us is an artificial contrivance; unfortunately it can also deprive us of something far more essential – rob us of ourselves.'
[3] xiii 340.   [4] xviii 206.

an unnatural monster, an absurd clamping together of disparate cultures, 'a lion's head with a dragon's tail, an eagle's wing, a bear's paw, ["glued together"] in one unpatriotic structure of a State'.[1] The Jews, 'parasitic' money-lenders now,[2] were at least not self-worshippers; they are praised for not having made Palestine the source and centre of the world, for not having idealised their ancestors, and for not deriving their genealogy from gods and demigods (it is this last that has enabled them to survive the Diaspora).[3] Empires, especially multi-national ones (a 'wild mingling of various tribes and peoples under one sceptre'),[4] rest on force; they have feet of clay and must collapse. Theocracies that are founded upon some non-political principle, a spiritual or religious force – China or Egypt, for example, to take only non-Christian faiths – have proved correspondingly more durable. The sword of the spirit is better than mere brute force: not even the acutest poverty, the deepest squalor, still less ambition and love of power, entitle men to have recourse to violence. Like Möser, Herder laments the fact that the Germans are poor, hungry and despised; that Luther's widow had to beg for help from the King of Denmark; that Kepler died of hunger; that men of German speech have been scattered and exiled to England, America, Russia, Transylvania; that gifted artists and inventors are compelled to leave their country and lavish their gifts upon foreigners; that Hessians are sold and bought like Negro slaves while their families starve and perish. Nevertheless, conquest is not the answer. He dwelt on the folly and cruelties of imperialism all his life.

---

[1] xiii 385.   [2] xiv 67; cf. xiv 283–4.

[3] Herder was fascinated by the survival of the Jews; he looked upon them as a most excellent example of a *Volk* with its own distinct character (x 139). 'Moses bound the heart of his people to their native soil' (xii 115). Land, common language, tradition, sense of kinship, common law as a freely accepted 'covenant' – all these interwoven factors, together with the bond created by their sacred literature, enabled the Jews to retain their identity in dispersion – but especially the fact that their eyes remained focused upon their original geographical home (xii 115, viii 355, xvii 312) – historical continuity, not race, is what counts (xii 107). This is what creates historical individuality (xii 123, xxxii 207). On this entire subject, and especially the view of the 'Jewish problem' as not religious, but national and political, needing what later came to be known as the Zionist solution, see the interesting article by F. M. Barnard, 'Herder and Israel', *Jewish Social Studies* 28 (1966), 25–33. See also the same author's 'The Hebrews and Herder's Political Creed', *Modern Language Review* 54 (1959), 533–46.

[4] xiii 384.

In his first essay on the philosophy of history (*Auch eine Philosophie*, of 1774) he speaks of Roman conquerors as a compound of blood, lust and sinister vices.[1] For the next two decades, and, indeed, in the last years of his life, he continues to denounce the inhumanity of colonial rule, ancient and modern: 'Foreign peoples were judged [by Rome] in terms of customs unknown to them';[2] imposed by violence, this distorted the character of the conquered until 'the Roman eagle ... pecked out their eyes, devoured their innards, and covered [their] wretched corpses with its feeble wings'.[3] It was not a happy day when the bloody tyranny of Rome became united with Christianity.[4] Rome ruined Greece, and the Teutonic Knights and recently converted Poles exterminated the Prussians and enslaved the poor Balts and peaceful Slavs.

> Can you name a land [he asks in his *Letters on the Advancement of Mankind* (1793–7)] where Europeans have entered without defiling themselves for ever before defenceless, trusting mankind, by the unjust word, greedy deceit, crushing oppression, diseases, fatal gifts they have brought? Our part of the earth should be called not the wisest, but the most arrogant, aggressive, money-minded: what it has given these people is not civilisation but the destruction of the rudiments of their own cultures wherever they could achieve this.[5]

This is what the English have done in Ireland, in the Scottish Highlands, and Europeans have done in their colonies, the natives of which have 'developed a passion for fire-water', whereby they were considered 'ripe for conversion to our faith'.[6] In 1802, in his periodical *Adrastea*, he imagines a conversation between an Asian and a European; in the course of it the Asian (an Indian) says:

> 'Tell me, have you still not lost the habit of trying to convert to your faith peoples whose property you steal, whom you rob, enslave, murder, deprive of their land and their State, to whom your customs seem revolting? Supposing that one of them came to your country, and with an insolent air pronounced absurd all that is most sacred to you – your laws, your religion, your wisdom, your institutions, and so on, what would you do to such a man?' 'Oh, but that is quite a different matter,' replied the European, 'we have power, ships, money, cannon, *culture*.'[7]

---

[1] v 508; cf. v 515.   [2] xiv 201.   [3] ibid.   [4] xiv 202.
[5] xviii 222–3; cf. xiv 410.   [6] v 546.   [7] xxiii 498.

On this topic Herder remained uncompromising and passionate: ' "Why are you pouring water over my head?" asked a dying slave of a Christian missionary. "So that you can go to Heaven." "I do not want to go to a heaven where there are white men," he replied, and turned on his side and died.'[1] By this means Europeans are engaged in forging the chains with which other peoples will bind them.[2] Herder is as certain as Karl Marx that those who oppress and exploit others and force their own institutions on others are acting as their own grave-diggers – that one day their victims will rise against them and use their catchwords, their methods and ideals to crush them.

The German mission is not to conquer; it is to be a nation of thinkers and educators. This is their true glory.[3] Sacrifice – self-sacrifice – not the domination of one man over another, is the proper end of man. Herder sets his face against everything that is predatory, against the use of force in any cause but that of self-defence. The Crusades, no matter how Christian in inspiration, are hateful to him, since they conquered and crushed other human communities. Yet consent for him is a false basis of society, for consent is ultimately a form of yielding, however rational or voluntary, to strength, whereas human relations must rest upon respect, affection, kinship, equality, not fear or prudence and utilitarian calculation. It is when religions forget the ends of man and turn into empty, mechanical cults that they develop into a source of unintelligible mystification and their ceremonies decay into a recital of dead formulae, while the priests, who no longer understand their own faith, become instruments of other forces – in particular of the State and the men who control it. For him, as for Nietzsche, the State is the coldest of all cold monsters. Nothing in the whole of human history is more hateful to him than Churches and priests who are instruments of political power; of these he speaks with the same voice as Voltaire or Holbach; as for the State (he says in words that could have been Rousseau's), it robs men of themselves.[4] The State becomes a drug with the help of which men seek to forget themselves, a self-generated method of

[1] xviii 224.   [2] v 579.

[3] The most eloquent statement of Herder's conception of the German's earthly miseries and spiritual task is to be found in his epistle in verse, German National Glory, written in the 1790s, but effectively first published, posthumously, in 1812 (xviii 208–16), when the mood of many of his countrymen, whipped into a frenzy of nationalism by Jahn, Arndt, Körner and Görres, was wholly different.

[4] See p. 182 above, note 2.

escaping from the need to live, create and choose. Furthermore, the sheer exercise of bureaucratic activity is a form of self-intoxication, and he speaks of it as a kind of opium by which men are metamorphosed into mechanical functionaries. Profound differences, both personal and literary, came to divide Herder from Goethe and Schiller, but when, in their jointly written *Xenien*, they say

> Deutschland? aber wo liegt es? Ich weiß das Land nicht zu finden,
> Wo das gelehrte beginnt, hört das politische auf.

and

> Zur *Nation* euch zu bilden, ihr hoffet es, Deutsche, vergebens,
> Bildet, ihr könnt es, dafür freyer zu Menschen euch aus.

they speak for Herder too.[1] The State is the substitution of machinery for life, a prospect, and a reality, that frightened him no less than it did Rousseau.

What then is the right life for men? They should live in natural units, that is, in societies united by a common culture. Nature, moreover, does not make some nations intrinsically superior to others. Whatever the qualities of the ancient Germans, to look on them, for this reason, as the European people chosen by God, to which he has, in virtue of its native ability, accorded the right to own the entire world and to be served by other peoples – that would be the ignoble vanity of barbarians.[2] There is no *Favoritvolk*.[3] A nation is made what it is by 'climate',[4] education, relations with its neighbours, and other changeable and empirical factors, and not by an impalpable inner essence or an unalterable factor such as race or colour. All this, said late in his life, is the pure milk of the doctrine of the Enlightenment. Herder protests, not without a certain malicious satisfaction (as Hamann also did, with

---

[1] 'Germany? But where's it located? That's a country I cannot find. / Where the realm of learning begins, the realm of politics ends.' 'To mould yourselves as a *nation*, you seek, Germans, in vain. / Instead, and this you *can* do, mould yourselves ever more freely as human beings.' *Xenien* 95–6, 'Das deutsche Reich' and 'Deutscher Nationalcharacter': vol. 1, pp. 320–1, in *Schillers Werke*, Nationalausgabe (Weimar, 1943–   ).

[2] xvii 212.

[3] xviii 247; cf. xviii 248, where Herder says there must be 'no order of rank ... The Negro is as much entitled to think the white man degenerate ... as the white man is to think of the Negro as a black beast.'

[4] See iv 204–5, xiii 265–73.

equally ironical pleasure), that the great liberal Kant in his *Anthropologie* emphasised race and colour too much. He is equally indignant about Kant's proposition that 'man is an animal who needs a master';[1] he replies, 'Turn the sentence round: the man who needs a master is an animal; as soon as he becomes human, he no longer needs a master.'[2] He also denounces Kant's philosophy of history, according to which it is the vices of mankind – desire for power and mastery over the scarce resources of the earth – that stimulate competition, struggle, and thereby progress, with the corollary that the sufferings of the individual are indispensable to the improvement of the species (a doctrine that was destined to reach its richest development in Hegel, and in another form in Spencer's evolutionary doctrine and the vagaries of social Darwinism). Herder repudiates these doctrines in the pure spirit of liberal, individualist, Weimar cosmopolitanism. Indeed, the perception that cruel and sinister implications are contained in any doctrine that preaches the sacrifice of individuals on the altar of vast abstractions – the human species, society, civilisation, progress (later thinkers were to say race, State, class and a chosen élite) – has its true beginnings here.

Kant's unconcealed lack of sympathy for Herder's sweeping and imprecise generalisations, and his complaints that these were never supported by either adequate evidence or rigorous argument, may in part account for Herder's deliberate choice of the famous champion of the inexorable voice of duty, the moral equality of men, and the infinite value of the individual as the butt of his own passionate anti-racialism and anti-imperialism and of his defence of the right of all men and nations to develop along their own, self-chosen, lines. Variety does not, for Herder, entail conflict. He does not see why one community absorbed in the development of its own native talent should not respect a similar activity on the part of others. The Kant of the *Grundlegung* or the *Zum ewigen Frieden* might have agreed; but the Kant of the *Anthropologie* and the other essays on universal history evidently did not. Kant drew a sharp line of division between, on the one hand, individual morality, universal, absolute, free from internal conflict, based on a

---

[1] *Kant's gesammelte Schriften* (Berlin, 1900–), vol. 8, p. 23, line 5. But see also Kant's 'Beantwortung der Frage: Was ist Aufklärung?' (ibid., pp. 33–42) and Herder's letter to Hamann of 14 February 1785.
[2] xiii 383.

transcendent rationality wholly unconnected with nature and history and empirical reality, and, on the other, the disharmonies of the processes of nature, the aim of which was the preservation of the species, and the promotion of progress by competition and strife. Herder would have none of this. He found such dualism totally unintelligible. The hard and fast distinctions between orders of experience, mental and corporeal faculties, reason and imagination, the world of sense and the worlds of understanding or the ethical will or a priori knowledge, seemed to him so many artificial partitions, 'wooden walls',[1] built by philosophers, to which nothing corresponded in reality. His world is organic, dynamic and unitary: every ingredient of it is at once unique and interwoven with every other by an infinite variety of relationships which, in the end, cannot be analysed or even fully described. 'Similarities, classes, orders, stages', he wrote in 1775, 'are only ... houses of cards in a game. The creator of all things does not see as a man sees. He knows no classes; each thing resembles only itself.'[2] 'I am not sure that I know what "material" and "immaterial" mean. I do not believe that nature erected iron walls between these terms ... I cannot see them anywhere.'[3] He is anxious not to lose any part of reality, not to obliterate or elide or smooth out irregularities in order to fit them into a system, get them neatly covered by a general formula. He inherits from his teacher Hamann the desire to seize the whole in its fullness, in all its peculiar, complex, historically changing manifestations (this is what fascinated and permanently influenced the young Goethe when they met in 1770), and goes a good deal further than Montesquieu, who raised the banner of revolt against the *grands simplificateurs*.[4] The springs of life are mysterious, hidden from those who lack the sense of the inwardness of the spirit of a society, an age, a movement – a sensibility killed by the dissection practised by French *lumières* and their academic German imitators. Like Hamann he is convinced that clarity, rigour, acuteness of analysis, rational, orderly arrangement, whether in theory or practice, can be bought at too high a price. In this sense he is the profoundest critic of the Enlightenment, as formidable as Burke, or Maistre, but free from their reactionary prejudices and hatred of equality and fraternity.

---

[1] viii 315.   [2] ibid.   [3] viii 193.

[4] See, e.g., *De l'esprit des lois*, book 24, chapter 18: vol. 1 B, p. 290, in *Oeuvres complètes de Montesquieu*, ed. A. Masson (Paris, 1950–5).

IV

As for Herder's doctrine of expression, it is for him profoundly connected with the ways in which and by which men live. What determines the units in which it is 'natural' for men to live? Despite his tendency to look upon the family and patriarchal institutions as the basic forms of human association, Herder does not explicitly affirm Aristotle's (and Rousseau's) doctrine that a 'natural' or satisfactory human society is constituted only by small human groups in which men can know each other face to face and where (in Aristotle's phrase) one herald can be heard by all. Human groups, large and small, are products of climate, geography, physical and biological needs, and similar factors; they are made one by common traditions and common memories, of which the principal link and vehicle – indeed, more than vehicle, the very incarnation – is language. 'Has a nation . . . anything more precious than the language of its fathers? In it dwells its entire world of tradition, history, religion, principles of existence; its whole heart and soul.'[1] It is so because men necessarily think in words or other symbols, since to think is to use symbols; and their feelings and attitudes to life are, he maintains (as Vico did before him), incorporated in symbolic forms – worship, poetry, ritual. This is so whether what they seek are pleasures or necessities: the dance, the hunt – primitive forms of social solidarity expressed and preserved by myth and formalised representation – in fact, the entire network of belief and behaviour that binds men to one another can be explained only in terms of common, public symbolism, in particular by language.

Herder had derived from Hamann his notion that words and ideas are one. Men do not think, as it were, in thoughts and ideas and then look for words in which to 'clothe' them, as one looks for a glove to fit a fully formed hand. Hamann taught that to think was to use symbols, and that to deny this was not so much false as unintelligible, because without symbolism one was led fallaciously to divide the aspects of a single experience into separate entities – the fatal doctrine of Descartes, who spoke of mind and body, thought and its object, matter and mind, as though they were independent existents. Such distinctions as we draw between thought and feeling (and their 'objects'), physical sensation and

[1] xvii 58.

intellectual or moral or aesthetic awareness, are, according to Hamann (where one can understand him), an attempt to draw attention now to this, now to that facet of a single experience; a tendency which, pushed too far, tends to separate and abstract one facet from another, and, pushed further still, to lead to the invention of imaginary abstract objects, or idealised entities – to transform reality into a collection of artificial figments. This springs from a craving for tidy scientific classification, but it distorts the facts, congeals the continuous flow of the living sense of nature and of God into dead fragments, and kills the sources of the true sense of reality – the imagination, consciousness of divine revelation, direct acquaintance with reality, obtained through the senses – which men unspoiled by the logic and metaphysics of rationalism always have.

Hamann was a Christian touched by mysticism: he looked upon the world, upon nature and history, as the speech of God to man; God's words were hieroglyphs, often tormentingly dark, or they were allegories, or they were symbols which opened doors to the vision of the truth, which, if only men saw and heard aright, answered the questions of their heads and hearts.[1] Hamann was not himself a visionary. He had had no special revelation; but when, in the midst of an acute spiritual crisis, he turned to the Bible, he was overwhelmed by the realisation that the history of the Jews embodied a universal, trans-historical truth: for it symbolised his own – and every man's – painful quest for God. Men were made in God's image, but as Hamann's pietist ancestors had taught, man was sinful and weak, he stumbled and fell and rose again as he sought to hear the voice of his father and master, the Christ within him and without, who alone could make him whole. Man was healed only by surrendering himself to the unity of life, by allowing his entire being – spirit and flesh, mind, will, and above all senses – to take in that which God was saying to him directly in Holy Writ, and also signified by means of the working of nature and by the pattern of human history. Nature and history were symbols, cryptograms, of the Logos, to be read by those who were not perverted by metaphysical subtleties. Sin was denial of divine grace and of what God had given men: passions, desires,

---

[1] The sources of this view in Christian mysticism and Neoplatonism, and its form in other philosophical systems – for instance, that of Berkeley – have not as yet been sufficiently investigated.

The dogmatic certainty of fanatical sectarians about what this or that sacred text must mean is therefore irrational and groundless. Knowledge of philology – the historical development of languages – alone yields the story of changing uses and meanings. Herder is anti-mechanistic: but he is an empiricist, in direct descent from Occam and the English naturalists. Only assiduous historical research, sympathetic insight into the purpose of the speaker, a grasp of the machinery of communication whereby human beings understand each other, whether directly, or across the centuries, can bridge the chasms between different, yet never wholly divorced, civilisations. Language expresses the collective experience of the group.[1]

Has a nation anything more precious? From a study of native literatures

> we learn to know ages and peoples more deeply than along the deceptive, desolate path of their political and military history. In the latter we seldom see more than the manner in which a people was ruled, how it let itself be slaughtered; in the former we learn how it thought, what it wished and craved for, how it took its pleasures, how it was led by its teachers or its inclinations.[2]

Hence Herder's stress on the importance of genetic studies and the history of language, and hence, too, the great impulsion that he gave to studies of comparative linguistics, comparative anthropology and ethnology, and above all to the great philological movement that became the pride of German scholarship towards the end of his life and in the century that followed. His own efforts in this direction were no less suggestive or speculative than those of Vico. After declaring, in language borrowed from Lavater, that the 'physiognomy of languages'[3] is all-important, he insisted, for example, that the languages which preserved genders (such as Russian, with which he came into contact during his Riga years) implied a vision of a world different from the world of those whose languages are sexless; so too did particular uses of pronouns. He insisted that verbs – connected with action – came before nouns, connected with contemplation of objects; that active nations employ different linguistic modes from passive ones; that nuances of language are pointers to differing forms of experience (*Weltanschauungen*). Logic for him is only an abstraction from languages

[1] See, e.g., xi 225, xvii 59, xviii 346, xxx 8.   [2] xviii 137.   [3] xiii 363.

living or dead. There is no 'deep' logical structure presupposed by all forms of rational thought; in his *Sprachphilosophie*, logic is an approximation to what is common in isomorphic languages, which themselves point to a high degree of similarity in the experiences of their users. Anthropology, not metaphysics or logic, whether Aristotelian or Leibnizian or Kantian, is for Herder the key to the understanding of human beings and of their world. It is the history of language that most clearly and continuously reveals such phenomena as social growth – the cycles of infancy, youth, maturity, decay – that are common to individuals and nations.

The relation of language to thought, although in a sense they are one, is an ambivalent one. At any rate, the art of writing, the incorporation of thought in permanent forms, while it creates the possibility of a continuity of social self-awareness, and makes accessible his own and other worlds to an individual, also arrests and kills. What has been put down in writing is incapable of that living process of constant adaptation and change, of the constant expression of the unanalysable and unseizable flow of actual experience, which language, if it is to communicate fully, must possess. Language alone makes experience possible, but it also freezes it. Hamann spoke of the valley of dry bones which only 'a prophet'[1] (such as Socrates, St Paul, Luther, and perhaps himself) could cover with flesh. Herder speaks of corpses – forms of linguistic petrifaction – against which, in due course, men revolt. The history of linguistic revolutions is the history of the succession of cultures, the true revolutions in the history of the human race. Was there once a language common to all men? He does not wish to assert this. On the one hand, he clings to the notion of one world, one basic human personality, the 'organic' interrelation of everything; he insists on the folly and danger of abstraction, of fragmentation, of splitting the human personality into separate faculties, as not only Wolff but Kant, too, had done in their psychologies and in their strict division of body from soul, nature from spirit, the empirical from the a priori, the historical from the eternal. Yet he is a Christian, too, and he is committed to the Aristotelian and biblical doctrine of natural kinds. Man is unique; Lord Monboddo and the naturalists must be mistaken. That, no doubt, is why language had to be a direct gift of God, and not the product of a gradual process of emergence of rational beings out of

[1] W ii 176.13.

some pre-rational state of nature – from the animal kingdom and subhuman forms of sentience, or even from insentience.[1] The contradiction is never reconciled.

The only identification that Herder never abandons is that of thought and action, language and activity. Poetry, particularly early epic poetry, is for him pure activity. He was taken in by Ossian, like many of his contemporaries. It is probably from these poems rather than from Homer – although he speaks of the Homeric poems as improvisations, not a dead artefact – that he derives his notion of poetry as activity. Poetry, particularly among early peoples, is, he maintains, magical in character; it is not cool description of nature or of anything else: it is a spur to action for heroes, hunters, lovers; it stimulates and directs. It is not to be savoured by the scholar in his armchair, but is intelligible only to those who have placed themselves in situations similar to the conditions in which such words sprang into existence. During his voyage from Riga to Nantes, he observed the sailors during rough seas. These dour men under a savage discipline, who lived in terror of, and in constant intimate contact with, the elements which they sought to dominate, resurrected for him the dark world of Skalds and Vikings and the Eddas,[2] a world scarcely intelligible to tranquil philologists in their studies or detached literary epicures who turn over the pages idly, without the power to re-create the world of which these works are the vision and the voice. Words, rhythms, actions are aspects of a single experience. These are commonplaces today, but (despite Vico) they were far from being such in Herder's time.

'The more savage, that is, the more alive and freedom-loving a people is (for that is the simple meaning of the word), the more savage, that is, alive, free, sensuous, lyrically active, its songs must be, if it has songs', he wrote in 1773.[3] He compares 'the living presentness of the imagery' of such songs with songs 'written for paper'. 'These arrows of a savage Apollo pierce hearts and carry souls and memories with them.'[4] 'All unpolished peoples sing and act; they sing about what they do and thus sing histories. Their songs are the archives of their people, the treasury of their science and religion ... a picture of their domestic life in joy and in

---

[1] G. A. Wells, op. cit. (p. 169 above, note 1), p. 43, advances this view, which seems to me very illuminating.
[2] See below, pp. 211–12.   [3] v 164.   [4] ibid.

sorrow, by bridal bed and graveside... Here everyone portrays himself and appears as he is.'[1] Language, content, tone tell us more about the outlook, beliefs, origins, history, mingling of nations than travellers' tales. Then artifice begins. When the words were divorced from music, when the poet began to write 'slowly, in order to be read',[2] art may have gained, but there was a loss of magic, of 'miraculous power'.[3] What do our modern critics, the 'counters of syllables', 'specialists in scansion', masters of dead learning, know of all this? 'Heart! Warmth! Blood! Humanity! Life!'[4] 'I feel! I am!'[5] These are Herder's mottoes; no wonder that the poets of the *Sturm und Drang* recognised themselves in his writings.

He dreams of a visit to the Northern seas reading 'the story of Utal and Ninetuma in sight of the very island where it all took place'. His voyage to France, which took him past the shores of Scandinavia and England, transported him: 'This was a living and creative Nature, between the deeps of sea and sky',[6] very different from the world in which he was living, where 'we scarcely see or feel, only reflect and reason',[7] in which poets invent imaginary passions and qualities of soul unknown to them or anyone, and compare verses about objects about which one cannot think or feel or imagine anything at all. He feels a kindred spirit in the English scholar Robert Wood, who gazed upon the ruins of Troy, a volume of Homer in hand.[8] He must go to the Scottish Highlands, to see the places described by the great Ossian himself and 'hear the living songs of a living people'.[9] After all, 'The Greeks, too, were once... savages, and in the best period of their flowering far more of nature remained in them than can be descried by the narrow gaze of a scholiast or a classical scholar.' Homer goes back to ancient sagas, Tyrtaeus to ballads, Arion and Orpheus are 'noble Greek shamans', Sappho's songs are like nothing so much as the songs of a Livonian girl of our own time.[10] Our scholars and translators have no inkling of this. Consider the translation of a Lapp song by the minor poet Christian Ewald Kleist:

---

[1] ix 532. This quotation, and those earlier in this paragraph, are based on the translations in Burton Feldman and Robert D. Richardson (eds), *The Rise of Modern Mythology 1680–1860* (Bloomington/London, 1972), pp. 229–30.

[2] viii 412. [3] See viii 390. [4] v 538. [5] viii 96. [6] v 169. [7] v 183.

[8] v 169. [9] v 167. [10] ix 534.

I would willingly give up for this song a dozen of Kleist's imitations. Do not be surprised [he writes to his fiancée Caroline], that a Laplandic youth who knew neither school nor writing, and scarcely knows God, sings better than Major Kleist. After all, the Lapp improvised his song while he was gliding with his reindeer over the snow, and time dragged so slowly on the way to Lake Orra where his beloved lived.[1]

Swiss and English scholars had celebrated Homer, Dante, Shakespeare, Milton. Hurd, Young, Percy, Lowth and Blackwell revived the study of ancient poetry. Enthusiasm for the achievements of the collective genius of primitive societies, under the impulsion of Rousseau, was transformed into a European movement by Herder's passionate advocacy.

All genuine expressions of experience are valid. They differ because lives differ: perhaps because the earth's axis is inclined by twenty-four degrees. This generates different geophysical 'climates', different experiences, different societies. Anything that seems to Herder authentic delights him. He has his preferences: he prefers the Greeks, the Germans and the Hebrews to the Romans, the ancient Egyptians or the Frenchmen of his own time or of the previous century. But, at least in theory, he is prepared to defend them all; he wishes and thinks he is able to penetrate – 'feel himself'[2] (*Einfühlen* is his invention, a hundred years before Lipps or Dilthey or Croce) – into their essence, grasp what it must be like to live, contemplate goals, act and react, think, imagine in the unique ways dictated by their circumstances, and so grasp the patterns of life in terms of which alone such groups are to be defined. The central concept here is that of natural growth, biological, emotional, intellectual. Nature *is* growth – what Bodmer and Breitinger had spoken of, perhaps echoing Vico's *nascimento*, as *Naturwüchsigkeit* – spontaneous natural growth, not the static 'true nature' of Boileau's aesthetics, or Batteux's *la belle nature*, which the artist must learn to discern and reveal from the welter of mere experience.

Everything that is natural is valuable. The notion (for example, the Marquis de Sade's) that vices or decadence or aggression are not less natural than the rich and harmonious development of all human potentialities is not allowed for. In this respect Herder is a true child of the Enlightenment at its most naïve as well as at its most imaginative and penetrating. Arthur Lovejoy was surely right

---

[1] Letter to Caroline Flachsland, 2 January 1771.   [2] v 503.

when he included Herder among the thinkers (perhaps the majority in the West) who identified the 'must' of natural laws that caused things to be as they are, and governed the world inexorably, with the 'ought' of the normative rules, derived, apparently, from the selfsame nature, obedience to which alone conducts men towards happiness and virtue and wisdom. But this consensus has its limits. Herder sharply differs from the central thought of the French Enlightenment, and that not only in the respects that all his commentators have noted.

What is usually stressed is, in the first place, his relativism,[1] his admiration of every authentic culture for being what it is, his insistence that outlooks and civilisations must be understood from within, in terms of their own stages of development, purposes and outlooks; and in the second place his sharp repudiation of that central strain in Cartesian rationalism which regards only what is universal, eternal, unalterable, governed by rigorously logical relationships – only the subject-matter of mathematics, logic, physics and the other natural sciences – as true knowledge.

But Herder rebelled against the *Aufklärung* in an even profounder way, by rejecting the very notion of impassable barriers in nature or experience – barriers between types of consciousness or faculties or ideas or natural objects. What repels him equally in such deeply disparate thinkers as Descartes and Kant and the French *philosophes* is their common insistence on rigid divisions between 'faculties' and types of experience, which they seem to him to have introduced merely to make it possible to classify and generalise. He admires Leibniz more than Kant: he recognises the logical gulf between mathematical truths and those of fact, but he regards the former (probably following Hume) as

---

[1] At various points in this essay I describe Herder as a relativist. Although the general tenor of my remarks makes it clear, I hope, in what sense I use this term, what I say has led to some misunderstanding of my views (see, for example, Arnaldo Momigliano, 'On the Pioneer Trail', *New York Review of Books*, 11 November 1976, 33–8). I have attempted to clarify my position in an article entitled 'Alleged Relativism in Eighteenth-Century European Thought', reprinted in one of my collections of essays, *The Crooked Timber of Humanity* [see p. viii above, note 1]. Essentially, in the present study of Herder I sometimes use 'relativism' not to mean a species of ethical or epistemological subjectivism, as the term has very often been understood, but to refer to what I have elsewhere identified, I hope more perspicuously, as objective pluralism, free from any taint of subjectivism. I.B. 1996.

tautologies, statements unconcerned with nature.[1] He is a thoroughgoing empiricist in matters of epistemology. Kant's transcendental categories, which claim to determine experience a priori, seem to him a monstrous conflation of analytic and synthetic: he rejects the 'synthetic a priori' as a hideous confusion.[2] Reality for him admits of no a priori laws; Kant's attempt to distinguish contingent from necessary judgements about experience seems to him to be far more misleading than the distinction between intuited necessities and observed contingencies out of which Spinoza and Leibniz built their systems. Categories, rigorous distinctions of kinds of truth about the nature of reality – like the similar distinctions drawn between words and concepts – distort judgement not only in epistemology and logic, but in politics and ethics and the arts, and indeed all regions of experience. All activities, he insists, express the whole and undivided man whom Descartes and Kant, in their several ways, have done their best to carve up into compartments with their faculty psychology of 'reason', 'imagination', 'intuition', 'feeling', 'will'.[3] He declares that he knows of no criteria for distinguishing such Kantian faculties as *Erkennen, Empfinden, Wollen* – they are indissolubly united in the organic personality of living men.

The attack on Kant in the *Metakritik* of 1799 merely summarises a lifelong attitude. The black-and-white terms these neo-scholastics use to describe man – an inexhaustibly complex organisation – seem to Herder wilfully absolute and arbitrary. Instead, for example, of asking themselves how free men are, free from or for

---

[1] xxi 36.   [2] xxi 38.

[3] According to Herder the soul evolves a pattern from the chaos of things by which it is surrounded, and so 'creates by its own inner power a one out of the many, which belongs to it alone' (xiii 182); cf. xv 532 and H. B. Nisbet, op. cit. (p. 169 above, note 1), p. 63. That the creation of integrated wholes out of discrete data is the fundamental organising activity of human nature is a belief that is central to Herder's entire social and moral outlook: for him all creative activity, conscious and unconscious, generates and is, in turn, determined by its own unique *Gestalt*, whereby every individual and group strives to perceive, understand, act, create, live. This is the idea which dominates his conception of social structure and development, of the nature of an identifiable civilisation, and, indeed, of what men live by (see v 103–5). Nisbet seems to me entirely justified in describing Herder as a forerunner of gestalt psychology. On this see also Martin Schütze's articles, 'Herder's Psychology', *Monist* 35 (1925), 507–54, and 'The Fundamental Ideas in Herder's Thought', *Modern Philology* 18 (1920–1), 65–78, 289–302; 19 (1921–2), 113–30, 361–82; 21 (1923–4), 29–48, 113–32.

what, and where and when, and in what respects, or what renders
them more or less free, these thinkers dogmatically pronounce
man to be free, wholly free in some absolute sense, as against
animals who are wholly mechanical, or at least wholly lack
freedom. They speak of man as distinguished by his possession of
reason (not as being less or more rational), and define him in terms
of selected properties that one must either possess wholly or not
possess at all; they describe him in terms of sharp, artificial
dichotomies that arbitrarily break up the interwoven, continuous,
at times irregular, fluid, shapeless, often unanalysable, but always
perceptible, dynamic, teeming, boundless, eternal multiplicity of
nature,[1] and so provide distorting lenses both to philosophers and
historians. Attempts to bring manifestations so complex and so
various under some general law, whether by philosophers seeking
knowledge, or by statesmen seeking to organise and govern,
seemed to Herder no better than a search for the lowest common
denominator – for what may be least characteristic and important
in the lives of men – and, therefore, to make for shallowness in
theory and a tendency to impose a crippling uniformity in practice.
Herder is one of the earliest opponents of uniformity as the enemy
of life and freedom.

One of the central doctrines of the Western tradition, at any rate
since Plato, has maintained that the good is one, while evil has
many faces; there is one true answer to every real question, but
many false ones. Even Aristotle, for whom Plato's ideal of an
unchanging, wholly unified society is too rigid, since it does not
allow for the variety of human characters and wishes, merely
reports this as a fact, not as something desirable in itself. The
central current in ethics and politics, as well as metaphysics and
theology and the sciences, is cast in a monist mould: it seeks to
bring the many into a coherent, systematic unity. Herder is an
early and passionate champion of variety: uniformity maims and
kills. The 'ferment' of the Middle Ages did at least, he wrote in
1774, 'hold at bay the devouring jaws of despotism' whose
tendency is

> to crush everything into deadly uniformity. Now is it better, is it
> healthier and more beneficent for mankind to produce only the lifeless
> cogs of a huge, wooden, thoughtless machine, or to rouse and activate

[1] See xiii 194.

lively energies? Even if institutions are not perfect, even if men are not always honest, even if there is some disorder and a good deal of disagreement, it is still preferable to a state of affairs in which men are forced to rot and decay during their own lifetime.[1]

Even Montesquieu, so widely praised for his novel sense of the differences between societies and of the 'spirit' that animates their laws and institutions, has tried to press these teeming varieties of human life and culture into the straitjacket of three basic types: 'three wretched generalisations! ... the history of all times and peoples, whose succession forms the great, living work of God, reduced to ruins, divided neatly into three heaps... Oh, Montesquieu!'[2]

All regionalists, all defenders of the local against the universal, all champions of deeply rooted forms of life, both reactionary and progressive, both genuine humanists and obscurantist opponents of scientific advance, owe something, whether they know it or not, to the doctrines which Herder (with a far wider and more magnificent sweep than Möser or Burke or Ferguson) introduced into European thought. Vico might have achieved something of this. But he was (and is) not read; as Savigny remarked, he came into his own too late to have a decisive influence.

However much lip-service Herder may have paid to 'natural kinds', in general he conceived of nature as a unity in which the *Kräfte* – the mysterious, dynamic, purpose-seeking forces the interplay of which constitutes all movement and growth – flow into each other, clash, combine, coalesce. These forces are not causal and mechanical as in Descartes; nor insulated from each other as in the *Monadology* of Leibniz; his notion of them owes more to Neoplatonic and Renaissance mysticism and, perhaps, to Erigena's *natura naturans* than to the sciences of his time. For Herder reality is a kind of symbiosis of these *Kräfte* (whose character remains obscure) with an environment that is conceived in somewhat static terms; if the environment is altered too abruptly, the result is some kind of collapse.

Herder found more and more evidence for this. Transplanted flowers decay in unsympathetic climates; so do human beings. Greenlanders do not thrive in Denmark. Africans are miserable and decay in Europe. Europeans become debilitated in America. Conquest crushes, and emigration sometimes leads to enfeeblement

[1] v 516.   [2] v 566.

– lack of vital force, the flattening out of human beings, and a sad uniformity. The *Ideen* is full of such examples. Like Fourier after him, Herder believed in the complete realisability of all potentialities ('All that can be, is; all that can come into being, will come into being; if not today, then tomorrow'),[1] since everything fits somewhere. Only artificiality is destructive, in life as in art. Marriages of convenience, coldly entered into, ruin children, and are worse for them than pure animality. The patriarchs at times exercised severe and cruel authority: but at least this is more 'natural' – and therefore less harmful – than the artificial reasonings of philosophers. Herder harbours a Rousseau-like suspicion of 'reasoning'. He does not think that Voltaire's desiccated maxims or Wolff's syllogisms are better for children than the stern but natural behaviour of primitive men. Anything is preferable to a system which imposes the ideal of one culture on another and arranges, adjusts, makes for uniform 'physiognomies', as opposed to a condition which is 'natural', in a state of creative disorder, where alone individuality and freedom live and grow. Hence his condemnation of all theories which over-categorise men – into racial types, for example, or social orders – and thereby divide them from each other. Centralisation and *dirigisme* are the enemies: even some degree of inefficiency is preferable to 'a state of affairs in which men are forced to rot and decay during their own lifetime'. In the same spirit 'political reform must come from below',[2] since 'even when man abuses his freedom most despicably he is still king; for he can still choose, even if he chooses the worst; he can rule over himself, even if he legislates himself into a beast'.[3] His differences from his fellow opponents of the French *lumières* – Möser, Kant, Rousseau, Burke – are obvious enough.

He condemns the anthropologies which treat men in general and leave the individual drained of too many differentiating characteristics. Even tradition, which otherwise acts as a preservative of the most vital characteristics of human groups, can be a danger when it becomes too mechanical and acts as a narcotic, as it seems to him to have done in Asia, which it put to sleep by eliminating too many of the other ingredients of a healthy life, too many other *Kräfte* that are indispensable to life and activity. This thought is incapable of precise formulation; but, as always with Herder, it is suggestive and has a clear general direction. 'The savage who loves himself, his

[1] xiv 86.   [2] xxxii 56.   [3] xiii 147.

wife and his child ... and works for the good of his tribe as for his own ... is in my view more genuine than that cultivated ghost, the ... citizen of the world, who, burning with love for all his fellow ghosts, loves a chimera. The savage in his hut has room for any stranger ... the saturated heart of the superfluous cosmopolitan is a home for no one.'[1] He repeats throughout the *Ideen* that originality – freedom of choice and creation – is the divine element in man. When a savage speaks with vigour and precision he is superior to the civilised man who stands on a pedestal built by others.[2] There is much talk in the *Ideen* (this is later echoed by Fichte) about men who live on other men's accounts: they are viewed as 'superfluous cosmopolitans', men whose feelings have been drained away, dehumanised creatures, victims of nature or history, moral or physical cripples, parasites, fettered slaves.

How do men come to lose their humanity? By living on others and by the labour and ideas of others. Herder, in opposition to the primitivists, welcomed invention – the arts and sciences are fruits of the creative powers of man, and through them he rises to the full height of his purposive nature. Inventions as such do not corrupt (in this Herder differs from the Rousseau of the first and second *Discourses*); only if one lives on the inventions of others does one become mechanical and devitalised.[3] Here, too, as in the writings of Mably, Rousseau and Friedrich Karl von Moser,[4] begins that lament, still more characteristic of the following century, and perhaps even more often heard in our own, for the youth that is gone for ever – for the lost virtues of an earlier, more vigorous epoch in the life of mankind. Herder, no less than Mill or Carlyle or Ruskin, speaks with gloom about the triviality and lifelessness of modern men and modern art, in contrast with the full-blooded, doughty, independent human beings of the morning hours of humanity – the creators of the great epics and songs, of an anonymous but more robust age. Before Henri de Saint-Simon he

---

[1] xiii 339.   [2] xiii 371-2.

[3] In his essay on Ossian, Herder speaks of this as the source of the fatal division of labour which creates destructive barriers among men, classes and hierarchies, and the division of spiritual from manual labour which robs men of their humanity. Material progress may march hand in hand with cultural decline; this theme is taken up by Goethe and Schiller and developed by Marx and Marxists. (I owe this point to Professor Roy Pascal.)

[4] Especially in Moser's *Von dem deutschen Nationalgeist*, published in 1765-6, which speaks of the Germans as despised, disregarded, mocked, and preyed upon by everyone.

draws a contrast between the creative and the relatively sterile epochs in the history of culture. Herder has his optimistic moments, when he supposes that a renewal is possible: that if man can only 'cease to be in contradiction with himself' and 'return to himself', and if peoples can only 'find themselves' and learn not to 'think in other people's thoughts',[1] they can recover and revive and create new works of art, in modern terms, as noble and expressive of their true nature as anything that men have created in the past. There is only one course against which Herder sets his face absolutely: that is, any attempt to return to the past. Here there is no salvation. To sigh after the Greeks and wish to return to them, of which he suspects Winckelmann, is absurd and imposs-ible: Winckelmann's idealisation of the Greeks as the originators of art, which among them attained to a sublime height never reached by, say, the Egyptians, is wholly unhistorical and nothing but a terrible delusion.[2]

The dangers to free development are many. In the first place, there is the centralised State; it can rob us of something essential: it can rob us of ourselves. There are foreign cultures that devour German folk-song 'like a cancer'[3] – folk-song that is a response to the deepest human cravings, to collective desires that seek to embody common experiences in symbolic forms not dreamed of in Voltaire's philosophy. There is the more specific danger of foreign languages: I am able to stammer with immense effort in the words of a foreign language; its spirit will evade me. Yet to this we devote the best years of our life![4] But we are not Greeks; we are not Romans; and we cannot become such. To wish to return is to be dominated by a false vision, a crippling illusion as fatal as any for which it attempts to be the cure. Imitation is a terrible curse: human nature is not identical in different climes; 'the worlds of

---

[1] xiii 160–1. Such phrases are almost verbally exact echoes of sentences in which Hamann deals with what much later came to be called the problem of 'alienation'.

[2] viii 476–7; compare the following (v 565) from *Auch eine Philosophie*: 'There is no country the civilisation of which has been able to take a backward step, and become for the second time what it has once been. The path of destiny is as inflexible as iron ... can today become yesterday? ... You Ptolemies could never again create an Egypt, nor you Hadrians a Greece, nor Julian a Jerusalem.' These cultures have had their day. 'The sword is worn out, the empty scabbard lies in pieces.'

[3] xxv 11.   [4] iv 388–9, xxx 8.

things and sounds are different'.[1] What then must we do? We must seek to be ourselves. 'Let us be characteristic of our nation, language, scene, and let posterity decide whether or not we are classical!'[2] Perhaps Klopstock's *Messias* was less successful than it might have been because it was not 'national' enough.[3] It is here that Herder utters his most ardently nationalist sentiments: 'But now! I cry yet again, my German brothers! But now! The remnants of all living folk-life [*Volksdenkart*] are rolling into the abyss of oblivion ... the light of so-called culture is devouring all about it like a cancer.'[4] 'We speak the words of strangers and they wean us from our own thoughts.'[5] He sees no merit in peasants in wigs, much as Hamann talks of 'false noses'.[6] He appeals to the Germans to know themselves, to understand their place and respect their role in the cosmos, in time and in space.

V

Is this nationalism? In an obvious sense it is. It is anti-French – the voyage to Nantes and Paris (like the later journey to Rome) depressed Herder acutely. He met some of the most distinguished of the *philosophes*, but evidently failed to achieve any degree of communication with them. He suffered that mixture of envy, humiliation, admiration, resentment and defiant pride which backward peoples feel towards advanced ones, members of one social class towards those who belong to a higher rung in the hierarchy. Wounded national feeling – this scarcely needs saying – breeds nationalism, but it is important to realise that Herder's nationalism was never political. If he denounces individualism, he equally detests the State, which coerces and mutilates the free human personality. His social vision is antagonistic to government, power, domination. Louis XIV and Frederick the Great (like Caesar and Charlemagne before them) represent a detestable ideal. Herder does not ask for power and does not wish to assert the superiority of his own class or culture or nation. He wishes to create a society

---

[1] iv 38.   [2] ii 57.

[3] v 259; cf. i 268. Rouché, op. cit. (p. 170 above, note 2), p. 98 (cf. ibid., p. 52), is understandably surprised by the spectacle of a Christian clergyman complaining that the central theme of Christian religion is perhaps too foreign a topic for a German poem.

[4] xxv 11.   [5] iv 389.   [6] B vii 460.27.

in which men, whoever they are, can live full lives, attain to free self-expression, 'be someone'; and he thinks that the less government they have the better. We cannot return to the Greek *polis*.

This may, indeed, have been the first stage of a development destined in its later stages to become nationalistic and chauvinistic in the full, aggressive sense. Whether or not this is historically and sociologically true, it is clear that Herder did not himself harbour these sentiments. Even though he seems to have coined the word *Nationalismus*, his conception of a good society is closer to the anarchism of Thoreau or Proudhon or Kropotkin, and to the conception of a culture (*Bildung*) of which such liberals as Goethe and Humboldt were proponents, than to the ideals of Fichte or Hegel or political socialists. For him *die Nation* is not a political entity. He is repelled by the claims of contemporary Celtomaniacs and Teutomaniacs who rhapsodised over the ancient Gaels or Northmen. He celebrates German beginnings because they are part of, and illuminate, his own civilisation, not because German civilisation ranks higher than that of others on some cosmic scale. 'In the works of imagination and feeling the entire soul of the nation reveals itself most freely.'[1] This was developed by Sismondi, Michelet and Mazzini into a full-scale political-cultural doctrine; but Herder stands even closer to the outlook of Ruskin or Lamennais or William Morris, to populists and Christian socialists, and to all of those who, in the present day, are opposed to hierarchies of status or power, or to the influence of manipulators of any kind. He stands with those who protest against mechanisation and vulgarisation rather than with the nationalists of the last hundred years, whether moderate or violent. He favours autarky, but only in personal life; that is, in artistic creation and the rights of natural self-expression. All his invocations of the *Nationalgeist* (an expression probably coined by Friedrich Karl von Moser), and of its many aliases – the *Geist des Volkes*, *Seele des Volkes*, *Geist der Nation*, *Genius des Volkes* and the more empirical *Nationalcharakter*[2] – are intended to stress what is ours, not theirs, even though theirs may intrinsically be more valuable, viewed on some vaster scale.

Herder admits no such scale: cultures are comparable but not commensurable; each is what it is, of literally inestimable value in

[1] xviii 58.
[2] i 263; ii 160; iii 30; v 185, 217; viii 392; xiii 364; xiv 38, 84; xxv 10; and *passim*.

its own society, and consequently to humanity as a whole. Socrates is for him neither the timeless cosmopolitan sage of the Enlightenment, nor Hamann's destroyer of pretentious claims to knowledge whose irony and self-confessed ignorance opened the path to faith and salvation. Socrates is, above all, an Athenian of the fifth century; and that age is over. Aristotle may be more gifted than Leibniz, but Leibniz is ours, Aristotle is not; Shakespeare is ours, other great geniuses, Homer or Moses, are not. Individuality is all; artificial combinations of old and new, native and foreign, lead to false ideas and ruinous practice.[1] Let us follow our own path; let men speak well or ill of our nation, our literature, our language: they are ours, they are ourselves, and let that be enough.[2] Better Germans, whatever they are, than sham Greeks, Frenchmen, Englishmen.[3] But when he says, 'Awake, German nation! Do not let them ravish your Palladium!',[4] declares that fearful storms are coming and warns men not to lie asleep like Jonah in the tempest, and when he tells men to take warning from the terrible example of partitioned Poland,[5] and says, 'Poor, torn, crushed Germany, be hopeful!'[6] and 'Germans, speak German! Spew out the Seine's ugly slime!',[7] it is difficult to avoid the thought that this may indeed have fed the sinister nationalism of Görres and Jahn, Arndt and Treitschke, and their monstrous modern successors. Yet Herder's own sentences refer to purely cultural self-determination; he hates *policirte Nationen*.[8] Nationality for him is purely and strictly a cultural attribute; he believes that people can and should defend their cultural heritage: they need never give in. He almost blames the Jews, despite his passionate addiction to their antiquities, for not preserving a sufficient sense of collective honour and making no effort to return to their home in Palestine, which is the sole place where they can blossom again into a *Nation*. He is interested not in nationality but in cultures, in worlds, in the total experience of peoples; and the aspects of this experience that he celebrates are personal relationships, friendship and enmity, attitudes to nature, war and peace, art and science, ways in which truth, freedom and happiness are pursued, and in particular the relations of the great civilising leaders to the ungrateful mob. He fears organisation as such, and, like the early English romantics,

---

[1] xiv 227; xv 321; xviii 248. [2] xviii 160–1. [3] i 366–7. [4] xvii 309.
[5] xxix 210. [6] viii 433. [7] xxvii 129. [8] See v 555; cf. v 524.

like Young or Thomas and Joseph Warton, he wants to preserve what is irregular and unique in life and in art, that which no system can wholly contain.

His attack on political centralisation and intellectual polarisation springs from the same source. When he imagines the world as a garden which can contain many flowers, and when he speaks of the possible and desirable harmony between all the national cultures, he is not simply ignoring the aggressive potentialities of nation States or blandly assuming that there is no reason for conflict between various nationalisms. Rather, he is deeply hostile to the growth of political, economic, military centralisation, but sees no reason why culturally autonomous communities need clash. It may, of course, be unrealistic and unhistorical to suppose that one kind of autarky need not lead to other and more dangerous kinds. But it is not the same kind of unrealism as that with which he, and the Enlightenment generally, are usually charged. His faith is not in nationalism, collectivism, Teutomania or romantic State-worship, but in something that is, if anything, incompatible with these ideals. He is the champion of those mysterious *Kräfte* which are 'living and organic'.[1] For him, as for Shaftesbury (one of those English thinkers who, like Young and Carlyle, influenced the Germans far more than his own compatriots), there is, in the end, only one great creative *Kraft*: 'What is alive in creation is, in all forms, shapes, channels, one spirit, one single flame.'[2] This is scarcely an empirical or scientific notion. He sings paeans to the *Seele des Volkes* which is the social incarnation of the Leibnizian *vis viva*, 'wonderful, unique . . . inexplicable, inextinguishable, and as old as the *Nation*'.[3] Its most vivid expression is, of course, not the State, but 'the physiognomy of its speech'.[4]

The point that I wish to stress is that the true heir of this doctrine is not power politics but what came to be called populism. It is this that acquired such momentum among the oppressed people of Eastern Europe, and later spread in Asia and Africa. It inspired not *étatistes* but believers in 'grass roots' – Russian Slavophils and *Narodniks*, Christian Socialists and all those admirers of folk art and of popular traditions whose enthusiasm assumed both serious and ridiculous shapes, still not unfamiliar today. Populism may often have taken reactionary forms and fed

---

[1] xiii 172; cf. xiii 177.   [2] viii 178.   [3] xiv 38.   [4] xiii 364.

the stream of aggressive nationalism; but the form in which Herder held it was democratic and peaceful, not only anti-dynastic and anti-élitist, but deeply anti-political, directed against organised power, whether of nations, classes, races or parties. I have called it populism because this movement, whether in Europe or outside it, seems to me the nearest approximation to Herder's ideal. It is, as a rule, pluralistic, looks on government as an evil, tends, following Rousseau, to identify 'the people' with the poor, the peasants, the common folk, the plebeian masses,[1] uncorrupted by wealth or city life; and, to this day, animates folk enthusiasts and cultural fanatics, egalitarians and agitators for local autonomy, champions of arts and crafts and of simple life, and innocent Utopians of all brands. It is based on belief in loose textures, voluntary associations, natural ties, and is bitterly opposed to armies, bureaucracies, 'closed' societies of any sort.

Historically, populism has, of course, become closely interwoven with real nationalism, and it has, indeed, often provided the soil in which blind xenophobia and irrationalism grew to dangerous heights; and this is no more accidental than the alliances of nationalism with democracy or romanticism or liberalism at various points in the nineteenth century. Nevertheless, it is a historical and moral error to identify the ideology of one period with its consequences at some other, or with its transformation in another context and in combination with other factors. The progeny of Herder in, let us say, England or America are to be found principally among those amateurs who became absorbed in the antiquities and forms of life (ancient and modern) of cultures other than their own, in Asia and Africa or the 'backward' provinces of Europe or America, among professional amateurs and collectors of ancient song and poetry, among enthusiastic and sometimes sentimental devotees of more primitive forms of life in the Balkans or among the Arabs; nostalgic travellers and exiles like Richard Burton, Doughty, Lafcadio Hearn, the English companions of Gandhi or Ibn Saud, cultural autonomists and unpolitical youth movements, as well as serious students and philosophers of language and society.

---

[1] This strain is strong in Herder, particularly in his early years: e.g. 'Philosopher and plebeian, unite in order to be useful!' (xxxii 51), written in 1765, when Herder was twenty-one. There is also his insistence, already quoted, that political reform must always come 'from below' (xxxii 56).

Perhaps Herder's most characteristic descendants were to be found in Russia, in which he took so abiding an interest. In that country his ideas entered the thought of those critics and creative artists who not merely developed national and pseudo-national forms of their own native art but became passionate champions of all 'natural', 'spontaneous', traditional forms of art and self-expression wherever they manifested themselves. These admirers of ethnic colour and variety as such, Mussorgsky, Stassov, and some of the musicians and painters whom they inspired, so far from supporting authority and repression, stood politically on the left, and felt sympathy for all forms of cultural self-expression, especially on the part of persecuted minorities – Georgians, Poles, Jews, Finns, but also Spaniards, Hungarians and other 'unreconstructed' nations. They denounced, however unjustly and intemperately, such 'organ-grinders' as Rossini and Verdi, or neo-classical schools of painting, for alleged cosmopolitanism, for commercialism, for a tendency to destroy regional or national differences in favour of flat and mechanical forms of life – in short, for rootlessness (a term which afterwards became so sinister and ominous in the mouths of obscurantists and chauvinists), heartlessness, oppression and dehumanisation. All this is typically Herderian.

Something of this kind, too, may have entered Mazzini's ideal of the Young Italy which was to live in harmony and mutual understanding with Young Germany – and the 'Youth' of all nations – once they had thrown away the shackles of oppressive imperialism, of dynastic autocracies, of the denial of the rights of all 'natural' human units, and attained to free self-determination. Such views may have been thoroughly Utopian. But if they were nationalistic, they were so in a sense very different from the later – and pejorative – sense of the word. Populism may have been in part responsible for isolationism, provincialism, suspicion of everything smooth, metropolitan, elegant and socially superior, hatred of the *beau monde* in all its forms; but with this went hostility to centralisation, dogmatism, militarism and self-assertiveness, or, in other words, all that is commonly associated with the full-grown nationalism of the nineteenth century, as well as with deep antipathy to mobs – Herder carefully distinguishes the *Pöbel auf den Gassen* ('the rabble') from the *Volk* (that is, the body of the nation), however this is done[1] – and with a hatred of violence and

---

[1] xxv 323.

conquest as strong as any to be found among the other Weimar humanists, Goethe, Wieland and Schiller. The faithful followers of Herder may often have been – and can still be – confused, sentimental, impractical, ineffective and sometimes ridiculous, but not managerial, calculating or brutal. No one made more of this profound contrast than Herder himself.

VI

In this connection it is worth considering Herder's attitude to three great eighteenth-century myths which fed the stream of nine-teenth-century nationalism. The first is that of the superiority of a particular tribal culture. His denunciation of patriotic boastfulness – the *Favoritvolk* doctrine – has already been referred to. One of the most quoted sentences from *Yet Another Philosophy of History* tells us that 'Every nation has its own inner centre of happiness, as every sphere its own centre of gravity.'[1] This is what the historian, the critic, the philosopher must grasp, and nothing is more fatal than the attempted assimilation of the *Mittelpunkt* of one culture with those of others. One must 'enter the time, the place, the entire history'[2] of a people; one must 'feel oneself into [*sich hinein-fühlen*] everything'.[3] This is what contemporary historians (he is referring specifically to Schlözer) conspicuously fail to do.[4] To understand Hebrew scripture it is not enough, he tells us, to see it as a sublime work of art, and compare its beauties with those of Homer, as the Oxford scholar Robert Lowth had done; we must transport ourselves into a distant land and an earlier age, and read it as the national poem of the Jews, a pastoral and agricultural people, written in ancient, simple, rustic, poetic, not philosophical or abstract, language. 'Be a shepherd among shepherds, a peasant in the midst of an agricultural people, an oriental among the primitive dwellers of the East, if you wish to enjoy these creations in the atmosphere of their birth.'[5] Germans are not ancient Hebrews;

[1] v 509.   [2] v 502.   [3] v 503; cf. ii 118, ii 257, v 536.   [4] v 436–40.
[5] x 14 (written in 1780–1). This is less than fair to Lowth, who, a good deal earlier than his critic, spoke of biblical verse as words that 'burst forth in sentences pointed, earnest, rapid, and tremulous' and declared that 'we must see all things with their eyes ... we must endeavour ... to read Hebrew as the Hebrews would have read it'. Robert Lowth, *Lectures on the Sacred Poetry of the Hebrews* (1753), trans. from the Latin by G. Gregory (London, 1787), Lectures 1 and 5 (vol. 1, pp. 37 and 113).

biblical images are drawn from a world alien to them. When the poet of the Bible speaks of the snows of Lebanon or the pleasant vineyards of Carmel, these are empty words to a German poet.[1] 'The dreadful storms from the sea passing over their land to Arabia were for them thundering steeds bearing the chariot of Jehovah through the clouds.'[2] He says that it would be better for a contemporary poet to sing of electric sparks than copy these Judaean images; for the Bible the rainbow is the footstool of the Lord's house; for the Skalds it is a fiery bridge over which the giants sought to storm heaven.[3] All this is at best only half intelligible to us. The Germans are not biblical Jews, nor are they classical Greeks or Romans either.[4] Every experience is what it is. To understand it is to grasp what it meant to those who expressed it in the monuments through which we try to read it. All understanding is necessarily historical. The *Aufklärer* – Gottsched, Lessing and Moses Mendelssohn – not only lack all historical perspective, they tend to grade, to give marks for moral excellence. Herder, in this (what he would regard as a Spinozan) mood, warns, at any rate in 1774 in *Auch eine Philosophie*, against moral evaluation (prone though he was to it himself, then and later), and urges the critic to understand above all that if one must condemn and praise, this should be done only after an exercise of sympathetic insight – of one's capacity for *Einfühlen* ('empathy').

Auch eine Philosophie contains the most eloquent description of the newly discovered sense of history, with its uncanny resemblance to that of Vico, whom, so far as we can tell, Herder did not read until twenty years later:

---

[1] i 258–9.   [2] i 264.   [3] ibid.

[4] 'Oh accursed word "classical"! It has transformed Cicero for us into a classical school-rhetorician, Horace and Virgil into classical school-poets, Caesar into a pedant, Livy into a phrasemonger. It is the word "classical" that has divided expression from thought, and thought from the event that has generated it.' This word has become a wall between us and all true education, which would have seen the ancients as living exemplars. 'This word has buried many a genius beneath a heap of words ... crushed him under a millstone of a dead language' (i 412). When a German poet is described as a second Horace, as a new Lucretius, a historian as a second Livy, that is nothing to be proud of; 'but it would be a great, rare, enviable glory for us if one could say about such writers: "This is how Horace, Cicero, Lucretius, Livy would have written if they were writing about this topic, at this particular stage of culture, at this particular time, with this particular purpose, for this particular people, with its particular outlook and its own language"' (i 383).

How unspeakably difficult it is to convey the particular quality [*Eigenheit*] of an individual human being and how impossible it is to say precisely what distinguishes an individual, his way of feeling and living; how different and how individual [*anders und eigen*] everything becomes once his eyes see it, once his soul grasps it, his heart feels it. How much depth there is in the character of a single people, which, no matter how often observed, and gazed at with curiosity and wonder, nevertheless escapes the word which attempts to capture it, and, even with the word to catch it, is seldom so recognisable as to be universally understood and felt. If this is so, what happens when one tries to master an entire ocean of peoples, times, cultures, countries with one glance, one sentiment, by means of one single word! Words, pale shadow-play! An entire living picture of ways of life, or habits, wants, characteristics of land and sky, must be added, or provided in advance; one must start by feeling sympathy with a nation if one is to feel a single one of its inclinations or acts, or all of them together.[1]

Greece, he continues, was not Athens. It was inhabited and ruled by Athenians, Boeotians, Spartans, Corinthians. Egyptians were traders no less than Phoenicians. Macedon was a conqueror like Rome. The great Greek thinkers had speculative minds as sharp as those of moderns. Yet (Herder repeats in and out of context) they were Egyptians, Romans, Greeks, Macedonians, and *not* inhabitants of our world. Leibniz is ours; Plato is not. Similarity is not identity; one must see both the wood and the trees, although only God can do this completely. All history is an unending conflict between the general idea and the particular; all general ideas are abstractions, dangerous, misleading, and unavoidable. One must seek to see the whole, however unattainable this goal may be. Exceptions and deviations will amaze only those who insist upon forcing an idealised image on the manifold of reality. Hume and Voltaire, Robertson and Schlözer are denounced for using the measuring-rod of their own time. All civilisations are incommensurable.[2] The critic must, so far as he is able, surrender to his author and seek to see with the author's eyes.

Herder disagrees with Diderot's justly celebrated theory of the actor who is inwardly detached from a role when he plays it.[3] The true interpreter must seek to penetrate — lose himself in — the original which he, as it were, recreates, even if he can never wholly

[1] v 502.   [2] v 509.
[3] 'Nous sentons, nous; eux, ils observent': *Oeuvres complètes de Diderot*, ed. J. Assézat and Maurice Tourneaux (Paris, 1875–7), vol. 8, p. 368.

achieve this. Genuine translation from one language – that is, way of life – into another is, of course, impossible; no real idiom is literally translatable: the olives sacred to Minerva that grew round the Academy cannot be taken beyond the frontiers of Athens. 'Even when Sparta ravaged Athens, the goddess protected her grove. So no one can take the beauties of our language from us: beauties woven into its texture, glimmering like Phryne's bosom beneath her silken veil.'[1] To translate is – for better or for worse – to create; the translation must be an *Originalarbeit* by a *schöpferisches Genie*;[2] and, of course, because the creator is what he is, and not someone or somewhere else, a great deal is, and must be, lost. Egypt must not be judged by Greek criteria, or by Shaftesbury's modern ones; the schoolboy is not joyless because he takes no pleasure in the avocations of a grown man, nor were the Middle Ages worthless because they do not please Voltaire: there is more in the great ferment of the Dark Ages than the absurdities of Ripuarian or Salic laws. The medieval culture of the West must be seen as a great revolt against the suffocating centralisation of Rome, a 'rewinding of the gigantic, run-down clock'.[3] To denounce or idealise it is equally absurd: 'I am by no means disposed to defend the constant migrations and devastations, the feudal wars, the hordes of monks, the pilgrimages, the crusades. I want only to explain them: to show the spirit that breathed through it all, the ferment of human forces.'[4] This was original enough in 1774. The Middle Ages are not a corridor to the Renaissance, nor is paganism an ante-room of Christianity. One culture is never a mere means to another; even if there is a sense in which mankind as a whole is advancing,[5] each of the stages is an end in itself: men are never means to ends beyond themselves. No less than his opponent Kant, he fervently preaches the doctrine that only persons and societies, and almost all of these, are good in themselves – indeed they are all that is good, wholly good, in the world that we know. These maxims, which now (at least in the West) seem so platitudinous, were antinomian heresies in the middle of the eighteenth century in Paris and its intellectual dependencies.

So much for the myth of the Dominant Model. Still bolder was

---

[1] ii 44.   [2] i 178.   [3] v 526.   [4] ibid.
[5] Herder does not make clear what he means by the progress – *Fortgang* – of mankind: relativism is, on the face of it, incompatible with belief in objective progress. But see the discussion beginning on the next page.

Herder's rejection of the historical myths of the century;[1] of the French myth of classical culture created by the Gallo-Romans, in which lay the true soul of France, and which the barbarians destroyed, and equally of the counter-myth of the superiority of the Frankish conquerors, to which support had been given by Montesquieu, Mallet and Boulainvilliers. Similarly Herder has no truck with the Renaissance myth of the sunlit pagan world killed by the gloomy, pleasure-destroying Christian religion: he uses harsh words about the monks who suppressed the old German songs; but this does not mean that the Middle Ages are the dark haunt of the demons, slaves, diabolical priests and tyrants[2] painted by Voltaire, Gibbon, Hume and, later still, Heine and all the neo-pagans. But neither does he uphold the growing German-Protestant legend of the uncorrupted, fearless, Cheruscan warrior Hermann canonised by Klopstock as Arminius, and then, in the shape of the young Siegfried, placed by Wagner in the German nationalist pantheon. These fantasies offer no avenue of escape. All attempts to flee, whether to modern Paris or to the dark German woods, are condemned by Herder as being equally deluded. Those who, for whatever reason, will not face reality are doomed.

The third great myth of the eighteenth century was that of steady progress, if not inevitable, at least virtually certain; with consequent disparagement of the benighted past, which entailed the view of all earlier centuries as so many steps toward the superior life of the present and the still more wonderful life of the future. Herder rejects this completely. Each culture is a harmonious lyre – one must merely have the ear to hear its melodies. Those who seek to understand must learn to grasp the respects in which Abraham or Leonidas or Caesar are not men of our time – to see change as it occurs, not in juxtaposed segments which can be detached, compared and awarded marks for merit, for the degree to which they approach our standards of enlightenment. Is there, then, no progress? Are all cultures equally valuable? This is not Herder's view. There is *Fortgang*, but this is not the same as the notion of progress enunciated by, say, Turgot or Condorcet, or, in particular, by Voltaire (for example, in *La Philosophie d'histoire*

---

[1] Rouché, op. cit. (p. 170 above, note 2), esp. pp. 17 ff., deals with this far more faithfully than Herder's better-known German commentators.

[2] v 486.

par feu l'abbé Bazin), against whom, together with the Swiss philosopher of history Iselin, Herder's thunderbolts are specifically directed. Theirs is a shallow, unhistorical delusion. Diversity is everything. This is the central thesis of, to give it its full title, *Auch eine Philosophie der Geschichte zur Bildung der Menschheit*, as of almost all Herder's early writings:

> The general, philosophical, philanthropic temper of our age seeks to extend 'our own ideal' of virtue and happiness to each distant nation, even to the remotest ages in history . . . Those who have thus far taken it upon themselves to explain the centuries of progress have mostly cherished the notion that it must lead to greater virtue and happiness. In support of this they have embroidered or invented facts, played down or suppressed facts that belie it . . . taken words for works, enlightenment for happiness, greater intellectual sophistication for virtue, and so invented the figment of 'the general progressive improvement of the world'.[1]

Others realised that this was a dangerous delusion, and fell into hopeless scepticism like Montaigne, Bayle, Hume, and ultimately even Voltaire and Diderot.

This rests on a misconception of what progress is. It lies in a variety of cultures, incommensurable with each other and incapable of being arranged on some single scale of progress or retrogression. Each society, each culture, develops in its own way. Each age is different, and 'each has the centre of its happiness within itself. The youth is not happier than the innocent, contented child; nor is the peaceful old man less happy than the vigorous man in the prime of life.'[2] The Middle Ages are full of 'abominations, errors, absurdities',[3] but also possess 'something solid, cohesive, noble and majestic'[4] which our age, with its 'enervated coldness . . . and human misery',[5] can scarcely understand. 'Light does not nourish men',[6] order and affluence are not enough; still less technical accomplishment 'in the hands of one person, or of a few, who do the thinking' for everyone.[7] There are many ways of life and many truths – to believe that everything is either true or false is a wretched general illusion of our progressive age. True *Fortgang* ('advance') is the development of human beings as integrated wholes and, more particularly, their development as groups –

[1] v 511.   [2] v 512.   [3] v 527.   [4] v 524.   [5] v 527.   [6] v 525.   [7] v 538.

tribes, cultures and communities determined by language and
custom, creating out of the totality of their collective experience,
and expressing themselves in works of art that are consequently
intelligible to common men, and in sciences and crafts and forms of
social and political and cultural life that fulfil the cravings (conscious and unconscious) and develop the faculties of a given
society, in its interplay with its alterable, but not greatly alterable,
natural environment.

> To bind and interrogate this Proteus, which is usually called national
> character and which shows itself certainly not less in the writings than
> in the usages and actions of a nation – that is a high and beautiful
> philosophy. It is practised most surely in poetry; for in the works of
> ... imagination and feeling the entire soul of the nation reveals itself
> most freely.[1]

This is what the classical Greeks succeeded in doing so marvellously. Despite all Hamann's anathemas, Herder cannot refrain
from expressing his passionate admiration for the culture of Athens
– a feeling that he shared with Goethe and Hegel, Hölderlin and
Schiller, and, indeed, with the majority of the civilised Germans of
his time, romantic and anti-romantic alike. Herder thinks the
Greek achievement is in part due to the beauty of nature in Greece,
a beauty which inspired principles that those fortunate inhabitants
(mistakenly but excusably) regarded as objective and universally
valid. But there must be no *Favoritvolk*; he hastens to add to the
list Kashmiris and Persians, Bokharans and Circassians, who also
lived in beautiful natural surroundings, grew handsome themselves
and produced beautiful cultures (unlike the Hebrews, whose merits
are not aesthetic). The Greeks advanced; they developed their own
faculties harmoniously and triumphantly, because nature was
propitious and because no great natural accidents arrested this
development. But they are not a hallway to the Romans, whose
civilisation must be judged in terms of its own internal criteria, its
own 'centre of gravity'.

What Herder calls *Fortgang* is the internal development of a
culture in its own habitat, towards its own goals; but because there
are some qualities that are universal in man, one culture can study,
understand and admire another, even though it cannot return to it

---

[1] xviii 58.

and will only make itself foolish if it tries. At times Herder speaks like Bossuet: as if history were not an episodic story but a vast drama; as if the finger of God guided the destinies of humanity in some teleological fashion, in a play of which each great cultural epoch was an act. He does not develop this notion, which led Bossuet to see each act as in some degree a link between its predecessor and its successor. More often he speaks as if history were indeed a drama, but one without a dénouement: as if it were like a cosmic symphony of which each movement is significant in itself, and of which, in any case, we cannot hear the whole, for God alone does so. The later movements are not necessarily closer to, or a prefiguring of, some ultimate goal, and, therefore, superior to the earlier movements. Life is not a jigsaw puzzle of which the fragments must fit into some single pattern in terms of which alone they are all intelligible, so that what seems, taken in isolation, irrational or ugly, is seen to be an indispensable ingredient in the great harmonious whole – the world spirit come to full self-consciousness of itself, in Hegel's famous image. Herder believes in the development of each movement of the symphony (each act of the drama) in terms of its own ends, its own values, which are none the worse or less morally valuable because they will pass or be destroyed and be succeeded by others.

There is a general purpose to be achieved by human life on earth, which he calls *Humanität*. This is a notoriously vague term, in Herder and the *Aufklärung* generally, connoting harmonious development of all immortal souls towards universally valid goals: reason, freedom, toleration, mutual love and respect between individuals and societies, as well as physical and spiritual health, finer perceptions, dominion over the earth, the harmonious realisation of all that God has implanted in his noblest work and made in his own image.[1] This is a characteristically all-inclusive, general and optimistic formula of Weimar humanism, which Herder does, indeed, adopt, particularly in his later works, but which he does not seem to have used (for it has no precise connotation) as a universal criterion either of explanation or of value.

He wants above all to be comprehensive and fair. He dislikes Gothic architecture, despite the eloquence on its behalf with which he made so deep an impression on Goethe in Strasbourg; he is repelled by chivalry, by medieval values in general, but he defends them against Voltaire, against caricatures. He placed no great value,

[1] See the remarks on *Humanität* at xiii 154 ff.

particularly towards the end of his life, upon primitivism as such, and in this respect differed from its true admirers in the eighteenth century. Yet colonial subjugation of native populations, ancient and modern, in and outside Europe, is always represented as being morally odious and as a crime against humanity. If paganism requires to be defended against Christian attack, and Homer against Klotz and the *Encyclopédie*, so must Christianity be defended against Holbach, Voltaire and the Sinophiles, and the Chinese and Mongols in their turn against the arrogance of Europeans. The shamans of central Asia, he insists, are not just deceivers; nor are myths simply false statements about reality invented by wicked priests to bamboozle and acquire power over the masses, as Bayle and Voltaire had made the world believe; nor are the inventions of poets merely intended to give pleasure or to instruct. Here he stands with Vico, some time before he read him (one wonders whether he ever more than merely glanced at his work). Shamans express in the form of myth and superstition objects of men's natural wishes – a vision of the world from which poetry naturally springs and which it expresses. Whole worlds are created by such poetry, worlds worthy of man and his creative powers, worlds not commensurable with other worlds, but all equally worthy of our interest and in need of our insight, because they are worlds made by men; by contemplating them we may succeed in grasping what we, in our turn, can be and create. We do this not by learning the lessons of the past (he sometimes says that the past repeats itself, but his central doctrine, in opposition to Hume or Voltaire, is that each page is unique), but rather because the vision of past creation inspires us to find our own centre of gravity, our own *Mittelpunkt* or *Schwerpunkt* or that of the group – nation, region, community – to which we belong.

Without such belonging there is no true creation and no true realisation of human goals. Hence to foist a set of alien values on another *Nation* (as missionaries have done in the Baltic provinces, and are doing, for example, in India) is both ineffective and harmful.[1] Worst of all are those who have no group, because they are exiled or self-exiled, physically or spiritually (for Herder the two are not very different), and are doomed to sterility. Such disintegration seemed to him to threaten the Germans in his own day. Indignantly some of his modern critics point out that he

[1] viii 210; cf. viii 303.

condemned France – the France of the eighteenth and nineteenth centuries! – as being an exhausted society. But whatever his failings as a prophet (and he speaks with many voices, some of them far from distinct and often uttering contradictory sentiments), as a social psychologist he rose above his generation; more clearly than any other writer, he conceived and cast light upon the crucially important social function of 'belonging' – on what it is to belong to a group, a culture, a movement, a form of life. It was a most original achievement.

<h2 style="text-align:center">VII</h2>

It is the composer's duty, as a member of society, to speak to and for his fellow human beings.

I believe in roots, in associations, in backgrounds, in personal relationships ... my music now has its roots in where I live and work.

Benjamin Britten[1]

The notion of belonging is at the heart of all Herder's ideas. His doctrine of the unity of theory and practice, like that of his populism, is intelligible only in terms of it. To belong is not a passive condition, but active co-operation, social labour. 'Complete truth is always only the deed.'[2] Whether one reads the last books of his *Ideas about the Philosophy of History of Mankind*, the earlier treatise *On Hebrew Poetry*, the essays on Shakespeare, Ossian, Homer, the critical 'Groves', or the late *Adrastea* or *Kalligone*, one finds that what dominates them all is the notion that there are central patterns in terms of which each genuine culture – and the human beings who constitute it – can, and indeed must, be identified. For Herder, to be a member of a group is to think and act in a certain way, in the light of particular goals, values, pictures of the world: and to think and act so is to belong to a group. The notions are literally identical. To be a German is to be part of a unique stream of which language is the dominant element, but still only one element among others. He conveys the notion that the ways in which a people – say, the Germans – speak or move, eat or

---

[1] *On Receiving the First Aspen Award* (London, 1964), pp. 12, 21–2.

[2] 'Die vollständige Wahrheit ist immer nur That,' he wrote in 1774 (viii 261), long before Fichte or Hegel.

drink, their handwriting, their laws, their music, their social outlook, their dance forms, their theology, have patterns and qualities in common which they do not share, or share to a notably lesser degree, with the similar activities of some other group – the French, the Icelanders, the Arabs, the ancient Greeks. Each of these activities belongs to a cluster which must be grasped as a whole: they illuminate each other. Anyone who studies the speech rhythms, or the history or the architecture, or the physical characteristics of the Germans, will thereby achieve a deeper understanding of German legislation, music, dress. There is a property, not capable of being abstracted and articulated – that which is German in the Germans – which all these diverse activities uniquely evince. Activities like hunting, painting, worship, common to many groups in widely differing times and places, will resemble each other because they belong to the same genus. But the specific quality which each type of activity will show forth will have more in common with generically different activities of the same culture[1] than with specifically similar activities of another culture. Or, at the very least, that which the various activities of the same culture will have in common – the common pervasive pattern in virtue of which they are seen to be elements in one and the same culture – is more important, since it accounts for the characteristics of these activities at a deeper level, than their more superficial resemblances to the corresponding activities of other cultures and other human groups. In other words, what German epic poetry has in common with German family life, or German legislation, or German grammar, determines the patterns of these activities – runs through them more deeply – than that which German poetry has in common with Hindu or Hebrew poetry.

This common property is not occult; no special non-empirical faculty is needed to detect it; it is a natural attribute and open to empirical investigation. Despite his theology, his belief in the primacy of religion, and his use of such metaphysical notions as the collective 'soul' and 'spirit', despite the mysterious *Kräfte*, despite occasional lapses into acceptance of the dogma of natural kinds, Herder was far more of an empiricist from the beginning to the end of his life than Leibniz, Kant or even Helvétius. This was obscured by the fact that the following generation of German metaphysicians, whom he influenced, dealt freely in transcendent formulae.

[1] This notion is to be found in Hamann.

Yet in his own day he was at times suspected by the stricter among his fellow churchmen of inclining dangerously toward materialistic heresies. The heart of his empiricism lay in the importance that he attributed to the discovery of patterns in history and nature. It is this directly perceptible, but literally unanalysable, pattern quality, in virtue of which what Germans think or do or say is, as a rule, characteristically and unmistakably German – it is this *Gestalt* quality[1] that, in his view, makes us attribute the doer and the deed, the thinker and the thought, to a specific German culture at a specific stage of its development.

To fit into such a pattern is to belong: it is for this and no other reason that a German exiled from the milieu of his fellow Germans, perhaps a Saxon or a Prussian forced to live elsewhere, will not feel at home there; and whoever does not feel at home cannot create naturally, freely, generously, unselfconsciously, in the manner that Schiller called 'naïve', and that Herder, whether he admits it or not, most admires and believes in. All his talk about the national character, the national genius, the *Volksseele*, the spirit of the people and so forth in the end comes to this alone. His notion of what it is to belong to a family, a sect, a place, a period, a style is the foundation of his populism, and of all the later conscious programmes for self-integration or re-integration among men who felt scattered, exiled or alienated. The language in which he speaks of his unfortunate fellow countrymen, driven by poverty or the despotic whims of their masters to Russia or Transylvania or America to become blacks and slaves, is not simply a lament for the material and moral miseries of exile, but is based on the view that to cut men off from their living centre – from the texture to which they naturally belong – or to force them to sit by the rivers of some remote Babylon, and to prostitute their creative faculties for the benefit of strangers, is to degrade, dehumanise, destroy them.[2]

No writer has stressed more vividly the damage done to human beings by being torn from the only conditions in which their history has made it possible for them to live full lives. He insists

[1] Since originally writing this, I was glad to find it strongly confirmed by H. B. Nisbet, 'Herder, Goethe, and the Natural "Type" ', *Publications of the English Goethe Society* NS 37 (1967), 83–119.

[2] 'No Tyrtaeus', he wrote in 1778, 'will follow our brothers who have been sold to America as soldiers, no Homer will sing of this sad expedition. When religion, people, country are crushed, when these very notions are grown shadowy, the poet's lyre can yield only muted, strangled sounds' (viii 434).

over and over again that no one milieu or group or way of life is
necessarily superior to any other; but it is what it is, and
assimilation to a single universal pattern, of laws or language or
social structure, as advocated by the French *lumières*, would
destroy what is most living and valuable in life and art. Hence the
fierce polemic against Voltaire, who, in his *Essai sur les moeurs*,
declared that 'Man, generally speaking, was always what he is
now',[1] or that morality is the same in all civilised nations.[2]
Hence, by definition, it seemed to follow that the rest were
barbarous or stupid: Gauls are 'a disgrace to nature'.[3] Hence, too,
the attack on Sulzer for demanding a universal philosophical
grammar, according to the rules of which one would be enabled to
judge of the degree of the perfection of a people's language, and, if
need be, correct its rules in the light of the universal rules. Needless
to say, this for Herder was both false in principle and the death of
poetry and the springs of all creative power. Every group has a
right to be happy in its own way. It is terrible arrogance to affirm
that, to be happy, everyone should become European.[4] This is so
not because, as Voltaire maintained, other cultures may be superior
to ours, but simply because they are not comparable. 'No man can
convey the character of *his* feeling, or transform my being into
his.'[5] 'The Negro is as much entitled to think the white man
degenerate . . . as the white man is to think of the Negro as a black
beast . . . The civilisation of man is not that of the European; it
manifests itself, according to time and place, in every people.'[6]
Again, there is no *Favoritvolk*. Herder assumes only that to be
fully human, that is, fully creative, one must belong somewhere, to
some group or some historical stream, which cannot be defined
save in the genetic terms of a tradition, a milieu and a culture,
themselves generated by natural forces – the *Klima* (that is, the
external world) and physical structure and biological needs which,
in interplay with every individual's mind and will, create the
dynamic, collective process called society.

This theory entails no mythology. For Herder all groups are
ultimately collections of individuals; his use of 'organic' and
'organism' is still wholly metaphorical and not, as in later, more

[1] *Oeuvres complètes de Voltaire*, [ed. Louis Moland] (Paris, 1877–85), vol. 11,
p. 21.
[2] cf. *Le philosophe ignorant*, section 31: ibid., vol. 26, pp. 78–9.
[3] ibid., vol. 11, p. 260.   [4] xiii 333–42, esp. 342.   [5] xiii 333–4.
[6] xviii 248–9.

metaphysical thinkers, only half metaphorical. There is no evidence that he conceived of groups as metaphysical 'super-individual' entities or values. For Herder this is no mystique of history, or of a species to which individuals were to be sacrificed, still less of the superior wisdom of the race, or of a particular nation, or even of humanity as a whole. Nevertheless, to understand men is to understand them genetically, in terms of their history, of the one complex of spiritual and physical 'forces' in which they feel free and at home. This notion of being at home, and the corresponding notion of homelessness (nostalgia, he once remarked, is the noblest of all pains) which lies at the heart of his reflections on the emptiness of cosmopolitanism, on the damage done to men by social barriers, oppression by strangers, division, specialisation – like the connected concepts of exploitation and of the alienation of men from each other, and, in the end, from their own true selves – derive from his one central conception. Those who have grasped the notion that men are made miserable not only by poverty, disease, stupidity or the effects of ignorance, but also because they are misfits or outsiders or not spoken to, that liberty and equality are nothing without fraternity; that only those societies are truly human which may follow a leader but obey no master,[1] are in possession of one of Herder's *idées maîtresses*. His writings radically transformed the notion of relations of men to each other. Hegel's famous definition of freedom as *Bei-sich-selbst-seyn*,[2] as well as his doctrine of *Anerkennung* – reciprocal recognition among men – seem to me to owe much to Herder's teaching. The proposition that man is by nature sociable had been uttered by Aristotle and repeated by Cicero, Aquinas, Hooker, Grotius, Locke and innumerable others. The depth and breadth of Herder's writings on human association and its vicissitudes, the wealth of concrete historical and psychological observation with which he developed the concept of what it is for men to belong to a community, made such formulae seem to be thin abstractions and drove them permanently out of circulation. No serious social theorist after Herder dared advance mechanical clichés of this type in lieu of thought. His vision of society has dominated Western thought; the extent of its influence has not always been recognised, because it has entered too deeply into the texture of ordinary thinking. His immense impact, of which Goethe spoke and to

[1] cf. pp. 186–7 above.   [2] op. cit. (p. 56 above, note 4), vol. 11, p. 44.

which J. S. Mill bore witness, is due principally to his central thesis – his account of what it is to live and act together – from which the rest of his thought flows, and to which it constantly returns. This idea is at the heart of all populism; and it has entered every subsequent attempt to arrive at truth about society.

VIII

So much for Herder's specific contribution to the understanding of men and their history. There are two implications of his conception of men that have received little attention from his interpreters. These are, first, his doctrine of the indivisibility of the human personality and, as a corollary of this, his conception of the artist and his expressive role in society; and, secondly, his pluralism and the doctrine of the incompatibility of ultimate human ends.

Herder was, as everyone knows, much occupied with aesthetic questions, and tried to seek out all manifestations of art in their richest and fullest forms. He tended to find them in the creations of the early ages of man. For Herder, art is the expression of men in society in their fullness. To say that art is expression is to say that it is a voice speaking rather than the production of an object – a poem, a painting, a golden bowl, a symphony, all of which possess their own properties, like objects in nature, independently of the purposes or character or milieu of the men who created them.[1] By the very appropriately called *Stimmen der Völker in Liedern*, and by explicit argument, Herder seeks to demonstrate that all that a man does and says and creates must express, whether he intends it to do so or not, his whole personality; and, since a man is not conceivable outside a group to which, if he is reasonably fortunate, he continues to belong (he retains its characteristics in a mutilated state even if he has been torn from it), conveys also its collective individuality[2] – a culture conceived as a constant flow of thought, feeling, action and expression. Hence he is bitterly opposed to the view, influential in his day as in ours, that the purpose of the artist is to create an object whose merits are independent of the creator's personal qualities or his intentions, conscious or unconscious, or of his social situation.

[1] A doctrine maintained, so it seemed to Herder, by such despotic Paris arbiters of artistic beauty as the disciples of Boileau – the abbés Dubos, Batteux and the like.

[2] v 502.

This is an aesthetic doctrine that reigned long before the doctrine of art for art's sake had been explicitly formulated. The craftsman who makes a golden bowl is entitled, according to this view, to say that it is no business of those who acquire or admire his creation to enquire whether he is himself sincere or calculating, pious or an atheist, a faithful husband, politically sound, a sympathetic boon companion or morally pure. Herder is the true father of the doctrine that it is the artist's mission, above others, to testify in his works to the truth of his own inner experience;[1] from which it follows that any conscious falsification of this experience, from whatever motive – indeed any attempt merely to satisfy the taste of his customers, to titillate their senses, or even to offer them instruction by means that have little to do with his own life or convictions, or to use techniques and skills as a detached exercise, to practise virtuosity for its own sake or for the sake of the pleasure it brings – is a betrayal of his calling.

This was implicit in the artistic movement which came to be called *Sturm und Drang*, of which Herder was one of the leaders. To view oneself as a professional who in his works of art plays a role, or performs with a specialised part of himself, while the rest of him is left free to observe the performance; to maintain that one's behaviour as a man – as a father, a Frenchman, a political terrorist – can be wholly detached from one's professional function as a carpenter, doctor, artist – this view, to which Voltaire, if he had considered it, could scarcely have offered any objection, is, for all the writers of the *Sturm und Drang*, a fatal misapprehension and distortion of the nature of man and his relations with other men. Since man is in fact one and not many (and those who are genuinely divided personalities are literally no longer sane), it follows that whether a man be an artist, a politician, a lawyer, a soldier, anything that he does expresses all that he is.

Some among the *Stürmer* remained individualistic – Heinse, for example, or Klinger. But Herder is uncompromisingly hostile to such egomania. The individual, for him, is inescapably a member of some group; consequently all that he does must express, consciously or unconsciously, the aspirations of his group. Hence, if he is conscious of his own acts (and all self-consciousness is embryonic assessment and therefore critical), such awareness, like

---

[1] But Vico anticipated him: see p. 110 above, note 1.

all true criticism, is inevitably to a high degree social criticism, because it is the nature of human beings to be socially aware: expression is communication. Herder feels that all history shows this to be so. To divide (and not merely to distinguish as facets or aspects of one substance) body and soul, science and craft or art, the individual and society, description and evaluation, philosophical, scientific and historical judgement, empirical and metaphysical statements, as if any of these could be independent of one another, is for Herder false, superficial and misleading.

The body is the image, the expression, of the soul, not its tomb or instrument or enemy. There are no 'iron walls' between body and soul;[1] everything can pass into everything else by the insensible transitions of which Leibniz had spoken in his *Nouveaux Essais*. Once upon a time men 'were all things: poets, philosophers, land surveyors, legislators, musicians, warriors'.[2] In those days there was unity of theory and practice, of man and citizen, a unity that the division of labour destroyed; after that men became 'half thinkers and half feelers'.[3] There is, he remarks, something amiss about moralists who do not act, epic poets who are unheroic, orators who are not statesmen, and aestheticians who cannot create anything. Once doctrines are accepted uncritically – as dogmatic, unalterable, eternal truths – they become dead formulae, or else their meaning is fearfully distorted. Such ossification and decay lead to nonsense in thought and monstrous behaviour in practice.[4]

This doctrine was destined to have a great flowering, not merely in the application of the concept of alienation in the writings of the young Marx and his friends in their Left-Hegelian phase, and among those who have used these ideas in our own time, but more particularly among pre-Marxist Russian radicals and revolutionaries. No body of men ever believed so devoutly and passionately in the unity of man as the Russian intelligentsia of the last century. These men – at first dissident members of the nobility and gentry, later members of many classes – were united by a burning faith in the right and duty of all men to realise their creative potentialities (physical and spiritual, intellectual and artistic) in the light of the

[1] viii 193.   [2] viii 261.
[3] ibid. The celebrated description in the introduction to Karl Marx's *German Ideology* of what a full human life could be seems to be a direct echo of this doctrine.
[4] xiii 195.

reason and the moral insight with which all men are endowed. What the eighteenth-century French *philosophes* and the German romantics preached, these men sought to practise. Light to them came from the West. And since the number of literate – let alone well-educated – men in Russia was infinitesimal compared to the number who lived in ignorance, misery, hopeless starvation and poverty, it was plainly the first duty of any decent man to give all he could to the effort to lift his brothers to a level where they could lead a human existence.

From this sprang the conception of the intelligentsia as a sacred order called upon by history to dedicate their lives to the discovery and use of all possible means – intellectual and moral, artistic and technological, scientific and educational – in a single-minded effort to discover the truth, realise it in their lives, and with its aid to rescue the hungry and the naked, and make it possible for them to live in freedom and be men once more. Man is one and undivided; whatever he is and does flows from a single centre; but at the same time he is as he is within a social web of which he is a constituent; to ignore it is to falsify the nature of man. The famous doctrine that the artist, and above all the writer, has a social obligation to express the nature of the milieu in which he lives, and that he has no right to isolate himself artificially, under the cover of some theory about the need for moral neutrality, or the need for specialisation, the purity of art, or of its specifically aesthetic function – a priestly task that is to be kept uncontaminated, especially by politics – this entire conception, over which such ferocious battles were fought in the following century, stems from Herder's doctrine of the unity of man.

'Everything that a man sets out to achieve, whether it is produced by deed or word or by some other means, must spring from all his powers combined; all segregation is deplorable.'[1] This principle of Hamann's, so much admired by Goethe, formed Herder, and became (through Schiller and Friedrich Schlegel) the creed of the Russian radical critics. Whatever a man does, if he is as he should be, will express his entire nature. The worst sin is to mutilate oneself, to suppress this or that side of oneself, in the service of some false aesthetic or political or religious ideal. This is

[1] The form of words is Goethe's, in *Dichtung und Wahrheit*, book 12: vol. 28, p. 108, line 25, in op. cit. (p. 113 above, note 2). It is quoted by Roy Pascal on pp. 9–10 and 134 of his *The German Sturm und Drang* (Manchester, 1953), in which he gives an admirable account, the best in English, of this entire movement.

the heart of the revolt against the pruned French garden of the eighteenth century. Blake is a passionate spokesman of this faith no less than Hamann or Herder or Schleiermacher. To understand any creator – any poet or, for that matter, any human being who is not half dead – is to understand his age and nation, his way of life, the society which (like nature in Shaftesbury) 'thinks in him'. Herder says over and over again that the true artist (in the widest sense) creates only out of the fullness of the experience of his whole society, especially out of its memories and antiquities, which shape its collective individuality; and he speaks of Chaucer, Shakespeare, Spenser as being steeped in their national folklore. About this he may be mistaken, but the direction of his thought is clear enough. Poetry – and, indeed, all literature and all art – is the direct expression of uninhibited life. The expression of life may be disciplined, but life itself must not be so. As early poetry was magical, a spur to heroes, hunters, lovers, men of action, a continuation of experience, so, *mutatis mutandis*, it must be so now also. Society may have sadly disintegrated since those days, and Herder concedes that the rhapsodical Klopstock may now be able consciously to express only his own individual, rather than the communal, life; but express he must whatever is in him, and his words will communicate the experience of his society to his fellow men. 'A poet is a creator of a people; he gives it a world to contemplate, he holds its soul in his hand.'[1] He is, of course, to an equal extent created by it.[2] A man lives in a world of which, together with others, he is in some sense the maker. 'We live in a world we ourselves create.'[3] These words of Herder's were destined to be inflated into extravagant metaphysical shapes by Fichte, Schelling, Hegel and the Idealist movement in philosophy; but they are equally at the source of the profoundest sociological insights of Marx and the revolution in the historical outlook that he initiated.[4]

Herder may be regarded as being among the originators of the

---

[1] viii 433.   [2] ii 160–1.   [3] viii 252.

[4] It is odd that one of Hamann's most fruitful observations – that the poetry of Livonian peasants in the country round Riga and Mitau, which he knew well, was connected with the rhythms of their daily work – evidently made no impression on his disciple. Herder is fascinated by the intimate relation of action and speech, e.g. in his theory of why it is that (as he supposed) verbs precede nouns in primitive speech, but ignores the influence of work. This was made good much later under Saint-Simonian and Marxist influence.

doctrine of artistic commitment – perhaps with Hamann the earliest thinker consciously to speak (as one would expect of the founder of populism) in terms of the totally *engagé* writer, to see the artist as *ipso facto* committed and not permitted to divide himself into compartments, to separate body from spirit, the secular from the sacred, and, above all, life from art. He believed from the beginning to the end of his life that all men are in some degree artists, and that all artists are, first and last, men – fathers, sons, friends, citizens, fellow worshippers, men united by common action. Hence the purpose of art is not to exist for its own sake (the late *Adrastea* and *Kalligone* are the most ferocious attacks on this doctrine, which he suspected both Kant and Goethe of advancing) or to be utilitarian, or propagandist, or to purvey 'social realism'; still less, of course, should it seek merely to embellish life or invent forms of pleasure or produce artefacts for the market. The artist is a sacred vessel who is shaped by, and the highest expression of, the spirit of his time and place and society; he is the man who conveys, as far as possible, a total human experience, an entire world. This is the doctrine that, under the impulsion of German romanticism and French socialism, profoundly affected the conception of the artist and his relation to society, and animated Russian critics and writers from the late 1830s until, at any rate, *Doctor Zhivago*. The theory of art as total expression and of the artist as a man who testifies to the truth – as opposed to the concept of him as a purveyor, however gifted and dedicated, or as a priest of an esoteric cult, entered the practice of the great Russian novelists of the nineteenth century, even of such 'pure' writers as Turgenev and Chekhov. Through their works it has had a great, indeed a decisive, influence, not only on the literature and criticism, but on the moral and political ideas and behaviour, of the West, and indeed of the entire world. Consequently, Herder was perhaps not altogether mistaken when he so confidently proclaimed the part to be played by the artist in the world to come.

Whether as an aesthetic critic, or as a philosopher of history, or as a creator of the notion of the non-alienated man, or as the most vehement critic of the classifiers and dividers, Herder (with Hamann) emerges as the originator of the doctrine of the unity of art and life, theory and practice. He is the most eloquent of all the preachers of the restoration of the unbroken human being by the growth of civilisation, *Humanität*, whether by an act of spiritual water-divining whereby the buried stream of the true humanist tradition may be found and continued, or, as Rousseau demanded, by some social transformation that will destroy the shackles that crib and confine men, and will allow them to enter or re-enter the Garden of Eden which they lost when they yielded to the temptation to organise and dominate one another. Once the walls that separate men are knocked down, walls of State or class or race or religion, they will return to themselves and be men and creative once again. The influence of this part of his teaching on the ideas of others, who spoke more articulately and acted with greater political effect, has been very great.[1]

IX

Finally, I come to what is perhaps the most revolutionary of the implications of Herder's position, his famous rejection of absolute values, his pluralism.

Men, according to Herder, truly flourish only in congenial circumstances, that is, where the group to which they belong has achieved a fruitful relationship with the environment by which it is shaped and which in turn it shapes. There the individual is happily integrated into the 'natural community',[2] which grows

[1] Like other passionate propagandists, Herder pleaded for that which he himself conspicuously lacked. As sometimes happens, what the prophet saw before him was a great compensatory fantasy. The vision of the unity of the human personality and its integration into the social organism by 'natural' means was the polar opposite of Herder's own character and conduct. He was, by all accounts, a deeply divided, touchy, resentful, bitter, unhappy man in constant need of support and praise, neurotic, pedantic, difficult, suspicious and often insupportable. When he speaks about the 'simple, deep, irreplaceable feeling of being alive' (xiii 337) and compares it with the carefully tended, over-arranged world of, say, the critic Sulzer, he is evidently speaking of an experience which he longed for but must often have lacked. It has frequently been remarked that it is tormented and unbalanced personalities – Rousseau, Nietzsche, D. H. Lawrence – who celebrate with particular passion physical beauty, strength, generosity, spontaneity, above all unbroken unity, harmony and serenity, qualities for which they had an insatiable craving. No man felt less happy in the Prussia of Frederick the Great, or even in the enlightened Weimar of Goethe and Wieland and Schiller, than Herder. Wieland, the most amiable and tolerant of men, found him maddening. Goethe said that he had in him something compulsively vicious – like a vicious horse – a desire to bite and hurt. His ideals seem at times a mirror image of his own frustration.

[2] This is the real community which was later (even before Tönnies) contrasted with the artificial *Gesellschaft*; e.g. Fichte's *Totum* as contrasted with his *Compositum*. But in Herder there are still no explicitly metaphysical overtones:

spontaneously, like a plant, and is not held together by artificial clamps, or soldered together by sheer force, or regulated by laws and regulations invented, whether benevolently or not, by the despot or his bureaucrats. Each of these natural societies contains within itself (in the words of *Yet Another Philosophy of History*) the 'ideal of its own perfection, wholly independent of all comparison with those of others'.[1] If this is so, how must we answer the question, put by men throughout recorded history and settled with such clarity and authority by the great *lumières* of the eighteenth century, namely: What is the best life for men? And, more particularly: What is the most perfect society?

There is, after all, no dearth of solutions. Every age has provided its own formulae. Some have looked for the solution in sacred books or in revelation or in the words of inspired prophets or the tradition of organised priesthoods; others found it in the rational insight of the skilled metaphysician, or in the combination of scientific observation and experiment, or in the 'natural' good sense of men not 'scribbled over' by philosophers or theologians or perverted by 'interested error'. Still others have found it only in the uncorrupted heart of the simple good man. Some thought that only trained experts could discover great and saving truths; others supposed that on questions of value all sane men were equally well qualified to judge. Some maintained that such truths could be discovered at any time, and that it was mere bad luck that it had taken so long to find the most important among them, or that they had been so easily forgotten. Others held that mankind was subject to the law of growth; and that the truth would not be seen in its fullness until mankind had reached maturity – the age of reason. Some doubted even this, and said men could never attain to such knowledge on earth; or if they did, were too weak to follow it in practice, since such perfection was attainable only by angels, or in the life hereafter. But one assumption was common to all these views: that it was, at any rate in principle, possible to draw some outline of the perfect society or the perfect man, if only to define how far a given society or a given individual fell short of the ideal.

the *Kräfte* realised in communal life – the dynamic forces which he probably derives from Leibniz – are not discovered, nor do they act, in any a priori or transcendent fashion: but neither are they described as being susceptible to scientific tests; their nature, a puzzle to his commentators, evidently did not seem problematic to Herder.

[1] xiv 227.

This was necessary if one was to be able to compare degrees of imperfection.

But this belief in the final objective answer has not been absolutely universal. Relativists held that different circumstances and temperaments demanded different policies; but, for the most part, even they supposed that, though the routes might differ, the ultimate goal – human happiness, the satisfaction of human wishes – was one and the same. Some sceptical thinkers in the ancient world – Carneades, for example – went further and uttered the disquieting thought that some ultimate values might be incompatible with one another, so that no solution could logically incorporate them all. There was something of this doubt about the logic of the concept of the perfect society not only among the Greeks, but in the Renaissance too, in Pontano, in Montaigne, in Machiavelli, and after them in Leibniz and Rousseau, who thought that no gain could be made without a corresponding loss.[1] Something of this, too, seemed to lie at the heart of the tragedies of Sophocles, Euripides, Shakespeare. Nevertheless, the central stream of the Western tradition was little affected by this fundamental doubt. The central assumption was that problems of value were in principle soluble, and soluble with finality. Whether the solutions could be implemented by imperfect men was another question, a question which did not affect the rationality of the universe. This is the keystone of the classical arch which, after Herder, began to crumble.

If Herder's view of mankind was correct – if Germans in the eighteenth century cannot become Greeks or Romans or ancient Hebrews or simple shepherds, still less all of these together – and if each of the civilisations into which he infuses so much life by his sympathetic *Einfühlen* are widely different, and indeed uncombinable – then how could there exist, even in principle, one universal ideal, valid for all men, at all times, everywhere? The 'physiognomies' of cultures are unique: each presents a wonderful exfoliation of human potentialities in its own time and place and environment. We are forbidden to make judgements of comparative value, for that is measuring the incommensurable; and even though Herder himself may not always be consistent in this respect, since he condemns and praises entire civilisations, his doctrine, at least in his most original works, does not permit this. Nor can it be doubted

[1] See p. 237 below, note 5.

that he himself made valiant efforts to live up to his earlier principles: for all his dislike of the rigidly centralised Egyptian establishment, or Roman imperialism, or the brutal chivalry of the Middle Ages, or the dogmatism and intolerance of the Catholic Church, he sought to be not merely fair to these civilisations, but to represent them as each realising an ideal of indefeasible validity which, as an expression of a particular manifestation of the human spirit, was valuable in itself, and not as a step to some higher order.

It is this rejection of a central dogma of the Enlightenment, which saw in each civilisation either a stepping-stone to a higher one, or a sad relapse to an earlier and lower one, that gives force, a sense of reality, and persuasive power to his vast panoramic survey. It is true that in the *Ideen* he enunciates the general ideal of *Humanität* towards which man is slowly climbing, and some of Herder's interpreters have faithfully attempted to represent his earlier relativism as a phase of his thought which he 'outgrew', or else to reconcile it with his hazy notion of a single progressive movement towards *Humanität*. Thus, Max Rouché thinks that Herder conceives of history as a drama, each act, perhaps each scene, of which can and should be understood and evaluated independently; which does not prevent us from perceiving that, taken together, these episodes constitute a single progressive ascent.[1] Perhaps Herder did come to believe this, or to believe that he believed it. But it remains a vague conception; his skill and imagination, even in the *Ideen*, go into the evocation of the individual cultures and not of the alleged links between them. The whole thrust of the argument, both in such early works as the *Älteste Urkunde des Menschengeschlechts*, *Von deutscher Art und Kunst*, *Vom Geist der ebräischen Poesie*, the *Kritische Wälder*, and in the late and mildly worded *Briefe zu Beförderung der Humanität*, and the *Ideen* itself, not to speak of his classical statement of historical relativism in *Auch eine Philosophie der Geschichte*, is to show and celebrate the uniqueness, the individuality and, above all, the incommensurability with one another of each of the civilisations which he so lovingly describes and defends.[2]

[1] Rouché, op. cit. (p. 170 above, note 2), esp. pp. 9, 48 ff., 62 ff.

[2] Meinecke discusses this in *Die Entstehung des Historismus* (Munich and Berlin, 1936), vol. 2, p. 438 – p. 339 in the translation by J. E. Anderson, *Historism: The Rise of a New Historical Outlook* (London, 1972) – and his conclusions are subjected to penetrating criticism by G. A. Wells in 'Herder's Two Philosophies of History', *Journal of the History of Ideas* 21 (1960), 527–37,

But if all these forms of life are intelligible each in its own terms (the only terms there are), if each is an 'organic' whole, a pattern of ends and means which cannot be resurrected, still less amalgamated, they can scarcely be graded as so many links in a cosmic, objectively knowable, progress, some stages of which are rendered automatically more valuable than others by their relationship – say, proximity to, or mirroring of – the final goal towards which humanity, however uncertainly, is marching. This places Herder's *Weltanschauung*, so far as it is consistent at all, despite all the insights that it shares with them, outside the 'perfectibilian' philosophies of modern times, as remote from the divine tactic of Bossuet (or even Burke) as from the doctrine of progress determined by the growth of reason preached by Lessing or Condorcet, or of Voltaire's *bon sens*, or from the ideal of progressive self-understanding and self-emancipation, spiritual or social, Hegelian or Marxist.

If Herder's notion of the equal validity of incommensurable cultures is accepted, the concepts of an ideal State or of an ideal man become incoherent. This is a far more radical denial of the foundations of traditional Western morality than any that Hume ever uttered. Herder's ethical relativism is a doctrine different from that of the Greek sophists or Montesquieu or Burke. These thinkers were agreed, by and large, that what men sought was happiness; they merely pointed out that differences of circumstance and the interplay of environment – 'climate' – with men's nature, conceived as fairly uniform, created different characters and outlooks and, above all, different needs which called for dissimilar institutional means of satisfaction. But they recognised a broad identity or similarity of purpose in all known forms of human activity, universal and timeless goals of men as such, which bound them in a single human species or Great Society. This would, at least in theory, enable a socially imaginative and well-informed universal despot, provided he was enlightened enough, to govern each society with a due regard to its individual needs; and to advance them all towards a final universal harmony, each moving by its own path toward the selfsame purpose – happiness and the rule of wisdom, virtue and justice. This is Lessing's conception,

---

at 535–6. Despite Wells's strictures, Meinecke's central thesis – that the heart of Herder's doctrines is a systematic relativism – still seems to me, for the reasons given above, to be valid.

embodied in the famous parable of the three rings in *Nathan the Wise*.[1]

Herder had deep affinities with the *Aufklärung*, and he did write with optimism and eloquence about man's ascent to ideal *Humanität*, and uttered sentiments to which Lessing could have subscribed, no less Goethe. Yet, despite the authority of some excellent scholars,[2] I do not believe that anyone who reads Herder's works with the *Einfühlung* for which he asks, and which he so well describes, will sustain the impression that it is this – the ideal of enlightened Weimar – that fills his mind. He is a rich, suggestive, prolix, marvellously imaginative writer, but seldom clear or rigorous or conclusive. His ideas are often confused, sometimes inconsistent, never wholly specific or precise, as, indeed, Kant pointedly complained. As a result, many interpretations can be (and have been) put upon his works. But what lies at the heart of the whole of his thought, what influenced later thinkers, particularly the German romantics and, through them, the entire history of populism, nationalism and individualism, is the theme to which he constantly returns: that one must not judge one culture by the criteria of another; that differing civilisations are different growths, pursue different goals, embody different ways of living, are dominated by different attitudes to life; so that to understand them one must perform an imaginative act of 'empathy' into their essence, understand them 'from within' as far as possible, and see the world through their eyes – be a 'shepherd among shepherds' with the ancient Hebrews,[3] or sail the Northern seas in a tempest and read the Eddas again on board a ship struggling through the Skagerrak.[4]

These widely differing societies and their ideals are not commensurable. Such questions as which of them is the best, or even which one should prefer, which one would judge to be nearer to the universal human ideal, *Humanität*, even subjectively conceived – the pattern most likely to produce man as he should be or as one thinks he should be – are, therefore, for a thinker of this type, in

---

[1] It found an unexpected re-incarnation in Mao Tse-tung's celebrated image of the many flowers.

[2] e.g. Rudolf Stadelmann, *Der historische Sinn bei Herder* (Halle/Saale, 1928); Robert Arnold Fritzsche, 'Herder und die Humanität', *Der Morgen* 3 (1927), 402–10); Hermann Vesterling, *Herders Humanitätsprincip* (Halle, 1890).

[3] See p. 211 above, note 5.　　[4] See v 169.

the end, meaningless. 'Not a man, not a country, not a people, not a national history, not a State, is like another. Hence the True, the Beautiful, the Good in them are not similar either.'[1] Herder wrote this in his journal in 1769. The cloven hoof of relativism, or rather pluralism, shows itself even in his most orthodox discussions of universal ideals; for he thinks each image of *Humanität* to be unique and *sui generis*.[2] It is this strain in his thought, and not the language of commonplace universalism which he shares with his age, that struck, and perhaps shocked, the *Aufklärer*, the Kantians, the progressive thinkers of his time. For this goes directly against the notion of steady progress on the part of mankind as a whole, which, despite difficulties and relapses, must, or at least can and should, go on; a proposition to which the German no less than the French or Italian Enlightenment was fully committed.[3]

Herder is not a subjectivist. He believes in objective standards of judgement that are derived from understanding the life and purposes of individual societies, and are themselves objective historical structures, and require, on the part of the student, wide and scrupulous scholarship as well as sympathetic imagination. What he rejects is the single overarching standard of values, in terms of which all cultures, characters and acts can be evaluated. Each phenomenon to be investigated presents its own measuring-rod, its own internal constellation of values in the light of which alone 'the facts' can be truly understood. This is much more thoroughgoing than the realisation that man is incapable of complete perfection, which, for instance, Winckelmann allowed,[4] Rousseau lamented, and Kant accepted; or the doctrine that all gains entail some loss.[5] For what is here entailed is that the highest

---

[1] iv 472. [2] xiv 210.

[3] Among modern thinkers, Herder's relativism most resembles Wyndham Lewis's protest against what he called 'the demon of progress in the arts'. In the tract which bears this title (London, 1954) that acute, if perverse, writer denounced, with characteristically vehement and biting eloquence, the notion that valid universal criteria exist in terms of which it is possible to assert or deny that a work of art of one age is or is not superior to one that belongs to an entirely different tradition. What meaning can be attached to, say, the assertion that Phidias is superior or inferior to Michelangelo or Maillol, or that Goethe or Tolstoy represents an improvement on, or decline from, Homer or Aeschylus or Dante or the Book of Job?

[4] e.g. in his *Geschichte der Kunst des Altertums* (Dresden, 1764), book 4, chapter 2, section 21, where he speaks of 'perfection, for which man is not a suitable vessel'; Herder echoes this almost verbatim (v 498).

[5] *Die philosophische Schriften von Gottfried Wilhelm Leibniz*, ed. C. I.

ends for which men have rightly striven and sometimes died are strictly incompatible with one another. Even if it were possible to revive the glories of the past, as those pre-historicist thinkers (Machiavelli or Mably, for instance) thought who called for a return to the heroic virtues of Greece or Rome, we could not revive and unite them all. If we choose to emulate the Greeks, we cannot also emulate the Hebrews; if we model ourselves on the Chinese, whether as they are in reality, or in Voltaire's *opéra bouffe* version, we cannot also be the Florentines of the Renaissance, or the innocent, serene, hospitable savages of eighteenth-century imagination. Even if, *per impossibile*, we could choose among these ideals, which should we select? Since there is no common standard in terms of which to grade them, there can be no final solution to the problem of what men as such should aim at. The proposition that this question can, at least in principle, be answered correctly and finally, which few had seriously doubted since Plato had taken it for granted, is undermined.

Herder, of course, condemns the very wish to resurrect ancient ideals: ideals belong to the form of life which generates them, and are mere historical memories without them: values – ends – live and die with the social wholes of which they form an intrinsic part. Each collective individuality is unique, and has its own aims and standards, which will themselves inevitably be superseded by other goals and values – ethical, social and aesthetic. Each of these systems is objectively valid in its own day, in the course of 'Nature's long year' which brings all things to pass. All cultures are equal in the sight of God, each in its time and place. Ranke said precisely this: his theodicy is a complacent version of Herder's theses, directed equally against those of Hegel and moral scepticism. But if this is so, then the notion of the perfect civilisation in which the ideal human being realises his full potentialities is patently absurd: not merely difficult to formulate, or impossible to realise in practice, but incoherent and unintelligible. This is perhaps the sharpest blow ever delivered against the classical philosophy of

Gerhardt (Berlin, 1875–90), vol. 3, p. 589; [Henri de] Boulainvilliers, *Histoire de l'ancien gouvernement de la France* (The Hague and Amsterdam, 1727), vol. 1, p. 322; Rousseau in the letter to Mirabeau of 26 July 1767. Herder could have come across this in Wegelin's essay of 1770 on the philosophy of history: see [Jakob von Daniel] Weguelin, 'Sur la philosophie de l'histoire: premier mémoire', *Nouveaux Mémoires de l'Académie royale des sciences et belles-lettres*, 1770 (Berlin, 1772), 361–414.

the West, to which the notion of perfection – the possibility, at least in principle, of universal, timeless solutions of problems of value – is essential.

The consequences of Herder's doctrines did not make themselves felt immediately. He was thought to be a bold and original thinker, but not a subverter of common moral assumptions. Nor, of course, did he think so himself. The full effect was felt only when the romantic movement, at its most violent, attempted to overthrow the authority both of reason and of dogma on which the old order rested. The extent of its explosive potentialities was not fully realised until the rise of modern anti-rationalist movements – nationalism, Fascism, existentialism, emotivism, and the wars and revolutions made in the name of two among them; that is to say, not until our own time, and perhaps not altogether even today.

X

Herder's works, as might be expected, bristle with contradictions: on the one hand, 'The power which thinks and works in me is in its nature as eternal as that which holds together the sun and the stars ... Wherever and whoever I shall be, I shall be what I am now, a force in a system of forces, a being in the immeasurable harmony of God's world.'[1] Whatever can be, will be. All potentialities will be realised. Herder believes in plenitude, in the great chain of being, in a nature with no barriers. Influenced by the naturalists, by Ritter, by von Haller, he sees man as an animal among animals: man is what he is because of slowly working natural causes, because he walks upright, or because of a cavity in his skull. Yet he also believes, with Aristotle and the Bible, in natural kinds, and in the special act of creation. He believes in a general human essence, a central human character: it is, as Leibniz taught in the *Nouveaux Essais*, like a vein in marble, to be brought out by reason and imagination; men are the Benjamins, the 'darlings of Nature's old age', the peak of the creative process. Yet he also believes that this human essence takes conflicting forms; types differ and the differences are unbridgeable. He makes a curious effort to bring together the monistic notion of the logically rigorous interconnection of all real entities, as in Spinoza's world (although in Herder's case it takes the form of something more

---

[1] xiii 16.

flexible and empirical), with the dynamic, self-developing individuated entities of Leibniz.[1] There is a tension between Herder's naturalism and his teleology, his Christianity and his enthusiastic acceptance of the findings of the natural sciences; between, on the one hand, his respect for some, at any rate, of the achievements of the French Encyclopaedists, who believed in quantitative methods and precision and a unified schema of knowledge; and, on the other, his preference for the qualitative approach of Goethe and Schelling and their vitalistic followers. Again, there is a contradiction between his naturalistic determinism, which at times is very strong, and the notion that one can and should resist natural impulses and natural forces;[2] for people who do not resist are overwhelmed. The Jews were crushed by the Romans; their disastrous destiny is ascribed to natural factors; yet he holds that it could have been averted; so, too, the Romans are held to have succumbed to vices which they could have resisted successfully. Herder was not sensitive to the problem of free will as, say, Kant was; there are too many conflicting strains in him. He may have believed, like most self-determinists, that men were free when they did what they chose, but that it was, in some sense, idle to ask whether men were free to choose, since they obviously were not; yet his writings give little evidence that he sought escape in this time-honoured, but hardly satisfactory, 'solution'.[3] Again, there are the separate strands of *Humanität* as a general human ideal (to be realised fully, perhaps, only in the world to come) and the 'Gang Gottes unter die Nationen'[4] – a phrase and a concept which Hegel later appropriated – and, on the other side, his more frequent and characteristic pluralism and relativism. There is noticeable tension between his passion for ancient German tribal life, real or imaginary, as he conceived it – spontaneous, creative and free – and his reluctant admiration for Rome, and even more for the Church, with their universalism and order and capacity for rational organisation. More far-reaching still is the contrast

[1] This is developed at length in *God: Some Conversations* (xvi 401–580), in which he defends Spinoza against Jacobi's charges of atheism and pantheism.

[2] See the magnificent paean to human freedom and man's powers of resistance to nature, xiii 142–50.

[3] *Pace* G. A. Wells, who argues strongly for this interpretation: op. cit. (p. 169 above, note 1), pp. 37–42.

[4] v 565; cf. Georg Wilhelm Friedrich Hegel, *Grundlinien der Philosophie des Rechts* [= *Sämtliche Werke* (op. cit., p. 56 above, note 4), vol. 7] (Stuttgart, 1928), p. 336.

between, on the one hand, his notion of the continuity of
overflowing nature, *natura naturans*, the energy that is one in
magnetism and electricity, in plants and animals and men, in
language and in art – a universal, continuous life-force of which
everything is a manifestation, of which laws can be discovered in
the form both of the physical sciences of his time, and of biology,
psychology and the particular brand of historical geography and
anthropology that he favoured – and, on the other hand, the crucial
role attributed to the unaccountable leaps of genius, miraculous
events, sheer chance, the unanalysable process of true creation, and
the consequent impossibility of achieving anything great or lasting
solely by the application of techniques; and, what goes with this,
the incommunicability of the central core of what individuates men
or cultures and gives them all the colour and force and value they
possess, something that is open only to the eye of imaginative
intuition, incapable of being reduced to communicable, teachable
scientific method. Finally, there is the ban on moralising, but at the
same time the impassioned apostrophes to the great moments of
human existence, the curses heaped on the enemies of human unity
and creativity – the bloodstained conquerors, the ruthless central-
isers, the shrivelling of the spirit by narrow and superficial
systematisers, with, at the head of them all, the odious Voltaire,
with his devitalising ironies and pettiness and lack of insight into
what men truly are. All the confusions of his time seem richly
reflected in his shapeless, sprawling, but continuously suggestive
works.

XI

Herder is in some sense a premonitory symptom, the albatross
before the coming storm. The French Revolution was founded on
the notion of timeless truths given to the faculty of reason with
which all men are endowed. It was dedicated to the creation or
restoration of a static and harmonious society, founded on unaltering principles, a dream of classical perfection, or, at least, the closest
approximation to it feasible on earth. It preached a peaceful
universalism and a rational humanitarianism. But its consequences
threw into relief the precariousness of human institutions; the
disturbing phenomenon of apparently irresistible change; the clash
of irreconcilable values and ideas; the insufficiency of simple
formulae; the complexity of men and societies; the poetry of action,

destruction, heroism, war; the effectiveness of mobs and of great men; the crucial role played by chance; the feebleness of reason before the power of fanatically believed doctrines; the unpredictability of events; the part played in history by unintended consequences; the ignorance of the workings of the sunken two-thirds of the great human iceberg, of which only the visible portion had been studied by scientists and taken into account by the ideologists of the great Revolution.

This, too, could be said of the Russian Revolution. Its ideals are too familiar to rehearse; and its results, too, threw doubts, whether justified or not, on the effectiveness of the kind of democracy for which liberals and radicals in the nineteenth century had pleaded; on the ability of rational men to allow for and control the forces of unreason; on revolution as an instrument for the promotion of freedom, a wider culture and social justice. It awakened men forcibly to the effectiveness of resolute conspiracies by disciplined parties; the irrationality of the masses; the weakness of liberal and democratic institutions in the West; the force of nationalist passions. As Durkheim, Pareto and Freud stand to the Russian Revolution – with their views on the uncritical use of such general terms as democracy and liberty, and their theories of the interplay of rational and irrational factors in making for social cohesion and disintegration, ideas which have deeply influenced thought and action in our day – so Herder stands to the events of 1789. The craving for fraternity and for self-expression, and disbelief in the capacity of reason to determine values, dominated the nineteenth century, and even more our own. Herder lived until 1803. He did not attempt to draw the moral of his own doctrines in relation to the fate of Germany or Europe, as Saint-Simon and Hegel and Maistre, in their very different fashions, had attempted to do. Perhaps he died too early in the century. Nevertheless, he, more than any of his contemporaries, sensed the insecurity of the foundations of faith in the Enlightenment held by so many in his time, even while he half accepted it. In this sense, those who thought of him as endowed with special powers – we are told that he was sometimes called a magician and was a model for Goethe's Faust[1] – did him no injustice.

[1] e.g. by Günter Jacoby in *Herder als Faust: eine Untersuchung* (Leipzig, 1911). Goethe himself detested such identifications. For a discussion of this see Robert T. Clark, Jr, *Herder: His Life and Thought* (Berkeley and Los Angeles, 1955), pp. 127 ff.

THE MAGUS OF THE NORTH

*J. G. Hamann and the Origins
of Modern Irrationalism*

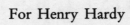For Henry Hardy

EDITOR'S PREFACE

ISAIAH BERLIN's first publication about Hamann appeared in 1956, in the form of a chapter in his selection from the eighteenth-century philosophers.[1] Thereafter he has discussed Hamann in some of his essays,[2] but has not treated him in any published work in the depth one might have expected, given the central position Hamann's ideas have undoubtedly occupied in his study of intellectual history. I had thought of this disappointing lack as irremediable until I encountered a collection of draft material dating from the 1960s, which, taken together, clearly represented the greater part of a much more detailed study of Hamann's ideas. So thoroughly had Berlin dismissed this material from his mind that, until I found it, he assured me that nothing of the kind existed. It did, and this book is based upon it.

The stimulus for the composition of the drafts was an invitation to deliver the Woodbridge Lectures at Columbia University in New York in 1965. The title given to the lectures was 'Two Enemies of the Enlightenment'; the other enemy was Joseph de Maistre.[3] The original plan was to publish a revised version of the typescripts on which the lectures were based, but although Berlin did a certain amount of further work after the lectures were delivered, he remained dissatisfied with what he had written, and

[1] *The Age of Enlightenment: The Eighteenth-Century Philosophers* (Boston and New York, 1956; Oxford, 1979), pp. 270–5.

[2] Least briefly in 'The Counter-Enlightenment' (1973) and 'Hume and the Sources of German Anti-Rationalism' (1977), both reprinted in *Against the Current* (see p. vii above, note 2); the former essay is also included in *The Proper Study of Mankind* (see p. ix above, note 1). See also the previous essays in the present volume.

[3] There were four lectures in all: one whole lecture and part of another were devoted to Hamann. In the case of both Hamann and Maistre there is a great deal in the typescripts which could not be drawn on in the time available for the lectures.

the drafts were laid aside. Twenty-five years later the material on Maistre was rescued, in the form of a long essay in Berlin's most recent collection;[1] Hamann has had to wait a little longer.

Something should be said about the establishment of the text, if only as a necessary background to the expression of my many debts of gratitude. Collation of the surviving typescripts revealed a substantial and crucial gap (of several pages, it turns out) at the end of the chapter on language. Without this missing material, publication would scarcely have been practicable. By a happy accident some of the dictated recordings on which the drafts were based had not been discarded; but they were made on 'Dictabelts', a technology long superseded, so that they seemed, at first, to be indecipherable. However, with the aid of the National Sound Archive, an example of the relevant machine was found in London's Science Museum. Once this had been put in working order, it was possible to transfer to modern cassettes the sound preserved on the Dictabelts. Miraculously, as it seemed at the time, the surviving recordings did include the missing pages of the text; indeed, they also provided further passages whose absence would not otherwise have been apparent. I pay tribute to Benet Bergonzi, Timothy Day and their colleagues at the National Sound Archive for their unfailing helpfulness and their technical expertise, without which this book could not have appeared in its present form, if at all.

Up to the point at which this gap occurred, the book is principally based on a largely continuous draft typescript. The remainder of the text was represented by a number of discontinuous passages of varying length, not all of which had been assigned a definite position in the overall structure; it is clear that they were destined for incorporation, but the project was abandoned before the final synthesis was performed. My aim in grafting these passages on to the main typescript has been to assemble, so far as I could manage, a readable text in which topics are discussed in a natural order: I trust that any remaining seams and imperfections are not too obtrusive. Isaiah Berlin has kindly read through the result, approved it, and improved it enormously;[2] to revisit and

---

[1] 'Joseph de Maistre and the Origins of Fascism', in *The Crooked Timber of Humanity* (see p. viii above, note 1).

[2] The text has not been revised in any systematic way to take full account of more recent work on Hamann, which in any case does not invalidate its central theses.

revise a somewhat disjointed draft laid aside decades previously is a deeply unappealing task, and I am extremely grateful to him for his willingness to undertake it.

My other principal concern has been to trace, check and provide references for as many as possible of the numerous quotations which the text contains.[1] This work, which has led me down some unexpected and occasionally unfrequented byways, could not have been completed without the help of a number of scholars, to whom I should like to express my thanks. Professor James C. O'Flaherty, the leading expert on Hamann in the English-speaking world, has given of his time and knowledge in abundance, with unstinting generosity, when he has been hard pressed by other preoccupations: it is no exaggeration to say that his help has been indispensable, and my gratitude to him is proportionate.[2] Professor Renate Knoll's remarkable store of information about Hamann and his world enabled her to solve for me several problems that might otherwise have proved intractable. Roger Hausheer has, with unflagging patience, put his knowledge of German and of the history of ideas at my disposal on innumerable occasions, to the great benefit of the book. Patrick Gardiner has read more than one draft of the text and enabled me to make a number of significant improvements. I have received help on individual points from Professor Frederick Barnard, Gunnar Beck, Dr Julie Curtis, Dr Anne Hardy, Veronica Hausheer, Professor Arthur Henkel, Dr Leofranc Holford-Strevens, Dr Aileen Kelly, Professor Ze'ev Levy, Professor T. J. Reed, Dr John Walker and Dr Robert Wokler. And I have been assisted, sometimes well beyond the call of duty, by many librarians: most directly in the line of fire in Oxford have been Adrian Hale, Librarian of Wolfson College, and

---

[1] Berlin's notes, where they survive, frequently contain the necessary clues, but other notes seem to have disappeared. Hamann scholars may like to know that one important source, not usually mentioned in Hamann bibliographies, was V. A. Kozhevnikov, *Filosofia chuvstva i very v eya otnosheniyakh k literature i razionalizmu XVIII veka i k kriticheskoi filosofii* [The Philosophy of Feeling and Faith in its Relations to the Literature and Rationalism of the Eighteenth Century and to Critical Philosophy], vol. 1 (Moscow, 1897), which contains a very extensive treatment of Hamann.

[2] Professor O'Flaherty has not only helped in the search for sources, but has thrown light on numerous matters of substance. It should not therefore be assumed, of course, that he is in agreement with the author's judgements. Isaiah Berlin takes sole responsibility for what is said in the book.

the staffs of the Bodleian Library and the Taylor Institution Library.

I have three more general sources of benefaction to mention. In the first place, it is a pleasure to acknowledge the very generous support of three charitable foundations, without whose help it would have been impossible to undertake the larger project of which this volume represents a first instalment. Next, I must confess that I can find no words adequate to describe the practical or psychological importance of the assistance provided by Pat Utechin, the author's secretary. Finally, Lord Bullock knows that I tell the truth when I say that it is only through his original intervention on my behalf that I have been in a position to incur any of the other obligations mentioned above.

Wolfson College, Oxford   HENRY HARDY
April 1993

Postscript

After the first impression of the UK edition of this book had been printed, chapters 1, 2 (to page 268) and 7 were published in the *New York Review of Books*, 21 October 1993, pp. 64–71. A number of minor changes were made by the author in this connection, and I have now incorporated most of these in the book. At the same time I have taken the opportunity of eliminating a handful of slips and infelicities that had come to light since the book went to press, and I should like to thank those who brought them to my attention. I should also like to take this opportunity of thanking – belatedly – Hugo Brunner, Gail Pirkis and their colleagues at John Murray for the patience and professionalism with which they have withstood my particularity.

October 1993

FOREWORD TO THE GERMAN EDITION

MY ACCOUNT of Hamann, as Henry Hardy makes clear in his Preface, is in all essentials a text prepared as the basis for a pair of lectures delivered nearly thirty years ago. I did not, on that occasion, claim to deal with the entire range of Hamann's thought; indeed it would have been absurd to try to do so in the time at my disposal – and I make no pretence of doing so in this largely unaltered version of what I wrote at that time. I wished to do no more than discuss that which seemed to me (and does so still) the most striking, original, important and influential of Hamann's central theses – namely his opposition to the entire rationalist trend of European philosophy, from the Greeks to medieval scholasticism, the Renaissance, and above all the French *philosophes* of his own time, and by implication their disciples in the following two centuries. There is a very great deal in Hamann's writings – especially, of course, the religious ideas which lie at the heart of all he was and felt and believed – which I did not feel myself competent to examine, quite apart from the fact that it could not be contained within the narrow confines of my two hours.

I am well aware that a great deal of scholarly work has been done on Hamann since I first read him, above all in Germany. Had I been writing today, I should naturally have discussed some of the recent accounts of Hamann, especially since one of their main tendencies is to cast doubt on the characterisation of the Magus as an opponent of rational methodologies; to present him, indeed, as in some sense a champion of true reason and enlightenment. Nevertheless, my portrayal of Hamann would not, I believe, have been radically altered. To the extent that some of these recent interpretations are to be understood as a substantive disagreement with previous accounts, rather than as a dispute about the proper use of words, especially 'reason', I am not persuaded by them. Had

I been so, I should not have agreed to publish my account in its present form.

The dispute is largely about Hamann's conception of reason and rational thought. There are those who agree with one of the friendliest, most perceptive and most learned of my critics, the eminent American scholar Professor J. C. O'Flaherty of Wake Forest University in the USA, who believes that Hamann was no irrationalist, but 'a child of the Enlightenment',[1] a defender of true reason properly understood – not indeed what he calls 'discursive reason' but 'intuitive reason', in his view a legitimate use of the term.

I understand his term 'discursive reason' to mean that which is involved in formulating ideas, concepts, propositions, descriptions, rules, hypotheses, arguments, demonstrations, theories and the like, as they constitute the content of the natural sciences and mathematics, and equally of the great bulk of the humanities – philosophy, history, law, social studies, criticism and so on. This is the kind of reason – rational methods – that Hamann is, or in my view should be, commemorated by historians of modern thought for attacking.

Some of those who disagree with me cite such passages in Hamann's writings as his contrast between 'correct and authentic' reason on the one hand, and, on the other, 'scholastic reason', which makes a distinction between idealism and realism that he described as wholly imaginary.[2] Of the latter they quote Hamann as saying: 'What is this highly praised *reason*, with its universality, infallibility, overweeningness, certainty, self-evidence? An *ens rationis* . . .';[3] and again, 'People talk about reason as if it were a real being.'[4] And they then go on to oppose to the reason which was for Hamann an *ens rationis*, a figment, his idea of 'authentic' reasoning (so far as he may be said to have one). But this notion seems to me to be closely related not to what is commonly called rational thinking, but to his identification of thought and language, one of his most important and original discoveries, best stated in the famous passage in one of his letters to Herder, quoted by all commentators: 'Reason is language, *logos*. On this marrowbone I gnaw, and shall gnaw myself to death on it.'[5]

[1] *New York Review of Books*, 18 November 1993, p. 68.
[2] B vii 165.13.   [3] W iii 225.3.   [4] B vii 26.34.   [5] B v 177.18.

Of course I do not wish to say that Hamann condemns ordinary reasoning, in the sense in which we speak of reasonable people or actions. It seems to me that his idea of the *Vernunft* which guides ordinary thinking is closer to what we mean by 'understanding', *Verstehen* as opposed to *Wissen*, which leads to a true sense of reality, God's creation; an eye for the concrete, the individual, the unique, the flow of living life; the encounter with the real, face to face. It is this that appealed to Jacobi and Goethe: the imaginative or quasi-artistic insight which Wilhelm Dilthey and his followers developed so richly, and which so irritated the great systematiser Hegel, and for that reason alone might have stirred the enthusiasm of Kierkegaard. For Hamann this deep interrelationship of God, man and nature stems from the divine *Logos* which 'was in the beginning'[1] and by which the world came to be. It is this profoundly religious approach that is conveyed by such words as 'Without *language*, we would have no reason; without reason, no *religion*',[2] and again, 'Where there is no *word* there is no reason – and no world.'[3] This surely refers to the creative power of the *Logos* which gives reality to all there is, and which animates human souls, for which nature, history, Holy Writ and much else is God's voice that speaks to us. This is scarcely what is meant by the reason of the sciences, or the generalising scientific or rational methods of the Cartesians, the French *philosophes*, the entire tradition of the European Enlightenment. It is this rational outlook that Hamann opposed with all his strength. It is this rebellion against systems, objective, unbreakable uniformities, application of mathematical methods, calculation that I and others mean by speaking of his anti-rationalism – the banner of Counter-Enlightenment that he raised – and of the influence of this on some of the philosophers of the so-called Romantic school of thought which originated in Germany in the early nineteenth century, and their descendants.

To return to the claims of 'intuitive reason'. This is not an expression used, so far as I know, by Hamann. It was used ironically by Kant in a letter to him in which he asks for his help in interpreting a dark passage in Hamann's disciple Herder, but begs him to reply 'in human language, if possible; for I, poor mortal, am not at all *organised* to understand the divine language of *intuitive reason*'.[4] Nor am I so organised. One of the best of modern

---

[1] John 1: 2.   [2] W iii 231.10.   [3] B v 95.21.   [4] B iii 82.11.

historians of ideas, A. O. Lovejoy, appears equally puzzled by this conception of reason in his book *The Reason, the Understanding, and Time*. On this issue I am happy to align myself with the excellent scholar Rudolf Unger, to whose magisterial work *Hamann und die Aufklärung* I naturally owe a great deal. The *Vernunft* that Hamann attacked so passionately and at times so brilliantly, the use of reason against which he scored such palpable hits, is the principle on which not only the great rationalists of the seventeenth century, but no less so the French science-influenced *lumières* of his own time, claimed to base their thinking. These were the methods by which some if not most of the best-known later thinkers and philosophers, Jeremy Bentham, J. S. Mill, Franz von Brentano, William James, Bertrand Russell, the *Wiener Kreis*, and all the schools of analytic philosophy dominant in this century in English-speaking and Scandinavian countries, stated, explained and sought to justify their views, and by which they assailed those of their opponents.

The term 'reason' has been variously understood; there is a vast chasm between, for example, Hume's use of it and the divine *Logos*. But its common meaning among philosophers, both positivist and metaphysical, is that given to it by the thinkers listed above. It is the fact that Hamann was the first in modern times to reject this outlook, and to fight vehemently against it with all his considerable might, that constitutes his right to be recognised as the founder of the Counter-Enlightenment, indeed as the principal adversary of the application of reason and all its works, as commonly understood, to account for the reality of the direct everyday experience of mankind, especially in the realm of the spirit. Consequently I do not see in what way recent interpretations of Hamann's thought as an unfamiliar form of rationalism can affect my central theses. *Ho gegrapha, gegrapha* – what I have written, I have written – to be accepted or refuted by the critical reader.

February 1994   ISAIAH BERLIN

AUTHOR'S PREFACE

THE FAMOUS phrase 'God-intoxicated man' fits Hamann far better than the wildly romanticised Spinoza of the eighteenth-century German critics. For Hamann everything – all there is and all that could be – is not only created by God, and serves his inscrutable purposes, but speaks to us, his creatures, made in his image. Everything is revelation. Everything is a miracle. Causality is illusory. All that is created by God's will reveals reality, truth, speaks to those who have the eyes and ears to grasp it. *Te saxa loquuntur*; but not only stones and rocks speak the Lord, everything does: in the first place, of course, Holy Writ, and the words of the saints and the fathers and the doctors of the Christian Church, and of their forerunners in Judaea and Greece, and its dissident child, Islam. But in addition to this the whole of history, facts, events, all that human beings are, think, feel, do – and not only human beings: nature, fauna and flora, earth and sky, mountains and streams, and all natural events – speak to us directly; are the form and substance of the language in which God implants knowledge in us.

But Hamann is clear that we can receive it only if we can read this language – if its meaning is revealed to us – and that may well vary between individuals and societies. It is obfuscated by those who mistakenly believe that what matters are the inventions and creations of men, of individuals – the arts and the sciences, and above all theories, systems, artificial creations which deaden the living life of the universe in its continuous activity. Spontaneity is everything: imaginative intuition, not the logic and classifications and systems of the theorists, opens the windows through which the divine light comes to us. All that we are and do and make – including the arts and the sciences and the means by which we live our ordinary lives – has no meaning save as the expression of God's communication to us; all that there is – animate and inanimate – forms a single seamless whole. We cannot see it all, for we are finite beings, and can see only parts, fragments, but that is sufficient to give us understanding; understanding, not the knowledge of the experts, the scientists, those who arrange and order and collect and distribute and build systems. Goethe says that the living butterfly, with its bright, beautiful colours, once it is pinned down by Moses Mendelssohn turns into a grey lifeless corpse;[1] so Hamann too contrasts the intuitive insight, the imaginative grasp of reality with the lifeless material of the systematisers and the dissecters. That is the heart of his theory of cognition, experience, being and the world. No generalities, only the particular is real. Direct revelation, not analysis – that is the heart of his vision.

But I must own that Hamann's vision is not the subject of this essay: Hamann's theology and his religious metaphysics I find I am neither drawn to nor competent to discuss, except in so far as they are part and parcel of the rest of what he wrote. This has been done very well by others. My interest lies in the fact that Hamann is the first out-and-out opponent of the French Enlightenment of his time. His attacks upon it are more uncompromising, and in some respects sharper and more revealing of its shortcomings, than those of later critics. He is deeply biased, prejudiced, one-sided; profoundly sincere, serious, original; and the true founder of a polemical anti-rationalist tradition which in the course of time has done much, for good and (mostly) ill, to shape the thought and art and feeling of the West. I do not speak as a champion of Hamann's views, only as a witness of a great deal that is truly revealing in the scattered, unsystematic, passionate, and always deeply committed writings of this eccentric thinker – one of the important if often maddening irregulars of civilisation.

March 1993   ISAIAH BERLIN

---

[1] Letter of 14 July 1770 to Hetzler the younger: part 4 (*Goethe's Briefe*), vol. 1, p. 238, lines 19 ff., in op. cit. (p. 113 above, note 1).

1

INTRODUCTION

Do either nothing or everything; the mediocre, the moderate, is repellent to me: I prefer an extreme.
Hamann to J. G. Lindner, 20 May 1756[1]

Think less and live more.
Hamann to J. G. Herder, 18 May 1765[2]

THE MOST passionate, consistent, extreme and implacable enemy of the Enlightenment and, in particular, of all forms of rationalism of his time (he lived and died in the eighteenth century) was Johann Georg Hamann. His influence, direct and indirect, upon the romantic revolt against universalism and scientific method in any guise was considerable and perhaps crucial.

This may seem at first sight to be an absurd claim on behalf of a man whose name is scarcely known in the English-speaking world, who is barely mentioned, at best, in some of our larger or more specialised encyclopaedias as an esoteric writer, confused and obscure to the point of total unintelligibility, an eccentric and isolated figure, about whose views – beyond the fact that he was consumed by some kind of highly individual Christianity, usually described as a form of pietism, believed in the occult truths of divine revelation and the literal inspiration of the Bible, rejected the French atheism and materialism of his time, and was at most a minor figure in the German literary movement known as *Sturm und Drang* ('Storm and Stress') – virtually nothing is said. Literary histories and monographs sometimes speak of him as a minor contributor to the turbulence of the 'pre-romantic' German literature of the 1760s and 1770s; he occurs in the biographies of Kant as a fellow citizen of Königsberg, as being an unhappy dilettante, an amateur philosopher whom Kant once helped, then abandoned, and who criticised Kant without understanding him;

[1] B i 202.2.   [2] B ii 330.30.

and biographies of Goethe occasionally contain a few admiring quotations about him from Goethe's autobiography, *Dichtung und Wahrheit*.

But no definite impression emerges: Hamann remains in these histories (as he did in his life) in the margin of the central movement of ideas, an object of mild astonishment, of some interest to historians of Protestant theology, or, more often, altogether unnoticed. Yet Herder, whose part in altering historical and sociological writing can hardly be disputed, once wrote to him that he was content to be 'a Turkish camel-driver gathering up sacred apples before his ambling holy beast, which bears the Koran'.[1] Herder revered Hamann as a man of genius, looked upon him as the greatest of his teachers, and after his death venerated his ashes as the remains of a prophet. America was indeed called after Amerigo Vespucci, but it was Columbus who discovered that great continent, and in this case the Columbus, as Herder freely admitted, was Hamann.[2]

Hamann's disciple F. H. Jacobi transmitted much of his thought to the romantic metaphysicians of the beginning of the nineteenth century. Schelling regarded him as a 'great writer' whom Jacobi perhaps did not understand at all;[3] Niebuhr speaks of his 'demonic' nature and its superhuman strength;[4] Jean Paul says that 'the great Hamann is a deep heaven full of telescopic stars and many nebulae that no human eye can resolve',[5] and even for a

---

[1] B ii 315.35.

[2] Goethe saw Hamann as a great awakener, the first champion of the unity of man – the union of all his faculties, mental, emotional, physical, in his greatest creations – man misunderstood and misrepresented, and indeed done harm, by the dissection of his activity by lifeless French criticism. In book 12 of *Dichtung und Wahrheit* he expresses Hamann's central principle thus: 'Everything that a man sets out to achieve, whether it is produced by deed or word or by some other means, must spring from all his powers combined; everything segregated is deplorable.' loc. cit. (p. 228 above, note 1). Goethe wrote to Frau von Stein about his delight in grasping more of Hamann's meaning than most men. *Goethes Liebesbriefe an Frau von Stein 1776 bis 1789*, ed. Heinrich Düntzer (Leipzig, 1886), p. 515 (letter of 17 September 1784).

[3] *F. W. J. Schelling's Denkmal der Schrift von den göttlichen Dingen etc. des Herrn Friedrich Heinrich Jacobi...* (Tübingen, 1812), p. 192.

[4] *Lebensnachrichten über Barthold Georg Niebuhr aus Briefen desselben und aus Erinnerungen einiger seiner nächsten Freunde* (Hamburg, 1838), vol. 2, p. 482.

[5] Jean Paul, *Vorschule der Ästhetik*, part 1, § 14: p. 64 in Norbert Miller's edition (Munich, 1963).

romantic writer goes to unheard-of lengths to praise his unique, unsurpassed genius; in the same spirit J. K. Lavater says that he is content to 'collect the golden crumbs from his table',[1] and similarly Friedrich Karl von Moser, 'the German Burke', admires his eagle flight.[2] Even if some of this is due to the enthusiasm of contemporaries which left little trace on later generations, it is still sufficient to stir curiosity about the character of this peculiar figure, half hidden by the fame of his disciples.

Hamann repays study: he is one of the few wholly original critics of modern times. Without any known debt to anyone else, he attacks the entire prevailing orthodoxy with weapons some of which are obsolete and some ineffective or absurd; but there is enough force in them to hamper the enemy's advance, to attract allies to his own reactionary banner, and to begin – so far as anyone may be said to have done so – the secular resistance to the eighteenth-century march of enlightenment and reason, the resistance which in time culminated in romanticism, obscurantism and political reaction, in a great, deeply influential renewal of artistic forms, and, in the end, in permanent damage to the social and political lives of men. Such a figure surely demands some degree of attention.

Hamann is the pioneer of anti-rationalism in every sphere. Neither of his contemporaries Rousseau and Burke can justly be called this, for Rousseau's explicitly political ideas are classical in their rationalism, while Burke appeals to the calm good sense of reflective men, even if he denounces theories founded on abstractions. Hamann would have none of this: wherever the hydra of reason, theory, generalisation rears one of its many hideous heads, he strikes. He provided an arsenal from which more moderate romantics – Herder, even such cool heads as the young Goethe, even Hegel, who wrote a long and not too friendly review of his works, even the level-headed Humboldt and his fellow liberals – drew some of their most effective weapons. He is the forgotten source of a movement that in the end engulfed the whole of European culture.

---

[1] *Friedrich Heinrich Jacobi's auserlesener Briefwechsel*, ed. Friedrich Roth (Leipzig, 1825–7), vol. i, p. 438.
[2] B ii 230.9.

2

LIFE

HAMANN'S LIFE, at any rate in its outward aspects, was uneventful. He was born on 27 August 1730 in the East Prussian capital of Königsberg.[1] His father, Johann Christoph, came from Lusatia and was apparently a surgeon barber who became the supervisor of the municipal bathhouse, a fact in which he took some pride. His mother, Maria Magdalena, came from Lübeck. His social origins were therefore not very different from those of Kant and Schiller, and a good deal more humble than those of Goethe, Hegel, Hölderlin and Schelling, not to speak of the sons of the gentry and the nobility. The background of the family was pietist; that is to say, it belonged to, although it was not at all prominent in, that wing of German Lutheranism which, inspired by the revolt against book learning and intellectualism generally that broke out in Germany towards the end of the seventeenth century, laid stress on the depth and sincerity of personal faith and direct union with God, achieved by scrupulous self-examination, passionate, intensely introspective religious feeling, and concentrated self-absorption and prayer, whereby the sinful, corrupt self was humbled and the soul left open to the blessing of divine, unmerited grace.

This highly subjective wing of German Protestantism had its analogues in the Moravian Brotherhood, in the mysticism of Jakob Böhme's English disciples (Pordage, for example), of Weigel, Arndt, and the followers in the eighteenth century of William Law, of the Methodist preachers – the Wesleys and Whitefield – and of Swedenborg and his disciples, among them William Blake. It spread widely in Scandinavia, England and America, and in some of the Masonic and Rosicrucian lodges both in France and in

[1] Today part of the Russian Federation, and officially known since 1946 as Kaliningrad.

Germany. The German pietists were distinguished by a personal emotionalism and, in the second half of the century especially, a gloomy puritanical self-abasement and self-mortification, and a stern opposition to the pleasures of the world and especially the secular arts,[1] for which the Calvinists of Geneva, Scotland and New England had also been known.

Even if the ascetic and introspective quality of this outlook can be traced in Hamann's character and views, the bleak puritanism, of which there are notable traces in Kant – a child of a similar environment – is wholly absent. So too is the shallow and sometimes hysterical emotionalism of some pietist confessional writing. Hamann appears equally free both from the narrow hatred of learning which caused the expulsion of Leibniz's disciple, the philosopher Wolff, from Halle earlier in the century, and from the more exhibitionist forms of German Protestantism, though he did remain devoted to Luther's life and personality to the end of his days.

His education was somewhat desultory. He was instructed by a former priest who believed in teaching Latin without grammar. He and his brother wandered from one small and sordid school to another and never acquired respect for system of any kind. By the time he reached fifteen, the normal age for higher education in Germany at that time, he managed to scrape into Königsberg University, where he heard lectures on history, geography, philosophy, mathematics, theology and Hebrew, and displayed considerable gifts. He listened to the philosophical lectures of Knutzen, who had also taught Kant, and took some interest in astronomy and botany. He did not seem to be drawn to theology. He preferred, he tells us in his autobiography,[2] 'antiquities, criticism ... poetry, novels, philology, French authors with their peculiar gift for invention, description, and capacity for giving delight to the imagination'.[3] He deliberately evaded acquiring useful knowledge and obstinately pursued humane studies for their own sake, determined to remain a servant of the Muses.[4]

He lingered on for six years at the University, took part in student literary publications, made friends, and is described as a

---

[1] See the interesting account in *Anton Reiser*, the well-known novel by Goethe's admirer Karl Philipp Moritz.

[2] *Gedanken über meinen Lebenslauf* (W ii 9–54).

[3] W ii 21.3. [4] W ii 21.25.

man of passionate, affectionate and sensitive character, frank and impulsive, with a quick temper, in need of affection, timid, high-minded, with fastidious literary taste. His writings of that period are of no great interest. His style had not developed the eccentric attributes for which it – and he – became notorious in later years. At the age of twenty, in the literary periodical *Daphne*, he appears as a typical young German of the *Aufklärung*, uttering impeccably conventional sentiments derived from the fashionable French writers, with a tendency, not uncommon in German writers of that time, towards a heavy-footed style, an effort to imitate Gallic *esprit* and gaiety which in German hands often became clumsy, elephantine, embarrassing and pathetically lacking in wit. He read enormously and chaotically and began that vast accumulation of apparently unrelated information which cluttered his pages in later years.

After the University he was not sure what career to choose: he was regarded as a promising young littérateur, a disciple of the French *lumières*, who might make his mark as an essayist or journalist. In common with other poor students of the time, he became tutor to the sons of prosperous local bourgeois; he made friends with the brothers Berens, rich merchants in the city of Riga,[1] whither they persuaded him to accompany them. Christoph Berens was an enlightened man with a great faith in the then rising science of economics, and directed Hamann's attention to the French economic writing of the time. Hamann translated a book by the French economist Dangeul, adding an appendix of his own, in the course of which, after an autobiographical excursus – in imitation of Young's *Night Thoughts* rather than Rousseau – about his sad career as an usher, his misanthropy, and the various attacks of gloom and melancholia which he had endured, he manages to quote Terence, Cicero, Madame de Graffigny, Gellert, Xenophon, Montesquieu, Plutarch, Pope, Hume, the early Councils of the Church, Plato, Mandeville, Aeneas Sylvius, the Marchese Belloni, Mathurin Régnier and the political testament of the head of a gang of smugglers. He praises the French Encyclopaedia and ends with a great paean to merchants as such, men engaged in increasing material welfare, in cultivating the arts of peace, as against the robber barons, the idle and corrupt monks of the Middle Ages, the hideous wars that devastated mankind, to which

[1] In our day the capital of Latvia (then called Livonia, and part of the Russian Empire).

he favourably compares the eighteenth century as an age of peace.[1] If Plato and Aeneas Sylvius had lived now and had been acquainted with the Berenses they would not have looked down on trade and despised as they did the merchants of the Piraeus or the bankers of Italy. Trade is a form of altruistic benevolence, commerce brings blessings greater than Hobbes's or Machiavelli's bloodstained despots.

All this was conventional enough, and the Berenses must have been well pleased: they were progressive merchants and anxious to embellish their commercial activities with the works of polite culture. They liked to dabble in economics themselves, and although Hamann was obviously an odd fish, with an irregular imagination unlike that of the tidier imitators of the French style of which Germany could at that time boast a good number, he did honour to the house.

From time to time Hamann quarrelled with his patrons and became tutor in the houses of the German nobility along the Baltic coast. He was thin-skinned and resented the mixture of patronage and philistinism for which the Baltic barons were then (and indeed later) noted. His meditation on his mother's Christian death, with its epigraph from Young ('He mourns the Dead, who lives as they desire'),[2] is a totally conventional piece. In 1756 he could have been written down as a minor German imitator of French critics, with a special interest in economics,[3] a reader of Voltaire and Montesquieu and the abbé Coyer, a friend of liberty and equality, a defender of civic virtue and public spirit. In short, Hamann is at this stage a spokesman of the rising bourgeoisie, and against soldiers and nobles; one of those progressive youths who agreed with Kant and their common friend Berens that 'well earned' rightly fills the middle-class citizen with as much pride as 'well

[1] The Wars of the Spanish and Austrian Successions, the rumblings which culminated in the Seven Years War, and the Anglo-French wars, as well as the colonial wars in India and elsewhere, seem to have made no impact on him.

[2] Edward Young, *Night Thoughts* (1742–5) ii 24, quoted at W ii 233.

[3] He retained this interest even after he changed his central opinions, as is shown by his appreciation of the writings of the Neapolitan abbé Galiani. It should be added, though, that Galiani's views were somewhat unorthodox: he argued against free trade and *laissez-faire*, laid stress on non-economic considerations of a social 'welfare State' type, and was not uncritical of Montesquieu. See Ferdinando Galiani, *Dialogues sur le commerce des bleds* (London, 1770), and Philip Merlan, 'Parva Hamanniana: Hamann and Galiani', *Journal of the History of Ideas* 11 (1950), 486–9.

born' fills an aristocrat.[1] All this was shared by Lessing, Diderot, Quesnay and all champions of progress and private enterprise, peace and enlightenment, and was common enough at the time.[2] If Hamann had died then he would have deserved his present obscurity; but in 1756 he undertook a journey that was destined to alter his life.

It is not quite clear why Hamann was sent to London in 1756. We know that the firm of the Berenses entrusted him with a mission that he failed to fulfil. The exact nature of this mission remains, to this day, a mystery. There may be some grounds for believing that it was political as well as commercial. His task, so some researchers suppose, was to deliver a proposal to leading circles in British political life that they should consider the possibility of the secession of the 'German' Baltic area from the Russian Empire to form an independent or semi-independent State, a scheme likely to appeal to England because of its assumed fear of the expanding Russian power. If this is so, it came to nothing, and if any record of it exists, it has not so far been found.

The year 1756, according to Swedenborg, was to precede the Last Judgement, in which the old Church was to be consumed and the new, 'true' universal Church of true Christianity was to rise like a phoenix from its ashes. Although the world in general experienced no noticeable cataclysm of this type, this is precisely what occurred within Hamann himself. The crisis in his life transformed him and created the figure that was, in its turn, to do much to alter the thought of his time.

Of all the German provinces of the middle years of the eighteenth century, Prussia was the most consciously and vigorously progressive. Driven by the restless energy and ambition of Frederick the Great, the enlightened bureaucracy of Berlin was making a great and continuous effort to raise the social, economic and cultural level of Prussia to that of the admired lands of the West, in the first place of France, the supremacy of whose capital city was acknowledged by the entire civilised world. Industry and

---

[1] Berens's remark is quoted by Herder in *Briefe zu Beförderung der Humanität*: xvii 391.

[2] See Philip Merlan, 'Parva Hamanniana: J. G. Hamann as a Spokesman of the Middle Class', *Journal of the History of Ideas* 9 (1948), 380–4, and Jean Blum, *La Vie et l'oeuvre de J.-G. Hamann, le 'Mage du Nord', 1730–1788* (Paris, 1912), pp. 32–3.

trade, with State aid and control, were created, encouraged, developed; finances were rationalised, agriculture improved; foreign savants, especially Frenchmen, were invited and made much of at the court in Potsdam. The language of the court was French. Frenchmen were not only appointed to leading intellectual positions – of these Voltaire, Maupertuis and La Mettrie were only the most famous – but put in charge of administrative departments, to the distress of all true Prussians (particularly in the traditional Eastern part of the country), who grumbled but obeyed. Every effort was made to rescue the country from the long-drawn effects of the collapse of much of German life and civilisation as a result of the murderous Thirty Years War, and the national humiliation and the enormous social and cultural night that followed. The policy of relatively enlightened paternalism which had begun with Frederick William, the Great Elector of Brandenburg, and the ferocious martinet, his grandson, Frederick William I of Prussia, was raised to a new height of ruthless efficiency by the great King. He was himself an accomplished writer and composer, besides being a soldier and administrator of genius, and the emergence of enlightened merchants like the Berenses in East Prussia and the Baltic, and the intellectual revival, of which Kant and the Academy in Berlin were among the leaders, were in complete harmony with this new awakening of the national energies.

This was the world in which, it was hoped, the young Hamann would play his part. His friends knew that he was not a typical child of the Enlightenment, that his peculiar blend of religious and economic reading, his failure to distinguish himself in the Law, which he had officially studied at the University of Königsberg, the alternating indolence and spurts of sudden energy that drove him in unexpected directions, his lack of system, his spells of melancholia, his stammer, his morbid pride, which led him to quarrel with his patrons, his inability to settle down to any fixed occupation, did not make him an ideal official or littérateur in a centralised modern State consumed with desire for power and success, as well as a craving for the cultural development, influenced by Paris, of which such *Aufklärer* as Lessing, Mendelssohn, Nicolai were the leaders. Nevertheless, it was clear that men like Kant and his other Königsberg friends hoped that Hamann's natural abilities and imagination could somehow be disciplined and rendered useful. What they did not realise was that, despite his earlier, apparently

conformist, adherence to the Enlightenment, he was by temperament violently opposed to the whole system: that he was basically
a seventeenth-century man born into an alien world – religious,
conservative, 'inner-directed', unable to breathe in the bright new
world of reason, centralisation, scientific progress. Like Samuel
Johnson in England, he represented an older attitude: personal
relationships, inner life, meant more to him at all times than any of
the values of the external world. He turned out to have neither the
ideals nor the temperament of a typical 'progressive'; he hated the
great Frederick, the 'Solomon of Prussia',[1] and his secular
wisdom. Like the Russian Slavophils of the following century, he
saw the family as the basis of true human existence, and the loose
texture founded on affection, tradition, local – even provincial –
values, with the minimum of interference by trained experts and
remote officials, as the only tolerable foundation of a truly
Christian life. He was never an atheist or an agnostic. He seems
never to have been tempted by the new, intellectually free, anti-
clerical Franco-Prussian Establishment. He may not have known
this before the journey to London, and his bold economic views
and natural hatred of despotism may have deceived him, as it did
his friends, concerning his prospects and vocation. But they were
to learn with whom they were dealing soon enough.

After a leisurely journey through Berlin, where he made the
acquaintance of Moses Mendelssohn, Nicolai and the other leading
men of letters of that intellectual capital of the German world,
followed by visits to Lübeck, Bremen, Hamburg, Amsterdam,
Leiden and Rotterdam, he arrived in London on 18 April 1757.
After an apparently abortive call at the Russian Embassy on his
mysterious mission, he established himself in the house of a music
teacher and decided to taste all the pleasures of the rich life of this
great Western city. He tried to cure himself of stammering,
attempted to learn to play the lute, and plunged into what he later
described as a life of terrible dissipation. We have no independent
evidence of what occurred, save his own account, which is that of a
repentant sinner. At the end of ten months he was in debt to the
extent of £300 and in a state of utter loneliness, misery and, at
times, dreadful despair. He discovered accidentally that his host,
the musician, was involved in a homosexual relationship with a

[1] e.g. W ii 320.29, W iii 55–60.

'rich Englishman',[1] and the appalling shock seems to have been the occasion of the great spiritual crisis of his life.

His mission was a failure; he was penniless, alone – above all alone – and no one understood what he was saying. He prayed for a friend to lead him out of the hideous labyrinth. He returned to his earlier life; he left the musician's house, established himself in a humble boarding-house and returned to his pietist beginnings: he did what pietists did in states of spiritual oppression – he read the Bible from cover to cover. He had done so before, but now he found at last 'the Friend in my own heart, whither he had found his way when I felt nothing but void, darkness, desolation'.[2] He was starved of love and now he had found it. He began his real reading of the Bible on 13 March 1758 and, in pietist fashion, noted his spiritual progress day by day.[3] He wrote shortly afterwards, like a true disciple of Luther, that beneath the letter that is the flesh there is also an immortal soul, the breath of God, of light and life, a light burning in the darkness, which one must have eyes to see.[4]

Hamann emerged from this experience transformed. He had received no mystical vision, no specific revelation, as some converts to the new mystical trends then rising in Europe – partly in alliance with, partly in violent opposition to, the free individualist traditions of the Enlightenment – had often claimed to have had. There was no kind of connection between him and the Martinists or Freemasons or the many illuminist sects whose German centres were in East Prussia and Bavaria. He had been converted to the religion of his childhood, to Lutheran Protestantism. It is his application of this new light, which burned for him until the end of his days, that gives him historical importance.

To what was he converted? Not just to the simple faith of his

---

[1] W ii 37.7.   [2] W ii 39.40.

[3] Rudolf Unger, in his excellent if somewhat ponderous *Hamanns Sprach-theorie im Zusammenhange seines Denkens: Grundlegung zu einer Würdigung der geistesgeschichtlichen Stellung des Magus in Norden* (Munich, 1905) – incorporated, in expanded form, into his *Hamann und die Aufklärung* (Jena, 1911) – points to parallels in the instructions on the reading of the Scriptures by such pietists as Francke in 1693 and Joachim Lange in 1733. This is highly plausible, although Hamann never became an orthodox pietist and broke out in all kinds of – from the orthodox point of view of the movement – worrying and unaccountable directions. His relation to pietism is somewhat analogous to, say, Blake's relation to the Nonconformist and Swedenborgian currents in which he was brought up.

[4] W i 315.7.

266   THREE CRITICS OF THE ENLIGHTENMENT

childhood, but to the doctrine known to all those who are familiar
with the writings of the German Protestant mystics and their
followers in Scandinavia and England, according to whom the
sacred history of the Jews is not merely an account of how that
nation was guided from darkness to light by God's almighty hand,
but is a timeless allegory of the inner history of the soul of each
individual man. The sins of individuals are like the sins of nations.
Hamann's own religious conversion in London took the form of
discovering in himself all the crimes of the children of Israel: just as
they stumbled and fell and worshipped idols, so he fell into
hedonism and materialism and intellectualism and fell away from
God; and as the balm of divine grace enabled them to rise and
return to the Lord and repent their sins and resume their painful
pilgrimage, so he too returned to his Father and the Christ within
him, was born again, wept with bitter contrition and was saved.
The story of the wanderings of the Israelites, their *Reisekarte*, he
declared, was the story of his life, his *Lebenslauf*. This was the
inner sense of the biblical words. He who understood them
understood himself – all understanding of anything whatever was
self-understanding, for the spirit alone is what can be understood,
and to find it man need only, and must only, look within himself.
God's word was the ladder between heaven and earth sent to aid
weak and foolish children – it alone would vouchsafe them a
glimpse of what they were and why they were as they were, and
what their place was, and what they must do and what avoid. The
Bible was a great universal allegory, a similitude of that which was
occurring everywhere and at every instant. So indeed were human
history, and nature properly understood – understood with the
eyes not of analytical reason but of faith, trust in God, self-
examination, for all these were one.

The rest of his life story is comparatively irrelevant. He returned
to the house of his patron, Berens, who treated him with great
sympathy and immediately began to conspire with Kant to obtain
a new post for him. Kant suggested that they might write a
primer on physics together, but their difference of approach
made collaboration impossible.[1] Hamann proposed marriage to

---

[1] Nobody, Hamann says, can speak to children who cannot descend to their
level, that is, who does not love them. How can a crafty, vain intellectual do this?
(There may be something of Rousseau in this, the defence of the value of
emotional *rapport*, but Rousseau dealt in vast ideas, whereas Hamann insists on
concrete cases intuitively selected.) No philosopher will sacrifice enough *amour*

Berens's sister Katharina, but withdrew his offer, because her brother vetoed it. He made one or two journeys to his friends on the Baltic coast and then took an ill-paid post in the office of the Department of War and Crown Lands. This he kept for a while, but it brought in too little even for his modest requirements – he was fond of food and drink but otherwise his pleasures were few. He returned to his father's house and collaborated in the *Königsbergsche Gelehrte und Politische Zeitungen*, an enterprise financed by the bookseller Kanter, who had always been exceptionally kind to him, lent him books and encouraged him in every way. He began publishing his strange but arresting pamphlets: fragments, unfinished essays, peculiar amalgams of philosophy, literary criticism, philology, history and personal testimony, and attracted the attention of the Berlin literati, who tried to lure this strange talent into their circle – unsuccessfully, as they soon realised. He did not marry but lived with one of his father's servants, to whom he remained faithful all his life and by whom he had four children. She was a simple, illiterate and affectionate woman, and he was happy to use this as an excuse for declining posts that might embarrass her. From journalism he returned again to public service and in 1767 became an official in the General Excise and Customs Administration, then managed by one of Frederick's French experts, with whom Hamann remained on the worst of terms. He had by this time met Herder, who became his faithful and passionate disciple and, as he himself grew more famous and influential, spread his master's word throughout German-speaking lands.

Hamann occupied himself with attacks on liberal theologians – to him more contemptible than atheists – in obscure polemical pamphlets to which he gave grotesque titles. The flirtation with Mendelssohn, too, soon came to an end and was succeeded by one with F. K. von Moser, an enlightened bureaucrat who was fascinated by his originality. He corresponded with the Swiss pastor Lavater, who was the greatest champion of the varieties of illuminism and religious experience of his age, and became

---

propre to predigest food for children. Yet this is what God did for man – he abased himself, told him stories, descended to his level, became man, suffered. This is what the schoolmaster must do. Physics is too abstract. History or Natural History is better. Genesis is best of all. All this he embodied in a letter to Kant (B i 446–7), who did not reply.

celebrated for his theory according to which analysis of physiognomies provided the key to knowledge of the varieties of character, disposition and talent. He travelled occasionally to Western
Germany, and at least once to Poland. In later years he met the
philosopher F. H. Jacobi, one of the most famous thinkers of his
day, and conquered his head and heart; Jacobi replaced Herder in
his affections and became his most devoted and admiring pupil.
Towards the end of his life he gave up his post, which appeared to
him beset by unspeakable humiliations and acts of meanness
directed by his superiors against himself personally. He cannot
have been a very competent official: all his life he remained
obsessed by the thought that his hatred of abstraction was itself a
sufficient guarantee of his practical nature and capacities. His last
years were spent in comfort, for the affluent Jacobi introduced him
to an even richer religious seeker named Buchholtz and to an
exaltée lady, the Princess Golitsyn – the German widow of a
Russian diplomat. Although Buchholtz seems to have been a little
odd, Princess Golitsyn was perfectly sane – a Catholic who looked
upon Hamann as a saint at whose hands she obtained the greatest
spiritual comfort of her life. He died in her house in Münster in
1788, and is buried nearby – a peculiar and enigmatic figure to the
end.

Hamann was not unaware of some of his defects, and was
frequently self-deprecating. He declared: 'I feel at home in no
occupation, I am no use either as a thinker or as a businessman . . .
I cannot bear either high society or cloistered solitude';[1] 'I cannot
think badly enough of myself';[2] 'I have always been stupid';[3]
'imbecility is the proper word for me';[4] he was, like Socrates, an
'ignoramus';[5] his mind was 'blotting paper' and retained only
confused general impressions.[6] He constantly testifies that his
own appalling style inspired in him nothing but disgust and
horror, that he did not expect to be read much – for ninety-nine
readers out of a hundred his work is a hopeless business.[7] He
wished that he had remained a merchant. He knew that the sign of
genius is the elimination of the superfluous, the expression of the
most powerful thought in the smallest number of words, and that

---

[1] B vii 193.25.   [2] B vi 128.34.   [3] B vi 270.17.   [4] B v 365.17.
[5] B iv 4.16.   [6] B iv 7.4; cf. B vii 27.35.   [7] B ii 85.20.

he was far from attaining his goal. Yet in spite of all this he half accepted the recognition of his genius by Herder, Jacobi and his other disciples.

He had a certain desire to remain mysterious, a riddle to his contemporaries. When Kant begged him to talk in human language and even the loyal Herder confessed to being unable to make his way through some of the dark words showered upon him, he defended himself by saying that not everyone can be a system-building spider,[1] and that passion for system is a form of vanity.[2] True, he does not attain to precision and systematic exposition, he is only 'fit for fragments, leaps, hints',[3] but then system is an obstacle to the discovery of the truth.[4] This is a reference to Kant. '[M]a seule règle c'est de n'en point avoir.'[5] 'I look on the best demonstration in philosophy', he wrote to Kant, 'as the sensible girl looks on a love letter'[6] – with pleasure but suspicion.

He did not underestimate himself: he claimed to be original, to walk by himself, to put imitators to flight. He saw himself as a precursor, as an antinomian, a Socratic gadfly; he complacently accepted Herder's portrait of him as a Columbus who had discovered wholly new territories, and in a letter to Nicolai he wrote, '*genius* is a crown of thorns, *taste* is a purple cloak to cover a back torn by whips'.[7] And indeed his style is appalling: twisted, dark, allusive, filled with digressions, untraceable references, private jokes, puns within puns and invented words, cryptograms, secret names for persons in the past or present, for ideas, for the inexpressible contents of visions of the truth; where the spirit cannot be conveyed by the verbal flesh he attempts at once to imitate and emulate the cabbalistic utterances, justly forgotten, of mystagogues of the past, in phrases where it is impossible to tell where imitation ceases and parody begins. He remained unread, save for such discoverers as Kierkegaard, who revered him, and gives the impression that he thought him one of the only true philosophers of his time, speaking of his 'enormous genius'.[8]

---

[1] B ii. 203.37. The pun on *Spinne* (the German for 'spider') and Spinoza probably proved irresistible to Hamann; his work may well be fuller of puns than that of any other thinker.

[2] B i 367.13.　　[3] B i 431.30.　　[4] B vi 350.6.

[5] 'My only rule is to have no rules.' *Mittheilungen aus dem Tagebuch und Briefwechsel der Fürstin Adelheid Amalia von Gallitzin nebst Fragmenten und einem Anhange* (Stuttgart, 1868), p. 24.

[6] B i 378.32.　　[7] B ii 168.23.

[8] Howard V. Hong and Edna H. Hong (eds), *Søren Kierkegaard's Journals*

The fault is, quite deliberately, his own. 'What for others is style, for me is soul.'[1] Mendelssohn tells no more than the truth when he says that Hamann's style is too *outré*, too twisted, exaggerated, impenetrable, there are too many hobby-horses, family jokes intelligible only to esoteric cliques – 'what a mishmash of satirical fancies, wild spiritual leaps, flowery allusions, outlandish metaphors, critical vaticinations! – interlarded with passages from the Bible, decorated with Latin and English verse and frequent references to Plato, Bacon, Michaelis, Ausonius, Wachter, Holy Writ, Petronius, Shakespeare, Roscommon, Young, Voltaire and a

---

and Papers (Bloomington/London, 1967–78) [hereunder *Journals*], vol. 2, F–K, p. 252. [Kierkegaard's admiration for Hamann, though undoubtedly deep, was not unbounded, as he himself makes explicit in *Concluding Unscientific Postscript*: pp. 223–4 in the translation by David F. Swenson (London, 1941). Walter Lowrie's opinion, which has influenced other critics, is that Hamann 'is the only author by whom S. K. was profoundly influenced': *Kierkegaard* (London etc., 1938), p. 164. This seems to be an exaggeration: indeed, in *Johann Georg Hamann: An Existentialist* (Princeton, 1950), p. 4, Lowrie observes disarmingly that this view 'has perhaps more truth than evidence on its side'. Certainly he misused one piece of evidence, by sponsoring the odd myth that Kierkegaard called Hamann 'Emperor'. In *Kierkegaard*, Lowrie writes (pp. 164–5) that 'he hailed him reverently as "Emperor!" the very first time he made mention of him in the Journal'; he then refers to the journal entry for 10 September 1836. But apart from the fact that Kierkegaard refers to Hamann the day before (*Journals*, vol. 2, p. 158), in terms that suggest previous acquaintance with his work, Lowrie's reading of the entry for 10 September is bizarre. Here is the whole entry, translated by the Hongs: 'In an age when it is the order of the day for one author to plunder another, it is nevertheless pleasant at times to stumble upon men whose individuality so moulds and stamps every word with their portrait that it must compel everyone who meets it in a strange place to say to those concerned: "Render unto Caesar what is Caesar's"' (*Journals*, vol. 1, A–E, p. 53). In the first place, why is this passage thought to be about Hamann specifically? Kierkegaard does refer to Hamann in a postscript added the same day to an earlier passage (*Journals*, vol. 2, p. 199), but neither this nor his reference to Hamann on the previous day (in an entry principally about Goethe) seems conclusive. In the second place, whoever is referred to is plainly not being called 'Emperor' (though the Danish for 'Caesar' – 'Keiser' – can certainly be translated 'Emperor' in suitable contexts). Lowrie seems to have misread Kierkegaard's straightforward use of Jesus' well-known remark. (Another claim, that Kierkegaard called Hamann his 'only master', is perhaps equally without foundation. See Walter Leibrecht, *God and Man in the Thought of Hamann* (Philadelphia, 1966), p. 5, where no reference is given. I have been unable to find this phrase in Kierkegaard's works.) Ed.]

[1] B iii 378.36; cf. B iii 104.26.

hundred others"[1] – and gives up the case as desperate. Yet Mendelssohn felt that there was something remarkable about Hamann, that he was quite unlike any other writer who had lived. He realised that he had to do with a hostile genius who looked with contempt and indignation upon the doctrines of himself and his friends. And indeed Hamann's attitude towards the enlightened rationalists of Berlin was not unlike Rousseau's towards the *philosophes* and Encyclopaedists in Paris, only more so; still more like that of D. H. Lawrence towards Keynes, Russell, Moore and the whole of Bloomsbury, whose very existence appeared to him an insult to the forces of life and nature that he worshipped. Like Rousseau and Lawrence, Hamann was prepared to like individual members of this worthless group; he liked Kant personally and criticised him without bothering to understand his doctrines, much as Lawrence attacked English intellectuals; he accepted help from Kant without returning hatred for it, and called him a nice little homunculus, agreeable to gossip with, though plainly blind to the truth. He was flattered by the attentions of Mendelssohn and his friends, though in the end he turned against them, personally as well as ideologically; and he retained some admiration for Lessing, despite his deplorable Spinozism and calm rationalism, which seemed to Hamann to rob the world and the human spirit of all passion and colour. Lessing was not interested in him; but Mendelssohn, the most just and unprejudiced of the Prussian intellectuals, detected something unique and original and important. And he was not mistaken.

[1] *Moses Mendelssohn's gesammelte Schriften*, ed. G. B. Mendelssohn (Leipzig, 1843–5), vol. 4, part 2, p. 410.

3

THE CENTRAL CORE

WHAT IS it that is today worth resuscitating in Hamann's views and personality? Hardly his theosophy, central though this was to himself, and interesting and important in the history of Protestant religious belief. He was neither the first nor the greatest of those who believed that the only path to understanding was revelation; that prayer, meditation, the Christian life and innocence of spirit made it easier for the soul to be made whole; that nature in its entirety could be viewed as a book in which, in great and luminous letters, the whole history of the world and of man could be read by those who knew how to read; that all things and events were a great hieroglyphic script that needed only a key, which God's words alone provided, to reveal the nature and the fate of man and his relationship to the world and to God. This is in various forms already to be found in Eckhart and Tauler and Böhme and the whole German mystical tradition, of which pietism was an inward-looking Lutheran branch.

Even though this was the heart of Hamann's new transfigured outlook, what was truly – and deeply – original was his conception of the nature of man, the method by which he established it, and the polemical use that he made of it. He hated his century with an almost pathological hatred, and attacked what was most character-istic in it with an unparalleled sharpness and strength. He was the first writer in modern days to denounce the Enlightenment and all its works, and not merely this or that error or crime of the new culture, as for instance Rousseau, even at his most violent, does – for Rousseau shares more presuppositions with the Encyclopaed-ists than he denies, and in any case conceals his inconsistencies beneath a torrent of marvellous rhetoric. Hamann rose in revolt against the entire structure of science, reason, analysis – its virtues even more than its vices. He thought the basis of it altogether false and its conclusions a blasphemy against the nature of man and his creator; and he looked for evidence not so much in theological or metaphysical axioms or dogmas or a priori arguments, which the Enlightenment, with some justification, thought that it had discredited as methods of argument, as in his own day-to-day experience, in the empirically – not intuitively – perceived facts themselves, in direct observation of men and their conduct, and in direct introspection of his own passions, feelings, thoughts, way of life.

These were weapons which, in the end, the Enlightenment could not afford to disregard. Romanticism, anti-rationalism, suspicion of all theories and intellectual constructions as at best useful fictions, at worst a distorting medium – a form of escape from facing reality itself – virtually begin with Hamann. There is more than something of this among the Neoplatonists of the Renaissance, in Pascal, and still more in Vico. But the frontal attack was delivered by him. The fact that it was often ill-conceived, overdone, naïve, ludicrously exaggerated and irresponsible, or touched with bitter and savage obscurantism and a blind hatred of some of the noblest moral and artistic – as well as intellectual – achievements of mankind, does not lessen its importance, even if it diminishes its value. For some of what is most original in Hamann turned out to be in large measure disturbingly valid. His enemies are both those he calls the Pharisees – the supporters of the great dogmatic establishments, the Church of Rome or the French monarchy and its servants and imitators in German lands – and those he speaks of as the Sadducees – the freethinkers in Paris or Berlin or Edinburgh. And even though their achievements are, and remain, very great, while Hamann's unbridled and indiscriminate onslaughts on them are often patently unjust and, at times, absurd, humanity has had to pay a heavy price for disregarding that which he was able to see – to pay in terms not only of intellectual error, but of the defective practice and appalling human suffering to which the influence of the doctrines of both these mutually antagonistic establishments has helped to lead. This alone makes Hamann's single-minded but tortuous ideas worth examining in a spirit necessarily very different from his own.

There is no true development in Hamann's thought after his conversion, neither development nor orderly exposition. His views – on the nature of man; on his modes of cognition (belief, knowledge, understanding, imagination, reasoning, faith); on nature, history, God; on language, genius, expression, creation; on the senses, the passions, the relations of body, will, mind; on history and politics; on the ends of man and his salvation – remained from the age of thirty until his death at the age of fifty-eight virtually unaltered. It does not matter where in his writings one begins: nothing has a beginning or a middle or an end; everything is called forth by an occasion – the desire to instruct a friend, to refute some enemy or perverter of the truth, to intrigue or puzzle some old acquaintance or adversary. The thread of argument, such as it is, is constantly broken by other arguments or topics, digressions within digressions, sometimes within one vast paragraph, and the continuity of the thought emerges, after a long passage in underground channels, in some unexpected place, and is once again soon buried under the luxuriant, irrepressible, chaotic, scattered tropical growth of Hamann's ideas and images, which at once exhilarated and maddened even his most devoted and worshipping friends.

Yet within this wild and tangled wood, beside which even the works of such unsystematic writers as Diderot or Herder seem models of pedantic neatness, there is a unity of thought and outlook which no one who is not immediately repelled by his style and unparalleled obscurity will fail to grasp early in his reading. Neither his positive nor his negative doctrines are ever in serious doubt. The details may be puzzling or even exasperating; the main lines – for there are such – are firm and unchanged for over a quarter of a century of discontinuous but prolific writing. Goethe, who obtained from him, as from everyone else, precisely what he himself required, saw his thought as a kind of inner gesturing – the expression of his life by means of a kind of inward miming of it, which could be grasped only by feeling ourselves into his inner states, by a vision of the similes and allegories by which he sought to convey them.[1] Hamann's life, his style, his faith and his thought were one. His positive doctrines always developed as part of a furious onslaught on some falsehood to be rooted out: no man believed in or practised intellectual toleration less. So, for example, his doctrine of knowledge is rooted in a denunciation of Descartes' mathematical approach to natural science, and of the coherent structure of theoretical knowledge of man and nature embodied in

[1] Goethe's marvellous power of insight did not fail him: his remark that the Italians had their own Hamann in 'patriarch' Giambattista Vico (in whom he took little interest) is a brilliant observation. See p. 113 above, note 2.

the *Encyclopédie*, a work conceived and hatched in the hateful city of Paris – the work in which Kant, in one of his less tactful moments, suggested that Hamann, after he had returned from London out of a job and in debt, might find something to translate, for the benefit of his benighted fellow Prussians.

4

THE ENLIGHTENMENT

IT IS worth remembering that Hamann's attitude to the *philosophes* and all their works was undoubtedly connected with the fact that his formative years were dominated, like those of many German thinkers of this period, by the rise of the new doctrines of the Enlightenment, which, despite opposition offered by the Churches, both Catholic and Protestant, and occasional persecution by civil authority, both in France and in parts of Italy, swiftly rose to be the most powerful movement in European thought.

There were many divisions within the movement itself. Contrary to the traditional histories of the subject, not every French Encyclopaedist or German rationalist believed that men were by nature good, and ruined only by the follies or wickedness of priests or rulers, or by crippling institutions. Some, like Montesquieu and Helvétius, each in his own fashion, believed that men were born neither good nor bad, but were largely moulded by environment or education or chance, or all of these, into what they became. Others, like La Mettrie and at times Voltaire, believed that men were by nature cruel, aggressive and weak, and had to be restrained from developing these undesirable dispositions by deliberately imposed disciplines. Some among the new philosophers believed in the existence of an immortal soul, some did not; some were deists (or even theists); others were agnostics or militant atheists. Some believed that natural environment – climate, geography, physical and physiological characteristics of a scarcely alterable kind – exercised a causal influence that wholly determined human behaviour; others believed in the almost unlimited power of education and legislation, as weapons that men held in their own hands. Some, like Voltaire and Condorcet, paid attention to historical development; others, like Helvétius and Holbach, did not. Some, like d'Alembert and Condorcet, based their hopes upon the progress and application to human affairs of mathematics and natural science; others, like Mably, Rousseau, Raynal, Morelly, were inclined towards primitivism and dreamt about the restoration of a simple, innocent, pure-hearted society of 'natural' men, free from the deleterious influence of the corrupt life of the great cities and the tyranny of organised religion. Some believed in enlightened despotism, others in democracy; some, like Condorcet, believed in human equality; others, like Holbach and Kant, condemned the populations of entire continents as inferior races. Some conceived of the axioms and methods of discovery and knowledge as revealed a priori to special intellectual faculties or intuitive insight, and believed in natural law and natural rights; others believed that all knowledge rested on the experience of the physical senses, rejected all a priori certainty, and were rigorous empiricists. Some were determinists or utilitarians or teleologists; others believed in moral sense, or free will or chance.

Yet despite these disagreements – and they were far more profound than a cursory survey of the Enlightenment would indicate – there were certain beliefs that were more or less common to the entire party of progress and civilisation, and this is what makes it proper to speak of it as a single movement. These were, in effect, the conviction that the world, or nature, was a single whole, subject to a single set of laws, in principle discoverable by the intelligence of man; that the laws which governed inanimate nature were in principle the same as those which governed plants, animals and sentient beings; that man was capable of improvement; that there existed certain objectively recognisable human goals which all men, rightly so described, sought after, namely happiness, knowledge, justice, liberty, and what was somewhat vaguely described but well understood as virtue; that these goals were common to all men as such, were not unattainable, nor incompatible, and that human misery, vice and folly were mainly due to ignorance either of what these goals consisted in or of the means of attaining them – ignorance due in turn to insufficient knowledge of the laws of nature. Moreover, and despite the doubts expressed by Montesquieu and his followers, it was by and large believed that human nature was fundamentally the same in all times and places; local and historical variations were unimportant compared with the permanent central core in terms of which human beings could be defined as a single species, as minerals or plants or animals could be. Consequently the discovery of general laws that govern human behaviour, their clear and logical integration into scientific systems

– of psychology, sociology, economics, political science and the like (although they did not use these names) – and the determination of their proper place in the great corpus of knowledge that covered all discoverable facts, would, by replacing the chaotic amalgam of guesswork, tradition, superstition, prejudice, dogma, fantasy and 'interested error' that hitherto did service as human knowledge and human wisdom (and of which by far the chief protector and instigator was the Church), create a new, sane, rational, happy, just and self-perpetuating human society, which, having arrived at the peak of attainable perfection, would preserve itself against all hostile influences, save perhaps those of the forces of nature.

This is the noble, optimistic, rational doctrine and ideal of the great tradition of the Enlightenment from the Renaissance until the French Revolution, and indeed beyond it, until our own day. The three strongest pillars upon which it rested were faith in reason, that is, a logically connected structure of laws and generalisations susceptible of demonstration or verification; in the identity of human nature through time and the possibility of universal human goals; and finally in the possibility of attaining to the second by means of the first, of ensuring physical and spiritual harmony and progress by the power of the logically or empirically guided critical intellect, which was in principle capable of analysing everything into its ultimate constituents, of discovering their interrelations and the single system of laws which they obeyed, and thereby of answering all questions capable of being formulated by clear minds intent upon discovering the truth.

Naturally the enormous success and prestige of Newtonian physics, which seemed to have accomplished precisely this in the realm of inanimate nature, vastly added to the confidence of moral and social thinkers, who saw no reason why the application of the same methods in these spheres should not in time yield equally universal and unalterable knowledge. Despite hesitations and reservations of an obvious kind, there was an ever-growing movement, especially in the Protestant Churches – but to some extent in that of Rome also – in favour of attempting to apply these methods in metaphysical and theological matters too: or, at any rate, showing that Christian beliefs were not incompatible with, but in many cases identical with, or complementary to, the new rationalism. The disciples of Leibniz and Wolff in Germany, as well as the schools of natural theology in England and Scotland, moved along these lines. Rational religion, rational metaphysics, rational politics, rational law – these doctrines appeared to be moving forward with the irresistible power of liberated human reason. The spirit that inspired the most fearless and humane and enlightened writing on the need for reform in the often hideously oppressive and irrational legal systems or economic policies, or for the elimination of political and moral injustices and absurdities which are today by and large forgotten, was the same as that which inspired progress in the physical and biological sciences; it occasionally led to such oddities as Wolff's belief, enunciated in the course of an argument against miracles, that Christ was able to change water into wine, and Joshua to stop the sun at Gibeon, because they were endowed with superior – superhuman, indeed – chemical or astrophysical knowledge. All principles of explanation everywhere must be the same. Indeed, this is what rationality consisted in.

Not many thinkers of this period who are remembered today openly dissented from this central principle. Hamann was one of these. He attacked the entire outlook in every particular; and feeling himself a David chosen by the Lord to smite this vast and horrible Goliath, he marched to battle alone and unattended. He tried to attack the enemy along their entire front; and embodied his literally reactionary programme in three principal doctrines (if collections of beginnings without ends, ends without beginnings, riddles and epigrams and dark, though at times marvellously pregnant, sentences may be called that). These were: his view of the nature, the sources and the effectiveness of knowledge and belief; his theory of language and of symbolism generally; and his conception of genius, imagination, creation and the relation of God to man.

5

KNOWLEDGE

Historical, contingent truths can never be proofs of rational, necessary truths.

Lessing, 'Über den Beweis des Geistes und der Kraft'[1]

DESCARTES BELIEVED that it was possible to acquire knowledge of reality from a priori sources, by deductive reasoning. This, according to Hamann, is the first appalling fallacy of modern thought. The only true subverter of this false doctrine was Hume,[2] whom Hamann read with enthusiastic agreement. Indeed, it is not too much to say that the Bible and Hume are the two oddly interwoven roots of his ideas.

Hume had declared that the foundation of our knowledge of ourselves and the external world was *belief* – something for which there could be no a priori reasons; something to which all principles, theories, the most coherent and elaborate constructions of our minds, practical or theoretical, could in the end be reduced. We believed that there were material objects round us that behaved in this or that way; we believed that we were identical with ourselves through time. In Hamann's words: 'Our own existence and the existence of all things outside us must be believed and cannot be determined in any other way.'[3] And again: 'Belief is not the product of the intellect, and can therefore also suffer no casualty by it: since *belief* has as little grounds as *taste* or *sight*.'[4] Belief gives us all our values, heaven and earth, morals and the real

---

[1] Gotthold Ephraim Lessing, *Gesammelte Werke*, ed. Paul Rilla (Berlin, 1954–8), vol. 8, p. 12.

[2] Locke, of course, had declared that the only source of true knowledge is, not rational intuition or self-evident timeless truths which critical reason cannot reject or doubt, but experience, the brute fact of sensation – the fact that we see what we see, hear what we hear, form the images that we do. But Locke equivocated, allowing a considerable role to analytic reason.

[3] W ii 73.21; cf. B vii 167.10.   [4] W ii 74.2.

world. 'Know ye, philosophers, that between cause and effect, means and ends, the connection is not physical but spiritual, ideal; that is the nexus of blind faith.'[1] We do not perceive causes or necessity in nature; we believe them, we act as if they existed; we think and formulate our ideas in terms of such beliefs, but they are themselves mental habits, *de facto* forms of human behaviour, and the attempt to deduce the structure of the universe from them is a monstrous attempt to convert our subjective habits – which differ in different times and places and between different individuals – into unalterable, objective 'necessities' of nature.

Hamann read Hume with great attention. Hume was of course an unbeliever, an enemy of the Christian faith, but God spoke the truth through him all the same. He is a 'Saul among the Prophets',[2] a kind of Balaam, a reluctant witness to the truth, an ally despite himself.[3] Hamann translated Hume's *Dialogues concerning Natural Religion*, of which he thought most highly, and regarded Kant as a kind of Prussian Hume,[4] even though Kant ignored Hume's teaching on belief: where Hume is content to report that we can neither know nor reasonably ask why things are as they are, and must content ourselves with describing what we cannot help believing any more than we can help seeing, smelling, hearing, Kant attempts to erect these empirical habits into categories. 'Hume is always my man.'[5] The *Dialogues concerning Natural Religion* are 'full of poetic beauties' and 'not dangerous at all'.[6] 'To eat an egg, to drink a glass of water Hume needs belief;[7] ... but if belief is needed even for eating or drinking, why does Hume break his own principle when judging of things higher than eating or drinking?'[8] All wisdom begins in sense. '*Wisdom* is *feeling*, the *feeling* of a *father* and a *child*';[9] and again, 'The existence of the smallest things rests on *immediate impression*, and not on *ratiocination*.'[10] Faith is the basis of our knowledge of the external world. We may crave for something else: logical deduction, guarantees given by infallible intuition. But Hume is right, all we have is a kind of animal faith. This is the great battering-ram

---

[1] W iii 29.10.   [2] B i 380.6.

[3] See Philip Merlan, 'From Hume to Hamann', *Personalist* 32 (1951), 11–18.

[4] B iv 293.36.   [5] B iv 294.7.   [6] B iv 205.33, 34.

[7] Hamann delights in Hume's doctrine that even the most trivial act presupposes undemonstrable belief in certain uniformities.

[8] In his letter to Kant of 27 July 1759 (B i 379.35).

[9] B iii 35.1.   [10] B vii 460.6.

with which Hamann seeks to destroy the edifice of traditional metaphysics and theology.

Hume's principle was that from one fact no other fact can be deduced, that necessity is a logical relation, that is, a relation between symbols and not between the real things in the world, and that all proponents of doctrines that claim to know existential propositions that are not based on experience, or to infer other existential propositions by methods of pure thought, are deceiving either themselves or others or both. To this Hamann held steadily all his life: it is the basis of his entire attack on the methods and values of the scientific Enlightenment. There are no innate ideas in the sense in which the rationalists, Descartes, Leibniz and the Platonists spoke of them. We depend on metabolism with external nature: 'The *senses* are to the *intellect* what the *stomach* is to the vessels which separate off the finer and higher *juices* of the blood: the blood-vessels abstract what they need from the stomach ... our bodies are nothing but what comes from our or our parents' stomachs. The *stamina* and *menstrua* of our *reason* are properly only *revelation* and *tradition*.'[1] Tradition is accumulation of past beliefs; revelation is God's appearance to us through nature, or through Holy Writ.

Apart from the metaphysical implications of this, Hamann's constantly repeated point is that revelation is direct contact between one spirit and another, God and ourselves. What we see, hear, understand, is directly given. Yet we are not mere passive receptacles, as Locke had taught: our active and creative powers are empirical attributes that different men or societies have in different degrees and kinds, so that no generalisations can be guaranteed to hold for too long. Hamann boldly turns Hume's scepticism into an affirmation of belief – in empirical knowledge – that is its own guarantee: the ultimate datum, for which it makes no sense to ask for some general rationale.

In this way Hamann turns those very empirical weapons that were earlier used against dogmatic theology and metaphysics against rationalist epistemology – Cartesian, Leibnizian, Kantian – as his admirer Kierkegaard used them against the Hegelians. Nature and observation become weapons against a priori or quasi-a-priori guarantees of progress, or axioms for natural sciences, or any other large, metaphysically grounded, world-enveloping schemas. The metaphysician Fichte was right from this point of view to

[1] W iii 39.7.

exclaim that empiricism was or could be a danger to Rousseau and the French Revolution and the absolute principles which they had invoked. Hamann is among the earliest empiricist reactionaries who seek to blow up the constructions of audacious scientific reason by appeals – somewhat like Burke's, but much further-reaching and more radical – to asymmetrical, untidy reality, the reality revealed to a vision not distorted by metaphysical spectacles, or by knowledge of the certain existence of the cut and dried pattern which one professes to be attempting to find; for there is no knowledge without belief, unreasoned belief, at its base.

All general propositions rest on this. All abstractions are, in the end, arbitrary. Men cut reality, or the world of their experience, as they wish, or as they are used to doing, without any special warrant from nature, which has no grooves of an a priori kind. Yet our most famous philosophers cut away the branch on which they are sitting, hide with shame, like Adam, their unavoidable and agreeable sin;[1] they deny the brute fact, the irrational. Things are as they are; without accepting this there is no knowledge, for all knowledge reposes on belief or faith, *Glaube* (that is the transition that Hamann makes without argument), faith in the existence whether of chairs and tables and trees, or of God and the truth of his Bible, all given to faith, to belief, to no other faculty. The contrast between faith and reason is for him a profound fallacy. There are no ages of faith followed by ages of reason. These are fictions. Reason is built on faith, it cannot replace it; there are no ages that are not ages of both: the contrast is unreal. A rational religion is a contradiction in terms. A religion is true not because it is rational but because it is face to face with what is real: modern philosophers pursue rationality like Don Quixote, and will in the end, like him, lose their wits. Existence logically precedes reason; that is to say, what exists cannot be demonstrated by reason but must first be experienced itself, and then one may, if one wishes, build rational structures upon it whose reliability can be no greater than the reliability of the original base. There exists a pre-rational reality;[2] how we arrange it is ultimately arbitrary. This is in effect modern existentialism in embryo – its growth can be traced from Böhme and the German mystics to Hamann and from him to Jacobi and Kierkegaard and Nietzsche and Husserl; the route taken by Merleau-Ponty and Sartre springs from it too, but its twists and

[1] W iii 190.23.   [2] W iii 191.24.

turns are another story. In this chain Hamann's views are an irremovable link.

Among eighteenth-century German thinkers both the rationalist Lessing and the irrationalist Jacobi were profoundly troubled by the 'abyss' between the general statements of philosophy and empirical reality, between the universal 'truths of reason' and the 'truths of fact' that Leibniz had distinguished. Lessing agonised over the question of how necessary truths, 'quod ubique, quod semper, quod ab omnibus creditum est',[1] say the existence of God, or of the immortal soul, or universal objective moral truths – the 'truths of reason' – could be inferred from historical propositions, empirically known, and therefore contingent. God spoke to men at identifiable times, in particular places, Jesus was crucified in a particular place at a particular time, certain Apostles stated holy truths, had had experiences, commonly called supernatural, in specific places at specific times: can the eternal truths revealed by this *historia sacra* rest on accounts which no evidence could render absolute, infallible? How can this be accepted? He concluded by wondering whether, with the progress of human knowledge, knowledge of these contingent and empirical propositions would gradually lead to necessary truths, knowable a priori, guaranteed for ever; and concluded in turn from this that in the meanwhile all approaches towards them of all the various religions were but tentative efforts to arrive at the single central truth – hence that all these various avenues had an equal right to our respect and veneration; and deduced from this principles of universal tolerance embodied in the celebrated tale of the three rings in his play *Nathan the Wise*. Yet how could 'historical, contingent truths ... be proofs of rational, necessary truths'?[2] They cannot. 'This is the loathsome wide ditch', Lessing wrote, 'across which I cannot get, however often and earnestly I have attempted to leap over it',[3] and pathetically cries for light. Yet surely necessary truths exist? What then is their rational foundation? Jacobi maintained that Lessing died an atheist; Moses Mendelssohn hotly denied this – Lessing, he claimed, died a believer. Whatever the truth, the problem remained.

Jacobi in his turn was tormented by what he called the gap between his heart and his head: 'The light is in my heart,' he said: 'but as soon as I seek to carry it to my intellect it goes out.'[4] On

---

[1] See p. 59 above, note 3.   [2] loc. cit. (p. 280 above, note 1).   [3] ibid., p. 14.
[4] *Friedrich Heinrich Jacobi's Werke* (Leipzig, 1812–25), vol. 1, p. 367.

one side the chilly system of science, on the other hand the real world, which he is given only by the ardent fire of inner conviction – Jacobi cannot find the path between the direct experience of the heart and the general propositions of reason or science, which appear not to have any point of contact. He opts for the heart: the truths of faith. But does not the problem remain? Hamann attacks Lessing and tries to help Jacobi: but for him there is no real problem, no 'loathsome ditch', no abyss. What can it mean to wish to 'explain' existence? Thought – or rather thoughts, ideas, indeed all psychological events – are part of the furniture of the universe. There is no point outside the universe at which one can place oneself, from which the universe can be judged, condemned, justified, explained, proved. There is no chasm here: an infinity of reasons cannot be integrated into one trivial fact. In a letter to Jacobi Hamann wrote:

> Metaphysics has its own school and court languages ... and I am incapable of either understanding or making use of them. Hence I am close to suspecting that the whole of our philosophy consists more of language than of reason, and the misunderstandings of countless words, the personification of arbitrary abstractions ... have generated an entire world of problems which it is as vain to try to solve as it was to invent them.[1]

These problems are false problems. The whole world of the a priori is a fiction. Hamann is as certain of this as Bishop Berkeley was, or any modern positivist. One must avoid imposing one's own theoretical fancies upon the world. The tendency of reason is to invent entities, to start from what is given in sense and then inflate this into 'ideas of pure reason' or notions of 'pure being'. Nobody has ever understood what Aristotle or Kant really mean. Wisdom is one of the fruits of the tree of life. All evil comes from the tree of science. One should say 'est ergo sum', otherwise one will construct some brilliant fiction which one will worship as an idol. Jacobi thinks that there is some special faculty, a Pascalian 'reason of the heart', some irrational power, some special sense, whereby he will attain to ultimate reality and God; he oscillates between Spinoza and Plato, and chooses Plato. Hamann complains that what Jacobi is asking for is some special organ, a special set of contingent truths which will be more than contingent, and this is

[1] B v 272.3.

absurd. To know what there is we must look, feel, construct hypotheses perhaps, but suspect them as constructions of our own, above all not allow them to usurp the place of direct experience. The fact that experience differs from age to age, or even individual to individual, is nothing against it. Universalism is an idle craving, an attempt to reduce the rich variety of the universe to a bleak uniformity, which is itself a form of not facing reality, attempting to imprison it in some prefabricated favourite logical envelope – an insult to creation and a piece of foolish and unpardonable presumption on the part of those who try to do so. All forms of religious apologetics are this too, an attempt to apologise for, explain away, direct experience of God – whether in mystical revelation or by reading and understanding his word or decipher-ing his writing in nature – in terms invented by the puny intellect of the individual; an attempt to domesticate God, to place him in some tame herbarium of one's own.

In psychological terms it could be said that in Hamann the insulted faith of the defeated, humiliated Germans flared up against the Western oppressor with his levelling rationalism, and blasted a path for a general protest and campaign against the entire scientific-philosophical establishment, and in due course in every other province – in history, in literature, in politics, wherever the rational spirit made its home. Hamann sometimes says that he obtained these ideas from Young's *Night Thoughts*. If so, Young can hardly have known what a Pandora's box he was opening. Young preached the need for letting nature grow organically in the dark soil of faith and the past. But this turned into something much more formidable, into a general attack upon rationalism in all spheres, much as some of the most characteristic doctrines of our own century – existentialism in philosophy or Barthian anti-rationalism in religion, the doctrines of Heidegger and his pupils, emotivism in ethics, surrealism in art, and all the other manifesta-tions of rebellion against the positivism of the late nineteenth century and the early twentieth – are symptoms of a profound malaise. In this sense Saint-Simon and Maistre, from their very different points of view, correctly identified Luther as the earliest and greatest rebel against the established order – the incarnation of that force that destroyed order in France in 1789 and, despite all the Protestant quietism and advocacy of resignation, opened the door to the individual desire for self-assertion that had been outraged by the uniformity imposed upon it.

Direct experience for Hamann is a concrete fact – the basis of all true knowledge of reality. Its enemy is system, which of necessity is composed of words denoting abstractions or numbers. 'With *numbers*, as with *words*, one can do anything one likes.'[1] All these are *entia rationis*, which philosophers have taught us to confound with real things. How do such philosophers operate? By 'tearing up what nature has joined and uniting what it has divided'.[2] Analysis dismembers (although it cannot destroy), synthesis combines (although it cannot literally fuse).[3] 'Only a *scholastic reason* divides itself into realism and idealism; a correct and authentic reason knows nothing of such imaginary divisions.'[4] Analysis and synthesis are equally arbitrary.[5] The fault of all philosophers is to introduce arbitrary divisions, to shut their eyes to reality in order to build 'castles in the air'.[6] The language of nature is not mathematics – God is a poet, not a geometer.[7] Conventional signs are needed, no doubt, but they are unreal. Words like 'cause', 'reason', 'universality' are mere counters, and do not correspond to things. The greatest error in the world is 'to confuse *words* with *concepts* and *concepts* with *real things*'.[8] Philosophers are imprisoned in their own systems, which have become as dogmatic as those of the Church. Hamann said apropos of Kant: 'Every systematiser must be expected to look on his system precisely as every Catholic looks on his true Church.'[9] The geometrical method may do for spiders like Spinoza who catch flies in their nets,[10] but to apply it to living experience, to regard words like 'reason', 'existence' as referring to anything other than relationships that do not exist in reality, as being more than a mere aid to stimulate attention – that leads into private fantasies. 'If *data* are given, why use *ficta*?'[11] To ask for them is to lose the fruit of the tree of life for that of (illusory) knowledge.[12] The passion of philosophers for abstractions leads to the reification of relations,[13]

---

[1] B vii 441.22; cf. W iii 285.28–35.   [2] W iii 40.4.   [3] B vii 169.37.
[4] B vii 165.13.   [5] W iii 284.36.   [6] B v 265.37.
[7] This appealed to Goethe, who observed: 'Mathematics cannot eliminate prejudice, cannot mitigate wilfulness or allay partisanship; it can achieve nothing in the moral sphere.' Goethe, *Maximen und Reflexionen*, ed. Max Hecker (Weimar, 1907), No. 608 (p. 132).
[8] B v 264.36.   [9] B vi 350.17.
[10] B ii 203.36, B i 378.7. Elsewhere Hamann refers to Spinoza as 'the Jewish flycatcher' (B vii 181.6).
[11] B vi 331.22.   [12] B vi 492.9.   [13] e.g. B vii 173.8 ff.

for example those of time and space. Time comes to us in the cadence of music, the rhythms of our heartbeat and of breathing,[1] and is directly perceptible, not 'a form of the understanding' as Kant would have it. Space is a relation between figures that we paint or draw, gestures and the like; each relation is a particular, and to generalise them is to create a network of fictions. Moreover, nothing is intelligible save in its relationships, for the world hangs by 'threads which cannot be sundered without hurting oneself or others',[2] and this can only be perceived in each concrete particular. To generalise this into a doctrine of terms versus relations, substances versus their attributes, is once again to barter reality for figments.

For Hamann reason disrupts and fragments; time, for instance, is reduced by it to isolated 'instants'. What gives them continuity is the 'thread' by means of which Providence – and it alone – unites them. This thread alone 'ensures the continuity of the moments and parts of the flow in a manner so powerful and indissoluble that it is all of one piece'.[3] If it were not for this our analytic reason would disintegrate our experience into the fictitious units of the natural sciences and be unable to reassemble them again. Hamann loves the English poets, for 'they don't analyse, they don't dissect'.[4] The English poet Dyer, for instance, writes about wool, whereas Lessing's fables are nothing but vapid philosophising.

Hamann's general trend is clear, but it is equally clear that he suffers from genuine prejudice against the natural sciences as such. When Kant, in 1768, in the Königsberg garden of his friend the English merchant Green, said that astronomy had attained to such perfection that no new hypotheses were possible in it, Hamann was stunned.[5] To constrict God and the infinite possibilities of his creation? Was it against inexhaustible divine – and rational – fertility that Kant marched out his army of abstractions? No general proposition, still less theories, can catch the variety and the concreteness of life. It may be that Hamann's hatred of science (which he admits) is in part due to the danger to his piety.[6] This is rationalised into a general onslaught on the cut and dried universe, without spontaneity, without surprises, without inexhaustible possibilities, any one of which, without rhyme or reason, might be

---

[1] W iii 286.17.   [2] B iv 59.1.   [3] W i 126.3.   [4] B ii 78.33.
[5] B ii 416.29 ff.   [6] B ii 416.33 ff.

realised. Hence the denunciation of determinism, because it seems to impose a man-made straitjacket upon the unclassifiable, upon God-Nature – that which every man, according to him, lives in and for, but which he cannot express, for to express is to use symbols, and symbols limit, abstract, cut reality into arbitrary slices, destroy it for the sake of trying to communicate the incommunicable.

The first task is to expose the deleterious influence of abstractions and the false knowledge which is built upon and out of them. This is the task of the modern Socrates, as Hamann conceives himself. There is something ironical, as he well knows, in representing Socrates, the great saint of the Enlightenment, the father of rationalism, the martyr to prejudice and tradition and religion, as the critic and indeed enemy of the new orthodoxy. Socrates was much written about in the eighteenth century, and cast in many roles: for some he is the father of critical enquiry, the enemy of superstition, traditional values, all that resists the methods of reason and logical argument, wherever this may lead; for others he is principally a deist, or a freethinker; for still others he is a mystic guided by the inner voice of his 'daimon', which he is bound to follow in all his ways, or, again, an inspired precursor of Christianity (as he was to the Christian Platonists of the Renaissance, and, in a famous invocation, to Erasmus), or an early pietist in communion with his soul and its spiritual source, the Master of the universe, God himself. For Hamann Socrates is none of these avatars, but the opponent of the sophists, the gadfly of all the grand establishments, the fearless exposer of lies, hypocrisies, received opinions, delusions, all that is specious, clever, ingenious, the figments and fallacies of the arch-deceiver – the worldly, rootless intellect.[1] Helvétius and Voltaire, Descartes, Leibniz, Kant and Rousseau and Mendelssohn are the sophists of the present age. The first task of a man in pursuit of truth is to expose their hollow verbal fictions and declare that the task of reason is not the increase of theoretical knowledge – only the whole man, with his passions, emotions, desires, physiological reactions and all,

---

[1] Hamann knew something of Plato; but on Socrates he seems to have followed François Charpentier's *Life*, translated by Christian Thomasius. (Charpentier's 'La Vie de Socrate' was first published in his translation of Xenophon's *Memorabilia* in 1650, and revised more than once thereafter. Thomasius' 1693 translation was entitled *Das Ebenbild eines wahren und ohnpedantischen Philosophi, oder: Das Leben Socratis*; Hamann owned a copy of the second edition (Halle, 1720).)

can approach the truth – but the demonstration of the limits of knowledge, the exposure of man's ignorance and weakness.

This is what the *Socratic Memorabilia*, directed against the sophist Kant and the 'enlightened' merchant Berens, is meant to show. Socrates maddened the Athenians; Hamann is prepared to upset the bourgeoisie of Königsberg and Riga, to expose their *idées reçues*, to show that the official Christianity of the eighteenth century is nothing but paganism, that the real man of God is closer to thieves, beggars and criminals and to vagabonds and highwaymen – the irregulars of life – than to liberal Lutheran clergymen and rationalistic apologists for Christianity. A man of ironical doubt, ironical humility, inner light, hypnotic genius, a middle class *épateur* of all the bourgeois – this is Socrates, this is Hamann.

The Enlightenment seems to Hamann an inversion of natural values. In his diatribe against his friend F. K. von Moser's *Master and Servant* of 1759 – a treatise in praise of enlightened despotism – he identifies scientific method as casuistry, Machiavellian manipulation of men; he conceives the politics of enlightenment as a treatment of men as if they were machines; he protests against the usurpation of science, which has turned from a servant of man's fine and infinite creative capacity into a dictator which determines his position, morally, politically and personally.

Hamann does not offer a faculty for yielding propositions superior to those of science – revealed truths, say, or the axioms of natural law as conceived by either Aquinas or Grotius. He opposes to scientific rules the empirical knowledge – practical rather than theoretical – which belongs to any man who lives in a proper relationship to God and to nature (what these are still remains to be seen). Words are counters, he says, echoing Hobbes unconsciously; language is a currency: men of genius can use it, but officials turn it, as they turn everything, into a sterile dogmatism, which they proceed to offer for their own and popular worship. This turns human relations into mechanical ones, and makes of what were living truths, or a spontaneous capacity for acting in some appropriate fashion, a dead rule, an object for idolatrous worship. This is a sermon against dehumanisation and reification before those terms had been thought of.

Hamann's great enemy is necessity – metaphysical or scientific. Here he suspects that a specific human vision – a moment of illumination or ordinary understanding, in which a man grasped his situation and knew how to act, in order to achieve his spontaneously conceived ends – was turned into a pseudo-objective source of authority – a formula, a law, an institution, something outside men, conceived as eternal, unalterable, universal; a world of necessary truths, mathematics, theology, politics, physics, which man did not make and cannot alter, crystalline, pure, an object of divine worship for atheists. He rejects this absolutely. No bridge is needed between necessary and contingent truths because the laws of the world in which man lives are as contingent as the 'facts' in it. All that exists could have been otherwise if God had so chosen, and can be so still. God's creative powers are unlimited, man's are limited; nothing is eternally fixed, at least nothing in the human world – outside it we know nothing, at any rate in this life. The 'necessary' is relatively stable, the 'contingent' is relatively changing, but this is a matter of degree, not kind.

Any attempt to introduce a deep division between types of cognition or types of entities – any kind of dualism between 'reality' and 'appearance' – seems to him plain denial of the unity of experience and an escape into mythology. In this respect he is with the empiricist positivists against orthodox religion and the central tradition of Western metaphysics; the union of mysticism and empiricism as against rationalism here emerges in full strength for perhaps the first time. Hamann is a genuine nominalist, as is made clear in his theory of language. Hence his violent opposition to the notion that there is a world of eternal essences connected internally by logical relationships, or ontological bonds; a world whose bony structure an ideally clear language could mirror – as Leibniz certainly, and perhaps Descartes, believed. He rejects the very notion of an essence from which necessary characteristics or – still more insane – a necessary past and a necessary future could in principle be deduced. The world for him consists of persons and things and their *de facto* relationships, and the only evidence for them is experience, outside which there is nothing, save that such experience for him not merely includes but has as its very centre the relationship of man and God.

He pursues the devil of dualism wherever he sees it, and in his earliest writings he uses Hume's strict empiricism to destroy alleged necessary connections in nature together with their meta-physical guarantees and special non-empirical paths towards their discovery. Later he applies the very same method to refuting rationalist politics and ethics, for example in Mendelssohn's or

Lessing's attempts to divide one aspect of human life from another, say religion from civil law, 'inner' from 'outer' conduct, the State from the Church, and the like.

Mendelssohn's chief purpose in the work that Hamann attacked, *Jerusalem: A Plea for the Toleration of the Jews*, was to found both moral and political obligation on natural law and natural rights, which were to be distinguished from less perfect rights and less stringent laws and duties, as they developed in civil society. The specific points against Mendelssohn are of little interest now: the whole framework in which the debate was conducted has become largely obsolete. But what is characteristic is Hamann's indignation with Mendelssohn for supposing that man is a compound of reason and feeling who can be analysed into his individual ingredients, so that one can say that as a human being he has certain natural rights and duties, as a citizen other rights and other duties; that, for instance, the rights of man *qua* man, say to any religious opinions he may hold, cannot be cut into by his duties as a citizen, say to obey the government in the public sphere, which, *ex hypothesi*, must not impinge upon the private domain. These divisions – what a man owes God and what he owes Caesar, the 'public' and the 'private' – seemed to Hamann a fatal method of cutting human beings to pieces, like so much inanimate flesh. Man for him is one: feeling shapes belief and belief feeling. If religion is to be taken seriously at all it must penetrate every aspect of a man's life; if it is true, it is the heart and soul of a man's being; a religion that is confined to its 'proper' sphere – like an official with limited powers, to be kept in its place, not allowed to interfere – that is a mockery. Better deny religion altogether, like an atheist, than reduce it to a tame and harmless exercise within an artificially demarcated zone that it must not transgress.

Hamann's entire conception of Christian society rests on a passionate belief in the opposite of all this – that man is one and that if God (as he believed) not only exists but enters into every fibre, every nook and cranny, of human experience, the notion of confining him to his 'sphere', of creating frontiers against his worship, is a blasphemy and self-deception. If this leads to confusion of private and public, to interference and intolerance, Hamann does not mind at all: toleration of differences is a denial of their importance. Man is one, with all the uncomfortable consequences that this carries; attempts to show that all beliefs that continue to contribute to 'peace', 'harmony', 'rationality' –

whether religious, political or any other – are to be encouraged by the secular State (as advocated for example by Spinoza, Lessing and, in effect, the French utilitarians, Helvétius and Co.) seem to him tantamount to a denial that beliefs – truth – matter much. All efforts to demarcate the private from the public, the inner from the outer, contingent from necessary (here he mistakenly holds Kant to be particularly guilty – the mere words 'pure reason' infuriated Hamann, who misrepresented the *Critique of Pure Reason* to a quite fantastic degree), seemed to him nothing but efforts to evade reality, to label and classify various aspects of it and invent imaginary attributes and functions for them, intended to save men from the agony of being (as a later philosophy was to call it) 'authentic', of truly understanding themselves and their relations to others. All philosophical spectacles are for Hamann distorting lenses – efforts at escape from reality into the security of a theory from which the tangled avenues of real life have been kept out.

In a sense the great polemic against Mendelssohn and the humanistic liberals of Berlin reveals Hamann's position – at any rate as it was after his conversion in London – more vividly than even his more obviously theological writings. Mendelssohn is a characteristic representative of the Enlightenment, sincere, rational, humane, unoriginal, moderate, and exceptionally clear. Every one of these qualities irritated Hamann – even sincerity allied to a calm and conciliatory temper – for he believed that in serious matters detachment, dispassionate judgement, an attempt to do justice to opposite sides of the case, were merely a cloak for timidity and indifference. Theory for him was practice, and practice was the exercise of will, the self-commitment to what one not merely recognised but felt and, in a sense, willed to be true with every fibre of one's being in the perpetual battle for the word of God, for its realisation on earth – or against it. Indifference to this – suspension of judgement, coolness – is a contemptible aspect of failure to face reality.

Mendelssohn expounded the orthodox liberal doctrine of natural law, according to which the State was founded upon reciprocal promises or compacts between the ruler and the ruled, each to fulfil his proper, stipulated functions, and rested on the sanctity of promises, as ordained by natural law, recognised by all rational men – the law claiming universal obedience. He drew from this the normal liberal consequence, drawn by Spinoza before him, that since the promise was valid only if freely given, it entailed freedom of thought and expression, the absence of coercion towards men's beliefs, including their recognition of natural law, upon which the validity of promises was founded; for unless men were free to arrive at whatever conclusions were indicated by the operation of natural reason, the very notions of natural law and the obligations that sprang from it, and of a rational basis for government, could not be realised. While a government might have the right and duty to restrain or coerce action, it could not, without destroying the foundations of its own rights, dictate belief or persecute non-conformity which did not take violent forms or seek to disturb public order. This was the eighteenth-century distillation from the views of religious dissent in the seventeenth century held by Spinoza, Locke and all the fathers of the liberal enlightenment.

Hamann would have none of this. Everything in it seemed to him false: the notion of natural law, the notion that the State or any other human institution rested on some intellectual act of assent, for example a promise, seemed to him absurd. To keep one's word is to act normally as a thinking, feeling being. Society rests on this as a natural phenomenon.[1] The State was a form of human association that grew from natural needs which themselves could not be explained but were part of the general mystery of creation, that is, the mystery of why things were as they were and not otherwise – something that God had not chosen to reveal to us in any detail. God had spoken to men in manifold ways: through history, through nature, through Holy Writ – his words revealed by his prophets and by his only begotten Son.

To be a man was to understand in some degree what one's goal on earth was – this one understood only by understanding oneself, which one could do only in that human intercourse in which men were mirrors of one another, in which by understanding others – by communication – and by being understood by them, I understood myself; for if I were alone in the world, communication, and therefore speech, and therefore thought (which for Hamann were one), could never develop. Therefore the existence of a complex web of human relations was presupposed by the very possibility of thought, and did not need its products as its justification. Indeed, it needed no justification at all: it was a given fact to be accepted on pain of ignoring reality, and so being driven into error and madness.

[1] W iii 300.27 ff., 301.25 ff.

Hamann thought that the notion of justifying society – or for that matter the State – was as absurd as the attempt to justify the existence of speech, or love or art, or the existence of plants and animals in the world. Why should I obey the king, or indeed anyone? Not because I promised – this is neither historically true nor logically required, for why did I promise? For the sake of happiness? But that is not what I seek on this earth – only Frenchmen and utilitarians seek this (his tone at such points greatly resembles that of Nietzsche, especially on the English). It is because I am a man and seek to fulfil all my powers – to live, create, worship, understand, love, hate, eat, drink, procreate – in the way that I was created to do, and if I stumble and err I have but to read the Bible or study human history or look at nature to see what it is that God's creatures are meant to do; for there are parables and allegories everywhere around me. The story of Abraham, the story of Ruth, may be the story of an oriental patriarch or a Moabite woman, but they are also the stories of every man and every woman. Similarly, there are events in the history of my community, and there are phenomena in the nature that surrounds me, all of which are ways in which the Creator speaks to me, darkly sometimes, but in the end in such a manner that even the meanest soul can get some inkling of it – telling me what I am, what I can be, how to realise myself, not along paths logically deducible from contemplating my imaginary essence, but by understanding my relationship to God and to the world. This relationship can be realised only in action, in the actual act of living, in pursuing ends, in hurling myself against obstacles; the proper direction, the right things to do, faith alone can supply – that faith without which Hume could not eat an egg or drink a glass of water, without which there is for us no external world, no past, no awareness of objects or persons; that faith which cannot itself be bolstered by rational considerations, for it generates reason and is not generated by it; it is itself presupposed in every act of consciousness, and therefore cannot itself be justified, for it is that which justifies everything else.

So much for promises as the basis of political obligation. Natural law was for Hamann an equally hideous chimera, a great bleak construction of the rationalising intellect which has no reality at all. The word of God – faith – that saved him in London during the darkest hours of his life speaks differently to different men in different circumstances. There is no single, universal, public, objective structure – natural law or the rational structure of the universe, or anything else invented by philosophers – which can be contemplated by anyone at any time, and, provided he has adequate intellectual power, can be perceived in its immutable, eternal essence and authority. The whole of the rationalist construction of the Berlin sages seems to him a denial of activity, variety, energy, life, faith, God, and man's unique relation to him. And into his diatribe there enters, as one might expect, a note of personal violence, hatred of *raisonneurs*, heretics, and, as was not unusual, Jews.[1]

Mendelssohn had been a friend, in some sense a patron; nevertheless, Hamann is no more reluctant than other writers of his time and milieu – among them, at times, Kant, surprisingly enough – to denounce the materialistic, rationalistic unrealism and arrogant authority of anti-Christian liberal culture, a conception of a self-appointed élite of frozen dogmatists. He denounces Berlin as dominated by secular, liberal culture, positive, critical, atheist, analytical, disruptive; this note is to be found later in Maistre and in the entire anti-rationalist, anti-Semitic literature of the nineteenth century, until it finally reaches a point of violent hysteria in Austro-German racism and National Socialism. Jews, Wolffians, materialistic dwellers in the modern Babylon[2] – all are one to Hamann. The Jews emerge as the eternal critics, the detached, uncommitted judges of the Christian world. To tolerate them as an organised religion is a concession to that liberalism and rationalism that constitutes a denial of what men are for, to serve the true God, hear his words and feel and will and act them in every moment of their life on earth; this is known better to the common people than to the alienated wiseacres who dominate politics and intellectual

---

[1] Hamann's attitude to the Jews has been the subject of some dispute. See, for example, the essay by Ze'ev Levy on Hamann's controversy with Mendelssohn in Bernhard Gajek and Albert Meier (eds), *Johann Georg Hamann und die Krise der Aufklärung* (Frankfurt am Main etc., 1990), pp. 327–44. However, there is undoubtedly a scattering of anti-Jewish remarks in Hamann's writings (see, for example, W iii 146.34, 151.31, 395.11, 397.18; B vii 181.6, 467.26; as well as several passages in *Golgotha und Scheblimini!*); and although he was certainly concerned to defend what he saw as true Judaism against perversions of it, and well disposed to Mendelssohn as an individual, it is not plausible to maintain that he was free of what later came to be called anti-Semitism. In this he was, of course, entirely typical of his age.

[2] See W iii 397.18.

life – the tame philosophers at the courts of the enlightened despot. Hence again the combination of obscurantism, populism, fideism and anti-intellectualism, faith in the common people and hatred of natural science and criticism that was to have so powerful and so fatal an influence in the two centuries that followed.

Hamann's vision is that of human beings as children, to whom their father speaks, and who learn everything at his knee – much as his own ideas were intelligible to him only in terms of his own childhood, of the Bible that was at the centre of his pietist upbringing, and to which in moments of crisis and despair he constantly returned. Men must often be conceived of as deaf children whom one must painfully make repeat certain words whose very sound they cannot apprehend.[1] If they are docile they will never 'oppose their nature to their reason and of their habits make a necessity',[2] and so generate that dualism of nature, instinct, sense of kinship with others and with natural objects versus sceptical analytical individualising reason; or of creature versus creator; or of natural versus supernatural or anti-natural;[3] or of necessary versus contingent.

What is this category of nature and the natural to which French materialists are constantly appealing? Uniformities amongst the phenomena? But what guarantees have we of their continuance? Only God's will. 'What is there in nature, in the commonest of natural phenomena, that is not, for us, a miracle in the most precise sense of the term?'[4] It is a miracle because the causal nexus in terms of which we distinguish the normal and the miraculous is nothing but a fiction of our own making, a device, and not (as Hamann delights in saying that Hume pointed out) something that corresponds to reality, to an object of observation, or feeling, or any other direct apprehension on our part. From this he develops a view that is close to the occasionalism of Malebranche and Berkeley, and is one of the streams that fed those romantic philosophers who saw reality not as dead matter obeying unaltering laws but as a self-generating process, a thrusting forward of a living will – blind and unconscious in Schelling and Schopenhauer and Bergson, progressively attaining to greater and greater self-consciousness in the metaphysical systems of Hegel and Marx (whether in spiritual-cultural development, or in that of the more

[1] W i 14.19.   [2] W i 24.25.   [3] W i 24.27 ff.   [4] W i 24.30.

material struggle against nature or other men) or to the realisation of divine purpose that is intrinsic to the will of God, as in the metaphysics of the Christian religion.

Reason is said by the secular philosophers to be one and the same in all men: but this is not so, else there would not have been so many conflicting philosophies all claiming to be justified by the same faculty of reason. The only unitary source of truth is of course revelation – reason or the conflict of rationalisms has led to the Tower of Babel, which was laid in ruins; only when God descended to us and was made flesh was the possibility of a unitary faith made possible. This God is certainly not the abstraction of the deists, but creative and passionate – above all a person who speaks to us through history and nature, a person capable of being loved and worshipped, not the abstract unity and harmony of, say, Shaftesbury or Mendelssohn and his Christian friends. This is certainly, as Jean Blum says, the God of popular consciousness, not the shadowy deity of abstract thought. He adds: 'Hamann's thought is what those who do not normally think would think if they did think.'[1]

Since Hamann fervently believed in a personal God who made the heaven and the earth and governed them in accordance with his own will, he was a teleologist, but not a rationalistic one, still less an optimistic utilitarian. The three concepts that dominate him are those of creation, intentionality and its correlative, understanding. To understand is to understand someone; things or events or facts as such cannot be understood, only noted or described; by themselves they do not speak to us, they do not pursue purposes, they do not act or want or strive, they merely occur, are, exist – and come to be and pass away. To understand is to understand a voice speaking, or if not a voice, something else that conveys meaning, that is, the use of something – a sound, a patch of colour, a movement – to refer to, or stand for, something else. If we can claim to understand history, we can only mean by this that we understand not merely what occurred – that is mere transcription – but why, with what end in view; not merely what things are, but what they are at; and if they – the inanimate objects, say – are not at anything, are just a succession in a causal chain, events occurring in a certain identifiable order, then to say that we understand them must mean that we understand what those who produced them, consciously or unconsciously, intended them for; if nobody

[1] op. cit. (p. 262 above, note 2), pp. 47–8.

intended them for anything – if they just occurred for no reason – there is no understanding them, the category of understanding is inapplicable. But of course in history we understand the purposes of agents – not merely individuals who are fully conscious of what they are pursuing, and some among whom are aware of why they are pursuing it, but also groups of human beings, cultures, nations, Churches, which may be said to pursue collective purposes, although the analysis of this notion is far from easy. Hamann had no doubt that different civilisations pursued different ends and had different conceptions of the world, which were part and parcel of their ways of life, that is, of the civilisations that they were; and this notion he transmitted to Herder, who, apparently without the benefit of Vico's ideas – similar to his own and in some respects more original and profound – played a major part in transforming the human sciences and men's ideas about themselves.

But what, in that case, is nature, both as we contemplate it in ordinary life, as it forms the subject of sciences, and as, in interplay with active agents, it enters the web of human history as the weft to which the human agent is the warp? If the notion of understanding nature is to make any sense, it can only be because it too is at something, intends, strives, acts; or else is that whereby others do so. Hamann was not a pantheist. He was not an animist of any kind. He did not believe in active powers in stones or trees either as part of some omnipresent divinity or as independent centres of purposive action, as the pagans did. He believed in a personal deity, who created the world for his own often inscrutable purpose. To this degree he stands with the teleologists – Aristotle, Aquinas, Hegel. Where he sharply parts company from them is in denying that the divine (or cosmic) purpose is necessarily rational, that his relation to the universe is – even if in an infinitely higher degree or sense – identical with that of any earthly planner, whose reason is definable as a disposition towards thought in accordance with the laws of logic, the fitting of means to ends in accordance with proven principles, whether derived a priori or empirically, the test of which is consistency, systematic unity, generality and the like. This appears to him to attribute to God our own poor categories – poor in comparison with an infinity of ways that could exist in which an agent could act and not be capable of being caught in the net of our particular intellectual equipment. Since God exists, everything that he makes embodies his purpose; but to attempt to deduce his existence from the behaviour of the created world seems to him a particularly degraded kind of anthropomorphism – the notion that God is like a mathematician or an architect or some other kind of rational practitioner is an arbitrary and blasphemous assumption.

Hamann is strongly prejudiced against reason and the sciences, which seem to him to afford a poverty-stricken view even of human possibilities. The meaning of action for him is better exemplified in the infinitely various and rich world of individual self-expression: the effort of children to represent things to themselves and to communicate desires and fantasies, to express their personalities by creating works of art that convey their vision – that is, convey meaning by using primitive scrawls, or something not identical with themselves, to represent what they imagine or conceive to exist and to be worth identifying. What children do is in principle the same as that which all men do, from the simplest bodily gesture or scratch on the wall of a cave to the most sophisticated and profound spiritual expression in art, philosophy, literature, religion – identical, too, with entire styles of life through which nations and Churches and cultures express themselves.

God is inscrutable. But Hamann thought that if there was a key it was not in conceiving nature as a rational system from any part of which deductions could be made to any other part, following therein the divine logic of the plan on which it was constructed. He saw no evidence of this. The key for him was in understanding; that is, in having revealed to one what the Creator meant to convey. If we understand other human beings by having it revealed to us what a given set of marks on paper or sounds or artistic representation is meant to express or say – however this may happen, and this Hamann regards as always somewhat mysterious – then we must, to the extent of our powers, understand God's meaning by viewing his creation in this way.

It can come closer to us than that. In the Bible, Hamann believes, our Father spoke to us directly. We can only understand as much of this as we are capable of embracing within the particular concepts and categories of meaning that happen to have fallen to our lot as human beings, as Germans, as citizens of Königsberg; we can expand our powers by learning other languages, other styles of art, anything but the dead, artificial symbolism – the technical terminology of the sciences – that springs for him from no rich, imaginative source, and does not convey purpose and life in a sufficiently human fashion. Why should what God intends necessarily fit into our narrow, rational categories? It is at least a wider and more generous analogy – even if all analogies are inadequate – to assume him to be an artist whose purposes are manifold to a literally infinite extent; intelligible, understandable, only as we understand art, each concrete expression by itself as an individual whole, not as a link in some mechanical or logical system that a machine could operate, that one needs no imagination to comprehend. We understand nature as we understand art, as perpetual divine creation, in accordance with patterns that may illuminate divine purpose for us in some apparently remote field. A proper understanding of nature, the tracing of the divine purpose, however feebly and uncertainly, may cast light upon divine purpose in history, in my own individual life, or anywhere else.

This is Hamann's world: the union of the naïvely simple conception of God as the omnipotent Eternal Father, to whom I am bound by relations of awe and love and total dependence – perhaps the most widespread and primitive of all human attitudes – with a theory of creation, meaning, understanding that is by no means simple, and a full grasp of which created the humanities as we know them today, a late and sophisticated product of the human consciousness; together with the dogma that everything is created, that is, intended to do or stand for something by its creator – since if to assume that reason can unravel what an artist, or a lover, or an ordinary man in ordinary circumstances does and means is absurd, how much more is this so when applied to God. Where there is creation, there can always be revelation.[1]

Philosophy claims to be the explanation of life, but 'life is action',[2] not a static thing to be analysed like a botanist's specimen. An

---

[1] Of course there is much else in Hamann's conception of God. He is not only the poet who creates the world from the beginning, but also 'the thief at the end of days' (W ii 206.20; cf. Revelation 16: 15), that is, the final judge of all that he has made and now takes unto himself. Moreover he not only compassionately descended to the level of his creations, but displayed divine humility in the Incarnation – *forma servi*, as a mode of revelation. And his unity embraces opposites – infinite calm with infinite energy (W ii 204.10) – the *coincidentia oppositorum* of which Cusanus had spoken is of his essence. This is Hamann's theology, but far more striking is his doctrine of the relation of God to his creatures.

[2] B iv 288.29.

action cannot be described in the categories provided by the Cartesians, or even the Lockeans and Leibnizians, for all their talk of movement and change. The task of true philosophy is to explain[1] life in all its contradictions, with all its peculiarities; not to smooth it out or substitute for it 'castles in the air'[2] – harmonious, tidy, beautiful and false.

The first place in which to look is that which is most familiar to me – myself. 'Self-knowledge and self-love is the true norm of our knowledge of men and our love of men.'[3] And again, 'all our cognitive powers have *self-knowledge* as their object'.[4] The desire to know ourselves as we are and to be ourselves, and accept no substitutes – by the 'descent into Hell'[5] of self-knowledge – is the foundation of our entire activity.[6] 'Do not forget, for the sake of the *cogito*, the noble *sum*.'[7] Expel metaphysics, like Hagar,[8] and what do we discover in ourselves? Desire and passion and faith, which our heart sometimes seeks to satisfy with lies, for it is a born liar.[9] To suppress what we find in favour of the apotheosis of only one of our faculties – capacity for rational analysis – is a self-mutilation which can only lead to a perversion of our nature and distortion of the truth. Flesh has been given us, and passions; they do not sin by existing; they can be perverted, but the seducer is always cold reason, which desires to assert its own authority and usurp that of the other faculties.

Mystical rationalism despises the flesh and seeks to substitute for God's creation something of its own: that is what the Greeks sought to do at Eleusis. Philosophic rationalism is at a still further remove, a feeble substitute for the mystical variety. It preaches self-reliance, the attempt to construct the universe out of resources provided by logic, geometry, chemistry, and the other collections of useful figments that seek to substitute themselves for the direct vision of reality. Nothing is so insufficient for this purpose as reason. We are compounded of desires and passions as well as reason: our proper function is to learn from history, nature and God, their creator, and to create ourselves. Young had said that not only reason, but the passions too, have been sanctified by baptism. We must create with the whole of ourselves, not only our brains but the entire organic whole.

---

[1] W ii 199.1.   [2] B v 265.37.   [3] B iv 6.20.   [4] W i 300.17.
[5] 'Höllenfahrt', W ii 164.17.   [6] W iv 424.47.   [7] B vi 230.35.
[8] B vi 231.12.   [9] B i 297.12. St Paul was Hamann's favourite apostle.

Hamann's prose is full of reiteration of words like 'mutilation' and 'castration'. 'How can a man who has mutilated his organs feel?'[1] Bacon is quoted in the same passage as charging philosophers with mutilating nature by their abstractions. Passions are like limbs.[2] To maim them is to deprive us of the power not only of sensation but of understanding.[3] Philosophy can control and guide, but never initiate.[4] All energy is psycho-physical: it proceeds from the unity of body and soul. To tame the passions is to weaken spontaneity and genius. How then are vicious consequences to be avoided? By faith – self-surrender into the arms of Providence. Since God was made flesh this does not crush our body or passions. Sensualism in Hamann is combined with self-surrender; the abandonment of the latter leads to arid atheism, of the former to equally arid puritanism. Spontaneity is compatible with self-surrender but not with system.

Condillac wrote a treatise on sensations, in which Hamann, towards the end of his life, took some interest, but it is precisely such careful positivists as Condillac that he most detests, if only because they do not delve into the depths and splendours of the ravaged human soul, because they seek to make of nature an elegant front garden. (Goethe later claimed to be liberated from shallow classicism of this type by Herder, who in fact preached to him, at Strasburg, doctrines put forward by Hamann.) Modern writers have turned the savage violence of the Beasts of the Apocalypse into Lessing's harmless moral imagery, and Aesop's fierce vision into smooth Horatian elegance. To understand truly one must descend to the depths of the orgies, to Bacchus and Ceres.[5] Nieuwentyt's and Newton's and Buffon's discoveries cannot inspire poetry as mythology has done. For this there must be a reason.[6] Nature has been killed by the rationalists because they deny the senses and the passions. 'Passion alone gives to abstractions and hypotheses hands, feet, wings; images it endows with spirit, life, language. Where are swifter arguments to be found? Where the rolling thunder of eloquence, and its companion, the monosyllabic brevity of lightning?'[7] For this we must go to the artist, not to the modern philosopher; to the Bible and to Luther, not to the Greeks; to Milton, not to the French versifiers.[8]

[1] W ii 206.1.   [2] B i 442.32.   [3] W ii 206.1.   [4] W ii 162.33.
[5] W ii 201.4 ff.   [6] W ii 205.20.
[7] W ii 208.20; 'monosyllabic' because the German for lightning is 'Blitz'.
[8] Such passages are reminiscent of Burke's famous essay on the sublime and

If we are to pray for the whole of ourselves and avoid the fate of poor Origen or Abelard – austerity, dry intellectualism, passionless contemplation, self-castration are associated into one symbolic pattern in his mind – then we must not suppress our 'lower' nature: it was given to us by God as surely as all else. 'I have always sought to identify and pick out the *inferna* of a torso, rather than the *superna* of a bust,' he wrote to Herder in 1768; '. . . my coarse imagination has never been able to picture a creative spirit without *genitalia*.'[1] Why are the glorious organs of generation objects of shame? One must not speak of general human sentiment on this subject; it does not exist; '*children* are not full of prudery, nor *savages*, nor Cynic philosophers'.[2] Prudery is an inherited piece of morality – habit, due to consensus. And consensus is for Hamann the worst of authorities, appeal to good sense, tame middle-class sentiment, against the thunder of God and revelation. 'If the passions are mere *pudenda*, do they therefore cease to be the tools of virility?'[3] And again, 'the *pudenda* of our organisms are so closely united to the secret depths of our *heart* and *brain* that a total rupture of this natural union is impossible'.[4] To divide the flesh from the spirit is to blaspheme against God, who created us one. The truth is revealed to us in the Bible because the story is so simple, sincere and realistic, because it is childishly naïve, and so a true embodiment of human life. Since children are not ashamed of their bodies as the civilised man of the eighteenth century is, in this sense too we must take Christ's words literally and seek to restore within ourselves the less broken, more spontaneous view of life to be found among the innocent, those not bedevilled by doctrine or a despotic social organisation of enlightened autocrats either in politics or in the sciences or the arts.

Hamann's anti-rationalism, his emphasis on the fullness of life, and in particular on the importance of everything in man that is generative, creative, passionate – the sexual metaphors, the sensuality of his imagination at its most inspired and religious – have a

---

beautiful. Hamann certainly read Burke: and there is an affinity, particularly in the paean to the sublime as compared to the classically perfect. But the parallel should not be pressed too far. Joseph de Maistre, whose attacks on the French Enlightenment are not dissimilar, is unlikely ever to have heard of Hamann.

[1] B ii 415.20.   [2] W iii 199.28.   [3] W ii 208.11.   [4] B v 167.16.

clear affinity with the views of William Blake. When Blake says 'Without Contraries is no progression. Attraction and Repulsion, Reason and Energy, Love and Hate, are necessary to Human existence',[1] that is pure Hamann. So is

> Lo! A shadow of horror is risen
> In Eternity! Unknown, Unprolific?
> Self-closd, all-repelling ...
> Brooding secret, the dark power hid.[2]

The 'shadow of horror' is of course the 'Spectre', that is, cold reason, arid, hard, with lust for dominion, mad pride, ambitious, violent, hating, brutally and implacably egoistic, perverted, avid, as against the 'Emanation', which is tender, loving and creative. 'The Spectre is the Reasoning Power in Man';[3] 'The Spectre is, in Giant Man: insane';[4] 'An Abstract objecting power that negatives every thing',[5] 'brutish Deform'd ... a ravening devouring lust continually Craving & devouring'.[6] This echoes Hamann's very analogous sentiments. So does the contrast between 'Imagination the real & eternal World' as against the 'Vegetable Universe'[7] of ordinary life and the 'Vegetable Glass of Nature'.[8]

Blake differs from Hamann in regarding the external world as 'Dirt upon my feet, No part of me',[9] and in his general anti-empiricism, but the Spectre's boast – 'Am I not Bacon & Newton & Locke ... my two wings: Voltaire: Rousseau?'[10] – is much in Hamann's tradition. So is the hatred of man-made laws, laws needed to fence men off:

> And their children wept, & built
> Tombs in the desolate places,
> And form'd laws of prudence, and call'd them
> The eternal laws of God.[11]

---

[1] *The Marriage of Heaven and Hell*, plate 3. The text followed in these quotations from Blake is that to be found in *William Blake's Writings*, ed. G. E. Bentley, Jr (Oxford, 1978). References to this edition are given in parentheses, by volume and page, at the end of the relevant notes, thus: (i 77).

[2] *The First Book of Urizen*, plate 3, lines 1–3, 7 (i 241).

[3] *Jerusalem*, plate 74, line 10 (i 581).   [4] ibid., plate 37, line 4 (i 495).

[5] ibid., plate 10, line 14 (i 434).   [6] *Vala*, p. 84, lines 38–9 (ii 1196).

[7] *Jerusalem*, plate 77 (i 587).

[8] 'Vision of the Last Judgement', p. 69d (ii 1010).

[9] ibid., p. 95 (ii 1027).   [10] *Jerusalem*, plate 54, lines 17–18 (i 352).

[11] *The First Book of Urizen*, plate 28, lines 4–7 (i 282).

This is precisely Hamann's doctrine. So is the thunder against asceticism: 'Men are admitted into Heaven not because they have Curbed & governd their Passions or have No Passions but because they have Cultivated Their Understandings. The Treasures of Heaven are not Negations of Passion.'[1] And Hamann would have had profound sympathy for

> That they may call a shame & sin
> Loves Temple that God dwelleth in
> And hide in Secret hidden Shrine
>   The Naked Human form divine
> And render that a Lawless thing
>   On which the Soul Expands its wing.[2]

and

> Children of the future Age,
> Reading this indignant page;
> Know that in a former time,
> Love! sweet Love! was thought a crime.[3]

or for what he says in *Jerusalem*: 'I am not a God afar off, I am a brother and a friend ... Lo! we are One.'[4] He is still closer to Hamann in his passionate defence of free will against all forms of determinism, and in his doctrine of salvation through art, which he identified with a vision of God, until he arrived at the equation Christian = Artist. And 'Jesus & his Apostles & Disciples were all Artists';[5] this in sharp contrast to the Greek view of life, which for Blake was rational, scientific, secular, blind. Finally, nothing is more Hamannian than 'Art is the Tree of Life ... Science is the Tree of Death.'[6] D. H. Lawrence would have agreed.

As for Blake's political views and his mystical anarchism, that is another matter. Hamann, despite all his objections to the King of Prussia, was in the end a German and a Prussian – more the latter

---

[1] 'Vision of the Last Judgement', p. 87z (ii 1024).
[2] 'The Everlasting Gospel', p. 50 (ii 1060).
[3] *Songs of Experience*, plate 51 ('A Little GIRL Lost'), lines 1–4 (i 196).
[4] *Jerusalem*, plate 4, lines 18, 20 (i 422).
[5] 'Laocoon', aphorism 16 (i 665).
[6] ibid., aphorisms 17, 19 (i 665, 666).

than the former, as he indefatigably points out to Herder, whom he suspects of abandoning Prussia for Germany.[1] In part, this is to be explained by the fact that they were both influenced by Böhme, a child of East German culture, and Blake by Swedenborg, who lived in a climate of opinion not unlike that of Hamann in northern Europe.

The close connection of the notion of free creation with sexual fertility – and indeed of religious with sexual imagery – is familiar enough. Like Blake, Hamann identifies reason with repression. He was himself a sensual man and took pride in the fullness of his life. The unity of theory and practice was not a mere abstract doctrine for him: he genuinely detested anything that confined the human spirit, all rules and regulations as such. They were perhaps necessary, but if so they were necessary evils. Rules, he says, returning to his favourite field of metaphor, are like Vestal Virgins: only because a Vestal was violated did Rome acquire a popula-tion,[2] and if rules are not violated there is no issue; one must have rules but also break them.[3] Hagedorn says, 'We don't judge painters by the exceptions.'[4] Hamann answers: 'We poor readers do; for us, all the masterpieces in a cabinet of paintings are exceptions. He who cannot produce an exception cannot produce a masterpiece.'[5]

Passages in this vein, painstakingly collected by Hamann's exceedingly erudite student Rudolf Unger, are usually held to be only symptoms of his own richly sensual imagination. But they are far more than this: they are a passionate protest against what he regarded as the insane rationalism of the Enlightenment, the fact that, despite its professed empiricism, it did not pay sufficient attention to the irrational factors in man, whether in their normal

[1] For example: 'You pride yourself on being a German and are ashamed of being a Prussian, which is still ten times better' (B ii 434.5). Compare this remark in a letter to Kriegsrat Scheffner: 'I have scarcely any desire to be a German ... I am nothing more or less than an East Prussian' (B v 199.15). I owe these quotations to Gunnar Beck.

[2] 'Rules are vestal virgins who populated Rome, thanks to the exceptions which they perpetuated.' W ii 345.11. Romulus and Remus were the children by Mars of Rhea Silvia, a Vestal Virgin.

[3] W ii 362.16 ff.

[4] C. L. von Hagedorn, *Betrachtungen über die Mahlerey* (Leipzig, 1762), vol. 1, p. 150; quoted by Hamann at W ii 345.4.

[5] W ii 345.9.

or abnormal manifestations. The erotic writers – Crébillon, Parny and the like – trivialised the passions even further; the writings of the Marquis de Sade were not taken seriously at that time; nor did Diderot's remarkable explorations of sexual conduct attract much notice, even among the *philosophes*. Rousseau, whose influence was far wider, was prudish and morbidly puritanical about such matters. If he described them it was in a violent desire to confess, to draw attention to himself and his inescapable vices, and his passionate candour and freedom from hypocrisy. Hamann, and after him Blake, were among the few writers before the romantics who conceived the doctrine of the need for total self-expression as the object of the natural human craving for freedom, and wrote about it without excitement or terror, and with profound and sympathetic insight. The liberation of writers like Goethe and Schiller, Shelley and Wordsworth, even Hugo, from the despotism – moral as well as aesthetic – of the laws of fanatical eighteenth-century rationalism ultimately sprang from the revolt, which in this case took a religious form, against the enemies of man's unbroken nature.

The principal enemies for Hamann were Kant and Helvétius. Kant he accused of 'old, cold prejudice in favour of mathematics',[1] of a '*gnostic* hatred of matter' and a '*mystical* love of form',[2] though it is Helvétius (who was widely read in Germany) who preaches the shallow eudaemonism (*Glückseligkeitslehre*) which is the curse of Germany in his day. At least Rousseau and Diderot recognise the existence of spiritual conflict within man. Helvétius, who believes that public utility is all in all; that justice is public interest supported by power; that private honesty is of little importance to society, since vices can be harnessed as successfully to the public interest as virtues; that virtue without the support of public power is a pitiful absurdity; that to love the good for its own sake is as impossible as to love evil for its own sake; that the 'thermometer' of public evaluation of morals constantly alters,[3] hence absolute values are a conception absurd in itself; that genius is a product of artificial culture, and a reformed education can breed it as often and as much as may be needed by the society of the future; that personal liberty, if it is an obstacle to the rational organisation of society, may be suppressed – this man is Hamann's

[1] W iii 285.18.   [2] W iii 285.15.
[3] *De l'esprit*, essay 1, chapter 7: vol. 1, p. 116, in *Oeuvres complètes de M. Helvétius* (Liège, 1774); cf. essay 2, chapter 13.

natural enemy. Everything is false here: the psychology, the scale of values, the notion of what man's nature is, the total blindness to man's inner life, or the abysses of which Augustine and Pascal, Dante and Luther wrote, and which Helvétius and his friends blandly dismiss as an irrational aberration to be cured by a competent physician or 'engineer of human souls'.

Hamann is furiously angry and, as was often the case with other, particularly later, exasperated enemies of the triumphant march of science, falls into bitter and savage obscurantism: freethinkers are a danger not merely to sound religion, but to morals, to public order; they are inciters to political mutiny. The reference of everything to *bon sens* is in effect dangerous subjectivism: it offers the views of a group of atheists as an infallible criterion.[1] '*Obedience to reason* ... is a *call* to open *rebellion*.'[2] The bonds of subordination are broken, subordination becomes impossible, if reason is not submissive and denied.[3] Authority must be one and not many. It resides not in reason but in paradox, absurdity, in what is 'foolishness to the Greeks'.[4] (This is echoed by Kierkegaard in the following century.) There cannot be any peace between faith and reason. So far from religion being reason *in excelsis* as Thomism teaches, one must make up one's mind either for faith or for criticism; either to complete commitment or to open scepticism. An article in Nicolai's Berlin periodical, probably written by himself, mildly observed: 'There is room in the world for you and for us.'[5] This is precisely what Hamann denied. There is no room for truth and falsehood: one or the other must perish in the fight. The Jews must be kept in their place; so must all foreigners who bring disruptive ideas from the West. Yet he did not make common cause with the pamphleteers and clerical propagandists who attacked the Enlightenment. It is only after the death of Lessing that he allows himself to say that the notorious Pastor Goeze[6] may in his own way have been right. Whatever his

---

[1] W iii 385.29 ff.   [2] W iii 193.37.   [3] W iii 194.1.

[4] W iii 410.5, W iv 462.6; cf. 1 Corinthians 1: 23: 'But we preach Christ crucified, unto the Jews a stumblingblock, and unto the Greeks foolishness.'

[5] *Allgemeine deutsche Bibliothek*, supplement to vols 25–36 (1775–8), part 4, p. 2479 (reprinted in *Hamann's Schriften*, ed. Friedrich Roth (Berlin, 1821–43), vol. 8, ed. Gustav Adolph Weiner, part 1, p. 282).

[6] Lessing's most ferocious antagonist among the Lutheran clergy. An admirer of Lessing once said that he would rather be wrong with Lessing than right with Goeze.

influence on later reactionaries, Hamann was too independent, too eccentric, too unruly a subject of Frederick the Great to join in any man-hunt or collaborate in any government or Church campaign.

Far more typical of him is his defence of the letter *h*. In 1773 there appeared a volume entitled *Betrachtung über Religion* by C. T. Damm, an old Wolffian theologian much respected by the educated public of Berlin. Damm denounced the use of the letter *h* in many German words where it appeared to him to be superfluous, for instance between two syllables or after a consonant. Hamann published a riposte entitled *New Apology of the Letter H*.[1] This time he is no longer either Socrates or any of his more fearful impersonations – a crusading philosopher, a Rosicrucian knight on his death-bed, a sibyl, an apocalyptic mystagogue, Abelard Virbius, the Magus of the North,[2] the sage Aristobulus, the angry prophet from the Brook Kerith, a Northern Savage, Zacchaeus the Publican, Ahasuerus Lazarus, Elijah *redivivus*, the Mandarin Mien Man Hoam, or a Protestant Minister in Swabia. Now he is masquerading as a simple old Prussian schoolmaster called Heinrich Schröder; he smokes his pipe, he drinks his mug of beer in the evening, he has three classes to attend to, and the letter *h*, the first letter of his Christian name, is dear to him.

What are Damm's arguments? That the unpronounced *h* is otiose, and, perhaps worse, may teach children blind faith, may rob them of critical powers. Language ought to be rationalised; it ought

[1] W iii 89–108.

[2] This description, which he liked himself, and by which he was known to many of his contemporaries and is referred to throughout discussion of him by writers in German in the last two centuries, was originally given him by F. K. von Moser. It is connected not merely with the fact that in 1762 he wrote a little essay on the Magi of the East at Bethlehem, in which as a special nail in Helvétius' coffin he says that what the Magi did was prima facie absurd – they deserted their kingdoms and subjects, mistook an old Eastern legend for good tidings, sought the cradle of a foreign child with deplorable consequences, allowed the Tetrarch Philip to massacre the innocents (a disastrous enterprise) – yet the implication of it (as of all genius) is that an 'outer' act may seem absurd to contemporaries, but if God is truly within, the deed is immortal and beyond price. It is due even more to the fact that Kepler had predicted that the planet Venus would pass the solar orbit in June 1761; in that year Captain Cook set off for the Southern Seas; the learned orientalist Michaelis persuaded Frederick V of Denmark to send a learned expedition to Arabia. Hamann sat down to the study of the Koran. This concatenation of events brought together the notion of the Magi, a star, an expedition to the East, in the slightly ironical, affectionate sobriquet 'Der Magus in Norden'.

to be made sane, practical and free from all arbitrary elements. But this is impossible; a perfectly logical language is a chimera; all 'arbitrary' and non-logical elements cannot be taken out of life – that would leave it flat and dreary. The letter *h*, this parasitic letter, useless, a nuisance, embodies for Hamann the unpredictable element in reality, the element of fantasy in God's direction of the world. The tract grows into a diatribe against a spick and span, desiccated universe and a paean to irregularity and the beauty of the irrational. Reason is a 'lamentable, poor, blind, naked thing'.[1] 'Your life', says the letter *h*, addressing itself to Damm and his ilk[2] – 'Your life is what I am myself, a breath [*ein Hauch*].'[3] God has created poor little useless *h*, but it will not perish from the earth. A tremendous and most moving hymn to God follows. Deists who prove God by design have no faith in such as me; such a God exists only by the precarious logic of vain, puffed-up logicians – the logician is evidently logically prior to God. In such a universe I – *h* – could not survive, but thanks to the true God I do and shall.

It is no great distance from this to defending ancient institutions and usages as such for fear of killing the soul altogether with the body, as the French reformers seemed to Hamann on the way to doing. In a world built by Helvétius there would be no colour, no novelty, no genius, no thunder or lightning, no agony and no transfiguration. When the young Goethe spoke at Strasburg of how dark, how Cimmerian, how corpse-like Holbach's *System of Nature* appeared to him to be,[4] and spoke with rapture about the elemental, spontaneous poetry of Gothic cathedrals and the untamed German spirit, he supposed himself to be speaking under the influence of his new friend Herder; in fact both were echoing Hamann, who, in Germany at least, represents a solitary personal revolt against the entire embattled Enlightenment. He was a major force in transforming the ideas which hitherto had lived only in small, self-isolated religious communities, remote from and

[1] W iii 100.21.

[2] They are apostrophised as 'You little prophets of Böhmisch-Breda!', an allusion to *Le Petit Prophète de Boehmischbroda* (n.p., 1753), a pamphlet ostensibly reporting the vaticinations of a prophet born in a Bohemian village, actually by Baron Friedrich Melchior von Grimm, the celebrated Paris critic, a correspondent of Catherine the Great, a friend of Diderot, Holbach and many other figures of the Enlightenment.

[3] W iii 105.4.

[4] *Dichtung und Wahrheit*, book 11: vol. 28, p. 68, in op. cit. (p. 113 above, note 2).

opposed to the great world, into weapons in the public arena. His was the first great shot in the battle of the romantic individualists against rationalism and totalitarianism.

6

LANGUAGE

HAMANN'S VIEW of language is at once the most central and the most original doctrine in the rich and disordered world of his ideas, and perhaps the most fertile: from the seed that he planted – as always and as if on principle, he did not tend the plant, but let it grow as it would – developed Herder's linguistic historicism and psychologism, and (nothing would have horrified Hamann more deeply) a powerful factor in modern linguistic analysis.

The middle of the eighteenth century witnessed a celebrated controversy, launched by Condillac in 1746,[1] about the origins of speech, dividing those who believed that it was of human invention from those who supposed that it must have been given to mankind by God. Those who thought speech a human creation claimed it was a product of either nature or art, which, by analogy with the development in other respects of the human organism, sprang initially from biological needs, and developed, as for instance Maupertuis had maintained in 1756,[2] from gestures and natural cries. Something of the sort – though with considerable differences – was expounded by De Brosses in 1765.[3] Other 'naturalist' theories were contained in James Harris's *Hermes* (1751) and the famous treatise of Lord Monboddo, *Of the Origin and Progress of Language* (1773–92). Against this view arose an army of Christian theologians led by J. P. Süssmilch,[4] who argued, as indeed

---

[1] *Essai sur l'origine des connoissances humaines* (Amsterdam, 1746).

[2] 'Dissertation sur les différents moyens dont les hommes se sont servis pour exprimer leurs idées', a lecture delivered on 13 May 1756. *Oeuvres de Mr de Maupertuis* (Lyon, 1756), vol. 3, pp. 435–68.

[3] *Traité de la formation méchanique des langues et des principes physiques de l'étymologie* (Paris, 1765); translated into German as *De Brosse über Sprache und Schrift* (Leipzig, 1777).

[4] Johann Peter Süssmilch, *Versuch eines Beweises, daß die erste Sprache ihren Ursprung nicht vom Menschen, sondern allein vom Schöpfer erhalten habe*, dating

Rousseau had already claimed in his *Discours sur l'inégalité* of 1755, that if language was a human invention, something that man created to satisfy a need, it must have been a product of thought, since reflection was an indispensable precondition of language, just as language was of thought. But, according to Süssmilch, all thought used symbols, and therefore language, or at any rate symbolism, was presupposed in the act of inventing symbolism, which could not therefore be a pure invention. This perfectly valid argument – valid, that is, against the bald notion that language was a device created by man like the wheel or the screw – became a commonplace of theological argument and is much used by Bonald in his attempt at the refutation of Condillac. For the consequence that Süssmilch and others drew from this argument was that, since language is not a human creation, it was communicated to man by God – it was a miraculous gift of divine grace, like the human soul itself.

The greatest figure in this controversy was Herder, who attacked Süssmilch with weapons drawn from Hamann himself. The notion of a complete language springing forth fully armed, grammatical structure and all, before human reason had developed to a relevant degree of sophistication, is a chimera. All faculties grow; they are in a state of constant interplay (Hamann said '*jealousy*').[1] Language is one of the expressions of this organic growing together and mutual interpenetration of human faculties. It was neither invented nor revealed as a fully shaped instrument that one fine day fell into the lap of an astonished and overjoyed man like a delightful, precious and unexpected gift. Like everything else, it developed, *pari passu* with man's cognitive and emotional and other powers – *Kräfte* – in the course of time. No doubt, even though language was of human origin, 'it reveals *God in the light of a higher day*: his work is a human soul which itself creates and continues to create its own language because it is his work, because it is a human soul'.[2] It is no more and no less divine than any other human

from 1756 but first published ten years later (Berlin, 1766). One of Süssmilch's most eloquent and persuasive allies is Antoine Court de Gébelin later in the century.

[1] W iii 237.28.

[2] This was Herder's celebrated thesis in his work on the origin of language, *Abhandlung über den Ursprung der Sprache* (Berlin, 1772), at p. 221: v 146 in Suphan's edition (see p. xiii above). Hamann quotes the passage, with different emphases, at W iii 18.19.

activity. God works within us immanently – man, and all he is and does, is made in his image, his from first to last.

Hamann had nothing against the anti-apriorism and anti-rationalism of this approach, but he was outraged by its – to him excessive – degree of naturalism: it endowed man with too much power, and nature with too much creative capacity. He attacked Herder bitterly, and Herder in due course recanted and came closer to Süssmilch's position and the notion that language and symbolism and thought were miraculously – or at any rate for no natural cause that is in principle discoverable – added to the attributes of the human animal, who was thus transformed into man, an immortal soul, a being in constant dialogue with his Lord, unlike anything else in nature. This controversy between two Protestant theologians – for in essence Hamann was that no less, indeed rather more, than Herder – stimulated Hamann to expound his theory of language, as always in fragments and sudden digressions, footnotes, irrelevant parentheses, but nevertheless with characteristic boldness and life.

Hamann's claim was in effect this: the notion that there is a process called thought or reasoning that is an independent activity 'within' man, in some part of his brain or mind, which he can choose at will to articulate into a set of symbols that he invents for the purpose (or derives from others, fully formed), but which, alternatively, he can also conduct by means of unverbalised or unsymbolised ideas in some non-empirical medium, free from images, sounds, visual data, is a meaningless illusion – yet that is, of course, what men have often thought to be true, and indeed perhaps, for the most part, still think. Hamann is one of the first thinkers to be quite clear that thought *is* the use of symbols, that non-symbolic thought, that is, thought without either symbols or images – whether visual or auditory, or perhaps a shadowy combination of the two, or perhaps derived from some other sense, kinaesthetic or olfactory (though this is less likely in man as we know him) – is an unintelligible notion.[1] To think, in all the many senses of that concept, is to employ something – images, marks on paper, sounds – intentionally, that is, to denote objects: things, persons, events, facts. What symbols are used to do the denoting is

---

[1] There is a story that the economist J. M. Keynes, when asked whether he thought in words or images, replied, 'I think in thoughts.' This is amusing but, if Hamann is right, absurd.

another question: some may be traced to unconscious roots and biological and physiological causes, others to artificial invention, as of new words, technical terminology and the like. But in all cases thought (or language) is the employment of symbols. Vico had said something very close to this, but Hamann – like the rest of the learned world, apart from a few Italian savants – had evidently not read him.[1]

'Language is the first and last organ and criterion of reason,' said Hamann.[2] The Cartesian notion that there are ideas, clear and distinct, which can be contemplated by a kind of inner eye, a notion common to all the rationalists, and peddled in its empirical form by Locke and his followers – ideas in their pure state, unconnected with words and capable of being translated into any of them indifferently – this is the central fallacy that for him needed eliminating. The facts were otherwise. Language is what we think with, not translate into: the meaning of the notion of 'language' is symbol-using. Images came before words,[3] and images are created by passions.[4] Our images, and later our words (which are but images used in a systematic fashion according to rules, although Hamann, with his hatred of system, scarcely concedes even this; he would like to feel that language is a spontaneous outpouring, a kind of gesturing that others understand directly), are coloured, altered by the least change in our sense experience. Our art and thought and religion spring from the same root, our response to outside factors, in Hamann's case God, who speaks to us like a father and teaches us the rudiments of language, and thereby articulates our world for us; as our symbols go, so go our concepts and categories, which are but arrangements of symbols. This, if it is translated into non-theistic language, can be represented as a response to nature and to other human beings. Indeed, Hamann adds the latter: man thinks and acts in response to others like himself; his nature is not intelligible save in terms of perpetual communication – with God and with other beings – and

---

[1] He did order a copy of the *Scienza nuova* in 1777, and was disappointed when he received it, for he had assumed from its title that it dealt with the subject of political economy, which interested him; in any case, he formulated his own theory well before this; if there were Vichian influences via Italian Homeric scholars who were read in Germany, there is no evidence that the *New Science* directly influenced Hamann (cf. pp. 113–14 above).

[2] W iii 284.24.   [3] W ii 199.4 ff.   [4] W ii 208.20, 25.

by means of reminiscence of his own past self,[1] a reminiscence of something taught to him by God, or, as empiricists would say, by other human beings, his parents or teachers.

All speech, all art, all reflection are reducible to different uses of symbolism. Hamann's new aesthetics – here too he showed originality of a high order – is founded on the proposition that the language and the form of art are indissolubly one with the art itself, as against the dominant aesthetic theorists – Boileau or Batteux or Gottsched and their disciples – who maintained that rules existed for the purpose of rendering an identical 'content' into the best or most appropriate 'vehicle' or medium, and so distinguished content, form, style, language as independent and manipulable constituents of a compound substance – something that for Hamann was one indissoluble 'organic' entity. Sometimes he says of sense and reason that they are like angels moving up and down Jacob's Ladder, intermingling, in the end homogeneous and not sharply distinguishable.[2]

What is it to understand? If you wish to understand the Bible you must comprehend 'the Oriental character of the eloquence of the flesh that takes us to the cradle of our race and our religion'.[3] 'Every court, every school, every profession, every closed corporation, every sect – each has its own vocabulary.'[4] How do we penetrate this? With the passion of 'a friend, an intimate, a lover'[5] – faith and belief are the motifs again – above all, not by rules. The same applies even to theology. He was much excited by Luther's remark, which he found in Bengel, that theology was nothing but grammar concerned with the words of the Holy Ghost.[6] For what is theology but the study of the actual words of God spoken to us? Words – not ideas or truths which might have been articulated in some other fashion and symbolism, yet have borne literally the same sense: for sense and words are one, and all translation distorts. Some sentences may resemble one another, or carry similar meanings, but no sentence can literally be substituted for any other, for the connection of words and sense is organic, indissoluble, unique. Words are the living carriers of feeling – only pedants

---

[1] Language, like all learning, 'is not mere *invention*, but rather a *reminiscence*' (W iii 41.11).

[2] e.g. W iii 287.29.   [3] W ii 170.37.   [4] W ii 172.21.   [5] W ii 171.15.

[6] Johann Albrecht Bengel, *Gnomon novi testamenti in quo ex nativa verborum vi simplicitas, profunditas, concinnitas, salubritas sensuum coelestium indicatur* (Tübingen, 1742), preface, section 14, p. [xxiv]. See B ii 10.1 ff.

and scholars dilute them by analysis or kill them with devitalising formulae. A word is the stamp of life – the richer the better.

Goethe and Jacobi are witnesses to the magnetic force of Hamann's cryptic style – something that he deliberately adopted, half regretting his own obscurity, half accepting it as an antidote to abstraction, as the only way to attempt to convey the fullness of the inexhaustible particulars of which the world was composed. He was intent upon creating a sense of unplumbed depths, of unlimited vistas, and stopping efforts to define, delimit, close in tidy formulae; he applauds irregularity, luxuriance, the inexhaustible and indescribable, the astonishing, the miraculous, the strokes of lightning, the sudden momentary illumination of the dark. He spoke in riddles, but those who admired him were fascinated by this mysterious, deep man and the unusual, startling perspectives that he seemed to open. No man was ever in more conscious opposition to his age, with a fanaticism that often turned into blind perversity. 'For me', he said, 'every book is a Bible.'[1] And by this he certainly wished to imply no kind of pantheism, which he would have regarded as a shallow heresy. What he meant was that every author animates his book, that it is his living expression, that to understand it one needs direct insight, a sense of the author, his time, his intentions, the world that he inhabits, the vision of which his expression is a part, and this is needed above all to attain to even the most fleeting glimpse, the most insufficient knowledge, of what God said to us in his book, or in his nature, his history. It is this contrast between the sense of dialogue, communication, immediate understanding, achieved by what Herder was to call 'feeling into' (*Einfühlung*) a man, or a style or a period, with rational, rule-dominated analysis that to some extent Goethe may have derived from Hamann.

Whenever he embarks on amateur philological excursions of his own, what he seeks is the essence of the meaning of a word, a work of art, a ritual, a way of life, not an exotic vision into which to escape from the real world. For example, his suggestion that all mythological rivers are masculine, because not *flumen* but *vir* or *amnis* is the suppressed subject in their titles, shows a Vico-like desire to comprehend some inner process, a vision of the world on the part of men remote in time and space; it does not reflect a yearning to return to the Middle Ages, like that German linguistic

[1] B i 309.11.

nationalism which Swiss scholars such as Bodmer and Breitinger,
or even the liberal Gottsched, displayed, but which to Hamann
appears to be an unworthy unrealism and a rejection of the real
world in favour of some historical fiction. It is with this attitude
that he infected his disciple Herder, when he urged him to study
the poetry of the Letts, which, he suggested, may have had
something to do with the rhythm of their work,[1] or drew his
attention to a learned work on Icelandic sagas. Language and
thought are one, like God and his Shekinah and Tabernacle.[2]
'Where there is no *word* there is no reason – and no world.'[3] 'All
idle talk about reason is mere wind; language is its organon and
criterion!'[4] That is why Kant, who supposes himself to be
speaking about the categories and concepts of something that he
calls the understanding, is in fact speaking about forms of language
– a fluid, mercury-like substance that alters not only with entire
forms of life but with individuals, with attitudes, with professions,
with moods. To suppose that one is laying down, once and for all,
the eternal, unalterable laws of something called thought, translatable into any language and any symbolism – some inner, rock-like
reality, of which language is merely the cover or the glove, made to
fit, an artificial thing – that is the profoundest misunderstanding
of all.

There is no non-symbolic thought or knowledge. All thinkers
who have believed that actual forms of language conveyed error,
which could be detected by non-verbal means, and that a new
language could be invented to convey the truth more exactly – who
did not, in other words, use language as an instrument of self-
criticism, but tried to get in some sense behind it (as, for instance,
Leibniz and such modern philosophers as even the verbally
sensitive Russell have sometimes supposed themselves to be doing)
– appear to Hamann to be engaged upon a nonsensical undertaking, something that ignores the essence of the situation. For him, as
for Berkeley, the world is God's language; that is, just as we think
in symbols, God thinks in trees or battles, or rocks and seas, as
well as in the Hebrew and Greek letters of his inspired prophets,
who spoke not in their own name but in his. This vision never
leaves him:

[1] An idea which crops up in Henri de Saint-Simon and Marx, but not, so far as
I know, in Herder; cf. p. 229 above, note 4.
[2] W iii 237.10.   [3] B v 95.21.   [4] B v 108.6.

Every phenomenon of nature was a name – the sign, the symbol, the promise of a fresh and secret and ineffable but all the more intimate chosen union, communication and communion of divine energies and ideas. All that man in these beginnings heard with his ears, saw with his eyes, contemplated or touched with his hands, all this was the living word. For God was the Word. With the Word in his mouth and in his heart, the origin of language was as natural, as near and as easy as a child's game.[1]

This is how it was with Adam in Paradise, but then there was the Fall, arrogance, the Tower of Babel, an attempt to substitute for the immediacy of sense and direct perception cold constructions of theoretical reason.

For Hamann thought and language are one (even though he sometimes contradicts himself and speaks as if there could be some kind of translation from one to the other).[2] Because this is so, philosophy, which pretends to be the critique of things, or at best ideas about them, since it is nothing but words about words – second-order judgements – is in fact a critique of our use of language or symbols. If it had been the case that there was a metaphysical structure of things which could somehow be directly perceived, or if there were a guarantee that our ideas, or even our linguistic usage, in some mysterious way corresponded to such an objective structure, it might be supposed that philosophy, either by direct metaphysical intuition, or by attending to ideas or to language, and through them (because they correspond) to the facts, was a method of knowing and judging reality. But for Hamann this is a thoroughly fallacious conception, though time-honoured – indeed one on which the whole of European rationalism has been built. The notion of a correspondence, that there is an objective world on one side, and, on the other, man and his instruments – language, ideas and so forth – attempting to approximate to this objective reality, is a false picture. There is only a flow of sensations, inner and outer, colours, tastes, sights, sounds, smells, love and hatred, sorrow, pity, indignation, awe, worship, hope, remorse, rage, conflict; and above all faith, hope, love, directed towards persons – other human beings or the Creator and the Father of the world and of men, Almighty God.

We become conscious of this flow of experience – beyond which there are only nature and history, by which God speaks to us. Our

[1] W iii 32.21.   [2] e.g. 'To speak is to translate', W ii 199.4.

acceptance of these realities is founded on faith – or Hume's belief. We learn through the medium of symbolism, and our creative imagination conceives the past and the future that are absent, or the possibilities that are not yet and perhaps never will be, or what might have happened but did not, through the medium of the selfsame symbols. But the essence of symbolism is communication: communication between me and others or me and God, which is of the essence of being human at all. That, of course, is one of the reasons why it is absurd to suppose that human society is founded, or should be founded, on a promise or desire for utility or avoidance of danger or some other 'rational' consideration – that it was constructed by such calculation or can be justified in terms of it, so that if the justification were successfully refuted, we could, and rationally should, dissolve society and live in some other way. The truth is, of course, for Hamann, that man comes to recognise himself to be what he is only in the context of the relationships of which in a sense he is compounded, in the first place relationships to God, to other persons and to nature, in the second his own constructs out of these relationships – institutions, sciences, arts, forms of life, hopes and ideals. Above all, of course, this network of relationships is held together by the pervasiveness of the paternity and constant tutelage of God.

The image is, as it were, of an entity – man – engaged in perpetual activity, or construction of his own and others' lives, with bricks provided by sensation and imagination, called symbols, which are sometimes mistakenly denominated abstract notions, thought of as having an independent life of their own; sometimes still more mistakenly (as by medieval philosophical realists) viewed as non-sensuous, eternal characteristics of a transcendent world, called universals – eternal, unchangeable denizens of a supernatural world, which Plato conceived in one way and Descartes in another, and Kant (although Hamann misrepresents him gravely in this respect) in yet another. But in fact all there is is a world of persons, and their ways of conceiving their own experience – ways determined by the apparatus that determines their relationships. This is what he means by saying that creation is speech[1] or 'through [language] are *all things* made',[2] or when he describes human speech as a form of creative energy. That is why the cardinal sin is 'to confuse *words* with *concepts* and *concepts* with

[1] B i 393.28.   [2] B vi 108.24.

real things',[1] which is precisely what metaphysicians have done, hemming man in with imaginary entities of his own construction, which he then proceeds to worship as if they were real forces or divinities, and which distort his life (this is a vast and pregnant generalisation of Rousseau's and Diderot's notion of human alienation) because of the conflict between what man truly is – self-expressive, creative, loving (or hating) – and the standards that he has invented (without intending to), social, moral, aesthetic, philosophical, in terms of an imaginary being. This being, whose favour he seeks, to whom he seeks to approximate, to whom he wishes to justify himself, is a monstrosity of his own creation which he has set up in judgement over himself and calls 'public opinion' or 'the common morality of mankind' or 'the State' or 'the Church', or conceives as some more personal, and if anything more despotic, divinity, before which he quakes, whose authority he accepts as absolute, but which, on examination, turns out to be a figment, an obsession, due to some weakness or blunder, some blindness to reality, and the attempt to make up for this by a grotesque invention of man's perverted intellect or imagination.

Diderot, in the famous 'Paradox of the Comedian',[2] spoke of the contrast between natural action and assuming a role: 'The man of sensibility obeys only the impulses of nature, and utters nothing but a cry from his heart; as soon as he tries to moderate or force this cry it is no longer he, it is a comedian who is playing.'[3] And again: 'One is oneself by nature; one is another by imitation.'[4] This 'otherness', this acting of a role imposed upon one, imposed perhaps by the unintended consequences of the behaviour of one's self or one's fellows in the past, which comes to threaten and coerce one as if it were a real entity menacing one from outside – that is the phenomenon of alienation, to which Rousseau and Hegel, Kierkegaard and Marx, and much modern psychology and sociology have given a central role.

Hamann, although he does not call it by that name, is among those who originated this approach to man's condition. For him, as indeed for many a Christian thinker, man is alienated, a being who is estranged from the source of reality – God and other men, and the immediacy of feeling and sense-experience. As soon as man

[1] B v 264.36.
[2] *Paradoxe sur le comédien* (published posthumously in 1830): vol. 8, pp. 361–423, in op. cit. (p. 213 above, note 3).
[3] ibid., p. 387.   [4] ibid., p. 404.

starts to construct another world, to redress the balance of something that he has lost in this one – the abstract world of the sciences, the super-sensible world of metaphysics – he is done for. This is metaphysics, illusion, idolatry, self-frustration, of the most fatal kind. This is at the root of Hamann's new notion of language.

There are many stages in the fall from grace. First there is the effort on the part of the Enlightenment to cut reason off from custom and tradition and all faith in them.[1] This is called the autonomy of reason. Then there is an attempt to cut man off from his own individual experience and establish universal laws for all men as such, at any time and any place, as made, for instance, by Descartes or Kant. The worst of all is the divorce from words, the effort to suggest that one can grasp meanings in a naked, wordless state; but this always fails, for without words there is no thinking, and words are not timeless uniform entities, but change with every individual and social and historical tremor. He speaks of words, but to extend this to all symbols – anything intended to communicate – does not alter his meaning. Anyone who professes to be able to talk about pure form independently of its matter cheats in this way – that is what Kant is accused of with his '*gnostic* hatred of matter' and '*mystical* love of form'.[2] Kant speaks of paralogisms – the paradoxes of rationality – but they come not through the misuse of reason, whatever that may mean, but through the misuse of language, through not understanding how language functions in our perception and interpretation of reality, above all in our action, which is at one with our thought and feeling. This is a very modern doctrine, and when Hamann says to Herder, in one of the most profoundly felt of his tormented, seemingly endless pieces of self-examination, 'Reason is language, *logos*. On this marrowbone I gnaw, and shall gnaw myself to death on it',[3] he stakes out one of his greatest claims to immortality. It was a just summary of what preoccupied him all his life, and he had not long to live when he said it.

To be conscious – to discriminate – is to use symbols. Symbols or words are not invented by their user, but are given him as a free gift by divine grace, by the 'great *all-giver*'.[4] To understand or think is to participate in the drama that is the creation.[5] We are free to take part in the drama or to resign from it and perish –

[1] W iii 284.8. [2] W iii 285.15. [3] B v 177.18. [4] W iii 38.3.
[5] cf. B iii 104.26.

determinism is a scientific fiction. But we are not free to be what we wish, for we are created to be and do what we are and do. Herder is sharply criticised for supposing that language is a natural function, that it grows like the sense of smell or taste – for Hamann everything is a gift from a personal deity. Herder, after recanting, nevertheless leapt back into his naturalism towards the end of his life and attempted to give an empirical-genetic explanation of how different languages developed and what relations they had to the geographical, biological, and psychological and social characteristics of their users. Hamann thinks that there is an organic connection between all these attributes, and that history may indeed reveal it, but what is important for him is to insist that the connection created by God and history is itself only a kind of enormous living allegory. The facts, of course, occur as they do and the events that historians uncover did indeed occur, and it is possible to re-establish them by painstaking scholarship; but his point is that we can read in these patterns of events and facts what man is, what his purposes are, what God has created him for; and we can read this in the Bible also; we can read this in the economy of nature; and for Hamann that is all that is of importance.

It may be that others are interested in the facts for their own sake, to satisfy their curiosity; and invent or study sciences in order to satisfy this same curiosity; or perhaps they do so the better to control material forces. All this may be so, but to him this seems trivial beside the need to answer the ultimate questions: Why are we here? What are we at? What are our goals? How can we allay the spiritual agony of those who will not rest unless they obtain true answers to these questions? Nature is like the Hebrew alphabet. It contains only consonants. The vowels we must supply for ourselves, otherwise we cannot read the words.[1] How do we supply them? By that faith – or belief – of which Hume had spoken, without which we could not live for an instant; by our unbreakable certainty that there exists an external world, that there exists God, that there exist other human beings with whom we are in communication – this is presupposed by all other knowledge. To suppose it to be false, to doubt it, is nothing but self-refuting scepticism, the denial of that consciousness without which we could not even have formulated the doubt. *Cogito ergo est.*

Man begins with sensations and images and therefore with song

[1] B i 450.19.

and poetry, which precede prose[1] as forms of spontaneous self-expression – not under the pressure of solely material needs. Whereas Herder was inclined at times towards a historical materialism in his history of civilisation, Hamann will have none of this. 'As gardens come before the cultivation of fields, painting before writing, singing before speech, metaphors before reasoning, barter before trade',[2] so luxuries may come before necessities. Necessity is not the mother of invention, else why should orientals be the first to clothe themselves, while Red Indians shiver?[3] Rather than trace contemporary reason to primitive beginnings he prefers to note the signs of the survival of primitive unreason in modern life. Why should we assume that primitives are unthinking, semi-animal creatures whose whole life is exhausted in struggle, survival – in action? Although 'their movement was a tumultuous dance', yet they 'sat for seven days in silent meditation or amazement and opened their lips for wingèd words'.[4] In other words, in every stage of life, even the earliest, there is God, wonder, revelation, meditation, not just corporeal needs.

There is no evidence that Hamann knew anything about primitive man; such passages are pure imagination. Their value is only in illustrating his ever-present fear that the fullness of human life and the many-sidedness of human character may be misrepresented, narrowed, done injustice to, by being squeezed into the framework of some a priori scientific schema conceived by some fanatical arranger of facts. To understand the past we must in the first place understand the words used by those who made it. Scholars are often least gifted in this respect. The great orientalist J. D. Michaelis of Göttingen, in his book *The Dead Tongue of the Hebrews*, provides a characteristic example of 'philosophical myopia'.[5] The language of the Hebrews is not dead, only its treatment by Professor Michaelis is so. There is not a trace in his great work of any acquaintance with the spirit of the men who wrote in this language, because he has repressed within himself the

---

[1] Vico had said this before, but, as I have mentioned, nobody in the eighteenth century save perhaps a few scholars in Naples had paid attention to his work. The English scholars Bishop Lowth – in his *Lectures on the Sacred Poetry of the Hebrews* (1753) – and Blackwell, who said something of this sort, did not perceive its implications, and Voltaire, who reviewed Lowth in 1766, did not see them either.

[2] W ii 197.15.   [3] W ii 198.17 ff.   [4] W ii 197.18.   [5] W ii 123.12.

sensuous element and allowed the intellectual, reasoning faculty too much play; this produces a mountain of useless scholarship. How is this to be remedied? Only by abandoning the smooth Aristotelian methods of the eighteenth century, in which man is conceived as peacefully developing towards his appointed end – his preconceived purpose – in a rational, harmonious, inexorable way. We must delve into the depths and splendours of the ravaged human soul. The eighteenth century is not even blasphemous, simply blind to the abyss, and therefore blind to the grandeur of its creator. For this the pagan Goethe duly praises him, and so perhaps might Freud have done, who was no Christian either, and for the very same reason. Society is founded on language.[1] 'The *history* of a people is in its language.'[2] As the life of the people, so its language and its dialects. The relations of symbols are to Hamann not unlike the relations between persons.[3] There is no universal reason any more than a universal language – a 'natural language' is as absurd as 'natural religion', 'natural law' and all the other fictions of the metaphysicians. Everything is concrete, is and was where it is in the world, in its specific relations to other concrete entities, and cannot be grasped without some faculty other than the generalising faculty that analyses everything into uniform units, and then wonders where the variety, the colour, the meaning have gone. The German romantic school of philosophy was destined to make much of these polemical claims.

Hamann spoke out of a considerable knowledge of languages. He knew French and English, Latin and Greek, Italian, Portuguese and some Lettish as well as Hebrew and a certain amount of Arabic; he denounced translation, which loses precisely what distinguishes one type of inner experience from another; and he believed that a man can truly create only in his own native language. 'Who writes in his native tongue has the rights of the father of a family', and can fulfil his whole nature 'if he has the power to exercise these rights', whereas 'he who writes in a foreign tongue has to bend his spirit to it like a lover'.[4] A man, to create properly, must be master of his words, so that he can even misuse them if he will. Those who follow the rules of academies or the good taste of their society are like hired rhymesters who follow slavishly the thoughts of others. Authenticity is all. To be the

[1] W iii 300.31.   [2] B i 393.23.   [3] B v 40.16, 51.28.   [4] W ii 126.9.

servant of a master is ultimate degradation, even when the master is some impersonal authority, that is, not human, but official or imaginary (this again echoes Rousseau, whom on other grounds he thought much too abstract). Hence his objection to reform, whether of language or anything else – it seems to him a wilful revolt against God's order, in which alone we can harmoniously fulfil ourselves, or at least suffer those conflicts from the torment of which we shall emerge purified and strengthened. Hence his criticism of F. G. Klopstock[1] (whose sincere religious faith, patriotism and ecstatic flights he truly admired) for wishing to introduce syntactical reforms; all this emerges in an ironical form in *New Apology of the Letter H*, already referred to. It is all part and parcel of Hamann's passionate conviction that man is one, and his life is one; that letter is spirit, and spirit is letter; that letter without spirit is not even a letter; while spirit without letter does not exist at all.

He believes for this reason that private life cannot be sharply divided from public. Hence a State without a Church is a lifeless corpse, 'carrion for eagles',[2] while a Church without a State is a ghost, a scarecrow to frighten birds, and Mendelssohn and his rationalist friends, who wished to found a State on the need for security and public peace, were nothing but the reincarnation of the atheistical Hobbes – a man who wished to cut into the living flesh of society and turn it into a utilitarian device. This Hamann declares to be death and nausea – the turning of life into a mechanism, the killing of everything by which men live.[3] It was almost certainly he who inspired Herder with his interest in oriental literature and the Graeco-Roman classics, in popular speech, and in the intimate connections between language, thought, environment, and the physiological structure of different human types. This set Herder off on the road that led him to the creation of social psychology, of the view of men as deeply rooted in a texture of beliefs, institutions, forms of life, in terms of which alone they can be accounted for and their thought and action explained; to the creation of a new aesthetics of art as the sensual expression

[1] The famous and very pious German poet, author of the Christian epic *Messias*, about which Herder, the head of the Lutheran Church in Weimar, complained that it was not German enough.

[2] W iii 303.13.

[3] *Golgotha und Scheblimini!* (W iii 291–320), an attack on Mendelssohn's political tract, is entirely concerned with this theme.

of individual or collective personality, a form of moral social commitment, as against earlier theories of art as embellishment or imitation or instruction or inspired utterance detached from daily life. In spite of this Herder went his own way, and attempted to use the findings of the natural sciences of his day to explain the evolution of human society; while Hamann rejected the great advances in the midst of which he lived as abstract schemas – counterfeit goods, 'false noses',[1] 'empty sacks'[2] – and while passionately defending empiricism and glorifying Hume – an enemy who could not help speaking the truth – as against Kant, united it with a kind of mystical nominalism and belief in divine inspiration. As we cannot eat an egg without the faith for which no reason can in principle be given, so we know that God has spoken to us, and no one can argue us out of this, for all argument presupposes the faculty that guarantees the truth of divine revelation; and since one can understand only if one enters into the body and spirit of a symbolism which is the articulate expression of the soul, one must study and restudy the words of Holy Writ with which God created our world for us, and told us what to be, and revealed to us – as happened one night in London when Hamann saw his own life written large in the chronicles of the ancient Hebrews – what we are made of, what we must hope and fear and do.

Unger says that Hamann was both sensual and pious, and that in this way he was able to unite these two characteristics in a single doctrine. But the situation is odder than this. There is a union in Hamann's writings, not merely of sensual appetite and simple pietism, but of, on the one hand, a new and original theory of language and its relation to reality that was destined to celebrate its greatest triumphs in our own time, and, on the other, devout, passionate, uncritical absorption in every syllable of Holy Writ, and a polemic against the pretensions of reason far more vehement and far-reaching – and baseless – than that which Kant represented himself as attempting to achieve in order to make room for faith.[3] Kant's account of this faith is shadowy: Hamann's is passionate, vivid and concrete through and through. As a defender of the concrete, the particular, the intuitive, the personal, the unsystematic – this is the tendency which, for such cultural historians as

---

[1] B vii 460.27.   [2] B vii 172.33.   [3] See further the Appendix on p. 359.

Troeltsch and Meinecke, distinguishes, indeed divides, the Germans from the rational, generalising, scientific West – he has no equal. He is a true forerunner of Schelling, of Nietzsche and of the existentialists, and a dangerous ally of any supporter of organised religion.

7

CREATIVE GENIUS

In MOST histories of German and European literature Hamann – if he is mentioned at all – is considered as one of the inspirers of the German literary movement known as the *Sturm und Drang*, among the most prominent attributes of which were a belief in self-abandonment to spontaneous feeling and passion, hatred of rules, and a desire for unbridled self-expression and self-assertion on the part of the artist, whether in life or in the creation of his works – the conception of the poet, the thinker, as a superior being, subject to agonies not known to the common run of men, seeking to realise himself in some unique, violent, unheard-of fashion, obedient to his own passion and will alone. This is in part true. Hamann, who mildly scandalised his contemporaries by placing the emblem of a hornèd Pan on some of his works, by his writings probably helped to stimulate some of his contemporaries into violent outbreaks against classicism and order, and did emphasise the irrational sources of man's creative power. If he did not encourage divine frenzy, he had less against it than the champions of neo-classicism among whom he lived.

Nevertheless his romanticism needs a good deal of qualification. He was not a 'heaven-storming' irrationalist. When Lavater wrote to him confessing to spiritual agonies because he was not sure of his faith, Hamann replied: 'Eat your bread joyfully, drink your wine with good heart – for your work pleases God.'[1] To be concerned too deeply about one's own spiritual condition is to lack faith in God, that simple childlike faith upon which all rests; self-doubts and self-tortures (although Hamann was not a stranger to them) are mere pathological symptoms. To Jacobi, who complained that he could not reconcile his head and his heart, he replied in similar terms – submission, not Promethean struggle, is

---

[1] B iv 5.17.

the way to serenity and truth, however great the obstacles in our path. Our parents heard 'the voice of God walking in the garden in the cool of the evening'.[1] We may never be able to return to this, but that is the radiant vision in the light of which we must live. We are all God's children – so long as we live in this knowledge, we shall not go astray.

So, too, he told the Roman Catholic Princess Golitsyn, who was troubled by her unquiet conscience, about whether she had done all that it was right for a good Christian to have done, and lived a sufficiently pure and dedicated life, that she should sow her seed and trust in God. Do not wait for the seed to bloom; do not look for a quiet conscience too anxiously – one must learn to support one's 'nothingness' (Nichtigkeit) and have faith in God's mercy. One must do what appears right to oneself and then let well alone. To be preoccupied with one's virtue is appalling arrogance and a wall against God. She was particularly troubled about the education of her children. From her journal we learn that Hamann's tranquil sermon on the holiness of humility, on the need to learn to be contented, indeed happy, in one's own insignificance, liberated her from her self-torment. God speaks to us through his works, through the world that he gave us, and in particular to our senses – do not seek to reduce him or his world to some inner core, some irreducible and ultimate entity. Accept what is given – flesh, passions – and do not attempt to explain them, transform them, or deduce them. What is given is given; to learn to submit is to learn to understand.

Nevertheless Hamann naturally has thoughts about genius that are of interest. The notion of the free, spontaneous, creative impulse in man that knows no rules, or creates as the wind blows – this penetrates, as might be expected, everything that he wrote; he was not, of course, its originator, but he gave it a new and historically important direction. The notion that genius is a divine afflatus, so that the artist himself does not always know what it is that he is making, since he is but an instrument through which a higher – superhuman – power is speaking, is at least as old as Plato's Ion. Young's celebrated essay on the subject[2] released a great volume of pent-up German feeling on this topic. The second half of the eighteenth century is full of denunciations of narrowness and specialisation – of anything that cribs and confines men

[1] W iii 31.30, alluding to Genesis 3: 8.
[2] Conjectures on Original Composition (1759).

and prevents the richest realisation of the 'complete man', which is conceived as a harmonious process, prevented hitherto only by human error or vice and the destructive institutions that this has bred. This is not confined to German writers: Diderot, too, speaks of the battle between the natural and the artificial man within civilised man, and Rousseau's sermon on the destructive effect of man's institutions upon those who are brought up under them is well enough known. But the real revolt against neo-classicism is German, and directed against the ascendancy of the thinkers of Paris.

Although Hamann was among the earliest European thinkers to protest against the effect of French education and French doctrines based on a false psychology and a false view of God and of nature, this is not where his strongest claim to originality in this field lies. He is not principally interested in creating conditions in which a small group of the elect may be able to express themselves freely at the expense of, or at any rate beyond the horizon of, the common man. Nor is he interested in the social conception of genius as it was treated, for instance, by the French Encyclopaedists, some of whom thought that in a rationally organised society any man could in principle be transformed into a genius, as for example Trotsky seemed to believe (this is what Diderot, with his customary sense of reality, mocked so exquisitely in his essay on Helvétius' *On Man*); nor is he with Mendelssohn and Nicolai, who conceived of genius as consisting in the communication of ideas until they became universally accepted and so raised human life to a new level.

As against the stress on social conditions, Hamann believed that genius was individual and incapable of being bred or cultivated by social organisation; each man was as he was, saw what he saw, and spoke to those who understood him – not everyone, but those with whom he had special rapport; how large or small a number, there was no telling. Against Mendelssohn and Nicolai he maintained that only the free can understand or inspire or be inspired; and freedom consists in being at once one's master and one's most faithful subject; acceptance of general rules was always slavery – 'he who trusts the judgement of another more than his own ceases to be a man'.[1] Even though Winckelmann had said that by imitating the Greeks modern man would become inimitable, Hamann

[1] B i 377.35.

remained suspicious. Like Prometheus, we must steal the divine fire, not make a picture of it: he who wishes to rob the arts of fantasy and arbitrary freedom is making an attempt on their honour and their life. We must commit 'a Promethean *plagiarism* of the primal, animal *light of nature*';[1] hence the dichotomy of originality and slavery, spontaneity and abdication; hence, also, the hostility to classical models and utilitarian or other brands of moral and aesthetic didacticism.

But this is not Hamann's principal concern. He is not interested in the needs of the artistic élite. He is a moralist and a critic of life, and wishes to go to war with the enemies of mankind in general; he wishes to help to liberate human beings as such. His originality consists in translating the appeal to the authority of the individual conscience and the rejection of institutional authority, which came to him from his pietist upbringing, to the whole of life; save that by a self he means something that is in constant communication with others and with God, and sees the truth, practical and theoretical, only through the medium of these relationships and submission to them – self-knowledge (which for him is obtained in communion with God) is not a threat against one's freedom, not a painful act of artificial self-discipline. He rejects with both hands the puritanism of the pietists: the notion that man is no more than an unclean vessel, a mass of sin and corruption, and that since all men are accursed they must seek to root out of themselves all natural desires: 'Victory consists in death; life in dying', as a line of contemporary pietist verse runs.[2]

Hamann is as passionately opposed to this as he is to the utilitarian harmonisation of the passions, as advocated by the French *philosophes*. He goes so far as to accept the pietists' doctrine that reason is a poisonous snake, the arch-heretic, the great enemy of God and his truth – thus Johann Konrad Dippel,[3] who, like Schopenhauer after him, thought that all suffering was caused by a thirst that could never be satisfied, and tried to demonstrate this by instances of children who died ecstatically. But thereafter Hamann

---

[1] W iii 22.16.

[2] *Nordische Sammlungen, welche unterschiedene Exempel einer lebendigen und wahren Gottseligkeit, im Reiche Schweden, in sich halten...*, vol. [1] ([Altona], 1755), part 1, p. 123.

[3] *Christen-Statt auff Erden ohne gewöhnlichen Lehr- Wehr- und Nehr-Stand...* (n.p., 1700; published under the pseudonym 'Christianus Democritus'), pp. 18, 78–9, 111.

parts company with this grim sect far more sharply than does their other scion, Immanuel Kant. His words of praise for his peasant common-law wife[1] – indeed, his motive for living with her – are rooted in his love of what seemed to him healthy, innocent, natural, free from the self-torture to which the misuse of our God-given sense and languages leads the learned: better provincialism, roots in local life, than bloodless uniformity, hot-house plants, the death in life of sophisticated academics; the greatest crime is to divorce the intellect from 'the deepest abysses of the most tangible sensuousness'.[2] 'Let there be light!'[3] This is joy in creation, sensuous joy. God himself was made flesh, else he could not discourse to us, who also are flesh; but we have divided the spirit and the flesh. 'To gather the fragments together – *disjecti membra poetae* – is the work of a scholar; to interpret them, of a philosopher; to imitate them or shape them [*sie in Geschick bringen*], of the poet.'[4] Poetry gives unity and life. So, too, history is only a valley of dead bones,[5] unless 'a prophet' comes, like Ezekiel, to clothe them with flesh.

To live truly and to create is one: this is the gist of the 'rhapsody in cabbalistic prose' hurled at Michaelis' head in 1762 under the title of 'Aesthetics in a Nutshell'.[6] 'Leben ist *actio*'[7] – life is action, not some impersonal metaphysical power, the self-developing Idea of Hegel, or the *praxis* of Marx, which it is difficult to identify in concrete spatial or temporal terms, something which even in the most materialistic terminology retains the mythical quality of its metaphysical origins; but day-to-day action, faith in instinct, in that understanding without which there is no communication with others, in direct face-to-face encounters with things or men, in the fullness of life. This is how artists create, but it is also how all men achieve the realisation of what is most human in them, how societies achieve unity of spirit, their members that blend of practical wisdom and love and sensuous satisfaction that distinguishes full human beings from the absurd two-dimensional figments of theorists, and from that inner desiccation and aliena-tion in the theorists themselves which cause them to confound real

---

[1] B iii xxi.21 ff., B iii 263.1 ff.   [2] W iii 287.31.   [3] W ii 197.26.
[4] W ii 198.34.   [5] W ii 176.12.
[6] *Aesthetica in nuce* (W ii 195–217): 'A Rhapsody in Cabbalistic Prose' is Hamann's subtitle.
[7] B iv 288.29.

life with their bloodless, stylised categories. A connoisseur who sits in his study, contemplating now a picture upon his wall, now a volume upon his table, is not a living human being at all, but a marionette. The *beaux esprits* for whom the French are writing will never see the dawn of the rising day, for they do not believe in the resurrection of the flesh. No! Nature, to repeat, is Hebrew consonants from which the vowels are missing, an equation with at least one unknown, and we can fathom this unknown only by action, not by contemplation in accordance with rules.[1]

What kind of action? He speaks, as always, in metaphors. We must ravish nature, enter into and be at one with her: 'Nature is our old grandmother ... to commit incest with this grandmother is the most important commandment of the Koran of the arts, and it is not obeyed.'[2] How can fastidious modern connoisseurs do this, since they are ashamed of nature, cover her up, concern themselves only with the pretty clothes with which they hide her?[3] Hamann's denunciations of the rationalists, and insistence on the wisdom that comes from true participation in life – at its highest level by the genius, at every level by human beings seeking to fulfil themselves – are perhaps the earliest hymn to the rejection of rules and norms and contemplation in favour of action. 'Think less and live more,'[4] he said to Herder – in that long line of the champions of life against what Goethe famously called 'grey theory',[5] which begins in earnest with the German *Sturm und Drang*, from Heinse's *Ardinghello*,[6] with its passionate call to throw away all convention and let all passions fulfil themselves, no matter how destructively or how great the scandal to the respectable, to Jacobi's *Allwill* and *Woldemar* (with its central doctrine that 'What cannot be got wrong ... has not much in it; and what cannot be abused has little practical value'),[7] to the cult of unbridled individualism of Schlegel's *Lucinde*,[8] and continues towards Byron and Stirner and Nietzsche and Hamsun and D. H. Lawrence.

[1] B i 450.18.   [2] W ii 342.28, 33.   [3] W ii 347.8 ff.   [4] B ii 330.30.
[5] *Faust*, part 1, line 2038.
[6] Johann Jakob Wilhelm Heinse, *Ardinghello und die glückseeligen Inseln* (1787).
[7] *Eduard Allwills Papiere* (the titles of later revisions differ) was published in 1775, *Woldemar* in 1779. The quotation from *Woldemar* may be found in op. cit. (p. 284 above, note 4), vol. 5, p. 113.
[8] Published in 1799.

'Every creature has a natural right to appropriate all that surrounds it to the limits of its power'; these limits will be determined only by the resistance of other creatures. All calls to discipline are mere manifestations of 'bourgeois order, which ruins man', just so much 'barbaric legislation'.[1] These doctrines of Heinse, which he admits may seem wild, debauched, horrible to the mass of the philistine public,[2] but will govern the lives of the truly free, who will alone understand them, these are not the views of Hamann, who believed in submission to the laws of God as we feel them with our whole being; yet though he opposed the general spirit of this cry for anarchy he admired the novel in which it was contained. *'Beauty is the appearance of our entire being unfalsified,'* said Heinse,[3] and this was Hamann's doctrine also. Beauty is life in its most characteristic, whole, dynamic, palpable form, full of conflict and contradiction as it may be – not smoothed out and brought to order by some theory-ridden Frenchman in a wig and silk stockings. This is the doctrine that he communicated to Herder, and that was destined to influence German romanticism, and through it all European thought.

He detested the tame imitations of this attitude more even than the materialism of the French. He disliked Sterne, for example, who was greatly admired by the romantics, because although he broke through the conventions and the rules, he took too much pleasure in his own waywardness, his attitude was too narcissistic, not passionate and single-minded enough, not serious, a mere pretence at unconventionality while remaining deeply embedded in the convention, a mild titillation of the philistine and the orthodox; and he equally detested the 'Anacreontic' poetry of Wieland and his disciples, pseudo-idyllic exercises, remoter from *actio* than the wrong-headed but formidable activity of, say, Voltaire, whose brilliance and verve Hamann admired as much as he condemned his doctrines.

The reader may enquire why Rousseau is not included in this catalogue of anti-intellectual naturalism. The reason is that

---

[1] Wilhelm Heinse, *Ardinghello und die glückseeligen Inseln*, ed. Carl Schüddekopf [vol. 4 of his edition of Heinse's *Sämmtliche Werke* (Leipzig, 1903–25)], pp. 155, 111.

[2] Wilhelm Körte (ed.), *Briefe zwischen Gleim, Wilhelm Heinse und Johann von Müller* (Zürich, 1806), vol. 1 [*Briefe deutscher Gelehrten*, vol. 2], p. 123; cf. ibid., pp. 10, 55.

[3] ibid., p. 255.

Hamann's attitude to Rousseau, like that of many of the anti-rationalists, is exceedingly ambivalent. On the one hand *Émile* and *The Social Contract* are rationalist treatises with an artificial view of man worthy of Voltaire or Raynal or d'Alembert or the miserable Berlin rationalists, men who in the battle against fanaticism have themselves become rationalist fanatics, murderers, incendiaries, robbers, cheats of God and man. Rousseau is Utopian, a dabbler in abstractions; his theory of education is founded upon the absurd myth of 'beautiful nature, good taste and balanced reason';[1] school is not a peaceful harmony of teacher and pupil, as Rousseau would have it, but 'a mountain of God like Dothan, full of fiery chargers and chariots round Elisha'.[2] On the other hand there is a 'sensuous fascination'[3] in his novels greater than that of Richardson's, and his bitter indignation with the *salons* and convention, and his wish 'to serve men by his knowledge of the human heart acquired by his excesses and those of others',[4] are sympathetic. All this before he had read Rousseau's *Confessions*, before indeed these had appeared. And he had a kind word for Diderot, the most German among the French, who, in spite of his terrible rationalist views, realises that rules are not everything, that 'something more *immediate, intimate, **obscure, certain**'* is what matters.[5] Still, of course, Diderot follows a false philosophy – he occasionally repents of it, but is mostly in error. Hamann would have approved of Diderot's paean to genius (in a section of a *Salon* devoted to the painter Carle Van Loo) as something dark, farouche, unapproachable, as opposed to the twitter, the charm and sweetness, of the fashionable wits.[6] Yet Hamann is inconstant: he bursts forth with the most passionate admiration for *La Nouvelle Héloïse*, but later attacks it. Saint-Preux is an idiot and my Lord Edward is not an Englishman. Julie does not deserve love or admiration or the absurd sacrifice of these to the insupportable Wolmar: Rousseau's language is not that of the passions but of rhetoric. It is all false. It is all French.

Although Rousseau's tone, particularly in *La Nouvelle Héloïse* and the *Confessions*, is that of a free, rebellious spirit, what he advocates is the striking off of the old yoke – of convention or science or art – in order to impose anew one of those eternal laws

---

[1] W ii 356.26.   [2] W ii 356.16.   [3] B ii 104.19.   [4] B ii 105.22.
[5] B ii 84.11.
[6] Diderot, *Salon de 1765*: vol. 10, p. 251, in op. cit. (p. 213 above, note 3).

which are graven within our hearts: the old morality preached by Plato and all the true sages of all times and climes. This is not what Hamann advocated. He wished to destroy what seemed to him the fixed, frozen establishment of rules and regulations as such, in order to reawaken in man a sense of his unity with God, and make him live spontaneously in him – if in a troubled relationship[1] – obedient to no rules that could be embodied in letters of any kind, ephemeral or eternal, least of all eternal. Hence Rousseau, in the end, was for him what Protagoras was for Socrates, perhaps the best among the sophists, but still a sophist.

Goethe said of Hamann (to Chancellor Müller), 'He had a clear head in his day, and knew what he wanted,'[2] but Kant said, 'The late Hamann had such a gift for thinking of things in general, but he did not have the power to point out their principles clearly, or at least to detach anything specific out of this wholesale trade of his.'[3] This is both amusing and true. But Hamann remained untouched by what he knew of Kant's attitude to him, and was, indeed, confirmed in his view of Kant as an intelligent man but blind – his eyes shut tightly against reality in order to perceive his own internal, imaginary structure more clearly. He would have echoed the romantic dramatist Klinger, who said that 'Kant's iron Colossus of Rhodes – his imperative – or his fantastic touchstone swinging suspended over the moral world by a hair' was not a fit instrument by which to explain or judge mankind.[4] Hamann, who was not an altogether modest man, saw himself as a German Socrates, who refuses to engage in vain talk with the sophists,[5] and silences the importunate Athenians who pester him with too many questions, and gives his disciples courage to conquer their vanity by his example. His business was to blow up established values, both those of tradition and those of philosophy, and to organise a counter-revolution back towards simplicity and faith against the arrogance and optimism of the new science.

---

[1] W iii 312.36.

[2] Kanzler [Friedrich] von Müller, *Unterhaltungen mit Goethe*, ed. Ernst Grumach (Weimar, 1956), p. 99, 18 December 1823.

[3] See C. H. Gildemeister, *Johann Georg Hamann's, des Magus in Norden, Leben und Schriften* (Gotha, 1857–73), vol. 6: *Hamann-Studien*, p. 56.

[4] F. M. Klinger, *Betrachtungen und Gedanken über verschiedene Gegenstände der Welt und der Literatur*, § 55: vol. 11, p. 40, in *F. M. Klinger's sämmtliche Werke* (Stuttgart/Tübingen, 1842).

[5] W ii 73.2 ff.

Socrates attempted to do his work by means of analytical reason. Hamann saw himself as doing so by other methods, by breaking through established conventions and expectations with every weapon that could break the crust of custom or dogma. This was the justification, in his own eyes, for his hermetic style, his mysterious formulae, with which he hoped to puzzle, intrigue and awaken the reader, his frenzied scurrying from one topic to another, his deliberately disordered succession of ideas, the constant self-incarnation in fantastic personages drawn from mythology or poetry or his own wild, extravagant imagination – anything to stop the reader in his tracks, harry him, astonish, irritate, open windows on new vistas; above all, to break the normal train of association to which his own unselfcritical life or the authority of his spiritual or literary guides had accustomed him. Into the reader thus awakened he hoped to pour the true word of God – the unity of spirit and flesh, the oneness of life, the need to live and create, the paramountcy of belief, the feebleness of reason, the fatal delusiveness of all contrived answers, constructed theories, everything calculated to lull the spirit into the false dream of reality. The true image of the practical man is that of a sleepwalker, a man who, with infinite sagacity, reflection, coherence, talks, acts, executes perilous enterprises, and does this with greater sureness of touch than he would – or could – do it if his eyes were even a little open.

This paradox is echoed by nearly every romantic writer – the confidence of the sleepwalker which comes from his blindness: reality is disturbing, but must be faced. The only way to awaken such deluded beings is by breaking the spectacles through which they normally look at reality, by affectation of madness, by the methods used later by Novalis, Hoffmann, Gogol, and in our own day by Pirandello, Kafka and the surrealists. Of course, only men of original genius can achieve this, and Hamann certainly believed himself to be one, no less than Socrates. Genius is not healthy, but a divine malady which, as Hippocrates says, is at once divine and human – *panta theia kai panta anthropina*[1] – that which unites heaven and earth. Genius is mad in the worldly sense, for the wisdom of this world is folly; and the only use of reason is not to give us knowledge but to expose to ourselves our own ignorance – to conduce to humility. That we have learnt from Socrates. But, as

[1] *On the Sacred Disease* xxi, (mis)quoted at W ii 105.24.

Hume correctly says, reason taken by itself is impotent, and when it dictates it is a usurper and an impostor.

This is Hamann's central message, and his own justification for his method. If it was a rationalisation of the fact – supposing it was a fact – that he was unable to write clearly because his thoughts were turbid and chaotic, the apologia is ingenious and had a powerful historical effect. Kant was properly horrified: 'One can only laugh', he said, at these 'men of genius, or perhaps apes of genius' – 'one can only laugh and continue on one's own path with assiduity, order, clarity, paying no attention to these jugglers'.[1] He was, no doubt, right. Nevertheless, it is doubtful whether without Hamann's revolt – or at any rate something similar – the worlds of Herder, Friedrich Schlegel, Tieck, Schiller, and indeed of Goethe too, would have come into being. Herder owed Hamann a great deal, and he and Jacobi – who owed him even more – were, with the brothers Schlegel, the chief subverters of the tradition of order, rationalism, classicism, not only in Germany but in Europe. Madame de Staël's *De l'Allemagne* lifted the curtain on a part of this turbulence. The doctrines of Fichte and Schelling and even of Hegel, which strike the reader brought up in the Anglo-Saxon tradition of philosophy as wild irruptions into the well-ordered procession of sane and scrupulous rational European thinkers, could scarcely have taken place without this counter-revolution, which has cast alternate light and darkness upon the European scene, and, whether as cause or as symptom, is indissolubly connected with the most creative and the most destructive phenomena of our own time; this is the revolt of which Hamann was the first standard-bearer and perhaps the most original figure.

---

[1] Immanuel Kant, *Anthropologie in pragmatischer Hinsicht*, part 1, book 1, § 58: vol. 8, p. 226, line 10, in op. cit. (p. 187 above, note 1).

8

POLITICS

HAMANN'S POLITICAL views, such as they were, emerge most clearly, as always, in a protest against a particular position that irritated him: in this case one of Kant's best short essays, 'What is Enlightenment?' Kant's central thesis is that to be enlightened is to be responsible, even when obedience to legitimate authority is demanded, for one's own choices, to be independent, to determine oneself: not to allow others to lead one by the hand; not to be treated as a child, a minor, a ward. It is a passionate attack on paternalism, however benevolent, and a plea for individual freedom, equality and dignity, which Kant identifies with maturity and civilisation.

Hamann, of course, was outraged. Pride, independence, are the most fatal of all spiritual delusions. He protests, not of course against Kant's disapproval of childlike dependence on the part of subjects, but against his conception of the liberty of action due to truly enlightened men. Who has given the State, or its ruler and his hired professors, the right to tell others how to live? Who has certified them as ultimate authority – this self-appointed élite of sages and experts who have declared themselves infallible and presume to dictate to others? For him enlightenment and despotism – intellectual and political (for they are one) – march hand in hand. The *Aufklärung* is nothing but an aurora borealis – cold and illusory. He sees no good in the 'chatter' of those emancipated children (the philosophers) who constitute themselves guardians of the other guardians (the princes). All this rationalist patter seems to him like the cold light of the moon, which cannot be expected to illuminate our weak reason or warm our feeble will.[1] He looks for faith and finds it more readily among the untutored masses.

Hamann hated authorities, autocrats, self-appointed leaders – he was democratic and anti-liberal – and embodies one of the earliest

[1] B v 291.3 ff.

combinations of populism and obscurantism, a genuine feeling for ordinary men and their values and the texture of their lives, joined with acute dislike for those who presume to tell them how to live. This kind of reactionary democracy, the union of anti-intellectualism and self-identification with the popular masses, is later to be found both in Cobbett and in the German nationalists of the Napoleonic wars, and is one of the strands that was most prominent in the Christian-Social Party in Austria, in the chauvinist clerical politics at the end of the nineteenth century in France and, in due course, in Fascism and National Socialism, into which these streams in part poured themselves.

Yet Hamann does, with his customary penetration, point to the weakest parts of Kant's edifice. Kant, as a loyal Prussian subject, declared that if the prince or the sovereign orders me to do something that I deem to be wrong, I must as a private person – still more as an official – carry it out; I have no right to disobey; but as a rational being and member of a rational society I have a duty to criticise such an order. I am a combination: on the one hand a private person, on the other a publicist or philosopher or theologian or professor whose duty it is to speak out. Hamann does not think highly of this 'solution'. He asks whether, according to Kant, man is at once master and slave, guardian and minor, adult and not grown up. 'So the public use of reason and liberty is but a dessert, whereas the private use of these excellent things is the daily bread that we must give up, the better to taste the dessert.'[1] In public I wear the trappings of freedom, while at home I have nothing but the slave's rags? What is the use of this? Then he falls into his customary appeal to faith, for it alone gives us strength to resist the guardians and the tutors who not only kill our bodies but empty our pockets – faith, which is a concrete experience known to all, and not Kant's abstract 'good will', which is but an empty scholastic formula. Through it all he likes Kant; Kant is wrong-headed, hopelessly bemused by his own fantasies, but a decent old friend whose character one respects. It was a peculiar relationship.

Hamann admired Frederick the Great's greatness as a ruler, and his 'vital warmth'[2] as a man, but detested his policies and outlook, above all for putting reason, organisation and efficiency above

[1] B v 292.5.   [2] B vi 533.5.

humanity, God, variety, feeling; for creating a cold, elegant, magnificent, heartless social machine manipulated by logic-chopping sophists, *'political arithmeticians'*,[1] Frenchmen, Dutchmen and God knows what other imported dehumanised uniformed creatures; for despising Christianity, religion generally, for breaking up the old, intimate provincial Königsberg–Riga society. Hamann is the prophet Elijah and Frederick is the wicked king Ahab, whose subjects are corrupt and insolent and pagan and blasphemous and have starved and frozen the prophet almost to death. They have taken away five thalers a month from him, or at least the French administrator has – and this costs him his heating. The deduction is 'against all *rhyme* and *reason* – I am convinced that Your Majesty loves one and the other', he writes to him in the course of an appeal for justice.[2] Hamann is Jeremiah, he is the psalmist, he passes from curses and blessings to ponderous playfulness, indignation, melancholy, irony, prophetic fire. Let the King return to the Christian faith, let him dismiss his wicked, pagan Frenchmen, de Lattre and Guichard, who are eating his subjects' flesh. Frederick is Nero, he is Julian the Apostate,[3] again he is not Solomon, he is Ahab. The implication is that he treats Hamann as Ahab treated Naboth: he has taken away his *Hausrecht*.[4] Frederick is a philosophical anti-Christ who has taken the place of the Popish anti-Christ.[5] He has sold Prussia to a hollow cosmopolitan ideal, to foreigners, to sophists, lying prophets of this new Islam (perhaps Voltaire, perhaps a reference to Frederick himself). Hamann describes himself as one of 'les *petits* Philosophes de *grand-soucy*' as against 'les *grands* Philosophes

---

[1] W iii 60.18.

[2] ibid. In another letter, to the Prussian General Administration (W ii 325–6), he begs for permission to take one afternoon off from his duties in order to sell his books, for otherwise he cannot survive. Elsewhere he begs for a job as a minor official in the Salt Tax Office, and to obtain the post but not the garden of his Dutch predecessor. When Hamann forced the lock, he was reprimanded, humiliated, crushed, driven into debt.

[3] cf. W iii 145.9.

[4] There is something of the same sublimity of thought and miserable struggle for his salary and his rights in Giambattista Vico, in certain respects Hamann's forerunner: neither obtained his full due in his own century.

[5] B iv 260.26, in a letter to Herder dealing mostly with other matters; cf. Hamann's view that philosophy is *'popery* spiritualised by good sense' (W ii 290.36).

sans-soucy'.[1] Tyrants and sophists are enemies of mankind: they place themselves above the herd of common men.[2] Then follows a passage which is a caricature of Herder's description of man as lord of creation *vis-à-vis* the beasts of the field. Frederick is the 'Solomon of Prussia'[3] and he understands well that there are two ways of government. 'One must either *coerce* or *deceive* one's subjects.'[4] But of course rulers must hide this fact – hence their hypocrisy. Only God can love *and* reign. Charity and authority cannot be combined on earth. To love subjects is to be their dupe, like the great God himself; or their victim, like his well-beloved Son. But if one is to gain resources in this world one must turn one's back on both charity and authority. Blood and gold – which alone rule the world – are the Devil's weapons. That is, so goes the implication, what Frederick and enlightened despots of his type accumulate.

His references to Frederick acquire a certain pitch of hysteria. Frederick is the head and leader of the conspiracy of reason against faith, in thought and in action. At times he speaks of his homosexuality in obscene language. Yet, of course, Hamann remains a loyal subject, a quietist, against resistance, in this respect like his friend Immanuel Kant, Prussian, Lutheran, obedient to all forms of *Obrigkeit*, anxious to avoid disorder. The subversive note comes not from the left but from the right, from the old, vanishing, domestic, narrowly provincial, semi-feudal Prussia as against the *Rechtsstaat* and the notion of a civilised world without frontiers. His extreme hatred of the new political ideal communicated itself to Herder, who perhaps did not need it. Both felt more tenderly towards the customs and songs of the primitive natives of the Baltic coast than towards the new, well-administered modern State, resting on the basis of uniform, clearly intelligible, impartial laws administered by well-trained, enlightened officials with little respect for tradition or the crooked alleys of the ancient, familiar Prussian establishment, its roots lost in pre-Roman times. There is nothing that Hamann or Herder detested so much as new brooms that swept clean, no matter what frightful accumulation of injustice

---

[1] W ii 319.19.   [2] cf. W ii 302.17.   [3] cf. p. 264 above, note 1.

[4] W ii 302.16. 'There are two ways of government,' said an eminent British statesman in the nineteenth century, in an unpublished conversation, 'bamboozle or bamboo.'

and misery had built up beneath the ancient cobwebs of the traditional edifice.[1]

---

[1] This does not prevent Hamann from rebuking Frederick for pampering his pets at the expense of his subjects: 'It is not right to take the children's bread and cast it to little dogs.' W ii 293.20; cf. Matthew 15: 26, Mark 7: 28.

9

CONCLUSION

THERE IS much else that is of value in Hamann, and much absurdity too. His worship of Homer and Shakespeare is of little interest to us now, because this is a victory that he and his disciples have long won – though it was not as inevitable as it may now seem, if we remember not merely the notorious observations about Shakespeare by Voltaire, but the fact that the great French Encyclopaedia devoted no separate article to Homer, while Diderot's entry on Greek philosophy refers to him as 'a theologian, philosopher and poet'; it proceeds to quote the view of a 'well-known man' that he was unlikely to be read much in twenty years' time, although Diderot does protest that this 'shows a lack of philosophy and taste'.[1] Hamann read *Hamlet* with Herder, and although he does not say so, his references to his own lack of decision, stupidity, inability to cope with life, have led his interpreters to suppose that he partly identified himself with the Prince of Denmark. At the same time, there is no doubt that he saw himself as a genius and a prophet: Socrates was his only true predecessor.

> An angel came down . . . and troubled the Well of Bethesda, in the five grottoes of which many who were sick, blind, lame, consumptive lay waiting for the waters to be stirred. So the genius must lower himself to destroy the rules, else the waters remain still; once the waters are troubled, a man must be the first to step into them, if he wants to experience the virtue and effectiveness of the rules for himself.[2]

Good sense is the enemy: the sick, children and demigods cannot digest good sense, he told his great friend the pastor Lindner.[3] Lindner had asked him whether after all some rules were not

---

[1] loc. cit. (p. 174 above, note 1).   [2] W ii 362.1.   [3] W ii 361.1 ff.

needed to preserve order and decency, in art as in life; was not good sense, after all, the daily bread of philosophers and critics? Yes, he replied, 'infants need milk',[1] and human beings are, for these purposes, children looking up to their Heavenly Father, who as often as not astonishes them, hurls paradoxes at them, creates earthquakes, makes wars, and through the mouth of his chosen prophets says deeply upsetting things. Moses did not let the Children of Israel rest peacefully in the desert. Herder took great pleasure in describing Hamann's aesthetics as Mosaic. Hamann could speak to Herder, because Herder seemed to him childlike and to have a virginal soul like Virgil, while Kant was a frozen-up old pedant who understood nothing worth understanding. For Kant, the world – nature – is a dead, external object, to be observed, analysed, labelled; the relevant concepts and categories are to be properly examined, their connections established, and the great automaton that is the world for him can be described and explained by a cut and dried system which, if it is true at all, will remain true for ever. No doubt this is an improvement on the cruder mechanistic views of the French materialists, but the presuppositions are the same: that a series of logically intercon-nected propositions of a descriptive kind can account for every-thing, and that conduct and the vast universe of men, beasts, material objects, life, soul, heaven and earth can be classified and interpreted in terms of one systematic unifying instrument – the correct theory, something that any man, provided he is impartial enough, able enough, and sets himself to it, can invent or at any rate understand.

All his life Hamann struggled violently to deny and expose this. His doctrines and his style reflect each other and his view of the world as an unorderable succession of episodes, each carrying its value in itself, intelligible only by direct experience, a 'living through' this experience, unintelligible – dead – when it is reported by others. A man must live on his own account, not as a pensioner of others, and to live on one's own account is to report – or, as often as not, fail to report – what one has lived through, and to use theories only as crutches to be thrown away when direct experience presents itself. No complete account of anything can be achieved by these means. Kant has rightly won the day, but Hamann and his followers express a continual revolt against taking

[1] W ii 361.3.

so much so blandly for granted, against leaving out so much, perhaps necessarily, but with too little regret, with no qualms, as if what the theory cannot embrace is mere expendable rubbish: psychological idiosyncrasy, oddities and quirks, which the theory cannot notice and which in a rational universe will themselves be ironed out, so that the facts will be only such as the final infallible theory fits.

Hamann sees the same all-conquering monism in the Roman Church and in the dream of a universal science as preached by the French Encyclopaedia; this seems to him to ignore and obliterate differences in thought and feeling, and to sweep them aside in practice. He fears system, centralisation, monism, as such, and his view of the authoritative role demanded by the sciences of his day as something of a secular version of the claims of the Catholic hierarchy is echoed in the following century by Auguste Comte – save that this was an object of horror to Hamann and of complete approval to Comte. Hamann saw in this convergence yet another example of the 'coincidence of opposites', a doctrine originated by Nicholas of Cusa (Hamann mistakenly ascribed it to Giordano Bruno) – although it is not clear how far he understood it, and he certainly gives it a sense of his own. Nevertheless, this war on two fronts against the conflicting claims to all knowledge – of the Church on the right and of science on the left – is a position of which Hamann is perhaps the most single-minded and passionate, as well as the earliest, representative – and with which he imbued the romantics and after them the individualist liberals of the nineteenth century. When Herzen speaks of communism (of such writers as Cabet or the Babouvists) as simply tsarism stood on its head, an equally oppressive and individuality-ignoring system, and when Bakunin complains of Marx's authoritarianism, this is the tradition they continue – the terror of any establishment that hems in the individual and destroys his deepest values.

Hamann, in a very characteristic phrase, already quoted, summarises this in saying of Descartes' 'Cogito ergo sum', it is all very well about the *cogito* (that is, rationalism), but what about the 'noble *sum*'?[1] Any doctrine that stresses the general, the impersonal, the conceptual, the universal, seems to him likely to flatten out all differences, peculiarities, quirks – to obstruct the soul's free flight by clipping its wings in the interests of comprehensive

[1] B vi 230.35; cf. p. 302 above, note 7.

inclusiveness. The ambition to 'Newtonise' all knowledge tends to work against sensitiveness to each fleeting particular, to lower susceptibility to empirical impressions – to stress form at the expense of content, uniformity at the expense of variety, fullness of life, the kaleidoscopic metamorphoses of actual experience that slip through the meshes of the most elaborate conceptual net. Like William James more than a century later, Hamann is a champion of the individual, the complex and above all the unconscious and the unseizable. Far more than James, he defends the inarticulate, the mystical, the demonic, the dark reaches and mysterious depths. Virtue and philanthropy are no substitute for compassion, love, generosity of spirit. Hamann reacted against the bland neglect of the animal and diabolical element in men on the part of the eighteenth-century optimists and naturalists, and when Kant, in his *Religion Within the Limits of Reason Alone*, speaks of radical evil and calls for a rebirth – something that even Herder, let alone Goethe and Schiller, was remote from – Hamann understands this only too well. 'The defects and the holes – that is the deepest and highest knowledge of human nature, whereby alone man can rise to the ideal',[1] and 'nothing but the descent into hell [*Höllenfahrt*] of self-knowledge builds the path to becoming divine [*Vergötterung*]':[2] this is quoted by Kant.[3]

Hence also Hamann's passionate defence of freedom of the will:

Without freedom to be *wicked*, there is no *merit*, and without freedom to be *good*, no attribution of any *guilt*, indeed no *knowledge of good and evil* at all. Freedom is the *maximum* and *minimum* of all our natural powers, both the base and the goal of their entire direction, development and return.

Neither *instinct* nor *sensus communis* determines *man* . . . Each man is his own *lawgiver*, but also the *first-born* and *most immediate* of his *subjects*.[4]

Only indeterminism can explain the spiritual development of the human race, since without 'the law of freedom' man would be nothing but an imitator; 'for man is of all the animals the greatest *mime*'.[5] He believed this politically, morally and in the sphere of self-knowledge also.

The fear of monism in all its forms – whether as the

[1] B iii 34.33.   [2] W ii 164.17.
[3] op. cit. (p. 187 above, note 1), vol. 7, p. 55.   [4] W iii 38.8.
[5] W iii 38.20.

comprehensive scientific treatise or centralised religious or political establishment – is usually the cry of a trapped man (or class) who cannot be brought to see that to be regimented or eliminated is either inevitable or desirable; the idea he or others cling to may be unsatisfactory or even detestable, but to be torn away from it must evoke a cry of pain and despair. It may be that the old ways of life are to be condemned. Montesquieu cautiously advocates care and slowness in making changes because he thinks that the kind of radical reforms that even in his day men began to demand would be ineffective or too despotic. Hamann condemns monism because all generalisation for him embodies false values. Tom Paine accused Burke, who uttered conservative sentiments in his attack on the French Revolution, of admiring the plumage while ignoring the dying bird. Hamann is not guilty of Burke's particular form of complacency. Nevertheless, he too, in his own way, is blind to the cry of human misery, unless it is of an individual or spiritual character. Those who put an end to suttee, or cleared slums, or created tolerable conditions of life in the place of some crushing, poverty-stricken patriarchalism, have rightly not been condemned by the majority of mankind. Hamann speaks for those who hear the cry of the toad beneath the harrow, even when it may be right to plough over him: since if men do not hear this cry, if they are deaf, if the toad is written off because he has been 'condemned by history' – if the defeated are never worth attending to because history is the history of the victorious – then such victories will prove their own undoing, for they will tend to destroy the very values in the name of which the battle was undertaken. The cry from the heart of human beings pushed against the wall by Frederick's great new broom, which swept so clean, and in a sense so permanently, is what is heard in all Hamann's writings. He spoke for ultimate human values no less than did his enlightened opponents, Voltaire and Kant, who are rightly admired as defenders of human rights.

Hamann knows that not one reader in a hundred will understand his writings, but he begs, with a curious mixture of pathos and arrogance, that he be accorded the treatment accorded to Heraclitus by Socrates: who, it is said, believed the passages that he could not understand because of the great value of those that he did. He compares his own prose to an archipelago of isolated islands; he cannot throw bridges across them, for that is precisely what he is against, the construction of a system that obliterates what is most living, individual, real. The vision that obsessed him was that of a world in process of perpetual re-creation, a process that cannot be stopped. It has to be described in what are inevitably static terms. It is not a slow growth – Hamann is not a historicist; he does not believe, or at least is not interested, in development. For him the world grows neither better nor worse. But there is an original, transcendent pattern, as it were, of which everything is a reflection or an analogy or an intimation. In the Garden of Eden, before the expulsion from Paradise, Adam was acquainted with it: 'Adam was of God, and God himself brought in the oldest of our race so that he might possess in fief and heritage the world, and the world be fulfilled by the word of his mouth.'[1]

> Every phenomenon of nature was a name – the sign, the symbol, the promise of a fresh and secret and ineffable but all the more intimate chosen union, communication and communion of divine energies and ideas. All that man in these beginnings heard with his ears, saw with his eyes, contemplated or touched with his hands, all this was the living word. For God was the Word. With the Word in his mouth and in his heart, the origin of language was as natural, as near and as easy as a child's game.[2]

This dark and mystical passage, already quoted in connection with Hamann's views of language, is the nearest that we can get to the central vision. It is one in which Hamann conceives the unity of thought and object – which he calls word and world – as mystics and metaphysicians have often conceived it: the unbroken unity of thought and feeling, not yet of immediacy and knowledge, not yet broken into subject and object, the knower and the known, which man is perpetually attempting to transcend. Whoever, whenever and wherever they may be, men, according to Hamann, have a choice of two alternatives. The first is to seek truly to understand, which means to perceive what this primal pattern may be as well as they are able (although they can never see it all, being finite) through direct experience, whether of history or of nature, or by reading the words of the Bible, which is an attempt of the unity to express itself in language intelligible to finite men; the second alternative is to shield oneself from reality by the construction of systems, by belief in conventional institutions, by living life

[1] W iii 32.8.   [2] W iii 32.21.

according to the dictates of good sense. 'Three things . . . I cannot comprehend, possibly four: a *man of sound judgement* who looks for the philosophers' stone; the squaring of a circle; the extent of the sea; and a *man of genius* who *affects the religion of sound human reason*.'[1] God is a poet: the world is an act of perpetual creation in accordance with a pattern that cannot be reduced to rules, which can only be perceived by the reflection that each of God's creations is another thing – by the fact that all events and objects are themselves, but are also symbols of, hieroglyphs of, allusions to, throw light upon, every other thing.

Quite apart from the intrinsic value of this profoundly irrationalist spiritual vision, its importance in the history of ideas (and of practice) is as a glove thrown down against the claim of the sciences, whether empirical or a priori, to answer all the central human questions. Hamann in the end recognises only the individual and his temperament, and he thinks that all attempts to generalise lead to the creation of faceless abstractions that are then taken for the individuals who are the raw material for the abstractions, with the consequence that theories propounded in terms of these abstractions do not touch the core of the individuals whom they purport to describe or explain, and the legal, moral and aesthetic systems – every formulation of principles of action – either ignore the individuals from whose experience they are in the end drawn, or force them into some Procrustean bed of conformity to rules which certainly maim and may destroy them.

When Hamann inveighs against all abstraction, if what he says is taken literally it is pure nonsense. Without some generalisation there can be no symbols, no words, no thought. Wherever anything is used to stand for anything else – Hamann's favourite and most original field of speculation – some degree of generalisation occurs of whatever is used as a symbol: it is removed from its natural medium, whatever that may be, and made to stand for something else, in order to discriminate this something else from other things similar or dissimilar to it, so that both the symbol and the symbolised, if they are to be identified at all, can only be so by means of general terms. To forbid abstraction is to forbid thought, self-consciousness, articulation of any kind; to confine the agent to sensation and musing and dreams, whether by day or by night, with no power of naming them. Hamann certainly did not mean this, but he occasionally speaks as if he did; and his denunciation of

[1] W ii 294.6.

the sciences, which carry abstraction beyond common speech, turns into a denial of their necessary function in their own field, into an attack on thought as such, as opposed to sensation or the mystery of artistic creation.

The distinction that Hamann seeks to establish between abstract thought and concrete certainty is, as it stands, illicit, and when driven as far as he drives it turns into blind obscurantism, an attack on critical thought, the making of distinctions, the formulation of hypotheses, ratiocination itself, an onslaught which springs from anger and hatred of criticism and, in the end, all mental activity. But despite the fact that Hamann's words are often passionate rhetoric and not careful thought, his general trend is not obscure. Like Burke some years later, he thinks that the application of scientific canons to living human beings leads to an erroneous and ultimately a deeply degrading view of what they are – mere human material, a field for physical, chemical and biological causation – and, since nobody was ever more acutely conscious of the unity of theory and practice, an inhuman attitude towards men. The fact that an equal, if not a greater, degree of inhumanity was practised by those who rejected science and allowed men to live in remediable poverty, ignorance and oppression left him unaffected. Often men can see clearly out of only one window.

Hamann was a fanatic, and his vision of life, despite its sincerity and depth and the value that believers in God and theologians have perceived in it, is, as a general philosophy of life, grotesquely one-sided: a violent exaggeration of the uniqueness of men and things, or the absence in them of significant common characteristics capable of being abstracted and theorised about; a passionate hatred of men's wish to understand the universe or themselves in publicly intelligible terms and to rule themselves and nature in order to achieve ends common to most men at most times (to go no further) by taking such scientific knowledge into account. This hatred and this blind irrationalism have fed the stream that has led to social and political irrationalism, particularly in Germany, in our own century, and has made for obscurantism, a revelling in darkness, the discrediting of that appeal to rational discussion in terms of principles intelligible to most men which alone can lead to an increase of knowledge, the creation of conditions for free co-operative action based on conscious acceptance of common ideals, and the promotion of the only type of progress that has ever deserved this name.

The importance of Hamann consists not in his bitterly obscurantist particularism and denigration of systematic thought and of
the demand that actions be accountable in terms of freely and
openly debatable principles, even though that was his own
constant practice, as in his polemics with Kant; it lies in the
inspired insights which this uncommonly sensitive and painfully
candid man achieved into those aspects of human life which the
sciences are apt to ignore – perhaps must ignore, because of their
very nature as sciences. His cry came from an outraged sensibility:
he spoke as a man of feeling offended by a passion for a cerebral
approach; as a moralist who understood that ethics is concerned
with relations between real persons (under God as the ultimate
ruler whose will they try to obey as his servants); as a man who
was offended by the enunciation of principles that claimed a
pseudo-scientific objectivity not derived from individual or social
experience; as a German humiliated by an arrogant and, it seemed
to him, spiritually blind West; as a humble member of a dying
social order, trampled by the inhuman tempo of centralisation in
the political and cultural sphere. Forced by arrogant dictators,
Frederick and Voltaire, he rose in rebellion and instituted a fierce
campaign against reason. Nevertheless, as with most rebellions,
there was real oppression to fight against – in this case, a
suppression of individuality and irrational and unconscious forces
in men which sooner or later was bound to provoke an explosion.
Hamann, while apparently engaged in confused and incomprehen-
sible theological tracts, lit a fuse – I know of no one earlier or more
directly responsible for this (although who can tell whether
without him the course of human history, or even thought in
Germany, would have been very different?) – which set off the
great romantic revolt, the denial that there was an objective order, a
rerum natura, whether factual or normative, from which all
knowledge and all values stemmed, and by which all action could
be tested.

The revolution began in Germany – perhaps for political reasons
which inhibited social and political agitation, and indeed open
discussion, and forced criticism into what Alexander Herzen once
called the 'tranquil sea of aesthetic theory'.[1] At the centre of it
were: the identity of language and thought; the idea of art as
neither imitation of an ideal beauty, objectively accessible to all
men, nor a means of giving pleasure governed by rules open to

---

[1] *Sobranie sochinenii v tridtsati tomakh* (Moscow, 1954–66), vol. 9, p. 21.

anyone to verify; the combination of a Humean empiricism that killed the authority of a priori principles with an emphasis on the supreme value of individual self-expression; the unique working of God in each sentient spirit in its own inexplicable way, not necessarily reconcilable with that at work in any other. All this proved a violently explosive amalgam which, whether or not it was itself a consequence of social or economic tensions, proved to be a great and world-transforming power with all the terrifying consequences that Heine, almost alone among writers before our own century, so accurately prophesied when he warned the French not to underestimate the power of the quiet German philosopher in his study. If Hamann had not enunciated, in however peculiar a fashion, truths too contemptuously ignored by the triumphant rationalist schools, not only in his own century, but in the great Victorian advance and its continuation in countries that came relatively late to this feast of reason, the movement that he initiated would not have had its formidable consequences on both thought and action, not least in our own terrible century. This is sufficient reason for rescuing his memory from the pages of purely literary or theological specialists.

One has only to compare the attempts to rebut the doctrines of the Enlightenment made by the official apologists of the Churches on the one hand, and the attempts at compromise made by Hamann's *bêtes noires*, the liberal theologians, on the other hand, to realise the full extent of Hamann's originality. On the side of the Sorbonne and the Catholic opposition one finds, for the most part, either blind dogmatism together with eccentric denials of the reliability of scientific or historical investigation in their own fields, or feeble efforts to show that what the *philosophes* claim to do, the Church – in its slow but nevertheless rational fashion – can do better. Apart from organised opposition of this type, there were the Protestant sects and movements which protected themselves against rationalism by attitudes of hostile indifference, 'know-nothing' parties which turned towards inward meditation and holy living, opting out of the social and political world either voluntarily or because of political barriers. This left the spiritual opposition to the march of reason to the illuminist and Masonic lodges, which even in the writings of their most influential and distinguished representatives, such as, for example, Saint-Martin, were incomparably less original or concerned with the critical issues – either individual or social – than even Hamann's darkest and most eccentric pieces. His central charge, that writers claiming to understand man and nature by direct observation ignore the areas of life that are closest to them in their daily experience – the actual way in which men act and what they believe – and the justice, and poignant and uncompromising audacity, with which he plunges the knife into those wounds which were duly uncovered for all to see in the decades that followed his death, give him his unique importance in the history of thought.

Hamann was not a nostalgic medievalist who contrasted an imaginary past, seen as a better and nobler age, with the dreary mediocrity of the present. His fantasies were timeless and not historical. But like the later denouncers of industrial civilisation, he steadfastly ignored not merely the causes but the purposes of the secular reformers. The application of rational methods to social policy, whether in Frederick's Prussia or Napoleonic France or even Joseph II's Holy Roman Empire, had as its purpose the removal of glaring injustices and irrational conflicts, human misery and oppression; and its achievements form a bright page in an otherwise none too brilliant portion of human history. The very notions of progress and reaction were born in the course of the conflict between, on the one hand, those who desired to introduce rapid changes (in the course of which they overestimated their own power and the malleability of men, and made empirical errors which caused much unnecessary suffering) and, on the other, those who for one reason or another – whether because of the interests of their class or nation, or because the Utopianism of the reformers struck them as at once shallow and insane – resisted.

Hamann belonged to the latter category. The world that the reformers were seeking to build seemed to him a denial of all the values that he prized and that he believed to be most deeply embedded in the nature of men. Because this was so, he remained blind to the worst abuses of the regime in which he lived: he saw only the vices of the 'great simplifiers' who were seeking to destroy living men and women in the name of hollow abstractions – ideals like reason, progress, liberty or equality, vast, balloon-like constructions of unrealistic minds – all of which taken together were worth less than acquaintance with one concrete fact, one real human being, one hour in the true, that is inner, experience of one human soul and one human body, as they really were in all their painful imperfection.

The contrasts and conflicts between the categories of quantity and quality have been familiar for a long while and have taken many forms – aesthetic, ethical, political, logical. This is indeed, in its sociological form, still one of the most profound issues that dominates the attitudes of men. But in Hamann's day it was a relatively new issue. The possibility of applying quantitative generalisations not only to the physical world – there the battle had been won in the seventeenth century – but to social and personal life as well – in the organisation of life on scientific principles, the calculation of relative sums of satisfaction between human beings conceived as equal (or if unequal, with the inequalities reducible to some common standard of measurement) – was prophesied with enthusiasm by Condorcet. Quantification, verification of numerically statable hypotheses, and planning on this basis, whether for individuals or for groups or for larger bodies of human beings, had scarcely entered their first stage. If anything is destined to be selected as characteristic of the new age that began in the seventeenth century, it is the transition from qualitative to quantitative concepts that laid the foundation not merely of physics and biology but of all the social sciences and the moral and economic outlook associated with this, together with its by-products in ethics and aesthetics.

All this is by now a truism. To repeat myself: one of Hamann's greatest claims to our notice is that, earlier than any other thinker, he became conscious of this, and protested violently. If to attempt to resist the swelling current of thought of an age and a civilisation is to be reactionary, then certainly Hamann was a complete and vehement reactionary. He knew this, and gloried in it. He spoke out, in his cryptic but violent fashion, a quarter of a century before Burke uttered his famous lament for the passing of the age of chivalry and the arrival of the sordid mechanical men with their slide-rules and statistical tables.[1] After the great revolution in France, and when the consequences of the industrial revolution in England penetrated every sphere of life, the conservative reaction of men like Chateaubriand or Maistre or Coleridge or Friedrich Schlegel or Novalis was to be expected. Hamann belongs to the small class of acutely sensitive persons with the gift – or the

[1] 'But the age of chivalry is gone. – That of sophisters, oeconomists, and calculators, has succeeded; and the glory of Europe is extinguished for ever.' Edmund Burke, *Reflections on the Revolution in France* (1790): p. 127 in *The Writings and Speeches of Edmund Burke*, ed. Paul Langford (Oxford, 1981–), vol. 8, *The French Revolution*, ed. L. G. Mitchell.

misfortune – of divining the contours of the future, whether to welcome them or recoil, as he did, in fear and hostility. Such men as a rule scarcely have the vocabulary in which to express something that resembles feeling more than an articulated vision; nevertheless, being poets (whose naturally responsive – irritable – constitutions are the first to react to such profound changes in human life), they find words, however obscure and charged with subjective emotion, to express their sense of the approaching cataclysm. Such men are justly called prophets, and, whether they know it or not, are gifted with a historical sense beyond the usual degree. When they come too early, it is difficult for them to convey the sense of what they feel in every pore of their being to men with a more normal vision. To see what others cannot see as yet, particularly if it appears as the sure sign of an approaching doom, and to be unable not to speak, drives such living divining-rods into themselves or into escape to some province free from the darkening world in which they are compelled to live. It may be that members of backward communities on the edges of a culture that is being radically transformed, who at once feel powerless to alter the current and are tied more deeply to the older culture that is being displaced, are peculiarly sensitive to such change: Naples at the turn of the seventeenth century, and Königsberg half a century later, were not at the centre of events, either politically or intellectually. At any rate, an explanation in sociological terms – which was something that all his life Hamann resisted as a false interpretation of history – fits his case. The type of household in which he was brought up, the life lived by the Inspector of Baths, as his father was proud to be described, was being crushed out of existence by the reforms of Frederick and his genuinely enlightened administrators. The son never found a secure place in the new establishment, and like many men who conceive bold ideas and speak in fierce and sweeping terms, was himself timid, gentle, self-distrustful and exceptionally vulnerable. Despite the calm and serene advice that he gave to other troubled spirits to cease from fretting, to surrender themselves wholly to God, to eat their bread and drink their wine in contentment, he himself nearly went out of his mind when his salary was reduced by five thalers and the size of his garden was cut down. He struck the first blow against the quantified world; his attack was often ill-judged, but he raised some of the greatest issues of our times by refusing to accept their advent.

APPENDIX

Excursus to chapter 6

I ALLUDED in chapter 6 to the success in our own day of a theory of language like Hamann's; and to the odd combination of his view of language with his religious devotion and irrationalism.[1] A few more words may be said on these subjects.

Hamann in effect maintained the following:

(*a*) There is no objective 'structure' of reality of which a 'logically perfect language' would be the correct reflection.

(*b*) Propositions for which philosophers have claimed universal validity are therefore necessarily hollow.

(*c*) Rules and laws hold while they hold, but when they do not, they must be broken.

(*d*) Problems in theory (and mistakes in practice) are generated not by mistakes in logical or metaphysical or psychological theory so much as by fanatical belief in the universal and eternal validity of theories as such – by the belief that, if not this theory, then some other one will answer all our questions (even within a given sphere). It is this addiction to theory, and in particular to scientific theories, that breeds imaginary entities which are confounded with things in real life, and leads to mental confusions, and, at times, spiritual torments, due to an obstinate adherence to man-made figments that springs in its turn from the quest for universality – a philosophers' stone, as Hamann called this wish.

(*e*) Every language is a way of life, and a way of life is based on a pattern of experience which cannot itself be subjected to criticism, since one cannot find an Archimedean point outside it from which to conduct such a critical examination; at most, all one can do is to examine the symbolism by which the pattern of experience is expressed. This is so because to think is to use symbols, and as the

[1] See p. 328 above.

symbols so the thought. Above all, content and form cannot be divorced – there is an 'organic' connection between all the elements of a medium of communication, and the meaning lies in the individual, ultimately unanalysable, whole.

(*f*) Perfect translation between different vocabularies, grammars, etymologies, syntaxes is in principle impossible, and the quest for a universal language, from which the irrational accretions and individual idiosyncrasies of natural languages would be cleansed – for instance Leibniz's belief in the possibility of this (called by him the 'Universal Characteristic'), or the universal language of science, which would respond to all human needs, dreamt of by Condorcet, and after him by many positivist thinkers – is the most absurd chimera of all.

(*g*) A corollary of (*f*): one cannot truly understand what men are saying by merely applying grammatical or logical or any other kind of rules, but only by an act of 'entering into' – what Herder called 'Einfühlung' – their symbolisms, and for that reason only by the preservation of actual usage, past and present. Even dialects and jargons – in so far as these bear 'the stamp of life' – are at the heart of ways of living and creating which uniformity in language, by producing uniformity in life, would destroy.

(*h*) Consequently, while we cannot do without rules and principles, we must constantly distrust them and never be betrayed by them into rejecting or ignoring or riding roughshod over the irregularities and peculiarities offered by concrete experience.

This is surely a doctrine that was not wholly unfamiliar in the middle of our century among English-speaking philosophers.

If this conception of language and meaning is valid, it follows that there are no ethical, aesthetic, ideological, social or religious beliefs that are excluded. Yet another thing follows. Since all thought and speech for Hamann is communication, it must be communication between specific individuals. But if these individuals are to understand each other as fully as life on earth permits they must enter into the individual images and texture that are indissoluble from the specific content of what a man is saying or, if he is an artist, making. To ask for words or works of art that will be intelligible to anyone anywhere is as absurd as the quest for the universal language. The worst of all standards is that of *bon sens*, that universal human good sense of which Descartes had spoken approvingly and which to Hamann is a guarantee of shallowness, philistinism and the all-flattening power that reduces everything to equal triviality. Hence his defence of the esoteric as such. This may indeed have been an attempt to justify his own passion to remain mysterious, to speak only to the few who could understand him – but he generalises it into a doctrine according to which all art, all creation, is a mystery which by being given rules and made public is distorted and degraded: this is the crime of the ancient Greeks and the modern French, who have turned this profoundly private, individual and at times terrifying process into a mechanised craft that anyone may perform and anyone respond to, save that both activities would be deprived of value.

All his life Hamann had a certain taste for mystagogues, even when he knew them to be charlatans, like the 'prophet' Christoph Kaufmann in his goatskin who shocked and intrigued the citizens of Königsberg and with whom Hamann entered into an ambivalent but fascinated relationship. Hamann represented himself, not unwillingly, as a dispenser of secret wisdom, a man not intending fully to be understood, an ironical Socrates, a Rosicrucian knight, an 'apocryphal' sibyl and the like. Though he never expressed it in these terms, he wished to be a teacher of wisdom, a sage, a guru, a rescuer of the unfortunate victims caught in the great net of the Enlightenment.

BIBLIOGRAPHICAL NOTE

READERS who do not (easily) read German may be glad to have details of the few translations into English of Hamann's writings. I cannot claim that I have discovered them all, but details follow of the ones I have encountered in my work on Isaiah Berlin's text. I should add for readers of French that the second volume of Nadler's edition of Hamann's works contains most of the few pieces he wrote in that language (there is also one in the third volume).

Aesthetica in nuce:[1] *A Rhapsody in Cabbalistic Prose*, trans. Joyce P. Crick, in H. B. Nisbet (ed.), *German Aesthetic and Literary Criticism: Winckelmann, Lessing, Hamann, Herder, Schiller, Goethe* (Cambridge etc., 1985: Cambridge University Press), pp. 139–50, notes pp. 275–86.

Golgotha and Scheblimini!, trans. Stephen N. Dunning in his *The Tongues of Men: Hegel and Hamann on Religious Language and History* (Missoula, 1979: Scholars Press), pp. 209–28, notes p. 247.

Hamann's 'Socratic Memorabilia': A Translation and Commentary, by James C. O'Flaherty (Baltimore, 1967: Johns Hopkins Press).

Letter to Kant, 27 July 1759, in *Kant: Philosophical Correspondence 1759–99*, ed. and trans. Arnulf Zweig (Chicago and London, 1967: University of Chicago Press), pp. 35–43.

'The Merchant' (an anonymous translation of all but the opening and closing pages of Hamann's supplement to his translation of Plumard de Dangeul's *Remarques sur les avantages et les désavantages de la France et de la Gr. Bretagne, par rapport au commerce, & aux autres sources de la puissance des états*), in

---

[1] 'Aesthetics in a nutshell'.

Frederic H. Hedge (ed.), *Prose Writers of Germany* (Philadelphia, 1848: Carey and Hart), pp. 121–7.

Selections in Ronald Gregor Smith, *J. G. Hamann 1730–1788: A Study in Christian Existence, with Selections from his Writings* (London, 1960: Collins). Much of what is translated in this volume takes the form of extracts, but there are also several complete items, viz.: *Fragments*; *The Wise Men from the East in Bethlehem*; *New Apology of the Letter H by Itself*; review of Kant's *Critique of Pure Reason*; *Metacritique*.

Gwen Griffith Dickson, *Johann Georg Hamann's Relational Metacriticism* (Berlin and New York, 1995: Walter de Gruyter) includes translations of a number of works: *Socratic Memorabilia*; *Aesthetica in nuce*; the 'Herderschriften'; *Essay of a Sibyl on Marriage*; *Metacritique of the Purism of Reason*.

There are also a few other books on Hamann in English known to me, which I list here. Their bibliographies may be consulted for details of articles in English, and of the growing literature in other languages.

W. M. Alexander, *Johann Georg Hamann: Philosophy and Faith* (The Hague, 1966: Martinus Nijhoff).

Terence J. German, *Hamann on Language and Religion* (Oxford, 1981: Oxford University Press).

Walter Leibrecht, *God and Man in the Thought of Hamann*, trans. James H. Stam and Martin H. Bertram (Philadelphia, 1966: Fortress Press) [original German edition 1958].

Walter Lowrie, *Johann Georg Hamann: An Existentialist* (Princeton, 1950: Princeton Theological Seminary).

James C. O'Flaherty, *Unity and Language: A Study in the Philosophy of Johann Georg Hamann* (Chapel Hill, 1952: University of North Carolina; New York, 1966: AMS Press).

James C. O'Flaherty, *Johann Georg Hamann* (Boston, 1979: Twayne).

James C. O'Flaherty, *The Quarrel of Reason with Itself: Essays on Hamann, Michaelis, Lessing, Nietzsche* (Columbia, SC, 1988: Camden House).

Larry Vaughan, *Johann Georg Hamann: Metaphysics of Language and Vision of History* (New York etc., 1989: Peter Lang).

H.H.

INDEX

Compiled by Douglas Matthews